THOMAS HARDY

His Career as a Novelist

THOMAS HARDY

His Career as a Novelist

MICHAEL
MILLGATE

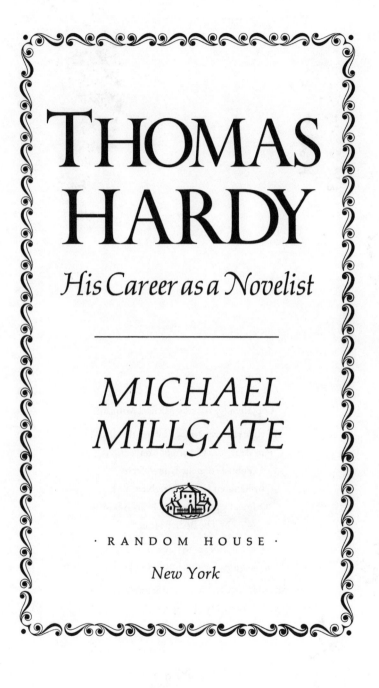

· RANDOM HOUSE ·

New York

ISBN: 0-394-46121-5
Library of Congress Catalog Card Number: 79-117656

Manufactured in the United States of America

2 4 6 8 9 7 5 3

FIRST AMERICAN EDITION

To Robin and Bronwen

CONTENTS

[7]

CONTENTS

[8]

ACKNOWLEDGMENTS

Quotations from published works of Thomas Hardy are made with the permission of Macmillan & Co. Ltd. Quotations from Florence Emily Hardy's *The Early Life of Thomas Hardy* and *The Later Years of Thomas Hardy* are made with the permission of Macmillan & Co. Ltd. and of Arcon Books, Hampden, Connecticut.

TEXTUAL NOTE

Unless otherwise indicated, the 24-volume Macmillan Wessex Edition (London, 1912–31) has been used throughout as the source of quotations from Hardy's novels and poems and as the basis for page references, whether in the notes or incorporated within parentheses in the text. The Wessex Edition is described in R. L. Purdy, *Thomas Hardy: A Bibliographical Study* (London, 1954, 1968), pp. 282–286.

Also incorporated within parentheses in the text are page references to *The Early Life of Thomas Hardy* (London: Macmillan, 1928) and *The Later Years of Thomas Hardy* (London: Macmillan, 1930), attributed to Hardy's second wife, Florence Emily Hardy, on their title-pages but known to have been largely the work of Hardy himself: see R. L. Purdy, *Thomas Hardy: A Bibliographical Study*, pp. 265–267, 272–273.

PREFACE

This study of Thomas Hardy's career and achievement as a novelist is primarily critical in aim and emphasis: it proceeds largely in terms of independent discussions of the various novels. But my endeavour throughout has been to bring the results of scholarly research directly to bear upon the processes of analysis and evaluation—to consider Hardy's fiction in the context of available biographical and bibliographical knowledge and in relation to the social and intellectual milieux within which he lived and worked at various periods. I have been particularly concerned to explore Hardy's creation and elaboration of the fictional world of Wessex, to determine the imaginative purposes served by that world, and—by invoking actual conditions in Dorset during the nineteenth century—to examine Hardy's credentials as a "regionalist" and as a chronicler of agricultural decline. In pursuing these questions I have drawn extensively upon the rich resources of Richard L. Purdy's bibliographical study and upon material from the early reviews, from the letters and reminiscences of those who knew Hardy, and from his own letters, notebooks, and manuscripts. The limitation of the book's scope to the actual period when Hardy was writing and publishing novels has been determined by its conception not as a biography but as a study of a literary career, and by practical considerations of length; the restriction implies neither a disregard for the importance of Hardy's earlier or later years, nor an insistence upon the superiority of his prose over his verse.

Hardy's letters and manuscripts are widely distributed throughout the British Isles and North America, and I should like to thank the following institutions which granted me access to materials in their possession and the members of their staffs who assisted me in my enquiries: Alderman Library, University of Virginia; Beinecke Library, Yale University; Berg Collection and Manuscript Division, New York Public Library; Bodleian Library; British Museum; Brotherton Library, Leeds University; Cambridge University Library; Colbeck Collection, University of British Columbia; Dorset County Museum; Fales Collection, New York University; Fitzwilliam Museum, Cambridge; Henry E. Huntington Library; Houghton Library, Harvard University; Library of Congress; Lilly Library, Indiana University; Magdalene College, Cambridge; Miriam Lutcher Stark Library, University of Texas; National Library of Scotland; Pierpont Morgan Library; Princeton University Library; Queen's College, Oxford; Royal Library, Windsor Castle. My thanks are particularly due, not only for access to materials but for generous hospitality, to Mrs Elfrida Manning, Mr Edwin Thorne, the late Miss Irene Cooper Willis, and, especially, Mr Frederick B. Adams, Jr., and Professor Richard L. Purdy.

I wish to thank the Trustees of the Hardy Estate for permission to make quotations from Hardy's letters and from previously unpublished materials in notebooks and manuscripts. I am also grateful to Mrs Christina Lloyd-Williams, Mrs Elfrida Manning, and Mr Alexander James for permission to quote letters by, respectively, Edward Arnold, Sir Hamo Thornycroft, and Henry James. I gladly acknowledge the gracious permission of Her Majesty The Queen for permission to quote from the manuscript of *The Trumpet-Major* in the Royal Library, Windsor Castle, and the permission of the following to quote manuscript material in their possession: Mr Frederick B. Adams, Jr.; the Henry W. and Albert A. Berg Collection of the New York Public Library, Astor, Lenox and Tilden Foundations; the Manuscripts Division of the Library of Congress; the Dorset County Museum; Magdalene College, Cambridge; Mrs Elfrida Manning; Mr Edwin Thorne.

The completion of this study has been materially assisted by the generous and sustained support of the Canada Council in the form of summer research grants and a Leave Fellowship. I should also like to express my warm appreciation of the hospitality extended to me, during the year in which the book was actually being written, by Rutherford College of the University of Kent at Canterbury, and especially by its Master and Bursar. Mrs

Muriel Waring and her assistants provided cheerful and efficient typing services as, at a later date, did Mrs Freda Gough. Among the numerous friends and colleagues who helped me with particular queries and problems I should particularly like to thank Dr C. J. P. Beatty, Professor Quentin Bell, Mrs Shirley Doughty, Professor Leon Edel, Miss Anne Freudenberg, Mr Colin Franklin, Mr E. G. H. Kempson, Mr David Masson, Professor James B. Meriwether, Dr A. N. L. Munby, Professor Harold Orel, Miss May O'Rourke, Dr William R. Rutland, and Professor Robert C. Schweik. Mr Roger Peers and Miss Maureen Samuel, Curator and Assistant Curator of the Dorset County Museum, have been unfailingly patient and helpful during the many visits I have made to the Museum in recent years. And to Professor Richard L. Purdy I am further indebted for advice, assistance, and the constant stimulus of his scholarly example. I have profited in many ways from the opportunity to discuss Hardy with Michael Collie, Ian Gregor, and W. J. Keith; Professors Gregor and Keith both took the trouble to read and criticise drafts of individual chapters, and the latter generously allowed me to make use of the results of some of his own research. The whole manuscript received meticulous and sensitive readings from Henry Auster, Caesar Blake, and Robin Biswas, and their suggestions enormously facilitated the process of final revision. My greatest debt, however, is to my wife, Jane Millgate, from whose wise and perceptive criticism my work has benefited immeasurably at every stage from inception to completion.

Prelude

THE POOR MAN AND THE LADY

The Poor Man and the Lady

Until his twenty-third year Thomas Hardy's experience had scarcely extended beyond the borders of his native Dorset. He was born, on June 2, 1840, in the hamlet of Upper Bockhampton; he went to school in the nearby county town of Dorchester; in 1856 he was articled to the Dorchester architect, John Hicks, specialist in the restoration of Gothic churches. Although during the later years of his pupilage Hardy took lodgings in Dorchester, returning to Bockhampton only at weekends, he had earlier continued to live at home, walking to and fro each day between "a county-town of assizes and aldermen, which had advanced to railways and telegraphs and daily London papers," and "a world of shepherds and ploughmen in a hamlet three miles off, where modern improvements were still regarded as wonders".[1] If the years with Hicks thus gave him an unusual opportunity of seeing "rustic and borough doings in a juxtaposition peculiarly close", they also enlarged his knowledge of the neighbouring country-side, into which he would often be sent to inspect churches on which restoration work was contemplated or actually in progress.

After the expiration of his articles, Hardy left Dorset for London and a job as an architectural assistant in the Adelphi office of Arthur (later Sir Arthur) Blomfield, the move no doubt recommending itself as an opportunity to further not only the career to which he had become committed through economic necessity (and his own talents with a pencil) but also his more private ambitions as a poet. Once arrived, he was immediately and profoundly fascinated by a city that, in April 1862, was still very much the London evoked by Dickens and Mayhew; he was no less excited by such specifically modern phenomena as the Great Exhibition of 1862, and by that tremendous mid-Victorian thrust of urban development and expansion which he was, as an architect working in the heart of the capital, in an unrivalled position to observe.

It is perhaps not surprising, therefore, that on March 18, 1865, Hardy should have initiated his career as a published writer of fiction with the appearance, in *Chambers's Journal*, of a lightly satirical piece on the current building boom. Yet "How I Built Myself a House" nonetheless constitutes a disturbingly un-characteristic debut, as its first sentence may sufficiently suggest: "My wife Sophia, myself, and the beginning of a happy line, formerly lived in the suburbs of London, in the sort of house called a Highly-Desirable Semi-detached Villa".[2] In almost every respect—the satirical archness, the use of a dramatised first-person point of view, the adoption of a specifically urban and middle-class persona—the sketch seems wholly out of key with Hardy's later work. It displays, like some of the early poems for which he had failed to find a publisher, a young writer searching for an effective method of literary processing, a means of transforming autobiography into art, and heralds the adoption of a similar formula two or three years later in his first—and unpublished—novel, *The Poor Man and the Lady*, "A Story with no Plot" narrated "By the Poor Man".[3]

The "Poor Man" persona allowed Hardy to draw much more immediately than in "How I Built Myself a House" upon his own experience, especially insofar as it had involved the juxtaposition of contrasted social worlds. From what is known of the lost manuscript of *The Poor Man and the Lady*, it also seems clear that the rhetoric of social criticism with which he sought to propel his autobiographical material into the stuff of fiction now became altogether more sweeping in scope and more assertive in tone. Certainly the letter submitting the novel to the firm of Macmillan on July 25, 1868, suggests an ambition whose direction may have been altered but whose confidence had in no way been dimin-ished by the decision of the young author to become, at least temporarily, a novelist rather than a poet. In writing the novel,

Hardy explained, he had had a number of considerations in mind:

That the upper classes of society have been induced to read, before any, books in which *they themselves* are painted by a comparative outsider.

That, in works of such a kind, unmitigated utterances of strong feeling against the class to which these readers belong may lead them to throw down a volume in disgust; whilst the very same feelings inserted edgewise so to say—half concealed beneath ambiguous expressions, or at any rate written as if they were not the chief aims of the book (even though they may be) —become the most attractive remarks of all.

* * *

That novelty of *position* and *view*, in relation to a known subject, is more taking among the readers of light literature than even absolute novelty of subject.

Hence the book took its shape, rightly or wrongly.[4]

As W. R. Rutland was the first to demonstrate effectively,[5] some impression of that "shape" can still be gathered by correlating available information about the manuscript of *The Poor Man and the Lady* with those sections of Hardy's published works which appear to have been derived, directly or indirectly, from it.

Once Hardy came to accept that the novel would not be published in its original form, he did not hesitate to excerpt or adapt substantial segments of it for use in works which could find a publisher. The "opening pictures of the Christmas Eve in the tranter's house" which John Morley praised in reporting on the manuscript to Macmillan[6] must have made an important contribution to the early chapters of *Under the Greenwood Tree*, and R. L. Purdy has suggested that "satiric details of London society" were incorporated into *A Pair of Blue Eyes* and probably *The Hand of Ethelberta*.[7] In 1925, in *Human Shows*, Hardy published a poem entitled "A Poor Man and a Lady", explaining in an accompanying note that it was "intended to preserve an episode in the story of 'The Poor Man and the Lady,' written in 1868, and, like these lines, in the first person; but never printed, and ultimately destroyed" (150). In 1934 the second Mrs Hardy reprinted the story "An Indiscretion in the Life of an Heiress" (first published in 1878 but never collected by Hardy himself), describing it as an "adaptation" of *The Poor Man and the Lady*.[8] While the adaptation must have been of a fairly radical kind, involving the abandonment of the "Poor Man" as narrator and the substitution of a third-person point of view, there seem good grounds for believing that the story does at least incorporate major narrative elements from the unpublished novel.[9]

The extant comments of its readers plainly suggest that the novel had a weak plot line (Morley complained that it hung "too loosely together") and that it proceeded largely in terms of contrasted scenes of what Alexander Macmillan distinguished as "country life among working men" and life "in drawing-rooms and ball-rooms".[10] As in so many of Hardy's later novels, much of the action derived from the pull of sexual attraction across social barriers, and the manuscript as a whole revealed strong class hostility: Morley referred to its "hard sarcasm" and "cynical description", while Macmillan suggested that its portrayal of the upper classes failed to convince simply because it was a "wholesale blackening", a "chastisement" likely to "fall harmless from its very excess".[11] In the same letter Macmillan commented: "The scene in Rotten Row—seen as it is and described by an outsider—is full of real power and insight".[12] Since Hardy's tentative approach to a literary career at this point would make it likely that he should draw first, as in *Under the Greenwood Tree*, on those sections of *The Poor Man and the Lady* which had been praised by its professional readers, it seems reasonable to link with Macmillan's remark the Rotten Row scene which occupies much of chapter 14 of *A Pair of Blue Eyes* and to speculate on the extent to which the published passage may reflect or even preserve the tone and manner of the novel which remained unpublished. In the serial version of *A Pair of Blue Eyes* the satiric comments put into the mouth of Mrs Swancourt are given at greater length than in any of the subsequent editions:

'You would hardly believe, would you, that members of a

fashionable world, whose professed zero is far above the highest degree of the humble, could be so ignorant of the elementary instincts of reticence.'

'How?'

'Why, to bear on their faces, as plainly as on a phylactery, the inscription, "Do, pray, look at the coronet on my panels;" or, "Look at the leaves and pearls in my coronet;" or, "Look at the leaves pure and unmixed in mine. I don't say," they seem to go on saying to the shabby people, "that I wish you to think us connected with the Norman Conquest of you, wretched Nobody-knows-who," or whatever the word of the season is for the poorer inhabitants of the country, "but we are, and there is our crest and significant motto." '

'O Mrs. Swancourt!' said Elfride.

'But I much prefer the manners of my acquaintance of that class to the way some of us, with no title but much wealth, look at the strugglers for gentility. There's a specimen—there's another. The glance in them is modified to "O, moneyless ones, this bracelet I wear, weighing three-quarters of a pound, is real gold! Solid, you know—s, o, l, i, d,—right through to the middle and out at the other side." '

'Really, Charlotte,' said the vicar, 'you see as much in faces as Mr. Puff saw in Lord Burleigh's nod.'[13]

As in chapter 36 ("The pennie's the jewel that beautifies a' "), which may also have originated in the manuscript of *The Poor Man and the Lady*, the satire seems ponderous, wholly disproportionate to its context, and it is perhaps significant that both chapters should have been substantially reduced in revisions made subsequent to serialisation.[14]

Successful or not, the satire is specifically class-conscious, representing a strain of overt social criticism which remained discernible in Hardy's work until after the publication of *The Hand of Ethelberta*. Though relatively quiescent in the deliberately pastoral *Under the Greenwood Tree*, the strain can be clearly detected even in a sensation novel like *Desperate Remedies*. The young architect Edward Springrove, forced to make his own way in the world, takes a cynical view of the paths of success for a professional man; at the same time, his educated independence makes him openly critical of the class attitudes of Miss Aldclyffe, who ruthlessly dismisses an old employee and exploits the misfortunes of her tenants as instruments in her own plans. Although Hardy did not write novels of manners, as that term is generally understood, the humble rank of so many of his characters should not be allowed to obscure the extent to which some of the most desperate battles in his fiction are fought out on the jealously guarded borders of the British class system. What we know of *The Poor Man and the Lady*, which had flung down a gauntlet in its very title, clearly suggests that Hardy originally conceived of his novels as social documents, even as social instruments: Thackeray "meant fun", Alexander Macmillan told him, "you *'mean mischief'*".[15]

Hardy told his friend Edward Clodd many years later that *The Poor Man and the Lady* was the most original thing, for its time, that he had ever written.[16] Its rejection, first by Macmillan and then by Chapman and Hall, must have been not only a bitter discouragement at the time but one of the sources of that wary unassertiveness which he so often displayed in his later dealings with publishers and editors. There seems, indeed, to have been an almost total collapse of self-confidence. Apart from "How I Built Myself a House" and a few unimpressive short stories, dramatised first-person narrative is wholly absent from Hardy's published fiction, and only at the very end of his career as a writer of prose did he again attempt anything resembling a novel of social purpose. If his first letter to Macmillan had amounted almost to a manifesto, he was soon humbly seeking advice as to "the sort of story you think I could do best, or any literary work I should do well to go upon?"[17] And his next book, *Desperate Remedies*, was to represent an excessively literal adoption of the suggestion of Chapman and Hall's reader, George Meredith, that he should write a novel with "a purely artistic purpose" and a much stronger plot.[18] The shift from manifesto to plea for advice both anticipates and images the movement from a commitment to "novelty of *position* and *view*, in relation to a known subject" to precisely the kind of resort to "novelty of subject" which had earlier been rejected. The new and exaggerated emphasis on plot in *Desperate Remedies* is the product of an over-reaction to the condemnation of "A Story with no Plot".

Once his original position had proved untenable, his self-confidence misplaced, Hardy embarked on that anxious search for new bearings which is directly reflected in the extraordinary disparateness of the three novels—*Desperate Remedies, Under the Greenwood Tree*, and *A Pair of Blue Eyes*—which belong to the period of his apprenticeship. It would scarcely be too much to say that the search never came to an end, that it was simply abandoned. Few novelists have produced work as varied in kind and in quality as did Hardy in the quarter century which separated *Desperate Remedies* and *Jude the Obscure*. Few literary careers of a major order have displayed a greater reluctance or incapacity to build progressively on previous achievements.

Yet there is, despite the discontinuity, an element of circularity. In his 1896 Preface to *Desperate Remedies* Hardy remarked that "certain characteristics which provoked most discussion in my latest story were present in this my first—published in 1871, when there was no French name for them" (viii). He had apparently come to feel that in its direct confrontation of social and sexual questions his first published novel could be linked with his last to give a satisfying sense of symmetry to his whole career as a novelist. Had *The Poor Man and the Lady* survived, the circularity would have been still more marked, and it is indeed conceivable that the title of *Jude the Obscure* deliberately embodied a private allusion to the abortive early manuscript: in *Jude* it had been Hardy's idea, *Later Years* (49) reports, "to use the difficulty of a poor man's acquiring learning at that date merely as the 'tragic mischief' (among others) of a dramatic story, for which purpose an old-fashioned university at the very door of the poor man was the most striking method". Hardy's unhappy experience with his first book seems to have taught him not that the concept of the social instrumentality of fiction was invalid, but that it was commercially impracticable, at least for a new and unknown author. In his first published novels he was thus forced to a radical confrontation with the problem of determining what sort of a novelist he was to be, of shaping his work to the circumstances of his time and the necessities of his own situation. The process seems to have involved not so much the surrender as the gradual repression, in terms of literary expression, of the kind of emotions, opinions, and attitudes which had gone into *The Poor Man and the Lady*—and which were only to return fully to the surface in the pages of *Jude the Obscure*.

One of the chief problems facing the critic of Hardy's fiction must be that of reconciling the discontinuity with the circularity, and both with the extraordinary inequality of achievement in successive books (such as *Tess of the d'Urbervilles* and *The Well-Beloved*) at every stage of his career. It is not the aim of the present study to argue a particular thesis about Hardy or his work, but rather to take a fresh look at both the texts and the contexts of his fiction, to explore—and to juxtapose—the world he inhabited as a man and the world he created as an artist. If the results of so speculative an investigation do not readily lend themselves to neat formulations, it may at least be possible to distinguish the directions in which they point—to suggest, for example, that although Hardy was from the beginning a conscious and indeed conscientious artist he seems never to have grasped comprehensively either the possibilities or the responsibilities inherent in the adoption of particular techniques, nor to have been entirely capable of judging the impact of his work upon its readers; that the elaboration of Wessex, though crucial to the creation of his finest novels, was a matter of slow and hesitant evolution rather than of instantaneous vision; that his concern with the fate of the agricultural community was inseparable from his discovery of subject and had relatively little significance in socio-political terms; that far from being an aggressive advocate of rigid social and philosophical positions he was, in all but his earliest and latest fiction, extremely hesitant and ambiguous in his handling of ideas, and reluctant to venture into the areas of politics and social policy.

The discontinuity in Hardy's career as a novelist can be associated with an attractive readiness to experiment with new settings and new kinds of subject-matter, but it must also be related to his persistent failure, as an artist, to learn from his own past experiences. The inequalities in his work can be partly explained in terms of biographical circumstances, but there remains a sense in which success or failure also depended upon creative accident, upon Hardy's discovering a theme and a story so compelling upon his imagination that it burned away in its intensity the kind of suffocating redundancies—sometimes contrived, often semi-autobiographical, always non-functional—to which he instinctively resorted when external pressures seemed inexorable and inspiration ran low. Artist though he was, Hardy never attained that kind of basic, unfailing competence in all branches of his trade which sustains even the least distinguished work of a novelist like Henry James. Yet when his imagination had been seized by a central dominating figure, or by an overpowering movement of human compassion, Hardy's fiction could generate a power to stir the profoundest emotions of its readers, to shape and subvert their previous vision of the world, which went beyond the range not only of his contemporaries but of almost any novelist who has written in English.

Part One
APPRENTICESHIP

DESPERATE REMEDIES
Published: March 1871

UNDER THE GREENWOOD TREE
Published: June 1872

A PAIR OF BLUE EYES
Serial: September 1872–July 1873
Published: May 1873

I

Desperate Remedies

The Poor Man and the Lady was written in late 1867 and the first half of 1868, after ill-health forced Hardy to return from Blomfield's drawing-office in London to his home in Bockhampton and a job with John Hicks, to whom he had first been articled more than ten years earlier. Submitted to Macmillan on July 25, 1868, the manuscript was rejected by them before the end of the year, and by Chapman and Hall the following February. Ignoring the advice of Meredith (with whom he had an interview in March) that publication would damage his future prospects as a writer, Hardy sent the manuscript on to the rather less fastidious publishing house of Tinsley Brothers. William Tinsley apparently responded with an offer to publish the book if Hardy himself would guarantee part of the cost, but on September 14, 1869, Hardy wrote to say that the terms proposed were beyond his reach and that the manuscript should be returned.[1]

It seems to have been at about this time, during Hardy's temporary employment as an architectural assistant with the Weymouth firm of G. R. Crickmay, that work on *Desperate Remedies* was begun. Weymouth, under the fictional name of Creston (changed to Budmouth in the 1896 edition), was to provide one of the chief settings of the new novel, and it was while Hardy was still living in the town during the winter of 1869–70, after his engagement with Crickmay had come to an end, that the bulk of the novel must presumably have been written. Early in February 1870 he returned home to Bockhampton, and on March 5, two days before setting out at Crickmay's request to inspect a dilapidated church at St Juliot in

Cornwall, he sent off to Alexander Macmillan his nearly-completed manuscript. A month later Macmillan rejected the book on the grounds of its sensationalism, John Morley having reported to him that it had excellent structural and stylistic qualities but turned on "a disgusting and absurd outrage" and contained a number of "highly extravagant" scenes, notably one "between Miss Aldclyffe and her new maid in bed". Morley added: "Yet the book shows *power*—at present of a violent and undisciplined kind".[2]

When the manuscript came back from Macmillan, Hardy must have sent it immediately on to Tinsley, who wrote acknowledging it, still without its final chapters, on April 7. Tinsley—who was not, of course, the "stranger" to Hardy that *Early Life* (100) suggests—later offered to publish the book if Hardy would contribute £75 towards the costs and make a number of revisions. These terms were accepted, and on December 9, 1870, Tinsley wrote to acknowledge the arrival of the *Desperate Remedies* manuscript—revised, completed, and with several chapters recopied by Miss Emma Lavinia Gifford, whom Hardy had met during his visit to St Juliot the previous March. On March 25, 1871, the novel was published anonymously in three volumes, and Hardy's career as a novelist began.

The consequences of Meredith's advice about writing a novel with a more complicated plot are evident throughout the book. The action turns upon the plight of a beautiful and penniless girl, Cytherea Graye, who finds herself at the mercy of wealth, represented by the ageing beauty, Miss Aldclyffe, in mysterious alliance with sensuality, in the person of Aeneas Manston, the sinister steward. Forced into marriage with Manston, whom she regards with mingled fascination and repulsion, Cytherea is saved only by a series of dramatic interventions and the revelation of Manston as the murderer of his first wife. In plot terms *Desperate Remedies* thus falls firmly within the sensation-novel category, allied to— if not, perhaps, greatly influenced by—the work of Wilkie Collins,[3] and with a wide range of effects heralded by the epigraph from Scott: "Though an unconnected course of adventure is what most frequently occurs in nature, yet the province of the romance-writer being artificial, there is more required from him than a mere compliance with the simplicity of reality". Hardy's early enrolment of himself among the writers of romance is significant for the whole pattern of his subsequent career. More immediately, the epigraph serves as an *apologia* for the contrivances of the plot and points towards such elements in the story as the heightened, melodramatic quality of much of the action and the way in which Cytherea is surrounded by forces of darkness: the "hot voluptuous" and "animal" (250) passion of Manston; the overpowering masculinity of Miss Aldclyffe, whom Cytherea associates with "deeds of darkness rather than of light" (129); and all the "ghastly" (66) suggestions which surround the old manor house.

Much of the novel—the gloomy ruin, the light-dark imagery, the hints at secret relationships and mysterious powers—seems unmistakably Gothic, although it is characteristic of Hardy and of *Desperate Remedies* itself that supernaturalism is rejected, no mystery or eerie effect left without its rational explanation. Some of the concealed relationships between the characters, for instance, are sufficiently exposed from a fairly early stage for an alert reader to bridge remaining lacunae for himself. Miss Aldclyffe's first name of Cytherea not only links her directly with Cytherea Graye but hints at the fact that she is the mother of *Aeneas* Manston. The villagers, however, suspect her of being Manston's mistress, and Hardy merges a false clue with a real one by allowing her to appear virtually as the Dido to Manston's Aeneas, as an ageing imperious beauty consumed by a hopeless passion for a younger man. It is not clear whether Springrove's name was intended to contain a suggestion of the Adonis myth and thus hint at an eventual partnership with Cytherea/Venus, but there can be no doubt of the self-consciously literary element in the novel, nor of the considerable care given to the detailed working out of the story.

Though Hardy may have written the novel against the grain of his instincts and original ambitions, he did not approach it casually. In early chapters a good deal of attention is devoted to the establishment of characterisation, setting, and social context, and although this concern progressively gives way to a preoccupation with plot manipulation and a somewhat tenuously sustained narrative suspense, Hardy keeps the novel firmly focused on the figure of Cytherea. As the quintessential victim, she is at the centre of the sensation-novel plot: it is her innocence and powerlessness which claim the reader's sympathy and give substance to a Gothic apparatus which would otherwise provoke scarcely a tremor. She is also the protagonist of that more realistic exploration of the personal predicament of a vulnerable young woman which is the novel's other major aspect. This is not to say that the action is consistently presented, explicitly or implicitly, from her point of view; rather that her experience is for Hardy the essential core of the novel, and to such an extent that his imagination seems scarcely capable of encompassing the thoughts and feelings of the other characters except insofar as they impinge upon Cytherea and her situation. It was perhaps for this reason that Hardy could allow Edward Springrove to remain so colourless—man of action though he proves—and be satisfied to create Manston in heavily conventional terms.

Cytherea is an embodiment of beauty and sexuality around whom the other characters, male and female, irresistibly hover. Her awareness of her own beauty is made clear by the scene in which she admires herself naked in the mirror (86), and it appears from the reactions of Mr Raunham, the ageing vicar, that she cannot help exploiting, albeit unconsciously, her sexual attractions. Essentially, however, she is passive—"docility was at all times natural to Cytherea" (106)—and thus all the more provocative to both Miss Aldclyffe and Manston. The novel contains several instances of quite explicit sexual comment. Cytherea, always extremely conscious of Manston's sexuality, feels him pressing threateningly upon her clothes (151, 254). Miss Aldclyffe, making her own approaches to Cytherea, is brutal in her sexual references: there is hardly a girl, she says, whose heart has not been "*had*" (93), and Cytherea herself seems like a "dusty highway" (94) because she has allowed a man to kiss her.

The emphasis on different kinds of sexuality is, by common agreement, one of the most remarkable aspects of *Desperate Remedies*, and it is not altogether surprising that Hardy should have been reported as saying in 1894 that *Desperate Remedies* had in 1871 contained "many passages exhibiting a similar plainness to *Tess*".[4] But if Cytherea certainly anticipates Tess in her combination of sexuality and passivity Hardy may have been thinking also of her role as victim. The poignancy of Cytherea's predicament is that she is deserted or threatened not only by those figures who conventionally menace the heroines of Gothic tales—the mysterious older woman, the would-be possessor— but also by figures not normally found in such roles, her father and her brother. The helpless orphan victim is common enough, but the early presentation of Cytherea's father suggests that he has almost wilfully precipitated her into that position through his casualness about money and personal safety. Her brother's failures as a substitute protector are also underlined, and his illness seems only a confirmation of a more fundamental weakness. Owen's capacity for deliberate evil should not be exaggerated— like Cytherea he is a victim of circumstance—but there is something in his behaviour which answers to his father's essential carelessness, and he moves from the mere passive inadequacy of allowing Cytherea to go boating with Springrove in a compromising manner to active propulsion of her in the direction of self-sacrifice and disaster, permitting her to go into service as a lady's maid and encouraging her to marry Manston.

If Cytherea's predicament is imaged by both the Gothic and the social elements of the story, it is made most explicit in her own outcry as an individual against all the pressures which have been brought to bear upon her:

'Yes—my duty to society,' she murmured. 'But ah, Owen, it is difficult to adjust our outer and inner life with perfect honesty to all! Though it may be right to care more for the benefit of the many than for the indulgence of your own single self, when you consider that the many, and duty to them, only exist to you through your own existence, what can be said? What do our own acquaintances care about us? Not much. I think of mine. Mine will now (do they learn all the wicked frailty of my heart in this affair) look at me, smile sickly, and condemn me. And perhaps, far in time to come, when I am dead and gone, some other's accent, or some other's song, or thought, like an old one of mine, will carry them back to what I used to say, and hurt their hearts a little that they blamed me so soon. And they will pause just for an instant, and give a sigh to me, and think, "Poor girl!" believing they do great justice to my memory by this. But they will never, never realize that it was my single opportunity of existence, as well as of doing my duty, which they are regarding; they will not feel that what to them is but a thought, easily held in those two words of pity, "Poor girl!" was a whole life to me; as full of hours, minutes, and peculiar minutes, of hopes and dreads, smiles, whisperings, tears, as theirs: that it was my world, what is to them their world, and they in that life of mine, however much I cared for them, only as the thought I seem to them to be. Nobody can enter into another's nature truly, that's what is so grievous.'

'Well, it cannot be helped,' said Owen. (278–279)

This is powerfully evoked and intensely moving; it is made more so by that abruptly unsympathetic reply from the brother who speaks with the voice of "duty to society" (278) and of self-interest, and by the placing of the outcry at a moment when the wedding with Manston has already taken place and all seems hopeless. If the passage stands out from the surrounding text, that is not simply because it is largely "prosed" from one of Hardy's early poems[5] but because it comes as the expression of feelings long suppressed and as a confirmation of the centrality of Cytherea's characterisation to the novel as a whole.

It would be wrong to try to make of *Desperate Remedies* something more cohesive than it really is. The "sensational" formulae and Gothic ingredients have been imported more opportunistically than systematically; Hardy's conceptions of appropriate narrative method remain largely scenic and strictly linear and reveal little appreciation of the possibilities and responsibilities inherent in the choice of point of view. The failure to achieve a satisfactory balance between the divergent aspects of *Desperate Remedies* has led critics to speak of Hardy's surrendering to the demands of sensational fiction only after abandoning an original attempt to write a novel of a more serious nature. What the book as a whole seems to reveal, however, is not so much a wavering between two opposed conceptions as a deliberate and reasonably consistent attempt to combine them—to accommodate within the framework of a sensation novel that kind of richness of treatment, of characterisation, and of human sympathy to which Hardy's instincts as an artist naturally impelled him. *Early Life* (268) records the following note of January 14, 1888:

> A "sensation-novel" is possible in which the sensationalism is not casualty, but evolution; not physical but psychical. . . . The difference between the latter kind of novel and the novel of physical sensationalism—*i.e.*, personal adventure, etc.,—is this: that whereas in the physical the adventure itself is the subject of interest, the psychical results being passed over as commonplace, in the psychical the casualty or adventure is held to be of no intrinsic interest, but the effect upon the faculties is the important matter to be depicted.

The inexperienced Hardy of 1870 was perhaps incapable of such discriminations, but the later note may nonetheless reflect the drift of his thinking at the time the book was being written. *Desperate Remedies* represents not a sacrifice of realism to sensationalism, nor even of sensationalism to realism, but an attempt to achieve, through the sensitively presented pivotal figure of Cytherea, a fusion of the two. Even if the attempt cannot be said to have succeeded, the failure was an interesting one, of which, so his successive prefaces would suggest, Hardy himself did not feel ashamed in later years.

2

"Ce Saxon autodidacte":
A Matter of Education

Although the first review of *Desperate Remedies* (in the *Athenaeum* for April 1, 1871)[1] deplored the novel's occasional coarseness of expression, it had warm praise for Hardy's plotting and characterisation. Despite this early encouragement, Hardy seems to have been defenceless in the face of the *Spectator* review later that same month: according to *Early Life* (111), "the bitterness of that moment was never forgotten; at the time he wished that he were dead". The bitterness, indeed, may have permitted some distortion to creep into the autobiographical account, which not only passes over the many favourable observations in the review in order to focus on the hostile opening paragraphs but incorporates a small yet significant misquotation: where the reviewer had written of his hope of stirring the author "to better things in the the future than these 'desperate remedies' which he has adopted for ennui or an emaciated purse",[2] *Early Life* (111) alludes merely to a "galling" suggestion "that the novel must have been 'a desperate remedy for an emaciated purse'". The omission of "ennui" stresses the insinuation of poverty; it also suggests Hardy's sensitivity to this implication at a moment of extreme financial vulnerability.

In 1871 Hardy had little reason to feel satisfied with his economic prospects. At the very moment when he was thinking of marriage to Emma Lavinia Gifford he was also contemplating the abandonment of the architectural career to which he had been trained in favour of a wholly new and hazardous career as a writer.

But the selective insistence on an "emaciated purse" perhaps hints at wider areas of Hardy's personality—at a more general uncertainty, at social and educational insecurity, at a fear of being somehow not quite acceptable in the literary world to which he now aspired. In an article published in 1881, in the *British Quarterly Review*, Hardy's friend Charles Kegan Paul spoke of the novelist's proud identification with the "race of labouring men" from which he sprang;[3] writing to Paul shortly afterwards Hardy gently insisted that his immediate ancestors had all been master-masons and employers of journeymen, never journeymen themselves.[4] Hardy seems indeed to have been justified in identifying himself, on this and other occasions, with the class of life-holders and independent tradesmen whose disappearance from the village community is lamented in the final paragraphs of his essay on "The Dorsetshire Labourer".[5] It has recently been pointed out, however, that the 1851 census of Stinsford parish listed Hardy's father as a brick-layer employing two labourers, and his brother James as a mason also employing two labourers.[6] Though independent, the Hardys seem not to have been in a very substantial way of business, and the resources available for educating and assisting young Thomas and the other children cannot have been great. Hardy received as a boy a very respectable education at Isaac Last's school in Dorchester, but he left school to become articled to John Hicks at the age of sixteen, and it is not easy to accept entirely at face value the suggestion in the *Early Life* (44) that, had not his friend Horace Moule advised him to concentrate on an architectural career, Hardy might have gone on to a university in his early twenties, "his father never absolutely refusing to advance him money in a good cause". Cambridge is the university most often mentioned in this connection,[7] but it seems permissible to question whether the family could in fact have afforded to send him there, or even whether his previous education and reading would have been adequate to ensure success. There seems little doubt that Hardy did at one time entertain ambitions of a university education, and markings in his copy of *The Popular Educator* show that he took particular interest in two articles dealing with the regulations for admission to the University of

London, both of them stressing that "self-taught students" were perfectly entitled to become members of the University if they could pass the requisite examinations.[8]

In his copy of F. A. Hedgcock's *Thomas Hardy, penseur et artiste* (1911), Hardy pencilled an objection to the description of himself as *"ce Saxon autodidacte"*, commenting: "This is not literary criticism, but impertinent personality & untrue, as he was taught Latin & French at School and college".[9] As with other annotations in the margins of Hedgecock's book,[10] the sharpness of the retort reflects a sensitivity about his background which had become exacerbated over the years by the social pretensions—impressive mainly in the tenacity with which they were advanced —of his first wife, and by his own developed fondness for the company of the upper classes. And, despite Hardy's protest, the question of his autodidacticism does raise issues which extend into the area of literary criticism. The extreme response to the *Spectator* review which had, in fact, many things to say in praise of *Desperate Remedies* is essentially of a piece with, for example, the readiness to modify or revise his texts in accordance with the objections of editors and reviewers, and with the tendency of the early novels to incorporate items of information of the most miscellaneous and incidental kind. Hardy was, as a young man, fascinated with technical terminology and eager to display his mastery not only of architecture but also of the kind of knowledge to be found in encyclopaedias and in educational works of the self-help variety. His library at the time of his death still contained not only *The Popular Educator*—published, as *Early Life* (32) observes, "by that genius in home-education, John Cassell"— but also such other volumes as *The Boys' Book of Science, Elements of Experimental and Natural Philosophy* (a gift from Horace Moule in 1857), John Timbs's *Things Not Generally Known, Familiarly Explained*, and *The Boys' Own Book*, purchased in 1853, from which Hardy apparently drew such items as the term *"en papillon"* for Sergeant Troy's method of treading water when he was swept out to sea in *Far from the Madding Crowd* and the technique of catching bullfinches advocated by Farmer Shiner in *Under the Greenwood Tree*.[11]

No reader can fail to notice—and few critics have failed to deplore—the ponderous allusions to literature and art which strew with their initial capitals the pages of Hardy's early novels. Traces of his deliberate and painstaking acquisition of the knowledge that these allusions represent remain in the reading lists preserved in *Early Life* and in surviving notebooks: a small notebook of 1865, for instance, entitled "Studies, Specimens etc"; another headed "12 May. 1863. Schools of Painting", possibly a survival from the period when Hardy thought of becoming an art critic; yet another, dated 1867 but lacking its first forty leaves, in which he jotted down quotations from authors as various as Zola and Sir Thomas Browne.[12] Throughout his life Hardy kept commonplace books both for factual information (usually gathered from newspapers old and new) and for literary and philosophical comment, often copying out long passages from such journals as the *Athenaeum*, the *Spectator*, the *Fortnightly Review*, and the *Revue des deux mondes*. A number of scrapbooks of cuttings, chiefly of reviews of Hardy's books, also survive.

To the student of Hardy these records must be of considerable interest, but they can also seem profoundly depressing. The so-called "Trumpet-Major Notebook" and the commonplace book labelled "Facts" both contain material which Hardy subsequently transposed into his fiction or his verse, while the volumes of "Literary Notes" offer occasional hints of specific influences which may have helped to mould both his thought and his imagination.[13] There remains, however, something disturbing and essentially sterile about this methodical storage of miscellaneous information, sustained over so many years that it must in some sense have been indispensable to Hardy's functioning as a man or as an artist, or perhaps as both.

If the notebooks provide a useful demonstration of the extent to which Hardy's imagination fed on literary and journalistic sources as well as on his own experience and observation, they also point to a fundamental lack of assurance which Hardy as an artist rapidly outgrew but which seems to have inhibited his personal life even into old age. Throughout his career, even in the days of his greatest reputation and success, Hardy was to remain acutely sensitive to hostile judgments, however casually advanced, however obscure their source. Whatever psychological reasons might be adduced for this extreme vulnerability—perhaps to be associated with his dislike of being touched[14]—something must certainly be attributed to his experience, as a young man, of social, economic, and educational insecurity. It is perhaps dangerous, Raymond Williams has suggested, to speak of Hardy as an autodidact, since his actual grasp of the world of contemporary thought and knowledge was greater than that of many men fortunate enough to have received a more extended formal education.[15] But if Hardy's letters show him to have been capable of sustaining a form of philosophical dialogue with such people as the Hon. Roden Noel, Sir Henry Newbolt, John Galsworthy, and J. McT. E. McTaggart,[16] some of his explicit statements of speculation or belief nonetheless reveal a sense of insecurity, an overanxious calculation of the reader's likely response, which seems directly analogous to the self-conscious allusiveness of the early fiction.

The mark of the autodidact is perhaps to be found not so much in what he knows as in how he regards the world of knowledge. Where Hardy's friend and contemporary Edmund Gosse succeeded with splendid if precarious verve in conquering that world, at least to the extent of escaping categorisation as the autodidact he most certainly was, Hardy himself seems always to have treated it with somewhat nervous deference. At Gosse's teaparties, Edward Marsh recalled, Hardy tended to be extremely uncommunicative,[17] and while the example of other novelists should alert us to the possibility that such withdrawals represented conservation of energy or comprehensive alertness of attention on Hardy's part, it would certainly appear that he had, at least until after the publication of The Dynasts, a serious reluctance to expound his own views in public—by which time, as W. R. Rutland pointed out, the "advanced" ideas of his younger days had become thoroughly unfashionable in their turn.[18] Even that serenity which marked his closing years, and to which so many younger men were to testify, seems to have inhered in a radiation of personality rather than in any dissemination of articulated wisdom. Hardy may have known more than many a man with a university education, but he lacked the kind of intellectual as well as social assurance that such an education might have given him, and if the hero of *Jude the Obscure* cannot in any direct sense be linked with its author, it seems obvious, despite all protestations to the contrary, that the novel carries a heavy freight of transferred autobiography, of deeply experienced personal frustration of an intellectual as well as a sexual kind.

3

Under the Greenwood Tree

Of the rural episodes in *Desperate Remedies* the *Spectator* reviewer had concluded: "The scenes allotted to these humble actors are few and slight, but they indicate powers that might and ought to be extended largely in this direction, instead of being prostituted to the purposes of idle prying into the ways of wickedness".[1] This sentence, prudently cut off at "direction", was quoted alongside similar praise of the rural scenes by the *Athenaeum* reviewer in Hardy's August 7, 1871 letter to Macmillan which accompanied the manuscript of *Under the Greenwood Tree*.[2] The general agreement among the reviewers as to the excellence of at least this aspect of his first published novel must have encouraged Hardy to entertain considerable hopes for the success of his new, entirely rural story, but there is no evidence that the reviews were in any sense influential upon its conception and composition. Indeed, when Horace Moule in the *Saturday Review* commended the cider-making scene in *Desperate Remedies* as "the same sort of thing in written sentences that a clear fresh country piece of Hobbema's is in art", he may well have been aware that Hardy had already submitted to Macmillan the manuscript sub-titled "A Rural Painting of the Dutch School".[3]

Alexander Macmillan returned the manuscript to Hardy on October 18, 1871, commenting on the slightness of the tale and making only a vague offer to reconsider it in the spring.[4] Presumably Hardy set some store by this half-promise—or very little store by the book itself—since, when he wrote to Tinsley on October 20, it was to sound him out on the prospects for *A Pair of Blue Eyes*, then in its early stages; *Under the Greenwood Tree* was referred to only in passing as "a little rural story" which he had relinquished in view of the favourable reception given by "critic-friends" to the heavily plotted *Desperate Remedies*.[5] The letter, however, was ostensibly framed as an enquiry about the sales of *Desperate Remedies*, and Tinsley in his reply seems to have confined himself to that not very encouraging topic. It was only in March 1872 that Tinsley raised the possibility of his publishing another book by Hardy; at this point Hardy sent off *Under the Greenwood Tree*, and towards the end of April he accepted the offer of £30 for the copyright. Publication, originally in two volumes, followed in early June of the same year.

Under the Greenwood Tree seems clearly to have originated in the abandoned manuscript of *The Poor Man and the Lady*, and especially in "the opening pictures of the Christmas Eve in the tranter's house" which John Morley had reported to Macmillan as being "really of good quality".[6] But what *Under the Greenwood Tree* owed to its unpublished predecessor was—as its original title, "The Mellstock Quire", perhaps suggests—the evocation of a particular setting and a particular community, not a story; it seems clear from the manuscript of *Under the Greenwood Tree* that even when Hardy began writing the novel its plot, minimal as it is, had not yet been fully worked out. In particular, the whole relationship between Parson Maybold and Fancy Day seems to have been introduced only at a late stage. Prior to the final paragraphs of Part the Second, chapter 7—the point at which Fancy and the Vicar are first seen together—the allusions to an actual or potential intimacy between them may well have been late additions to the manuscript: the paragraph in Part the First, chapter 6, beginning "By chance or by fate" (40) was inserted on a facing MS page, as were also the paragraph beginning "I fancy I see him" (71) and the two succeeding paragraphs in chapter 2 of Part the Second.[7] Farmer Shiner's interest in Fancy existed from the first, but Hardy seems to have introduced the plot complication revolving upon Parson Maybold's admiration of the heroine only when more than half the book had already been written.

This shift in emphasis may have determined Hardy's change of title. When submitting the manuscript to Macmillan Hardy had referred to it as *Under the Greenwood Tree*, but its first page must still have shown, as it does now, the deletion of "The Mellstock Quire". These words did not appear on the first edition title-page, but Hardy later brought them back as an alternative title, implying in the 1912 Preface that he would have restored them to their original position had it not seemed "undesirable to displace . . . the title by which the book first became known" (ix). It is difficult to share this preference for an inertly descriptive title, however appropriate to a genre painting "of the Dutch school", over one so richly suggestive. John F. Danby has argued, in an excellent article, that Hardy's original title placed the emphasis where it properly belongs, on the social and permanent aspects of the story rather than on the individual and transitory: "the importance of the love-story, in Hardy's view, . . . is that really it is unimportant: or not really important in the way those immediately concerned in it think it is".[8] Yet the familiar title seems no less evocative of precisely those aspects which Danby rightly stresses, and it goes much further than the other in calling attention to the whole frame of reference within which the novel is set. "The Mellstock Quire" adequately identifies the material and the main subject of the book; *Under the Greenwood Tree* suggests further the central theme and the underlying mode of treatment.

Clearly, the final title was not—as *Early Life* (113) implies— picked out casually from *The Golden Treasury* in order to satisfy a contemporary fashion for "titles from poetry". The phrase of course comes from the song in *As You Like It* (II.v,) a play which seems to have had a special fascination for Hardy. His poem, "To an Impersonator of Rosalind", shows that he was much impressed by the performance of Mrs Scott-Siddons in that role in 1867 (see also the later "The Two Rosalinds"), and the "neat figure" and "freedom of gesture" with which Mrs Scott-Siddons is credited in contemporary accounts[9] may conceivably have contributed something to the emphasis in *Under the Greenwood Tree* on Fancy Day's ease and grace of movement: "Flexibility was her first characteristic, by which she appeared to enjoy the most easeful rest when she was in gliding motion" (48). Fancy, indeed, has a good deal about her of the Shakespearean comic heroine, not least the quickness of wit she displays in her exchange with Farmer Shiner in the chapter on the honey-taking, and her early treatment of Dick suggests a less sophisticated version of Rosalind's teasing of the devoted Orlando—apparently a high-point of Mrs Scott-Siddons's performance.

The main function of the *As You Like It* allusion in the title of *Under the Greenwood Tree* is anticipated, interestingly enough, by an allusion to the same song in *Desperate Remedies*. Cytherea, just entering into service at Miss Aldclyffe's, gazes out of the window as she reflects on her unhappy situation:

> The petty, vulgar details of servitude that she had just passed through, her dependence upon the whims of a strange woman, the necessity of quenching all individuality of character in herself, and relinquishing her own peculiar tastes to help on the wheel of this alien establishment, made her sick and sad, and she almost longed to pursue some free, out-of-doors employment, sleep under trees or a hut, and know no enemy but winter and cold weather, like shepherds and cowkeepers, and birds and animals—ay, like the sheep she saw there under her window. (71–72)

The sheep are used in the following paragraphs to establish a narrative link, but their introduction here (as in the opening scene of *The Trumpet-Major*) helps to establish a specifically pastoral pattern of reference. The Shakespearean allusion fits into that pattern, and it again does so throughout *Under the Greenwood Tree*, where it is worked into the very fabric of the book—in terms, for instance, of the actual greenwood tree which provides the centre-piece for the wedding celebrations at the end of the novel, and of the final scene of all, with its reference, in the nightingale's "come hither", to the same song from *As You Like It*. As Fancy promises Dick that she will have no secrets from him "from to-day":

> From a neighbouring thicket was suddenly heard to issue in a loud, musical, and liquid voice—

[45]

'Tippiwit! swe-e-et! ki-ki-ki! Come hither, come hither, come hither!'

'O 'tis the nightingale,' murmured she, and thought of a secret she would never tell. (211)

Fancy's secret, unlike that of the nightingale, is of her own guilt, not of another's: in Arcadian Mellstock, clearly, as in the Forest of Arden, the ways of women may present a hazard at least as threatening as that of "winter and rough weather".

It would be too much to suggest that Hardy attempted or even contemplated any detailed pattern of correspondences between his novel and Shakespeare's play. Consciously and unconsciously, however, *As You Like It* was a lively presence in his imagination, prompting by its structural incorporation of music, song, and dance his own adoption of comparable techniques, encouraging and sustaining him in his choice of a pastoral theme and treatment, in the composition of a story with the patterned simplicity of a country dance and the time-honoured familiarity of a ballad. Because it is so simple, so familiar, and so highly patterned it is hard not to think of *Under the Greenwood Tree* as a kind of parable carrying with it the sort of mild moral always implicit in the simplest of pastorals—a moral, here, of individual transience and racial permanence:

> Yonder a maid and her wight
> Come whispering by:
> War's annals will cloud into night
> Ere their story die.[10]

Hardy seems to have conceived of *Under the Greenwood Tree* as a kind of woodland pastoral, moving in time with the procession of the seasons (an idea Hardy may have taken from Elizabethan pastorals, from Thomson, or from William Barnes) and in isolation from the world of great events. The characters are mostly musicians; their festivals and important occasions are musically celebrated. On the first page of the book Dick Dewy sings a song about sheep-shearing; in the final chapter the extended description of his marriage-day culminates in the dancing under the greenwood tree. The image of the dance, so persistent throughout

Hardy's work, is here especially pervasive, closely related as it is to the theme of choosing and exchanging partners. Dick's situation, for instance, is beautifully defined in terms of the dance of "Triumph, or Follow my Lover" during the tranter's party: in this dance, "according to the interesting rule laid down" (48), partners change from time and time, so that although Dick is initially successful in securing Fancy as his "prize" he has still to endure the sight of her coming down the room with Farmer Shiner "like two persons tripping down a lane to be married" (48)—just such a lane, it might be added, as the actual wedding party walks down in the chapter called "The Knot There's No Untying".

If the characters tend to range themselves dynastically, "two and two: every man hitched up to his woman" (201), they also tend in general conversation to bear an independent part as in a musical performance: each has his or her "note", and each—even Thomas Leaf—has his turn to sound it. The practical question of the church music is central to the story, and Parson Maybold's infatuation with Fancy reaches its height on the day of her first appearance as church organist. Music, indeed, is of such importance throughout the novel that responsiveness to it becomes—as so often with Shakespeare and the Elizabethan poets—a criterion of moral evaluation. We learn much of Fancy Day, Farmer Shiner, and Parson Maybold as—by one of Hardy's happiest devices—we are introduced to them in turn as the choir makes its rounds on Christmas Eve. Later in the novel it is Fancy's sensitivity to music which prevents her being regarded as the choir's enemy, while the essential coarseness of Farmer Shiner is confirmed by his singing unsuitable ballads in Fancy's presence. It is true that Dick criticises the rhymes of the ballad rather than its statements (159), but Hardy must have expected some at least of his readers to know that Shiner's ballad was, as he himself later remarked to a correspondent, "a coarsely humorous one" with a first stanza somewhat as follows:

> King Arthur he had three sons,
> Big rogues as ever did swing,

He had three sons of wh—s
And he kicked them all three out-of-doors
Because they could not sing.[11]

Of the musicians themselves it is William Dewy, the most
devoted to music, who displays the greatest magnanimity, and it
is with his point of view that Hardy's own position seems to be
most closely identified, insofar as he can be said to have taken a
position at all within the world of the novel. Harmony becomes a
dominant concept, and in the speech of these country people who
make their own music images of harmony recur with a marvellous
inevitability:

> Mrs. Dewy came up, talking to one person and looking at
> another. 'Happy, yes,' she said. "Tis always so when a couple
> is so exactly in tune with one another as Dick and she.'
> 'When they be'n't too poor to have time to sing,' said grand-
> father James. (209)

Grandfather James, not a musician, is the melancholy Jaques
of this greenwood—the correspondence of names may not be
accidental, although James was also a Hardy family name—and
his "inharmonious" (201) note of cold realism is consistently
disruptive of the idyllic surface. *As You Like It* is full of songs of
youth and love which find their echo in *Under the Greenwood Tree*,
but it also contains "Blow, blow, thou winter wind" as well as the
disquisition of Jaques on the seven ages of man, and these anti-
pastoral themes are also heard in Hardy's novel: the book is, as it
were, framed between grandfather William and grandfather
James. Much is made of the sequence, the conflict, and ultimately
the succession of the generations. The recurrent dances effectively divide the group into the children, the young, the middle-
aged, and the old, while the retrospective tendency of the conversation and the very antiquity of the customs being observed
all promote a constant awareness that those who are old were once
young and those now in the energy of youth will soon become old
in their turn. Dick Dewy becomes dimly aware of such truths as
he argues with his father about Fancy Day across the gap of a

generation, as he notes the curious similarities in the behaviour of all long-married couples or listens to their talk of their own courtships. And these are among the truths richly symbolised in the greenwood tree itself.

Under the Greenwood Tree is to some extent an ironic title, and fairly radical patterns of irony can be traced within the book itself—although "irony" may not always be quite the right term for that perpetual re-adjustment of the human balance which is what really seems to be going on. Each gain in the book has its counter-balancing loss, each happiness its sadness, each despair its triumph; there *are* enemies under the greenwood tree, nonetheless the "winter wind" does blow some people some good. Grandfather James's disenchanted comments have their due impact, but many of Hardy's effects are achieved in less explicit ways. In Part the Fifth, in particular, there is to the wedding of Dick and Fancy a quiet but audible undertone of foreboding, not so much of a troubled marriage ahead (though that suspicion is not entirely absent) as of the consequences which the passage of time will bring in its train. Dick, his romantic feelings already giving way to practical good sense, arrives late because he has paused to hive a swarm of bees: as grandfather James observes, "marrying a woman is a thing you can do at any moment; but a swarm o' bees won't come for the asking" (201). Fancy, six hours a wife, tries to look matronly, but there are plenty of pointers to suggest that she will be a matron all too soon: Nat Callcombe says the married couple have so much food and furniture "that anybody would think they were going to take hold the big end of married life first, and begin wi' a grown-up family" (198). The furniture removed to Dick's house has sadly depleted the keeper's cottage, and we have a sense of the Day household itself having been broken up. Enoch has left (as appears in an oddly disturbing episode at the end of the penultimate chapter), and Mrs Day, retreating ever further from reality, has gone upstairs to dust the second-best china. Life, it seems, has moved on and away from the keeper's cottage, and it may not be irrelevant to note that Dick's bees have swarmed while Mrs Day's have not.

The importance given to bees—they are persistently associated with crucial events in Dick's courtship of Fancy—exemplifies Hardy's extraordinary success in this novel in evoking large patterns in terms of trivial details, rooting the symbolic in the domestic and everyday. Whatever suggestions the bees may prompt—from thoughts of the fourth book of the *Georgics* and of the seasonal cycle to images of female domination—their presence in the book depends upon the importance of honey in the rural economy at a period when sugar was an imported luxury, expensive and heavily taxed. Similarly grounded in the realities of Dorset life in the first half of the nineteenth century, before that exodus of rural craftsmen which Hardy laments in "The Dorsetshire Labourer" and elsewhere, is the early episode in which Mr Penny dramatically places before his fascinated audience the boot belonging to Miss Fancy Day:

> Now, neighbours, though no common eye can see it,' the shoemaker went on, 'a man in the trade can see the likeness between this boot and that last, although that is so deformed as hardly to recall one of God's creatures, and this is one of as pretty a pair as you'd get for ten-and-sixpence in Casterbridge. To you, nothing; but 'tis father's voot and daughter's voot to me, as plain as houses.' (19)

The scene itself is superbly realised, with the glances of the men "converged like wheel-spokes upon the boot in the centre of them" (18): the heroine is auspiciously and (since Fancy is to prove quick-footed enough) appropriately heralded; one of the major themes of the novel, the inevitable procession of the generations, is stated early and in the most concrete of terms. Fancy's boot may lack the allusive potential of the greenwood tree in Part the Fifth, but it is a beautifully calculated embodiment of the book's abstract themes.

In praising the controlled composition of *Under the Greenwood Tree*—and it is the most nearly flawless of Hardy's novels—it is essential not to undervalue its immense page-by-page vitality and toughness of texture. The strength here comes primarily from the humour, all-pervasive though elusive of definition; from the dialogue, an unmistakably rural speech that avoids mere quaintness and dialectal eccentricity while achieving distinctiveness through a reassuring sufficiency of localisms; and from the discriminating use of "placing" detail in the evocation of setting and scene, as in the descriptions of the living-rooms of the Day and Dewy households. Hardy's intimate and affectionate familiarity with his material is fundamental to the success, and to the assurance, of *Under the Greenwood Tree*. The detailed descriptions of the various members of the Mellstock Quire, the account of Mr Penny at his work, the long passages of country conversation—these are by no means essential to the "story", the contest for the hand of Fancy Day, but they are the very stuff of the book.

As Hardy originally conceived of the book it may have been even more of a series of sketches and impressions—a kind of "Scenes from Rural Life"—than it is at present. The manuscript preserves indications of more numerous chapter divisions: the chapter called "Honey-taking, and Afterwards", for example, seems at one time to have been three separate chapters, "Honey-taking", "Emptying the hives", and "Dick pleads his cause".[12] The novel remains unusually rich in visual impressions, and the relevance of the sub-title, "A Rural Painting of the Dutch School", seems to extend beyond these to the deliberate delineation of customs, beliefs, attitudes, the whole fabric of rural life. The slight tale in its restricted setting is filled with figures, highly individualised as to both personality and social role, each of whom finds his place in the tightly-organised overall structure in terms not so much of plot as of what might in a painting be called composition: each has his position in the design, and whether that position be dominant or subordinate the figure itself appears in sharp focus.

The society presented in the novel is, in pastoral fashion, both remote and remarkably homogeneous: there is scarcely a murmur of the world outside, and Hardy may deliberately have excluded the inhabitants of the local manor-house in the interests of limiting the greenwood world to those who truly belong there.[13] Yet he insists, with a mild exploitation of pastoral for purposes of satire, that even Mellstock folk display a passionate preoccupation with questions of economic and social status, an intense concern for

niceties of behaviour and of domestic arrangement. Here as elsewhere Hardy anticipates Lawrence in stressing the perpetual
conflict between the women's striving towards gentility and the
unregenerate "animality" of the menfolk, and if vanity and social
ambition are dangerous flaws in the personality of Fancy Day,
her stepmother's obsession with "appearances" has reached a
point not far short of madness:

> The table had been spread for the mixed midday meal of
> dinner and tea which was common among frugal countryfolk.
> 'The parishioners about here,' continued Mrs. Day, not
> looking at any living being, but snatching up the brown delf
> tea-things, 'are the laziest, gossipest, poachest, jailest set of any
> ever I came among. And they'll talk about my teapot and tea-
> things next, I suppose!' She vanished with the teapot, cups,
> and saucers, and reappeared with a tea-service in white chain,
> and a packet wrapped in brown paper. This was removed,
> together with folds of tissue-paper underneath; and a brilliant
> silver teapot appeared. (105)

The second Mrs Day is, however, only sustaining a tradition
firmly established by the first. It is a crucial element in Fancy's
power to disturb both men and customs that she is of higher
educational and social standing than anyone in Mellstock apart
from Parson Maybold: her father's wealth is much discussed,
her mother was a governess, and she herself has been given an
education unusually good for a young woman in the first half of
the nineteenth century. The disruptive side-effects of Fancy's
education are evident enough: that she becomes entangled in
disagreements between the vicar, the church-warden, and the
choir is not simply because she is pretty but because she has been
taught to play the organ, and if she is not herself an active
innovator she is inevitably associated with the pressures making
for social change. Hardy also emphasises that she, like her father,
belongs not to Mellstock itself but to a neighbouring parish. Yet
the disappearance of the choir and of the traditions and values
which it embodied cannot be laid at Fancy's door. Choirs in other
parishes have already disappeared, and the Mellstock choir has

its internal weaknesses, among them the quiet cynicism of Reuben Dewy and the incipient defection of Dick. It is the chief pillar of the choir's strength, William Dewy himself, who is most indulgent towards Parson Maybold's innovation and most insistent that disbandment be accepted in a dignified and charitable manner. As for Fancy's specifically sexual role, it is notable that in the revisions which he made to the novel in 1896 and 1912 Hardy deliberately raised the social and economic status of Geoffrey Day —it is only in the 1912 edition that Day can contrast his earlier position as keeper with a situation in which he has "a dozen other irons in the fire as steward here for my lord" (163)—and, at the same time, significantly increased the dialect element in the speech of Dick Dewy.[14] The effect of these changes is to place Fancy, in socio-economic terms, further away from Dick and closer to Maybold, to re-emphasise her social location somewhere between the two men, and to increase both the credibility of Maybold's proposal and the reality of his threat. Farmer Shiner's vulgarity (Hardy seems originally to have conceived of him as a publican)[15] soon disqualifies him as a likely victor in the contest for Fancy's hand, but he too is a richer man than Dick and easily gains the support of Fancy's father.

Hardy once said that he was not interested in manners, and it may indeed have been that he did not feel particularly concerned with the manners of those urban middle and upper classes which had most often been made the subjects of nineteenth-century fiction. He had nonetheless a profound appreciation of the behavioural standards and social discriminations current among the country people he had known in his childhood and youth, and his fascination with these was sufficient to make *Under the Greenwood Tree* something very like a novel of rural manners. The book has already been referred to as pastoral, idyll, and potential parable; to define it also as a novel of rural manners may seem a little excessive. In fact, *Under the Greenwood Tree* cannot be precisely fitted into any terminological pigeonhole. While it displays elements of several literary modes it does not fully exemplify any one of them, and nothing in the book is more impressive than Hardy's refusal to allow it to become wholly predictable along the lines of a single formal precedent. Although the temptation in the final scenes to avoid reminders of Fancy's moment of weakness must have been a strong one, Hardy's chosen ending is far from conventional felicity, except in the sense that the book itself has by this time established its own conventions in terms of which the marriage of Dick and Fancy can be recognised as being reasonably fortunate—as marriages go. By the end of the novel something real if scarcely tangible has been lost, something detectable in the contrast between the air of unease and restraint which hangs over the dance under the greenwood tree and the comfortable enjoyment which marked the party at the tranter's in the opening pages.[16] For all the celebration of vanished woodland days and ways it is necessary to acknowledge that if *Under the Greenwood Tree* is an idyll it is one in which, at the end, many thing are less than idyllic.

4

Bockhampton and St Juliot:
The Exploitation of Autobiography

Despite John Morley's judgment that much of *The Poor Man and the Lady* read "like some clever lad's dream",[1] it seems clear that Hardy must in writing the novel have drawn freely upon his training as an architect and upon the experience of both country and city life which his Dorset childhood and his years in London had already given him. These same elements make a substantial contribution to *Desperate Remedies*. The father, brother, and both suitors of Cytherea are all architects, and the book incorporates scenes of rural and urban life quite as interesting in their socioeconomic implications as any in Hardy's later work: the matter of Farmer Springrove's leases, for instance, and the "depressing picture of married life among the very poor of a city" (350) which his son encounters while searching for Mrs Manston's workbox. Now, in *Under the Greenwood Tree*, Hardy drew immediately and intimately upon his own family background.

In his 1896 Preface to the novel he spoke almost as though it were simply a lightly fictionalised essay in historical reconstruction, "a fairly true picture, at first hand, of the personages, ways, and customs which were common among such orchestral bodies in the villages of fifty years ago".[2] The note is that of Hardy's letter published in the *Journal of the English Folk Dance Society* in 1927:

It is quite natural that my heretical query whether, after all, the country-dance might have been a successor to the true folk-dance should meet with opposition. I hold no strong views, but

I ask those who maintain otherwise to explain the following rather formidable facts:

1. Down to the middle of the last century, country villagers were divided into two distinct castes, one being the artisans, traders, "liviers" (owners of freeholds), and the manor-house upper servants; the other the "work-folk", i.e. farm-labourers (these were never called by the latter name by themselves and other country people till about 70 years ago). The two castes rarely intermarried, and did not go to each other's house-gatherings save exceptionally.

. . . .

3. Country-dances were introduced into villages about 1800 onwards by the first group or caste, who had sometimes lived in towns. The work-folk knew nothing of the so-called folk-dances (country-dances), and had to be taught them at mixed gatherings. They would lapse back again to their own dances at their own unmixed merry-makings, where they never voluntarily danced country-dances.

4. That in the London magazines of the eighteenth century, and by music publishers of that date, country-dances were printed, music and figures, as new dances.

Of course I speak only of the west and south-west of England; and don't wish to contest other explanations which may be possible. Also I speak of the Wessex village of seventy to eighty years ago, before railways, when I knew it intimately—and probably not many of your members did, not even the late Mr. Sharp, who gave such good labour to the subject—and know little of its condition in the present century.[3]

Hardy's letter was an episode in a larger controversy whose details need not be considered here. What does seem pertinent is the unyielding stance of disengagement and objectivity which Hardy adopts towards his subject. The strenuous insistence upon a strict village "caste" system conceivably carries an autobiographical resonance, but the discussion as a whole, though claiming to derive from intimate knowledge, suggests the viewpoint of a researcher rather than of an active participant in the tribal mysteries. The tone may of course have been deliberately calculated for a letter destined for publication in an antiquarian journal, and if the whole document seems a little disturbing in its apparent remoteness from such deeply personal material it none-theless reflects Hardy's continuing interest, in extreme old age, in music and the dance, in customs and manners long since vanished. It also offers a compact summary of that conception of Wessex village society which had been earlier embodied in the essay on "The Dorsetshire Labourer" and, more vitally, in such novels as *Far from the Madding Crowd, The Woodlanders*, and *Under the Greenwood Tree* itself.

Although Hardy's assertion that the book contained no family portraits may be strictly correct, it is clear from *Early Life* (14–15) that *Under the Greenwood Tree* evokes in a direct and affectionate way the Stinsford and Upper Bockhampton of Hardy's own childhood. The tranter's house seems, in essentials, to be the house in which Hardy himself was born;[4] grandfather James, like Hardy's own uncle James, follows the Hardy family trade of mason; the topographical descriptions, refined in successive revisions, are sufficiently localised for a recent pamphlet to be able to establish detailed correspondences between Hardy's Mellstock and the actual $2\frac{1}{2}$-inch Ordnance Survey map of the district.[5] The choir of Stinsford Church, with which the Hardy family had long been associated, seems to have been disbanded, and the choir gallery of Stinsford Church removed, at about the time of Hardy's birth in 1840, or within a year or two afterwards:[6] the drawing of the gallery with the choir in position which is reproduced in *Early Life* (13) carries the date "circa 1835". By speaking in 1896, however, of a period "fifty years ago" Hardy suggests that the action of the novel is set in the mid-1840s, and confirmation of such a dating can be found in the text: " 'Good guide us, surely 'tisn't a' empty house, as befell us in the year thirty-nine and forty-three!' said old Dewy" (28). This sentence, present in the manuscript[7] and in all editions of the novel, per-haps serves to distance the choir a little, to make it less specifically the Hardy choir; on the other hand, it brings the portrayal of "personages, ways, and customs" within the span of Hardy's own memory, and hence more credibly "at first hand".

Hardy may have meant no more by this last phrase than that he had himself known some of those who had served, directly or indirectly, as the originals of characters in the novel: Robert Reason, on whom the figure of Mr Penny was closely based, had died in 1819 and was an entirely imaginative recreation, but William Keates, apparently the original of the tranter, lived until 1870, James Dart, one of the musicians, died later in the 1870s, while Hardy's own father, the leading spirit in the choir at the time of its demise, survived until 1892.[8] The statement in *Early Life* that Hardy had never seen the choir "as such" (15) seems to leave open the further possibility that the practice of Christmas carolling, as distinct from regular performance in church, may have been continued for a number of years. As a boy Hardy must in any case have had many opportunities to watch and hear individual musicians of the old choir as they played on secular occasions, and *Early Life* (28–30) records that he himself often performed as a fiddler at village weddings and country dances, alone or in company with his father.

Although technically one of the most objective of Hardy's books, its action and characters held firmly at a distance from the author himself, *Under the Greenwood Tree* is thus—as a picture, an impression, an evocation of a particular community at a particular moment in time—an intensely autobiographical work in which Hardy drew lavishly upon some of the most cherished of his childhood memories: the members of the Mellstock choir, he once remarked, were his own favourites among all the characters he had created. Yet his concern for the authenticity of his portraiture, evident at every stage of composition and revision, seems not to have prevented Hardy in later years from feeling some dissatisfaction with his handling of the book's basic material. In the 1912 Preface to the novel he observed that "the realities out of which it was spun" (x) might have provided material for an altogether more sombre tale, and while this may not be a surprising remark to come from the author of *Tess of the d'Urbervilles* and the other late novels, it may have been prompted in part by a

specific historical episode of which he had apparently been unaware at the time of writing *Under the Greenwood Tree*. When in
the early 1880s he was going systematically through back files of
the local newspaper, the *Dorset County Chronicle*, he made in his
"Facts" notebook a detailed summary of a report he discovered
in the issue of January 24, 1828.[9] Because of its associations, of its
"period" interest, and of the way in which the prosecuting
counsel's tone of class superiority is so faithfully rendered, it
seems worth quoting the report directly and in full rather than
from Hardy's summary:

> *John Lock, Joseph Lucas, James Burt*, and *George Burt*, were
> indicted for creating a riot on the 24th Dec., and assaulting
> James Keates and Wm. Keates. As Counsel for the prosecu-
> tion, Mr. GAMBIER stated the case to the Jury, the circum-
> stances of which were as follows:—It appears that for many years
> past, there has been a co-partnership or corporation composed of
> individuals, who assume to themselves the designation of the
> Fordington mummers, and who conceive that they are en-
> titled from their prescriptive right to a monopoly in their
> profession of affording amusement to the good people of that
> parish and neighbourhood, during the convivial and merry-
> making time of Christmas. In the last year, however, a rival
> society has sprung up to pluck from them a portion of their
> laurels, in the neighbouring parish of Bockhampton, under the
> imposing title of the Bockhampton Band; and as the object of
> these latter was to afford a delicious titillation to the auricular
> nerves of the inhabitants of Bockhampton, Fordington, and the
> neighbourhood, by the performance of certain harmonious
> selections from the "first composers," the profits of the honour-
> able fraternity first mentioned were in a degree diminished. It
> was exceedingly natural that under this circumstance, a portion
> of hostility should exist; and as will be seen by the subjoined
> evidence, this hostility ripened on Christmas-eve last, into
> what may be almost termed a "battle royal".
>
> Joseph Keates sworn—is one of the Bockhampton band;
> knows Lucas and George Burt; they were with the mummers

on Christmas-eve. John Lock and James Burt are Fordington mummers. About 10 o'clock, witness was passing between Swan Bridge and Gray's Bridge, with the rest of the band; they were all proceeding homewards very quietly; they were followed by the prisoners and about a dozen others who came up to them. Witness and a man named Hardy were carrying the drum, when Lucas came up, and said he would break the drum, and pulled off his coat wanting to fight. G. Burt also wanted to fight Hardy. Witness and Hardy attempted to get away, but were followed by the whole of the mummers' party and others, amounting then to about 100; who came up and surrounded the band. Witness received a severe blow on his body, one in the back of his head and a gash in his forehead with a sword, (this wound was very visible, and appeared of no inconsiderable extent). Witness was obliged to go to a surgeon. The conduct of all four of the prisoners was very noisy, outrageous, and abusive, and they swore very much.

William Keates, Charles Keates, and John Hardy, were called, who corroborated the evidence of the last witness, and also proved an assault on William Keates, and that the wound in James Keates's forehead was inflicted by James Burt.

In their defence, D. O. P. Oakden, Esq., who presided, granted the prisoners every indulgence and opportunity for exculpating themselves or mitigating their offence, but they totally failed in every point they advanced.

They were found guilty of the riot and assault, and were sentenced as follows—James Burt, six months' imprisonment and hard labour; George Burt, John Lock, and Joseph Lucas, three months' imprisonment and hard labour.[10]

That there might be darker and less romantic aspects to the lives of village musicians is obvious enough from this passage, despite the heavy sarcasms of Mr Gambier. Within Hardy's own writings the members of the Mellstock Quire reappear in occasional short stories, but the most substantial hint of what the 1912 Preface calls "another kind of study of this little group of church musicians" (x) is contained in "The Rash Bride: An Experience of the

Mellstock Quire". First published in 1902, and first collected in *Time's Laughingstocks*, the poem opens with a scene strongly reminiscent of the beginning of chapter 5 of *Under the Greenwood Tree*, where Fancy Day appears at her window to thank the choir for their carols, but then develops out of basic materials remarkably similar to those in the novel a very different and far more tragic story:

> The rest is naught. . . We buried her o'Sunday.
>   Neighbours carried her;
> And Swetman—he who'd married her—now miserablest
>   of men,
> Walked mourning first; and then walked John; just
>   quivering, but composed anon;
> And we the quire formed round the grave, as was the
>   custom then. (365)

At the end of his life, when childhood memories had become even more precious, Hardy's regret about *Under the Greenwood Tree* was not so much that it lacked sombreness as that it lacked piety: he feared, so *Early Life* (15) records, that he had "rather burlesqued" the choir and given an inadequate reflection of "the poetry and romance that coloured their time-honoured observances". *Early Life* (97) also reflects Hardy's feelings, as an old man, about the autobiographical elements in his third published novel, *A Pair of Blue Eyes*: with few exceptions, it is insisted, the story "is so at variance with any possible facts as to be quite misleading". Yet, as R. L. Purdy observes, the novel was unquestionably based more closely upon actual experience, and especially upon his St Juliot courtship of Emma Lavinia Gifford, than Hardy was willing to acknowledge, although some of the devices of topographical semi-concealment were finally abandoned in the Mellstock edition of 1919.[11] Warmly praising *A Pair of Blue Eyes* in his article of 1881, Charles Kegan Paul spoke of "autobiographic hints" both in the presentation of the hero, Stephen Smith, and "in the relations, apart from those of rivalry in love, existing between the same young architect and his friend Henry Knight".[12] Hardy did not challenge this observation, and despite the insistence in *Early Life* (97) that Stephen was based on a pupil of John Hicks's, and that Hardy himself was closer to Knight in many ways, there seems little doubt that Knight owed much to Horace Moule and that something of Hardy's attitude towards the man who had helped and encouraged him is reflected in the Smith-Knight relationship—certainly in Stephen's admiration and gratitude but perhaps also, since it is the way of patrons to seem patronising, in his mild resentment.[13]

Precisely what aspects of Knight's curiously inhibited character were drawn from Horace Moule it is now impossible to say. Presumably the direct resemblances were not close; Moule, at any rate, remained on friendly terms with Hardy after the novel had been published.[14] But Hardy seems certainly to have drawn on Moule's literary career, especially as a reviewer, and he perhaps had in mind the pattern of that career in laying stress on Knight's sense of his own decline: from the reports of the inquest following Moule's suicide in September 1873 it appears that he too had been obsessed by feelings of personal inadequacy and failure.[15]

Moule had been something of a hero to Hardy as a young man, and in years long after his friend's death Hardy remained eager to pay tribute to him as scholar, critic, and poet. In 1918 he listed him alongside Patmore and Palgrave among the critics who had praised the work of William Barnes,[16] and in 1922 he supplied an appreciation to accompany a reprinting of Moule's poem "Ave Caesar":

> The author of the verses [wrote Hardy] was born at Fordington Vicarage, Dorchester, in 1832, died unmarried at Queen's [sic] College, Cambridge, 1873, and was buried at Fordington. He was Hulsean prizeman at the University, an accomplished Greek scholar and musician, and had early showed every promise of becoming a distinguished English poet. But the fates said otherwise. As a prose writer he was for many years on the staff of the old *Literary Gazette*, and on that of the *Saturday Review* in the eighteen-sixties under Cook and Harwood as editors. He was also an occasional reviewer in the *Quarterlies* of that date.[17]

Hardy places an extremely high valuation on Moule's literary attainments. That he was a good scholar and a gifted teacher there seems no reason to doubt, but his verse shows little evidence of real distinction and as a reviewer he allowed himself, like most of his contemporaries, a generous latitude in incorporating material from the works under consideration.[18] Moule's education and accomplishments were nonetheless of a kind to attract and dazzle a young man in Hardy's position, and during the 1860s at least he must have represented for Hardy not merely a friend to be consulted but an example to be followed. It was, conceivably, in an attempt to emulate Moule's knowledgeability that Hardy supplied *A Pair of Blue Eyes* with more than its share, even for an early novel, of gratuitous information about such matters as the tourist centres of Europe and the heights of cliffs along the coasts of Britain.

In 1913 Hardy told a correspondent: "It is very strange that you should have been attracted by 'A Pair of Blue Eyes'. The character of the heroine is somewhat—indeed, rather largely—that of my late wife, and the background of the tale the place where she lived. But of course the adventures, lovers, &c. are fictitious entirely, though people used sometimes to ask her why she did this and that—meaning incidents in the story that I invented."[19] While it is easy to accept the fictitious nature of the plot, and even the fictionalised character of the novel as a whole, it seems impossible to overlook the degree of correspondence between the Stephen-Elfride courtship and the impression of Hardy's own courtship of Emma Gifford which emerges from *Early Life* (96–99), from Emma's *Some Recollections*, from surviving drawings and sketches by both Hardy and Emma, and from some of Hardy's finest poems. The actual and the fictional romance are alike characterised by a naïve romanticism, exaggerated by the wildness and loneliness of the Cornish setting, by the legendary associations of nearby Tintagel, by the excitement of a meeting in so isolated a place between people so immediately sympathetic, and by the vital personality of the woman herself, with her literary aspirations, her fearless horsemanship, her in-experienced spontaneity and nervous femininity. Hardy's phrase, in a famous poem, about coming back "from Lyonnesse/With magic in my eyes"[20] only confirms what the weight of both factual and fictional evidence amply suggests: that Emma and St Juliot combined to cast a spell over Hardy—little more advanced emotionally at the age of twenty-nine, it would appear, than Stephen Smith, his twenty-year-old counterpart in the novel —and that it was precisely this all too brief and elusive moment of enchantment which Hardy sought again and again to recapture in the poems written after Emma's death.

The enchantment may already have suffered some evaporation by the time of their marriage in September 1874. If Emma's participation in the writing of *A Pair of Blue Eyes* (part of the surviving manuscript is in her hand)[21] was an episode in a court-ship, many things in the book stand out like warning signals: Emma, Hardy's junior by only a few months, could scarcely have taken such satisfaction in the difference in age between the youth-ful heroine and herself, nor—since her own tresses constituted her chief claim to beauty—in Knight's comments on thinning hair (312). It is important not to read the book too much in the light of hindsight, but a simple comparison of dates makes it abundantly plain that any inclusion of material relating to Emma in a book written in 1872–73 must have been not only highly personal but extremely delicate. The finished novel shows clearly enough that—like Charlotte Brontë in *The Professor* and D. H. Lawrence in *The White Peacock*—Hardy was much too close to his experiences to be capable of handling them either with assur-ance or with judgment. The success with which he had, in *Under the Greenwood Tree*, moulded autobiographical data into an almost flawless fictional unity no doubt encouraged him in his renewed resort to autobiography in *A Pair of Blue Eyes*. But in the earlier novel autobiography had merely provided a short-cut to the discovery of subject: its direct and essentially unrepeatable exploitation of childhood memories had opened up a rich rural and even pastoral world whose continued availability for fictional purposes would certainly remain dependent upon the circum-stances of Hardy's childhood but not necessarily upon the invo-cation of specific autobiographical detail. This fundamental lesson of *Under the Greenwood Tree* Hardy did not learn until *Far from the Madding Crowd*, after the recalcitrance and insufficiency of the much more recent and less fully absorbed material of *A Pair of Blue Eyes* had forced him to recognise the inadequacies of autobiography, however shrewdly it might be conjured into new patterns by ingenuities of plotting or of treatment.

5

A Pair of Blue Eyes

In October 1871 Tinsley had ignored Hardy's reference to his progress with another novel, "the essence of which is plot, *without crime*—but on the plan of D. R."[1]. On July 8, 1872, however, following the critical success of *Under the Greenwood Tree* (and perhaps a publishing emergency of his own), he wrote to ask whether Hardy could have the new story ready for serialisation in *Tinsleys' Magazine* from September onwards. Hardy promptly replied that the request was unexpected and the manuscript needed "a great deal of re-consideration", but that he would call and discuss the matter before leaving London later that month.[2] The results of that call appear in the letter to Tinsley of July 27, in which Hardy set out in detail the terms already discussed between them for the publication of "the story I have in preparation, 'A winning tongue had he' "—terms such as to lend plausibility to the anecdote in *Early Life* (118–119) about Hardy's having made a point of looking up the copyright laws beforehand.[3] It must have been at this moment, with an assurance of both serial and volume publication for his next book, that Hardy could for the first time begin to think of himself as a fully professional author, and it was during the composition of *A Pair of Blue Eyes* that he finally abandoned his original career as an architect.[4]

According to *Early Life* (98), Hardy had "thought of and written down" the plot of the novel long before his first meeting with Emma Lavinia Gifford. He can scarcely have worked it out in much detail, however, and the task of completion—begun in London, continued at Bockhampton and St Juliot—must have been anxiously and hurriedly carried through: the opening chapters were not merely in print but actually published by August 15.[5] Not surprisingly, surviving portions of the manuscript submitted to the printer show extensive correction, and many pages may represent first draft.[6] Nor is it surprising that Hardy, writing his first serial with inadequate preparation and under constant pressure from the printer, should resort to fictional exploitation of his own experiences. That generous introduction of extraneous material to which reference has already been made was no doubt prompted less by authorial vanity than by the sheer necessity of swelling out each instalment to the twenty pages stipulated in the agreement with Tinsley. The drawn-out account of boarding the steamer for Plymouth at the beginning of chapter 29 serves no narrative function—apart from the perhaps unconscious irony of introducing the image of an elderly and battered *Juliet*—and owes its presence in the novel to the need for padding and to the fact that Hardy had himself made just such an embarkation a month or two earlier.[7] Towards the end of the serial, remarkably enough, Hardy managed to gain ground; the final (July) instalment was sent off on March 12, 1873, permitting publication of the novel, in three volumes, at the end of May.[8]

A Pair of Blue Eyes became, under pressure of serialisation, a kind of rag-bag of information, ideas, descriptive vignettes, personal experiences, fragments of the author's brief literary past. Understandable as it was that Hardy should resort to such measures, the hastily inserted padding and ill-digested autobiography could only resist integration within a firmly controlled overall structure, obscure the central issues of the book (perhaps even from the author himself), and dangerously over-extend a story which may originally have been—particularly in view of its first title, "A Winning Tongue Had He", later incorporated into the thematic and structural pattern of *Far from the Madding Crowd*[9]—of almost ballad-like simplicity of outline. But if these are major reasons for the failure of *A Pair of Blue Eyes*, they are equally sources of its continuing interest. Simply because it is so unfinished, its material still so raw, the novel permits an unusually direct insight into Hardy's imaginative processes at this early point of his career; it also displays, however crudely, a wide range of narrative and descriptive techniques, some of them developed in later novels, others not to be found elsewhere in Hardy's work.

The setting and manipulation of scenes, for example, is often strongly theatrical: Stephen seen in profile in the act of kissing an unknown woman; the church nave left open to the moonlit sea; the Luxellian family vault described with the precision of a Shavian stage direction:

> The blackened coffins were now revealed more clearly than at first, the whitened walls and arches throwing them forward in strong relief. It was a scene which was remembered by all three as an indelible mark in their history. Knight, with an abstracted face, was standing between his companions, though a little in advance of them, Elfride being on his right hand, and Stephen Smith on his left. The white daylight on his right side gleamed faintly in, and was toned to a blueness by contrast with the yellow rays from the candle against the wall. Elfride, timidly shrinking back, and nearest the entrance, received most of the light therefrom, while Stephen was entirely in candlelight, and to him the spot of outer sky visible above the steps was as a steely blue patch, and nothing more. (297)

It was in such passages, rather than in his somewhat indiscriminate name-dropping, that Hardy's studies of painting really bore fruit. Like other scenes and settings, the Luxellian vault reappears later in the novel, and the vivid specificity with which it is evoked on this first occasion contributes substantially to the resonance, at once ironic and pathetic, of the book's conclusion.

Parallelism is the basic structural technique throughout. Though sometimes rather garishly melodramatic—as at the inconvenient reappearance of Elfride's lost earring—it proves sufficiently appropriate to Hardy's major themes, providing him with clear yet flexible guidelines in coping with the problems of serial publication and with the heterogeneity of his material. The introduction of a game of chess as at once an image and an actual battleground of sexual contest is hardly original with Hardy, but as developed here in two parallel scenes it operates as a cogent dramatic device. Hardy also makes some use of recurrent motifs, but so many of them seem to have been only half-realised that it is difficult to determine to what extent the technique is being deliberately developed. It is impossible not to remark the recurrence of graves and tombstones, or the contrasting preoccupation with jewellery, but even here Hardy seems not to have been engaged in any very systematic manipulation. Nor does anything beyond a persistent need for padding appear to link the numerous descriptions of sunrises or sunsets, although Hardy may vaguely have thought of them as appropriate—together with the jewels, the graveyards, and the mystifications of the plot—to that "romantic" and theatrical quality in the novel which looks back to the sensationalism of *Desperate Remedies* and forward to the pastoral melodrama of *Far from the Madding Crowd*.

A more consistent pattern is provided by the *Hamlet* motif. The play irresistibly suggests itself both as a source and as a point of deliberate reference for the first of the scenes in the Luxellian vault, and explicit allusions occur elsewhere in the novel: the epigraph comes from Laertes' warning to Ophelia that she should be wary of Hamlet's attentions, Knight's features are becoming "sicklied o'er by the unmistakable pale cast" (143), and Stephen tells him: "You out-Hamlet Hamlet in morbidness of mood" (401). Though the pattern of allusions is not elaborately worked out, the epigraph alone seems sufficient to suggest that Hardy saw Knight as the romantic intellectual whose essential nobility of soul cannot prevent him from bringing disaster upon himself and others. Knight's obsessions, like Hamlet's, emerge in indecision, morbidity, and disgust, and his internal struggle between an established dedication to the intellectual life and a late-emerging and perhaps ambiguous sexuality is strongly brought out. So, on a lighter level, is the contrast between his intellectual arrogance and dogmatism and his agonised indecision and incompetence in the everyday business of life, as in the purchase of earrings for Elfride:

It was with a most awkward and unwonted feeling that after entering and closing the door of his room he sat down, opened

[69]

the morocco case, and held up each of the fragile bits of gold-work before his eyes. Many things had become old to the solitary man of letters, but these were new, and he handled like a child an outcome of civilization which had never before been touched by his fingers. A sudden fastidious decision that the pattern chosen would not suit her after all caused him to rise in a flurry and tear down the street to change them for others. After a great deal of trouble in reselecting, during which his mind became so bewildered that the critical faculty on objects of art seemed to have vacated his person altogether, Knight carried off another pair of ear-rings. These remained in his possession till the afternoon, when, after contemplating them fifty times with a growing misgiving that the last choice was worse than the first, he felt that no sleep would visit his pillow till he had improved upon his previous purchases yet again. In a perfect heat of vexation with himself for such tergiversation, he went anew to the shop-door, was absolutely ashamed to enter and give further trouble, went to another shop, bought a pair at an enormously increased price, because they seemed the very thing, asked the goldsmiths if they would take the other pair in exchange, was told that they could not exchange articles bought of another maker, paid down the money, and went off with the two pairs in his possession, wondering what on earth to do with the superfluous pair. He almost wished he could lose them, or that somebody would steal them, and was burdened with an interposing sense that, as a capable man, with true ideas of economy, he must necessarily sell them somewhere, which he did at last for a mere song. Mingled with a blank feeling of a whole day being lost to him in running about the city on this new and extraordinary class of errand, and of several pounds being lost through his bungling, was a slight sense of satisfaction that he had emerged for ever from his antediluvian ignorance on the subject of ladies' jewellery, as well as secured a truly artistic production at last. During the remainder of that day he scanned the ornaments of every lady he met with the profoundly experienced eye of an appraiser. (214–215)

Though loosely written, the passage is nicely observed, down to the convincing detail of Knight's self-deceptive attempt to salvage an increment of knowledge from an expense of shame.

Elfride herself is also well done. William Dean Howells was ecstatic in her praise; Albert J. Guerard has pointed to the ways in which her "unused feminine energies" and "feminine nervous temperament" look forward both to Eustacia Vye and Sue Bride-head; H. B. Grimsditch and other critics have noted the similarities between the Elfride-Henry Knight relationship and the later Tess-Angel relationship.[10] Elfride's attraction towards a superior mind, her hesitation to confess her past conduct, Knight's obsession with purity, the essential coldness of his adherence to "principle"—in these and other respects the parallel with *Tess* is close, although Knight comes nearer to sharing Elfride's sexual nervousness than Angel's sexual hypocrisy. The most obvious parallel for Elfride in her relationship with her father is perhaps with Anne Garland of *The Trumpet-Major*, whose remaining parent also marries again; but Elfride, like Cytherea of *Desperate Remedies*, is a forerunner of all those Hardy heroines whose parents fail them through selfishness, insensitivity, or death. Bathsheba, Ethelberta, Eustacia, Anne, Paula, Elizabeth-Jane, Tess, and Sue are all forced to fight their own battles without parental help or in the face of actual parental opposition, though it is perhaps proper to observe that—as Jane Austen, Thackeray, and George Eliot had earlier realised—some removal or disqualification of parental direction is indispensable to the presentation of young women acting and choosing independently.

More nearly unique in Hardy's work, though perhaps with reverberations in the presentation of Farfrae and Henchard in *The Mayor of Casterbridge*, is the handling of the whole Smith-Knight relationship, especially as it is gradually modified in terms of Stephen's ever-increasing assurance and success and Knight's growing sense of failure. It would not be a difficult matter to render in diagrammatic form the curves described by the fortunes of Stephen and Knight, the points at which those curves intersect, and the relationship of each to the sad career of Elfride. Hardy's original conception of the book—hinging upon parallelism and other forms of ironic patterning—may well have partaken of the simplicity of such a diagram, perhaps along the lines of the ancient and fabular notion of two rivals for the love of the same woman becoming superseded, as a result of their own procrastination and folly, by an unsuspected and more decisive third suitor—who might, in the manner of moralities, turn out to be Death himself. Hardy's original twist, in the novel as published, was to resolve the primary pattern and then bring on Death as a fourth suitor.

The suddenness of Elfride's death has often been considered a serious flaw, and it might seem reasonable to suspect that it had not been foreseen by Hardy himself: even after he had finished the first instalment, according to *Early Life* (119), he still "had shaped nothing of what the later chapters were to be like". But such speculation is rendered untenable by the original opening of the novel. Extensively revised for volume publication, and again revised (to approximately its final form) in the one-volume edition of 1877, the first chapter began in the serial (as in the manuscript) with two paragraphs of ponderous generalisation and then proceeded as follows:

Elfride Swancourt is reading a romance.

She is sitting alone in the drawing-room of a remote country vicarage, hoping for a kindly ending to the story, or as it is put in homely phrase, that it may end well.

It happened that she was to be disappointed. The title of the novel it is not worth while to give, but it detailed in its conclusion the saddest *contretemps* that ever lingered in a gentle and responsive reader's mind since fiction has taken a turn—for better or for worse—for analysing rather than depicting character and emotion.

Elfride was just dismissing the second volume—its crimson covers making one pale pink hand that clasped them as intensely white by their contrast as the pallid leaf underlying the other caused that to tinge itself almost rosy. She read on with a pulse which, as each leaf was turned, quickened with misgiving. She began to suspect the trick of the issue, and dreaded it—as an inexorable fate with regard to the imaginary beings therein concerned—as she dreaded a wasp's sting in regard to herself.

She takes up the third volume, and opens it. The list of contents was disclosed, in which the author had, somewhat indiscreetly, too plainly revealed the sorrow that was impending. Elfride was too honest a reader to resolve her suspense into a more endurable certainty by taking a surreptitious glance at the end, yet too much of a woman to be satisfied with going straight on. Her eye strayed to the contents page to scan it, and so help her prognostication. No, even that was hardly fair: she would not look. She put her little palm over the relentless chapter-headings—to lift it after all, and look under at the suspicious group of terse phrases which meant so much to the initiated. Misgiving increased like Genevieve's at her lover's ditty of the Miserable Knight. Her heart still librating between hope and fear, fear permanently prevailed. Her hero died.

Elfride smothered an inward sigh and murmured, 'What a weak thing I am!'

She never forgot that novel, and those minutes of sadness. Not that the story was the most powerful she had ever read; not that those tears were the bitterest that had ever flowed. But for this reason: that it was the last time in her life that her emotions were ever wound to any height by circumstances which never transpired; that the loves and woes, expectations and despairs, of imaginary beings were ever able so much to emulate her own experiences as to make a perceptible difference to her state of mind for a whole afternoon.[11]

The chapters in *A Pair of Blue Eyes* are headed not by titles but by quotations. The message, even so, seems unmistakable, despite the fluttering coyness of the language in which it is delivered. Equally coy—and a good deal clumsier—was the serial version of the opening of chapter 7:

The history of the first wooing of our impressionable young heroine being to a great extent preliminary to the main story,

[73]

we hurry through it as rapidly as possible. In order, however, that the future position may be adequately understood, it is necessary to give the facts of the case seriatim.[12]

Hardy's belated good judgment in deleting this unfortunate paragraph as well as those early paragraphs of chapter 1 cannot be challenged. At the same time, these deletions left readers of the novel without the warnings given in the serial that the future held in store for Elfride things more serious than her girlish infatuation for Stephen, that even a romance could end unhappily.

Such deprivation would be unimportant if Hardy had achieved in the novel as a whole a greater consistency of tone and mood. Richard Carpenter, in the course of an excellent discussion of *A Pair of Blue Eyes*, has described the book as not so much a tragicomedy as a "comitragedy",[13] and certainly it has both an earlier and a greater tendency to the comic than it has to the tragic. But "comic" and "tragic" both seem unduly grandiose terms to invoke in this context, while to speak of the novel as a tragicomedy or even a comitragedy suggests an integration and interaction of comic and tragic elements wholly in excess of anything it actually offers. It seems more appropriate to turn again to *Hamlet* for the term "comical-tragical", which has the advantage of emphasising the separation of the two elements and of suggesting, even so, no more than an approximation to authentically comic and tragic effects. In *A Pair of Blue Eyes* the not quite comic and the potentially tragic are constantly in juxtaposition, but rarely brought into significant interrelationship.

Uncertainties of tone occur at the beginning of other Hardy novels, but *A Pair of Blue Eyes* is fundamentally disrupted by persistent alternations of mode, by shifts in authorial attitude towards the characters and towards the reader, and by a general failure to establish functional relationships between disparate elements of the total fiction. Nor can these difficulties be resolved simply by speaking of the book as a romance, as Hardy consistently did in later years,[14] since the central problem concerns precisely the transitions within the book from the lightly handled boy-and-girl affair of the early chapters, to the more heavily treated relationship between Elfride and Knight, and then to the abrupt conclusion. Painful as Knight's rejection of Elfride undoubtedly is, and not only because it brings *Tess* so strongly to mind, the wry comedy of the succeeding chapters seems still to promise a conclusion of a gently ironic kind. That the actual conclusion should seem not only unexpected but brutal—less an unknotting than an axe-stroke—is the result of a lack of preparation throughout the novel. That Elfride cannot be taken seriously as a tragic figure is chiefly the result of her removal from the foreground during the last four chapters, so that the revelations about her decline, marriage, and death come too late, too suddenly, and too much at second-hand, for them to be absorbed and assessed independently of the reactions of Stephen and Knight.

Hardy seems not to have regretted the conclusion; indeed he appears to have written to John Hutton (who had reviewed *A Pair of Blue Eyes* very favourably in the *Spectator*) of the essential truth of Elfride's death and of its contribution to the artistic integrity of the novel as a whole.[15] The book was well received by the early reviewers: Hutton called it "a really powerful story"; Horace Moule in the *Saturday Review* declared that "out of simple materials there has been evolved a result of really tragic power"; the *Pall Mall Gazette* had no fault to find except that the book was "undeniably sad".[16] Many years later, in urging Macbeth-Raeburn, the illustrator of the Osgood, McIlvaine collected edition, to visit the actual scenes of *A Pair of Blue Eyes* and not rely on photographs, Hardy commented that it was a book that had always sold well;[17] he also spoke of the novel as having been an especial favourite both of Tennyson and of Coventry Patmore, who regretted that it had not been written in verse.[18]

The mention of the authors of *Idylls of the King* and of *Angel in the House* is perhaps suggestive of the particular phase of Victorian sensibility which provided the context for the conception, publication, and popularity of *A Pair of Blue Eyes*. If it is not now possible to read the novel so sympathetically, or so much at its face value, it is at least possible to recognise the interest, the tragic potentialities, of Hardy's central subject. It is Elfride's misfortune, like that of later Hardy heroines, to be failed by all the

men on whom she depends, from her insensitive and egotistical
father onwards. Her own childishness and lack of force need to be
complemented by a personality much stronger than that of the
boyish (almost girlish) Stephen, whose incompetence and in-
experience is the root cause of many of her later difficulties. But
Knight, though he has the necessary strength of character, turns
out to be fundamentally lacking in flexibility and human warmth.
Neither Stephen nor Knight, in fact, wants Elfride for herself, or
even (to adapt Yeats) for her light-brown hair. Each seeks an
adjunct to his own personality: Stephen a queen, Knight a maiden
of spotless purity.

The one man who is portrayed as wanting Elfride in a direct
and unequivocally sexual way is Lord Luxellian, who gives her,
as early as chapter 14, "a manly, open, and genuine look of
admiration" (159). But if he can give Elfride such a look—and
subsequently get her pregnant—he cannot give her the kind of
intellectual companionship which she also needs and which, in
their different ways, both Stephen and Knight had been able to
offer. Elfride finds Lord Luxellian handsome; we are nonetheless
told that he has "no decided characteristics more than that he
somewhat resembled a good-natured commercial traveller of the
superior class" (156), and that his sole attraction is his musical
laugh: "People liked him for those tones, and forgot that he had
no talents" (157). He is also associated throughout the novel with
sickness and death: his first wife's, Mrs Jethway's, Elfride's.
Clearly he is less than an ideal husband for Elfride, and in this
sense there is perhaps, as Hardy claimed, a certain "truth", a
moral and aesthetic necessity in her death. Whether Hardy saw a
special appropriateness in her dying of a miscarriage it is impossible to say, but in a book written at such a crucial moment in
Hardy's career, and containing so much transposed autobiography, not the least remarkable thing is the shadowy suggestion
of underlying sexual themes in which the "nervousness" of
Elfride, the "manliness" of Lord Luxellian, the "prettiness" of
Stephen, might all fall into place in relation to the possibility that
Knight "was not shaped by Nature for a marrying man" (366).

Part Two
ACHIEVEMENT

FAR FROM THE MADDING CROWD
Serial: January–December 1874
Published: November 1874

THE HAND OF ETHELBERTA
Serial: July 1875–May 1876
Published: January 1876

THE RETURN OF THE NATIVE
Serial: January–December 1878
Published: November 1878

I

Far from the Madding Crowd

When *A Pair of Blue Eyes* appeared in its three-volume form in May 1873 Hardy's professional status was confirmed by the appearance of his name on a title-page for the first time. That status had earlier been signalled by his decision to abandon his architectural career, and by an invitation from Leslie Stephen to write a serial for the *Cornhill*. When Stephen wrote, on November 30, 1872, Hardy was ready with a suggestion for "a pastoral tale", though he seems to have reported only the title, *Far from the Madding Crowd*, and the occupations of the chief characters.[1] It was in the spring of 1873, following the completion of *A Pair of Blue Eyes* and a renewed enquiry from Stephen, that Hardy began serious work on the novel. Stephen accepted it at the beginning of that October on the evidence of the specimen chapters Hardy sent him; shortly afterwards Hardy agreed to an earlier publication date than had originally been contemplated, and the first part appeared in the *Cornhill* for January 1874. The novel was still far from completion at this point, and Hardy only finished work on it that summer.[2] The two-volume first edition appeared on November 23, 1874, Hardy having returned the proofs—with "very few" corrections, mainly to the opening chapter—to Smith, Elder on October 9, modestly requesting in the accompanying letter that his name be allowed to appear in "the announcement of the book".[3]

Coming after *A Pair of Blue Eyes*, *Far from the Madding Crowd* is a novel of astonishing confidence; as the successor to *Under the Greenwood Tree*, it is a book of extraordinary amplitude. Unmistakably a major work, it is nonetheless quite different in kind from Hardy's later fiction, and it seems the first duty of criticism simply to celebrate its unique virtues—the bold theatricality of the narrative progression, the rich yet strictly functional evocation of setting, the earth-bound poetry of the dialogue:

> 'Andrew Randle, here's yours—finish thanking me in a day or two. Temperance Miller—oh, here's another, Soberness—both women, I suppose?'
>
> 'Yes'm. Here we be, 'a b'lieve,' was echoed in shrill unison.
>
> 'What have you been doing?'
>
> 'Tending thrashing-machine, and wimbling haybonds, and saying "Hoosh!" to the cocks and hens when they go upon your seeds, and planting Early Flourballs and Thompson's Wonderfuls with a dibble.'
>
> 'Yes—I see. Are they satisfactory women?' she inquired softly of Henery Fray.
>
> 'O mem—don't ask me! Yielding women—as scarlet a pair as ever was!' groaned Henery under his breath.
>
> 'Sit down.'
>
> 'Who, mem?'
>
> 'Sit down.' (89)

Never again was Hardy to be quite so lavish in the humorous exploitation of rural dialogue, or even in the invention of incident: *Far from the Madding Crowd* includes, often in close juxtaposition, a profusion of natural and domestic disasters, mysterious disappearances and dramatic reappearances, the opening of a coffin, a revenge-murder, and a last-minute reprieve from the gallows. It is little wonder that Hardy could write to Frederic Harrison in 1901 that *Far from the Madding Crowd* had "a growing tendency to appear as the work of a youngish hand, though perhaps there is something in it which I could not have put there if I had been older".[4]

The novel displays throughout the excitement and assurance of a writer who has been given his great opportunity—serialisation in the *Cornhill*—at the moment when he begins to realise his proper subject. In *A Pair of Blue Eyes* the completion of a serial under pressure had proved nearly disastrous, and it was in relation

to *Far from the Madding Crowd* itself that Hardy made his
famous remark about wanting "merely to be considered a good
hand at a serial".[5] But he profited from his earlier experience, and
from the opportunity to plan his story further in advance, and
during the composition of *Far from the Madding Crowd* it was
precisely in responding, or even over-responding, to the demands
of the serial situation that he seems to have felt his way almost
instinctively towards a form—of strong outlines and rich possibilities for scenic presentation—which answered exactly to his
immediate creative needs, enabling him to develop the melodramatic romanticism which had marked the narrative method of
both *Desperate Remedies* and *A Pair of Blue Eyes* in terms of that
solidity of social context he had so far achieved only in *Under the
Greenwood Tree.*

Writing for the *Cornhill* also gave him, as R. L. Purdy has
pointed out,[6] the advantage of close editorial scrutiny from Leslie
Stephen, and although Stephen's interventions were later represented in *Early Life* (130–131) as having been characterised by an
excessive respect for the forces of Grundyism, they were often of
a far more important and positive kind. Thus the survival of the
manuscript pages which Hardy deleted from the scene of the
shearing supper makes it possible to see that Stephen was
perfectly right, in his letter of February 17, 1874, to recommend
some pruning at this point:

> I have read through your MS with very great pleasure;
> though I had seen most of it before. As you ask me for my
> opinion I will say frankly that I think the sheepshearing rather
> long for the present purpose. When the novel appears as a
> whole, it may very well come in in its present form. For
> periodical purposes, I think it rather delays the action un-
> necessarily. What I should be inclined to do would be simply
> to omit the chapter headed the "shearing supper" and to add
> a few paragraphs to the succeeding or preceding, just explaining
> that there has been a supper.... I don't know whether anything
> turns on the bailiff's story; but I don't think it necessary.[7]

If the proposed solution proved unnecessarily drastic, it was entirely to the good that Hardy should have been induced to delete from the scene the exchange involving Pennyways the ex-bailiff, which had indeed very little significance, and the subsequent conversation among Bathsheba's employees which, though sometimes amusing, was notably lacking in tension.[8] Earlier revisions had apparently been made at Stephen's suggestion—his letter of January 8, 1874, mentions that "the paying scene is judiciously reduced"[9]—and he was presumably responsible for the drastic curtailment of the drawn-out conclusion which Hardy originally wrote for the chapter describing Troy's "Adventures by the Shore".[10] Other substantial deletions were made, both within the manuscript itself and before the appearance of the serial,[11] and the book was unquestionably improved by this fining-down process, very largely carried out at Stephen's instigation. Even the deletions for which he has been specifically criticised can often be justified aesthetically. It may have seemed unduly fastidious of him to hint that he would "somehow be glad to omit the baby" from the scene in which Bathsheba opens Fanny Robin's coffin; but the suggestion had the happy result of removing from the novel the description of "both the silent ones" as they lay side by side, the baby "with a face so delicately small in contour & substance that its cheeks & the plump backs of its little fists irresistibly reminded her, excited as she was, of the soft convexity of mushrooms on a dewy morning".[12] It seems perfectly possible, indeed, that Stephen sometimes used the Grundian threat as a tactful cover for criticism of a more aesthetically significant kind.

The novel as published proceeds with immense assurance. If the opening pages reveal an initial uncertainty of tone in the way in which Gabriel Oak's ineptitudes of manner are made matter for shared amusement between sophisticated author and sophisticated reader, such infelicities may have resulted, at least in part, from the very need to create Gabriel "cold" in the opening pages. It seems to have been Hardy's preferred method to display his principal characters in dramatised episodes before introducing them directly to the reader, certainly before offering an analysis of their personalities or any internal view of their thoughts and feelings: it is thus that Bathsheba, Boldwood, and Troy are introduced. Unfortunately, Hardy had insufficient faith in his own power to reveal character in action, judging it necessary to insert "set-piece" analyses, unduly long and rather inertly abstract, of both Boldwood and Troy at the points where they are brought fully into the main narrative stream. He shows greater confidence in his dramatic creation of Bathsheba. Although the later crises in her life are presented largely in terms of a direct revelation of what she is thinking and feeling, the early chapters simply offer a series of vignettes of her—as tease, as tomboy, as "mistress of the farm", as manager of men—which are allowed to make their own impact with the minimum of authorial intrusion.

Some of these episodes take on an almost emblematic quality which forces the reader to register them quite consciously as portentous of future developments. The most notable of them, Gabriel's view of Bathsheba as she sits on the cart, surrounded by household impedimenta, admiring herself in the mirror, allows Gabriel himself to draw a lesson regarding Bathsheba's vanity, but it also hints at that display of femininity in the open air which will cause such damage when Bathsheba takes over Weatherbury Upper Farm and, not least, at that element of domesticity in her which Gabriel himself will finally discover. The whole Norcombe section—the five chapters which comprised the first serial instalment—operates along similar lines, standing in relation to the body of the novel almost as a kind of dumb show, offering a brief survey of what has gone before and a "type" or prefiguration of much that will follow. Hardy later adopted variations of this method in the early pages of such novels as *The Hand of Ethelberta*, *The Return of the Native* and, most powerfully, *The Mayor of Casterbridge*. In *Far from the Madding Crowd* itself it should perhaps be linked with other moments which cast a premonitory shadow: Bathsheba's singing of "Allan Water", Gabriel's encounter with Fanny Robin.

This last episode is one which Hardy may have added to the manuscript at a fairly late stage, and which he allows—almost in the manner of Dickens—to stand unexplained, quietly teasing the back of the reader's mind, while other strands of the story are taken up in successive chapters. What eventually becomes clear is that the scene has served to link Fanny Robin with Gabriel Oak, and thus to emphasise the contrast—in position and fortune as much as in personality—between Fanny and Bathsheba herself. Since Boldwood and of course Troy are also involved with the fate of Fanny, her relationship to Bathsheba becomes a strange shadow play of obvious contrasts and obscure rivalries. The pathetic scene in which Fanny pleads with Troy from outside the barracks is placed between Bathsheba's successful first appearance as mistress of the farm and the even greater triumph of her first appearance in the Corn Market; the pattern is later inverted when Fanny's unhappy death is transformed by Troy's declaration into a triumph for her and the most abject of defeats for Bathsheba.

Powerfully developed, skilfully connected with the lives of the central characters, Fanny's story is an instance of the extraordinary creative exuberance displayed throughout the novel. It remains, however, essentially subordinate to the main narrative line provided by the progress of Bathsheba's career as ruler of Weatherbury Upper Farm—though the "Squire Bathsheba" aspect of her role is much less strongly emphasised than it seems to have been in contemporary stage adaptations of the novel[13]— and by the developing pattern of her relationships with Oak, Boldwood, and Troy. In the novel as published, this pattern involves the violent opposition, culminating in insult and murder, between Troy and Boldwood, but there are indications that Boldwood's present role may have been a late addition to Hardy's conception of the story. When he first sketched for Leslie Stephen the basic idea of *Far from the Madding Crowd*, Hardy apparently described the chief characters as "a woman-farmer, a shepherd, and a sergeant in the Dragoon Guards",[14] and if the Boldwood-Troy rivalry is now the focus of violence, there survives from the first draft a scene in which Gabriel comes into open and even physical conflict with Troy. Since Boldwood's name is mentioned in this scene, Hardy may not so much have introduced a new character as developed an existing minor one;[15] in any case,

Boldwood's present role as Troy's opponent and antitype allows Oak to drop back into the relatively quiescent role which both his personality and his social position demand—to such an extent, indeed, that neither Troy nor Boldwood thinks seriously of him as a possible rival.

Clearly, the full elaboration of Boldwood's role demanded a certain delay in the eruption of Sergeant Troy upon the Weatherbury scene; it also involved, relatively to the book as a whole, a degree of narrative relaxation in the chapters (9–23) which are organised round the sheep-washing and sheep-shearing. It is part of the function of these chapters to provide time and opportunity for a credible development of Boldwood's courtship of Bathsheba, especially after the earlier reliance on the frail device of the valentine—convincing enough so far as Bathsheba is concerned, less so in its effect on Boldwood. But if Boldwood's role has to be somewhat slowly developed it grows eventually into one of Hardy's few male characterisations which can be even remotely compared with that of Henchard, remarkable, especially in its period, as a study in sexual obsession and the effects of sexual defeat. Few touches in the novel are more telling than the failure of an unmanned Boldwood to protect his ricks from the storm, or the discovery made at his house following the shooting of Troy:

> There were several sets of ladies' dresses in the piece, of sundry expensive materials; silks and satins, poplins and velvets, all of colours which from Bathsheba's style of dress might have been judged to be her favourites. There were two muffs, sable and ermine. Above all there was a case of jewellery, containing four heavy gold bracelets and several lockets and rings, all of fine quality and manufacture. These things had been bought in Bath and other towns from time to time, and brought home by stealth. They were all carefully packed in paper, and each package was labelled 'Bathsheba Boldwood,' a date being subjoined six years in advance in every instance. (442–443)

If the presentation of Troy does not offer quite the same richness, it nonetheless represents an admirably judged exploitation of the narrative and thematic possibilities inherent in such a figure.

The scene of the sword-exercise—characteristically "researched" by Hardy[16]—gives an occasion for what must to some extent have been a deliberate symbolism of sexual assault,[17] and while Troy's birth gives him qualities unusual in a soldier of his rank, the kind and degree of glamour which attaches to him—traditionally, and in ballad and melodrama—as a sergeant of cavalry becomes a precise measure of both the pathetic foolishness of Fanny Robin and the culpable indiscretion of Bathsheba; it also suggests how much the two women have in common. Perhaps originally conceived as a contrast to Oak, Troy is even more effective as a foil to Boldwood: where the latter is slow, massive, profoundly obsessive, Troy is quick, light, and casual; if they both neglect their ricks it is for utterly different reasons.

Troy is the more important figure in terms simply of the convolutions of the plot, and once he has encountered Bathsheba the narrative takes on its full amplitude, driving through with tremendous momentum to the day of his death. The quieter and more hopeful close is first heralded by the granting of a reprieve to Boldwood. On any reflection it must appear that a life sentence constitutes for a man so broodingly passionate a punishment far worse than hanging: it is in a determination to die that he gives himself up after his suicide attempt has been frustrated. But Hardy—needing to begin his upward movement, and presumably wanting Bathsheba not to have another death on her conscience—seeks to ensure that the reprieve is felt as a happy event: this is one of many occasions when his rustic chorus serves him well, and he is not afraid to use the cliché of the last-minute stay of execution to extort from the reader a sympathetic response.

Since the novel abounds in such melodramatic devices, it is scarcely surprising that Henry James, reviewing *Far from the Madding Crowd* for the New York *Nation* should have found it "inordinately diffuse, and, as a piece of narrative, singularly inartistic".[18] Curiously enough, Hardy had used similar phrases in remarking to Leslie Stephen that, though content at present to be judged "a good hand at a serial", he might "have higher aims some day, and be a great stickler for the proper artistic balance of the completed work".[19] It seems doubtful, however, whether

Hardy could ever have agreed with James as to what constituted "artistic balance". In *Far from the Madding Crowd* he shifts rapidly and almost indiscriminately between different versions of the omniscient viewpoint; dramatising, intervening, giving now external and now internal views—sometimes, as in the confrontation between Troy and Bathsheba over Fanny Robin's coffin, combining several methods in an unobtrusive and surprisingly successful manner.

At the same time, Hardy was, with his intense need and capacity for visualisation, acutely aware of the much less interesting question, technically speaking, of the actual physical vantage point from which incidents are observed by characters within the novel's world. His books are full of conversations overheard and meetings accidentally or deliberately observed, and *Far from the Madding Crowd* is no exception. Gabriel, who tells the time by pressing his face against other people's windows, watches Bathsheba unseen on a number of occasions, and she later sees him at his prayers. Troy crouches in almost physical contact with Bathsheba as she sits in the tent at Greenhill Fair; in a more complicated instance, he is himself observed as he stands outside the Malthouse listening to a conversation going on inside. It is tempting to dismiss this as little more than a rather literal-minded concern on Hardy's part for the question of how people know what they know, and perhaps as an almost indispensable lubricant for the complications of the plot.[20] Yet in *Far from the Madding Crowd* the position of the looker-on is characteristically one of deprivation: Troy's closeness to his wife reminds him of what he has lost, and what he might reclaim; Gabriel's pain at exclusion from Bathsheba's favour is balanced by her sense of lacking his security of mind; Fanny cries out to a Troy made doubly inaccessible by the barracks and the intervening river; both Gabriel and Boldwood, on different occasions, watch Troy appear at Bathsheba's bedroom window in all the arrogance of ownership.

The lookers-on *par excellence*—with whom the observation of their masters is both an occupation and a badge of their own inferior status—are the rustics who frequent Warren's Malthouse, most of them employees of Boldwood or Bathsheba.

Although it seems natural to speak of them as a kind of chorus, they discharge that particular function a good deal less obtrusively than do the lower-class characters in a more deliberately structured novel like *The Mayor of Casterbridge*. And they are perhaps less derivatively Shakespearean—despite the obvious echo of Silence and Shallow in the Malter's questions about Norcombe—than a first glance might suggest. They seem, indeed, to have owed a good deal to people Hardy had actually encountered, and in their speech he aimed at "scrupulously preserving the local idiom"[21] while yet avoiding the kind of phonetic eccentricities which rendered largely inaccessible the best work of a writer like William Barnes.

The scenes dominated by the workfolk—to use the local term on which Hardy insisted in his letter to the *Journal of the English Folk Dance Society* and his essay on "The Dorsetshire Labourer" —rarely make a very substantial contribution to the narrative, but they obviously offer something far more than an exhibition of local fauna: the book does not become static when such characters have the stage entirely to themselves. Partly this is because of their constant observation, and hence illumination, of the central characters; but it also seems obvious that Hardy deliberately invokes this collective voice of the agricultural community as an essential element in his pattern. His emphasis, most strongly brought out in the description of the great barn, is on the fact and value of continuity in the agricultural way of life.

One could say about this barn, what could hardly be said of either the church or the castle, akin to it in age and style, that the purpose which had dictated its original erection was the same with that to which it was still applied. Unlike and superior to either of those two typical remnants of mediaevalism, the old barn embodied practices which had suffered no mutilation at the hands of time. Here at least the spirit of the ancient builders was at one with the spirit of the modern beholder. Standing before this abraded pile, the eye regarded its present usage, the mind dwelt upon its past history, with a satisfied sense of functional continuity throughout—a feeling almost of

gratitude, and quite of pride, at the permanence of the idea
which had heaped it up. (164–165)

As well as the barn, Hardy touches in, with varying degrees of
detail, the Malthouse, the farms of Boldwood and Bathsheba, the
cottages of their employees, the Casterbridge corn market and
workhouse (associated respectively, and contrastively, with
Bathsheba and with Fanny), the Buck's Head Inn on the road
between the village and the town. The social detail, the evocation
of a village in its active life, is abundantly if unobtrusively present,
extending to the appearance of that rare phenomenon in Hardy's
novels, a village church with a parson who seems relevant to the
lives of his flock.[22]

The importance given to Weatherbury church in *Far from the
Madding Crowd* prompts reflection upon the derivation of the
novel's title from Gray's *Elegy in a Country Churchyard*:

> Far from the madding crowd's ignoble strife,
> Their sober wishes never learn'd to stray;
> Along the cool sequester'd vale of life
> They kept the noiseless tenor of their way.

Because of the novel's melodramatic and often violent character,
because its central figures scarcely lead lives of "noiseless tenor",
it is hard to think of the title as being other than ironic. Yet, as the
description of the Great Barn so firmly suggests, the allusion to
Gray seems to have been serious enough: Stinsford "*is* Stoke
Poges", Hardy is recorded as saying late in life.[23] Stinsford, of
course, is usually identified with the Mellstock of *Under the
Greenwood Tree*, while the Weatherbury of *Far from the Madding
Crowd* is associated with Puddletown. But Stinsford and Puddletown are in adjoining parishes, and Hardy told Stephen he had
decided to finish the novel at home because it was "within a walk
of the district in which the incidents are supposed to occur. I find
it a great advantage to be actually among the people described at
the time of describing them."[24] The road between Weatherbury/
Puddletown and Casterbridge/Dorchester which figures so pro-
minently in *Far from the Madding Crowd* passes through the

Yalbury Wood of *Under the Greenwood Tree*, and Keeper Day and his metheglin are recalled by Joseph Poorgrass.

Even more important than this placing of the two novels as near neighbours in space and time is the closeness of feeling and texture between the world of *Under the Greenwood Tree* and what might be called the permanent elements in the world of *Far from the Madding Crowd*. The frequenters of Warren's Malthouse differ in many respects from the guests at the tranter's party—for the most part, the latter are of higher social and economic standing —but the conversation of the two groups has a common *timbre*, reflecting, with marvellous richness of phrase and particularity of allusion, the immemorial features of the domestic life and rural economy of an area still almost untouched by the economic or social consequences of the industrial revolution. The villagers in *Far from the Madding Crowd*, unlike those in *Under the Greenwood Tree*, do not themselves play leading roles in the action, but they are directly involved in it; at the same time, they are so indispensable to the establishment of that action's social context as to demand consideration almost as an element in the setting. Quite as much as those passages of natural description for which the novel is rightly famous, the workfolk—Poorgrass, Coggan, Tall, Fray, and the rest—supply the novel's groundnote, that fundamental evenness of tenor which the title evokes, which Troy disturbs, and which the final chapters restore and reaffirm. That Oak—who has operated happily within the Malthouse group without ever being entirely of it—should join the choir at the end of the novel is perfectly in accordance with that religious faith of his which has impressed Bathsheba earlier on; but it is also, like walking to church to be married, a gesture of solidarity with the village community.

Gabriel's relationship with that community serves throughout the novel as a convenient measure of his current social status. One moment of advancement arouses local comment:

'Whatever d'ye think,' said Susan Tall, 'Gable Oak is coming it quite the dand. He now wears shining boots with hardly a hob in 'em, two or three times a-week, and a tall hat 'a-Sundays, and 'a hardly knows the name of smockfrock. When I see people strut enough to be cut up into bantam cocks, I stand dormant with wonder, and says no more!' (381)

The observation is unkind, but it is made in terms of those minute discriminations of dress which are so important in the world of *Far from the Madding Crowd*, as in that of *Under the Greenwood Tree*, and which can be made so readily in communities where a substantial wardrobe is unknown and where "five decades hardly modified the cut of a gaiter, the embroidery of a smock-frock, by the breadth of a hair" (166).

It is this isolation and slowness to change—a quality of permanence corresponding to the permanent features of the seasons and of the countryside—which Hardy chiefly suggests in his title. He described the book to Stephen as a "pastoral tale", and the progress of the narrative is marked throughout by the festivals and occupations of the agricultural year: lambing and shearing, haymaking and harvest, the hiring fair and the sheep fair, the shearing and harvest suppers, Saint Valentine's Day and Christmas. The bee-taking scene recalls Hardy's use of a specifically seasonal structure in *Under the Greenwood Tree*, and perhaps prompts the reflection that in its profusion of agricultural detail the novel occasionally runs the risk of becoming a kind of latter-day *Georgics*. These recurring moments in the pattern of Weatherbury life are set off, in their essential timelessness and changelessness, against the rapid and often strenuous action of the narrative itself, but they are also used, again and again, as both the setting and raw material of a series of magnificent scenes in which the seasonal moment, evoked in all its detail, becomes an integral part of the presented experience. So Troy meets Bathsheba in the hayfield; so Gabriel strips the blushing sheep under Bathsheba's modest but critical eye;[25] so the ironic uncertainties of Gabriel's relationship with Bathsheba are subtly defined by the seating arrangements at the shearing supper, where distinction of class merges with sexual rivalry; so Boldwood's obsession is displayed in all its grotesqueness by the sombre incongruities of his Christmas party.

[91]

The specifically pastoral aspects of the novel are emphasised in many of the images and allusions which Hardy evokes: *Lycidas*, for example, as well as Virgil's *Eclogues* and Old Testament narratives of herdsmen and their flock—Susan Tall's husband is called Laban, Boldwood speaks of waiting for Bathsheba as Jacob had done for Rachel. Gabriel, we are told, could play his flute with "Arcadian sweetness" (45), and at the shearing supper, when Bathsheba sings to Gabriel's accompaniment, the "shearers reclined against each other as at suppers in the early ages of the world" (179). Such allusions combine with others in the novel— for example, those implicit in the naming of Troy and Bathsheba[26] —and with the pastoral character of the setting and the continuing life of farm and village to throw into relief and into perspective the foreground narrative. As the ballads incorporated into the novel further stress, love is as natural and as immemorial as the seasons themselves, and there are ample precedents both for the ways of soldiers with "winning tongues" and for the patient devotion of shepherds.

It is of course to Gabriel, as the one specifically pastoral figure in the novel, that these allusions most persistently accrete, and there is clearly a sense in which he is linked with traditional presentations of the shepherd as rustic lover and philosopher. In the Norcombe chapters, where Gabriel is first introduced as a flute-playing shepherd, we hear of his "pastoral affairs" (27), and of the "Pastoral Tragedy" (37) when he loses his sheep; at the hiring fair he is sensitive to his fall from his "modest elevation as pastoral king" (43) to the level of hired man. But if Gabriel is very much the shepherd here, Bathsheba at Norcombe appears essentially as a milkmaid; both are seen caring for new-born creatures, and Gabriel's idea of courting Bathsheba is to take her a young lamb which has lost its mother. Within the context of these opening pages Gabriel's gesture, like the courtship itself, seems appropriate enough, and although Hardy handles the episode with gentle humour neither this nor Bathsheba's disdain removes the impression of a basic congruity between the couple or qualifies the firmness of Gabriel's declaration:

She contracted a yawn to an inoffensive smallness, so that it was hardly ill-mannered at all. 'I don't love you,' she said.

'But I love you—and, as for myself, I am content to be liked.'

'O Mr. Oak—that's very fine! You'd get to despise me.'

'Never,' said Mr. Oak, so earnestly that he seemed to be coming, by the force of his words, straight through the bush and into her arms. 'I shall do one thing in this life—one thing certain—that is, love you, and long for you, and *keep wanting you* till I die.' His voice had a genuine pathos now, and his large brown hands perceptibly trembled. (34)

If Gabriel's pastoral attributes in these early scenes do not greatly enhance the reader's sense of him as a man to be reckoned with in the affairs of the world, they certainly reinforce the impression of independence and integrity, of a loyalty and love that may be the more absolute for being capable of expression only in domestic gestures and homely terminology. In a real sense, Gabriel is not simply the hero but, quite specifically, the romantic hero.

Throughout the remainder of the novel, Hardy is at pains to keep Gabriel constantly in view, and in his role as shepherd. Bathsheba's, clearly, is a mixed farm, producing both corn and sheep after the standard pattern of Victorian high farming. But while all aspects of the farm's economy are evoked in their due season, the chief emphasis falls consistently upon the sheep, whose progress we follow from lambing-time onwards: as R. L. Purdy remarks, "the story moves by the shepherd's calendar".[27] Although the original of Greenhill fair was much more than a sheep-fair,[28] that is the aspect in which Hardy chooses to present it, and it is perhaps of some interest that in the discarded scene in which Oak fought with Troy the source of their difference was Troy's deliberate infection of the flock with sheep-rot—in order, as Hardy explains in technical language, to bring them to an early and illusory readiness for market.[29] The emphasis on the part played by sheep in the economy of Weatherbury Upper Farm is essentially an emphasis on Gabriel's contribution. When he is seen helping in the harvest field Hardy stresses that he "was not bound by his agreement" (249) to assist in this way, and it is, of course, part of the point of Gabriel's action in saving Bathsheba's ricks on two separate occasions that they lie outside the range of his responsibility as a shepherd.

It is in such episodes that Hardy stresses Gabriel's unfailing loyalty to Bathsheba and, at the same time, sustains a relationship between the two during the long period when Bathsheba's emotional life is engrossed by her involvements with Troy and Boldwood. Here, of course, the dual aspect of Bathsheba's role—as mistress of the farm and as inexperienced girl—allows Hardy unusual flexibility, as does the entirely convincing "*ficelle*" figure of Liddy, in whom, though they are mistress and maid, Bathsheba can with perfect naturalness confide. But the recurrent demonstrations of Gabriel's resourcefulness also sustain and expand the sense of him as a man of parts as well as of integrity, so that it seems entirely proper that at the end of the novel he should both marry Bathsheba and take over Boldwood's farm. The two achievements are, in fact, splendidly one.[30] If Bathsheba has learned through suffering to value Gabriel for what he is and what he represents, Gabriel has proved himself through resourceful endurance to be something more than "an every-day sort of man" (31)—to be worthy, indeed, as man and as farmer, both of Bathsheba's hand and of that social and economic role within the agricultural community which, as Boldwood's successor and Bathsheba's husband, he must necessarily perform.

2

Puddletown into Weatherbury:
The Genesis of Wessex

It was in the manuscript of chapter 50 of *Far from the Madding Crowd*—"Greenhill was the Nijnii [sic] Novgorod of Wessex"—that Hardy seems first to have used the term Wessex; its first appearance in print dates from the publication of the chapter in the *Cornhill* as part of the November 1874 serial instalment.[1] The term did not appear elsewhere in the serial or the first edition—other occurrences are the result of later revision—but its revival in the opening sentence of Hardy's next novel, *The Hand of Ethelberta*, confirmed beyond doubt that he was laying claim to a whole fictional region. A map of Wessex as it existed in 1874 would have been a simple affair: Budmouth and Melchester had been located, Casterbridge lightly sketched in, Mellstock and Weatherbury surveyed in some detail; a few other places had been mentioned, some of them under names later abandoned; the region as a whole had been placed in relation to the actual geography of England by the account of Bathsheba's journey to Bath. Wessex was to be much developed in later books and in the process of revision, but the publication of *Far from the Madding Crowd* established the name and the broad framework, while the overlapping of *Under the Greenwood Tree* and *Far from the Madding Crowd*, slight as it was, already demonstrated possibilities not only of greater expansion but of greater density.

Several of the early reviewers recognised the nature, if not always the quality, of Hardy's endeavour in these two early novels. Horace Moule referred to *Under the Greenwood Tree* as "the best prose idyl that we have seen for a long while past", while *The Times* praised *Far from the Madding Crowd* for its "delicate perspective faculty, which transforms, with skilful touch, the matter-of-fact prosaic details of every-day life into an idyl or a pastoral poem".[2] Late in 1875 Léon Boucher, writing at length on Hardy's work in the *Revue des deux mondes* under the title "Le roman pastoral en Angleterre", defined in very positive terms the achievement of *Far from the Madding Crowd*:

Peut-être même la plus grande beauté du nouveau roman a-t-elle échappé à bien des lecteurs, qui n'y ont vu qu'une histoire amusante et des situations dramatiques telles qu'on en peut trouver ailleurs. M. Hardy en effet a voulu faire quelque chose de plus : il a voulu rajeunir le genre antique et souvent ennuyeux de la pastorale, et il y a mis une telle vérité d'observation, une passion si profonde, une poésie si fraîche, un style si puissant, tant d'idéal et de réalité à la fois, que cette transformation peut presque passer pour une création originale.[3]

In September 1877 a general article on Hardy's work in the short-lived journal *London* linked him and R. D. Blackmore as novelists of the "British Boor", described as the "latter-day analogue" of the shepherds of Arcadia. Though generally hostile, the article does show by its use of such terms as "the Wessex rustic" how strongly Hardy's imaginative world had already impressed itself upon his contemporaries.[4]

There is a reference in *Early Life* (142) to Boucher's article, and since this and the other pieces were all preserved by Hardy in one of his scrapbooks one wonders whether they contributed anything to his own conception of the nature and function of his fiction. The question seems especially pertinent in relation to an article published anonymously in the *Examiner* on July 15, 1876. Entitled "The Wessex Labourer", it surveys Hardy's work up to and including *The Hand of Ethelberta*, refers easily to "Wessex novels" and "Wessex peasants", and praises Hardy's authentic portrayal of both the landscape and the labouring population of a little-known county. The article speaks of Dorset as "the very last county in England whose sacred soil was broken by a railroad, and those which now traverse it leave the very heart of the shire untouched. The narrow provincialism of the squires, which is in some measure the bane of all the more distant counties, is accentuated there; and though charity and kindliness are not wanting, the labourer and squire feel towards each other as though they were of different races." Later it adds: "Time in Dorset has stood still; advancing civilisation has given the labourers only lucifer-matches and the penny post, and the clowns in *Hamlet* are no anachronism if placed in a west country village of our own day."[5]

Hardy put this article, too, in his scrapbook, and obviously had it in front of him many years later when writing the preface to the 1895 edition of *Far from the Madding Crowd*. He mentions it specifically as the first occasion when the term Wessex was "taken up elsewhere" (viii), and adopts some of its phraseology in speaking of his appropriation of the old Saxon name for "a modern Wessex of railways, the penny post, mowing and reaping machines, union workhouses, lucifer matches, labourers who could read and write, and National school children" (vii). Hardy must have found, in 1876, great reassurance in the article's informed and unhesitating endorsement both of the method and of the authenticity of his work; he may also have been grateful for the defence of his fiction against those reviewers (among them R. H. Hutton in the *Spectator*)[6] who had found his rural characters extravagantly philosophical and articulate. The article argues that the Dorset labourer, although "in a different stage of civilisation" from readers of the *Examiner*, "is no fool in his own line, but rather very shrewd, racy, and wise, full of practical knowledge of all natural things, and of considerable powers of thought. Words are now and then lacking to him in which to clothe thought, for the vocabulary of those who live apart from books is everywhere restricted, but the dialect is yet vigorous and especially English." The hint of William Barnes in that last sentence is confirmed in the next by the suggestion that Hardy and Barnes, "both parts of that of which they write, ought to dissipate many popular fancies about their fair western county".[7]

The social and economic backwardness of Dorset had long been notorious. In 1830 the county had seen, especially on the southern fringes of the Vale of Blackmore, some of the worst outbreaks of what Hardy himself once called in a letter "the last peasant revolt",[8] and a few years later, in the southern part of the county, the "Tolpuddle martyrs" were convicted and transported for their primitive gestures towards rural unionisation. In the 1840s, when Hardy himself knew by sight a boy who died of starvation,[9] Lord Sydney Godolphin Osborne ("S.G.O.") aroused controversy about the condition of the Dorsetshire peasantry, and the corroborative reports of *The Times* investigator reinforced the national image of Dorset as (to use a phrase from Hardy's essay on "The Dorsetshire Labourer") the home of "Hodge in his most unmitigated form".[10] The 1867 Royal Commission on the Employment of Children, Young Persons, and Women in Agriculture, to which submissions were made by such Dorset figures as William Barnes and Henry Moule, gave ample coverage to Dorset as, by common consent, one of the areas where wages were lowest, cottages the least sanitary, landlords the most unenlightened, and the plight of the labouring class nearest to desperation.[11] Still more recently, Dorset, like many other parts of southern and eastern England, had seen a great upsurge of union activity under the leadership of Joseph Arch.

On December 5, 1872, two or three days after Hardy had received from Leslie Stephen the invitation which led to the appearance of *Far from the Madding Crowd* in the pages of the *Cornhill*, a large meeting of agricultural labourers was held in the Corn Exchange at Dorchester. Arch himself was not present, but the meeting was addressed by one of his warmest supporters, the Hon. Auberon Herbert, the Radical M.P., with whom Hardy was later to be on friendly terms.[12] Since, according to *Early Life* (121), Hardy spent the closing months of 1872 at Bockhampton finishing *A Pair of Blue Eyes*, he can scarcely have been unaware of this occasion, of the meeting's pledge of support to the National Agricultural Labourers' Union, or of the recommendation of emigration to Brazil which came from several of the platform speakers: "it being stated," reported *The Times*, "that the

Government of that country was prepared to assist 500,000 men in going there from England".

Hardy later made dramatic use, in *Tess*, of the illusory promises of the Brazilian Government to British farmers and farm labourers. In "The Dorsetshire Labourer" essay of 1883 he referred in genial terms to Joseph Arch himself, giving a sympathetic account of his programme and achievements and recalling a personal memory of a speech delivered by Arch during one of his "early tours through Dorsetshire".[13] Hardy perhaps heard Arch speak during the Dorchester Candlemas Fair of 1873, held on Friday, February 14, and reported by the *Dorset County Chronicle* in its issue of February 20:

THE HIRING FAIR.—This annual statute fair took place on Friday last, the attendance of labourers being larger than on any similar occasion for years past. The source of attraction was Joseph Arch, a star of the first magnitude amongst the agricultural labourers, who flocked into the town from all parts of the county. Passenger carriages were attached to the early down goods train on the Great Western Railway, and they were crowded, as was also the ordinary train due at Dorchester at 10.27. The higher part of the town was thronged towards eleven o'clock, the guardians of the peace pacing to and fro in the interests of order. A little commotion was got up near St. Peter's Church by a labourer, sporting blue ribbons in his cap, who delivered his mind, aided by a "wee-drap" beforehand. But the crowd soon wended its way up the street. Excepting this incident all was quiet. The farmers were conspicuous by their absence, indeed they are making strenuous efforts to discountenance the system of hiring at the fair, the Dorchester Farmers' Club having last year unanimously decided upon that course. Where agreements with non-unionists were effected 12s. with perquisites were given to ordinary labourers, the extras, of course, depending upon circumstances. Towards noon a procession was formed, and it moved in the direction of Fordington-green, being headed by Arch, Cox, and Co., who, from a waggon, harangued an assembly of nearly 1,000 men, women, and lads. The speakers strongly condemned the system of men hiring themselves for a year, comparing it to proceedings at a slave market. They seemed to forget that the farmers of Dorset themselves had discouraged the practice, and that the labourers had this year come to the fair chiefly to hear the agitators. The meeting lasted about two hours, a resolution to support the union being carried. At three o'clock there was a second meeting at the same place. On Cornhill there was the usual display of agricultural implements, and confection stalls occupied the pavement fronting St. Peter's Church. It is stated that steps will probably be taken by the farmers with a view to abolishing the system of hiring at the fair altogether, and the expediency of that course is particularly desirable on account of the drunkenness with which the day is finished, this year's fair being no exception in that respect.[14]

The contemporary realities of Dorset life in the early 1870s which figure in this report find little direct reflection in the worlds of Hardy's early novels. It is not until the early 1880s that the first clear indication of agricultural distress and discontent appears, somewhat unexpectedly, in *Two on a Tower*, where the labourers refer to themselves as "folks with ten or a dozen shillings a week and their gristing, and a load o' thorn faggots when we can get 'em" (96), and one of them braves a suspected ghost with the words: "Well, well; I've not held out against the spectre o' starvation these five-and-twenty year on nine shillings a week, to be afeard of a walking vapour, sweet or savoury" (165).

In *Far from the Madding Crowd*, indeed, Hardy seems to have chosen his setting with a deliberate eye to its remoteness from the current unrest. He had of course been familiar since childhood with the village variously known as Puddletown or Piddletown, but in selecting it as the original for the fictional Weatherbury he may have been influenced by a long report on conditions in the village which appeared, under the heading "Arcadians of Dorset", in the *Daily Telegraph* for April 30, 1872. Valuable in itself as an account of conditions in the county at the beginning of Arch's movement, the article is fascinating as a sketch of Hardy's Weatherbury the year before he began to re-create it in fictional terms. It presents Puddletown as "a model Dorsetshire village" where old ways still flourish within the as yet unacknowledged shadow of the new:

> Piddletown occupies the crest of a great ridge which shuts out the semi-urban environs of Dorchester from the genuinely rural centre of the county. It rejoices in most of the essentials of Arcadian felicity. The squire takes a direct and fatherly interest in his villagers. He has built them from time to time numbers of good cottages, and he has furnished them with ground for garden allotments. The tenants he has selected for his farms are men who make the best of a bad system of labour. They pay the full standard wages of the county—oftener, I believe, the nine shilling maximum than the eight shilling minimum. Though privileges as a matter of right and custom have almost died out in Dorsetshire, they linger on sufferance in Piddletown. One of them is the ancient perquisite of gristing, under which each labourer can claim a bushel per week of wheat for family use, at the uniform rate of five shillings. . . . The potato ground, which seems to prevail throughout the whole of the West of England, is granted here without any of the drawbacks and qualifications that are being introduced elsewhere. Small kindnesses are also practised by the farmers, which go a long way in promoting friendly feeling amongst the labourers. A man would very seldom be refused a truss of straw for his pig when he is so fortunate as to possess one. In a county so well timbered, it would be hard if something were not done to help to keep his pot boiling in winter. He stands a chance, provided he be faultless as a labourer, and properly deferential as an inferior, of having a hundredweight or two of firewood delivered at his door in the cold weather.[15]

The agricultural labourers of Puddletown are thus fortunate by comparison with those in many other villages; they receive ungrudgingly whatever custom and agreement have prescribed as theirs. It is nonetheless clear, the article continues, that their position remains precarious: Puddletown "depends a great deal on the grace of its suzerains. When they smile benevolently it stops a certain degree shorter of starvation than when they have to frown reprovingly. What might happen if in a moment of supreme displeasure they were to withdraw their pigstraw and firewood, the most vivid imagination in Piddletown cannot conceive. The bare money value of labour in the parish is just nine shillings per week." As yet, however, the labourers have shown no sign of taking concerted action to protect or improve their situation, receiving with near incredulity rumours of a strike threat in the adjoining parish of Milborne St Andrew: "Piddletown had not dreamed of any such insubordination as writing to a master about wages, much less had it dared to think of such a millennium as the possession of a weekly income of twelve shillings."[16]

Powerful though Arch's impact had been, it had not yet touched every part of Dorset, and Hardy, anxious throughout his career to avoid the slightest suggestion of political involvement, had evidently found in Puddletown, with or without the assistance of the *Daily Telegraph* correspondent, a village where unionisation had not yet become an issue. To strengthen his position still further he placed the action of the novel perceptibly, if somewhat vaguely, in the past. As R. L. Purdy has observed, several phrases in chapter 42 of the novel suggest a period more distant than the 1869–73 dating proposed by Carl J. Weber, and if the calendar for those years seems to fit the sequence of the action, so equally would the calendar for, say, 1858–62.[17] A date prior to the early 1870s certainly seems required by Cainy Ball's reaction to Bathsheba's crinoline; by the allusion to Keeper Day of Yalbury Wood, with its suggestion of a world not far removed in time or space from that of *Under the Greenwood Tree;* and by Hardy's hint some years later, through allusions to Bathsheba's uncle and to a "silent, reserved young man named Boldwood", that the action of *Far from the Madding Crowd* is to be imagined as taking place some ten years after the central action of *The Mayor of Casterbridge*, itself set at mid-century.[18]

A specific date is perhaps impossible to determine and not, in any case, of great importance. As Andrew Lang pertinently observed in his *Academy* review of *Far from the Madding Crowd*, "the country folk in the story have not heard of strikes, or of Mr. Arch; they have, to all appearances, plenty to eat, and warm clothes to wear, and when the sheep are shorn in the ancient barn of Weatherbury, the scene is one that Shakespeare or that Chaucer might have watched. This immobile rural existence is what the novelist has to paint." The world of Weatherbury, as other reviewers also saw, is fixed, arrested at a moment in time somewhere before the onset of the disruptive processes of rural mobility and depopulation: it is placed, just over the rim of the present, in a condition of timelessness. "No condition of society," Lang goes on, "could supply the writer who knows it well with a more promising ground for his story. The old and the new must meet here and there, with curious surprises, and our world may find itself face to face with the quaint conceited rustics of Shakespeare's plays." What prevents Hardy from making the best of his theme, Lang believes, is his tendency, because he is "telling clever people about unlettered people", to be somewhat patronising.[19]

It is of course possible to argue that a patronising attitude is implicit in Hardy's decision to avert his eyes from the actual conditions and issues of the day: by evoking a pastoral world remote from contemporary realities, "far from the madding crowd", he could disengage himself from the story, view the characters with affection and amusement, unblushingly confront his readers with a Shakespearean rustic. Yet the novel is rich and resilient in its dependence upon the pattern of the agricultural year and the techniques of rural trades, and if Hardy does not draw attention to the miseries of the farm labourer's lot he does not seek specifically to conceal them. He neither romanticises his rustics nor dwells explicitly upon the implications of a man like Joseph Poorgrass receiving a wage of 9s. 9d. a week in what are apparently prosperous times, or a man like Andrew Randle losing his job for telling the squire his soul was his own. The hiring fair in *Far from the Madding Crowd* is accepted, with neither criticism nor praise, as simply an economic fact. Hardy preserves, in short, a careful neutrality in all such matters, and his personal attitudes towards the labourer's situation are impossible to determine. He certainly never identified himself with the Dorsetshire labourers of whom he wrote, and he was anxious, especially as he grew older, to insist upon his father's status as a member of the lifeholding class celebrated in the closing paragraphs of "The Dorsetshire Labourer". But even had he felt absolutely in sympathy with Joseph Arch and his cause, his own experience with *The Poor Man and the Lady* must inevitably have impelled him towards the possibilities of neutrality and self-protection inherent in the choice of a remote setting and a past time.

3

The Hand of Ethelberta

In September 1874, after more than four years of courtship, Hardy married Emma Lavinia Gifford. By that time the serialisation of *Far from the Madding Crowd* was already well advanced, and it must have been both professionally and financially reassuring to Hardy to receive Leslie Stephen's letter of December 2, 1874, asking if he could supply another story for the *Cornhill*.[1] Stephen mentioned April 1875 as a possible starting date, but Hardy had as yet made little progress with his new novel and the first serial part did not in fact appear until July of that year. Stephen's letters during the composition of *The Hand of Ethelberta* again reflect editorial hesitancy about Hardy's habitual directness. On May 13, 1875, he wrote: "I read with much pleasure the chapters you sent me. I doubt (to mention the only trifle which occurred to me) whether a lady ought to call herself or her writings 'amorous'. Would not some such word as 'sentimental' be strong enough? But I am hypercritical perhaps."[2] He also reported, in the same month, the objections which had been raised to Hardy's sub-title, "A Comedy in Chapters",[3] and these words were omitted from the serial version, only to be restored to the first edition (published in two volumes, in April 1876) and retained in all subsequent editions. In *Early Life* (143) the argument that the novel was, as "a Comedy of Society", many years ahead of its time is supported by reference to the successful use of similar scenes and material "in a play in recent years by Mr. Bernard Shaw"—presumably *You Never Can Tell*.

It would perhaps be equally appropriate to say that the novel was written with a backward glance to Hardy's years in London during the 1860s and to the mode of *The Poor Man and the Lady*. If it seems unlikely that the actual manuscript of the first novel was drawn upon for *The Hand of Ethelberta*, it is at least conceivable that fragments from that quarry contributed to some of the "society" episodes and to the speeches of Ethelberta's mildly socialistic brothers. Ethelberta herself begins poor and becomes Lady Mountclere, thus enacting something of an inversion of the "Poor Man" pattern, and although the class theme is both qualified and distanced by the predominantly comic, sometimes satirical, tone—and by the demonstration that the daughter of a butler may marry a viscount and fail to please her family—a persistent ambivalence of attitude (especially towards Ethelberta's social achievements) suggests that material dating from the late 1860s is perhaps being reworked from a different point of view.

Central to *The Hand of Ethelberta* is its evocation of great and rapid social change. In revising the novel for the Osgood, McIlvaine edition of 1896 Hardy for some reason deleted a passage describing the re-orientation of the town of Anglebury since the coming of the railway,[4] but there are plenty of indications elsewhere in the book that a building boom is in progress:

We are accustomed to regard increase as the chief feature in a great city's progress, its well-known signs greeting our eyes on every outskirt. Slush-ponds may be seen turning into basement-kitchens; a broad causeway of shattered earthenware smothers plots of budding gooseberry-bushes and vegetable trenches, foundations following so closely upon gardens that the householder may be expected to find cadaverous sprouts from overlooked potatoes rising through the chinks of his cellar floor. But the other great process, that of internal transmutation, is not less curious than this encroachment of grey upon green. Its first erections are often only the milk-teeth of a suburb, and as the district arises in dignity they are dislodged by those which are to endure. Slightness becomes supplanted by comparative solidity, commonness by novelty, lowness and irregularity by symmetry and height. (364)

As in London, so in the smaller towns. Ethelberta moves into a

bright new villa in Knollsea, and her parents are installed at the
end of the novel—with what Hardy perhaps intended as a deliberate and ironic compromise between the urban and the rural—on
the new estate at Sandbourne:

> Mr. Chickerel and his family now lived at Firtop Villa in that
> place, a house which, like many others, had been built since
> Julian's last visit to the town. He was directed to the outskirts,
> and into a fir plantation where drives and intersecting roads
> had been laid out, and where new villas had sprung up like
> mushrooms. (455)

When Sandbourne—based on Bournemouth, that remarkable
product of the Victorian speculative builder[5]—reappears in
Hardy's fiction as the place where Tess murders Alec d'Urberville,
its newness and vulgarity ("a glittering novelty" juxtaposed against
the ancient heath)[6] are emphasised afresh. Hardy had seen the
London building boom at first hand while he was in Blomfield's
office—treating one aspect of it in "How I Built Myself a House"
in 1866—and he knew that it had been the source of many new
fortunes: so Lord Mountclere exclaims that Ethelberta's brothers
"may buy me up before they die!" (335); and by the end of the
novel Sol and Dan, set up by Ethelberta as builders in London,
have already "signed a contract to build a hospital for twenty
thousand pounds" (457).[7]

In a world where so much was changing, manners and social
attitudes must have seemed ripe for changes on a similar scale, and
Hardy treats Ethelberta's career almost as a parable of social
revolution. He knew as well as Thackeray and James that a
beautiful and talented young woman without inherited wealth and
position possessed the maximum potential for social mobility: she
could become a "lost woman" or a duchess, or even both in
succession; she could certainly move readily within "the meta-
morphic classes of society", Hardy's telling term for the rising
middle class (347–348). By making Ethelberta both a widow—an
unusual situation for a nineteenth-century heroine—and a professional teller of stories he gave her possibilities of social freedom
beyond those normally accorded to women of the time and per-

mitted her to appear almost as a pioneer of a more general emancipation:

> She stood there, as all women stand who have made themselves remarkable by their originality, or devotion to any singular cause, as a person freed of her hampering and inconvenient sex, and, by virtue of her popularity, unfettered from the conventionalities of manner prescribed by custom for household womankind.

* * *

> It will be seen that Ethelberta was the sort of woman that well-rooted local people might like to look at on such a free and friendly occasion as an archaeological meeting, where, to gratify a pleasant whim, the picturesque form of acquaintance is for the nonce preferred to the useful, the spirits being so brisk as to swerve from strict attention to the select and sequent gifts of heaven, blood and acres, to consider for an idle moment the subversive Mephistophelian endowment, brains. (262–263)

Bathsheba had, at her uncle's death, taken the management of the farm into her own hands. Ethelberta assumes responsibility for her family even during her father's lifetime and, as Lady Mountclere, proves herself entirely capable of running efficiently and successfully the affairs of a great landed estate. That she should at the same time be writing an epic poem (456) perhaps suggests that her emotional energies are far from absorbed by the life she leads; or it may be simply an ironic demonstration that success in the world of affairs need not be incompatible either with femininity or with poetry.

Yet "femininity" is perhaps not quite the term to use of Ethelberta. As a widow she has presumably had sexual experience, and the novel contains ample dramatisation of her attractiveness to men. But Hardy does not give a full physical description of her as he had done, often lavishly, with his previous heroines. At her first appearance he speaks simply of the elegance of her "diadem-and-sceptre bearing" (2) and contrasts it with her energetic impulsiveness as she runs to see the conclusion of the struggle between the duck and the duck-hawk. Subsequent references evoke not so much Ethelberta's person as her personality, and such specific details of her appearance as are supplied—for example, her neck "firm as a fort" and the "open full look" of her eyes (39)—often stress that masculinity of hers to which Albert J. Guerard has rightly drawn attention.[8]

Although *The Hand of Ethelberta* is ostensibly a novel about sexual selection it contains less genuine sexuality than almost any of Hardy's books, and if, as Richard Carpenter has suggested,[9] Ethelberta in her role as adventuress seems reminiscent of Becky Sharp (with Lord Mountclere as a feebler version of Lord Steyne), in her strength of will and capacity for self-repression she is closer allied to Hester Prynne. Christopher Julian, falling sadly short of the heroic promise of his name, may seem in no sense of the word a match for Ethelberta; yet we are apparently to read renunciation into her refusal to accept him as a husband. Ethelberta also rejects Neigh and Ladywell, both of whom hold some attraction for her, and there is a sense in which her determination to avoid womanly weakness ultimately makes her somewhat unwomanly. Her adopted role in life is specifically a masculine one, and this sexual inversion reinforces the more obvious social inversion involved in the whole pattern of her career.

Hardy thus asked his readers to accept a resolution which directly challenged their expectations and their prejudices. The butler's daughter does not prove to be out of place as the viscount's wife but actually fills her new role, as Christopher Julian recognises (453), more successfully than would most women who had been born into that rank of society. As Lady Mountclere, Ethelberta comes into her "own", as the suggestions of nobility in her name perhaps anticipate—and her "dominant" personality (342) finds appropriate expression in the governance of Enckworth Court and of a husband of distinguished lineage but tarnished reputation: "'Tis a sad condition [says the man who takes Christopher past Enckworth two and a half years after Ethelberta's marriage] for one who ruled womankind as he, that a woman should lead him in a string whether he will or no." (453)

Christopher catches only a glimpse of Ethelberta as she drives past, and in the Sequel as a whole we are given no direct indication of her feelings about her marriage. Clearly Ethelberta has fulfilled all her social aspirations, and more, and there is ample evidence of the new prosperity of her family; but Hardy has deliberately left unresolved the question of whether, for Ethelberta herself, achieved ambition also represents achieved happiness. She has longed for security and been attracted by power, and both of these she possesses in full measure. At the same time, she has renounced love and maternity, she sees little of her family, and the necessities of power have led her to be, in her father's expert opinion, "occasionally too severe with the servants" (456). There is, apparently, some basis for Sol's scolding of Ethelberta as "a deserter of her own lot" (424), and such fulfilment as she has gained must certainly be regarded as being of a strictly limited kind. But Hardy's chosen method of indirection enables him to sustain to the very end of the book that fundamental ambivalence in the presentation of his heroine which is implicit in the title itself. If the business of the novel is largely the traditional one of the disposal of the heroine's hand in marriage, Ethelberta's role is far more active than such an account would suggest, her "hand" is discernible in a multiplicity of schemes. Possibly there is also a sense in which she could be said to be "playing a hand", especially in the socio-sexual contest with Lord Mountclere.

That contest is evoked in a series of striking images: Ethelberta is "a fair galleon", Mountclere a "persevering buccaneer" (284); at the archaeological society meeting Mountclere busies himself round Ethelberta "like the head scraper at a pig-killing" (264). The incident in the opening chapter, in which Ethelberta watches the frustration of the hunting duck-hawk by the evasive tactics of its intended victim, seems remarkable not only for its "Darwinian" quality—its exemplification of the constant battle for survival in the world of nature—but for the intensity of Ethelberta's interest in the outcome: she has, it appears, an appetite for such life-and-death struggles and an instinctive sympathy for creatures cast in the role of victim. This in itself is relevant enough to her situation and to her readiness to confront directly the world of economic and social realities within which she must operate. But there is obviously a further sense in which she herself plays the duck—the victim turned vanquisher—to Lord Mountclere's hawk, and the social implications of the analogy are pressed home by the scene in chapter 3 in which the gentlemanly duck-shooters observe, from "ambuscade" (33), the bedraggled figure of Picotee. The final triumph of Ethelberta, born a member of the victim-class, is only the major element in a pattern of inversions which runs throughout the book and which is deliberately and carefully prefigured in these opening pages.

Other signals and prefigurations occur in the early chapters— the allusions to Lord Mountclere, the comments of the ostler on the interest taken by old men in young girls, the evocation of the inn at Anglebury (one of several recurrent settings in the novel), the mildly allegorical naming of some of the characters (Menlove, Ladywell, Neigh)—and they indicate the tight structural control which Hardy sought and generally maintained, despite the over-extension of some episodes and an occasional tendency to self-indulgent expatiation along "guide-book" lines, as in the potted history of Corvesgate Castle and some of the descriptions of Rouen. Hardy's sub-title, "A Comedy in Chapters", suggests a deliberate correspondence to the patterns of stage comedy: that he had Restoration and eighteenth-century comedy specifically in mind is indicated by the naming of the characters, the reference in the 1912 Preface to the "artificial treatment perceptible in many of the pages" (viii), the use of the chapter-headings to record the sequence of scenes and their settings, the presence of a witty, resourceful and generally dominant heroine, and the near-farcical elements involving a multiplicity of pursuing suitors and the subsequent moves and counter-moves of Ethelberta's contest with Lord Mountclere. The relationship of the novel to stage comedy and the fundamental pattern of inversion are both explicitly invoked in chapter 42:

'What a funny thing!' said the lady, with a wretchedly factitious smile. 'The times have taken a strange turn when the angry parent of the comedy who goes post-haste to prevent the undutiful daughter's rash marriage, is a gentleman from below stairs and the unworthy lover a peer of the realm!' (378)

Not all the comedy depends upon the convolutions of the plot. Occasional passages of the dialogue are unexpectedly successful, especially some of the exchanges between Sol and Lord Mountclere's brother, and between Ladywell and Neigh. Nor indeed is all the comedy of a straightforward kind: there are elements of incipient tragi-comedy and of what might now be called black comedy in the presentation of Picotee's personality and situation, in the almost Hawthornean characterisation of Faith Julian ("She had no outer world, and her rusty black was as appropriate to Faith's unseen courses as were Ethelberta's correct lights and shades to her more prominent career" [189]), in the hints of fundamental evil in the make-up of Lord Mountclere, in the "grotesque habits" (244) of Mr Doncastle's servants, and above all in that strangely disturbing episode in which Ethelberta and Picotee explore Neigh's estate and come suddenly, in the fog, upon the ghastly shapes of the dying horses.

Most of these instances can be related, in one way or another, to the question of appearance and reality which provides one of the novel's continuing themes: Faith's truth to herself is not matched by Neigh the knacker's heir, nor by other characters who set store by their social pretensions. Hardy seems to have been especially fascinated by the perpetually merging layers of reality and unreality implicit in the pattern of Ethelberta's career. She plays so many superimposed parts before audiences possessed of such differing degrees of initiation into her secrets that her "true" personality proves finally elusive—perhaps even to Hardy himself, though the deliberate indirection of the final view of her seems not so much an evasion of difficulty as a conscious choice of ambiguity, a decision to rest with the enigma. Hardy also makes a good deal of play with the question of point of view: as his 1895 Preface points out, the notion of presenting the upper classes "from the point of view of the servants' hall" (vii) is fundamental to the whole book, while Ethelberta is not only seen from many different angles but herself sees her world from radically opposed standpoints, as when she catches a glimpse of Ladywell as he drives past the gatehouse in which her family live.

The gatehouse itself, with that ambiguous appellation of

"Lodge" which causes Christopher Julian so much confusion, is one of several buildings in the novel which represent not Hardy's indulgence in (or desperate recourse to) reminiscences of his architectural past but his conscious attempt to use architecture as a thematic element, almost as a measure or standard of morality. The cramped quarters at Arrowthorne Lodge, the London house of many levels, the "ornamental villa" at Knollsea, the Chickerels' final home at Sandbourne—all serve both to chart and to image the changing fate of Ethelberta and her family. Of Lord Mountclere's house, Enckworth Court, Hardy writes:

> Without attempting to trace an analogy between a man and his mansion, it may be stated that everything here, though so dignified and magnificent, was not conceived in quite the true and eternal spirit of art. It was a house in which Pugin would have torn his hair. Those massive blocks of red-veined marble lining the hall—emulating in their surface-glitter the Escalier de Marbre at Versailles—were cunning imitations in paint and plaster by workmen brought from afar for the purpose, at a prodigious expense, by the present viscount's father, and recently repaired and re-varnished. The dark green columns and pilasters corresponding were brick at the core. Nay, the external walls, apparently of massive and solid freestone, were only veneered with that material, being, like the pillars, of brick within. (329–330)

That Hardy, despite the disclaimer in the first sentence, does intend an analogy between Lord Mountclere and his house is clear from a subsequent reference to the deceptively youthful appearance which Lord Mountclere himself achieves by dressing "with all the cunning that could be drawn from the metropolis by money and reiterated dissatisfaction" (354).

Architecture was to play a far more central role in *A Laodicean* than in *The Hand of Ethelberta;* but in the earlier novel Hardy had already felt his way to a realisation that the description and evocation of buildings—no less than of natural settings—might be introduced into fiction not merely as distinct and separate set-pieces but as essential elements in a total pattern. The conception

of architecture as a moral touchstone may well have dated from
the days of Hardy's professional training, but its first substantial
appearance in his novels had been in *Far from the Madding Crowd*,
with its marvellously rich evocation of the great barn as social,
historical, and moral fact, and it was in *The Hand of Ethelberta*,
with its multiplicity of settings and social levels, that he apparently
attempted for the first time to incorporate architecture more or
less systematically as an element in an overall value-system.[10]

If the attempt was neither as deft nor as successful as it might
have been, it nonetheless supplied an additional element in that
technical adventurousness of *The Hand of Ethelberta* which seems
—like the handling of contrasted rural and urban settings and of
conflicting class relationships—to demand a higher place for the
novel than it has customarily been accorded. It is usual to consider *The Hand of Ethelberta* as a distinctly minor and unfortunate
episode in Hardy's career—an aberration in many ways, but
chiefly in its departure from the Wessex pattern so lately established in *Under the Greenwood Tree* and *Far from the Madding
Crowd*. Yet concentration on what is unusual in the novel—the
concern with urban life and upper-class manners—has perhaps
led to an under-appreciation of what is more familiar. The book
opens in Wessex, the name of Wessex is invoked in the first sentence
(and was so invoked in the original serial), and the number of
scenes which take place in various settings in and near the
triangle of Sandbourne—Anglebury—Knollsea (corresponding to
the actual Bournemouth, Wareham, and Swanage) was sufficient
to lead Charles Kegan Paul to speak (in a letter to Hardy of April
13, 1877) of the novelist's having made that section of Dorset his
"own".[11]

It would be too much to suggest that Hardy thought to organise
his novel about a highly developed contrast between country and
town, between Wessex and a Cobbettian Great Wen, or that he
could yet have had sufficient confidence in his own achievement
to hope or intend that his allusions to Wessex in this novel would
carry with them any of the specifically pastoral implications of the
world he had created in *Far from the Madding Crowd*. Yet Wessex
does operate here as a kind of notation for the rural simplicities.

The "free old Wessex manners" (187) are implicitly opposed to those of a society in which a "complete divorce between thinking and saying" is regarded as "the hall-mark of high civilization" (213); as a new day begins in London the "swarthy columns of smoke" are "spoiling the sweetness of the new atmosphere that had rolled in from the country during the night, giving it the usual city smell" (253); Ethelberta's bearing among her brothers and sisters at Arrowthorne Lodge shows that "the free habits and enthusiasms of country life had still their charm with her, in the face of the subtler gratifications of abridged bodices, candlelight, and no feelings in particular, which prevailed in town" (109); Picotee is named for a flower, and when she is first described—as "an April-natured, pink-cheeked girl" (24)—both her charm and her complexion are specifically identified as rural, emphatically non-urban. Throughout the novel there is a sustained contrast between the freshness, honesty, and simplicity of country life and country ways and the tawdriness, deceit, and artificiality of the city. It is clearly no accident that Ethelberta's family carries the name of a small Dorset village just west of Weymouth[12]: they are of rural origin and their strengths of honesty, good-humour, and family cohesiveness derive essentially from rural virtues, though these are always in danger—certainly in young Joey, ambiguously in Ethelberta herself—of being corrupted by one form or another of urban sophistication.

Yet this town-country, London-Wessex opposition, fascinating though it is, seems to be present in the novel not so much for its own sake as to provide Hardy with one angle of attack, one standard of reference, in that satirical treatment of London society which seems to have remained his primary concern. What, indeed, is finally most impressive in the book is precisely the profusion of such angles and such standards of reference which Hardy was able to build into it. If *The Hand of Ethelberta* is very obviously a Comedy of Society, deliberately satirical and contemporary, it is also an ambitious exploration of social and moral values—not an aberration in Hardy's career but rather an experiment with techniques and areas of subject-matter which he had not previously exploited in print. The experiment was, in many respects, a successful one, and certainly Hardy had little reason to be seriously dissatisfied with its first reception.

Although some of the reviewers found the characters insubstantial, and at least one (in the *Graphic*) regretted Hardy's abandonment of rustic life, most of them wrote about the book enthusiastically and even perceptively. In the *Examiner* there was talk of a "carefulness in construction and regard for dramatic unity" which was "worthy of Ben Jonson himself"; in the *Spectator* the novel was seen as "a humorous fable illustrating the vices and weakness of the upper ten thousand"; while the critic in the *Athenaeum* remarked that Hardy seemed "to have finally chosen as his branch of fiction that which, for the want of a better name, may be called the modern-romantic. That is, he takes the present for his time, and such people as move among us at the present for his characters; but he makes his characters do things, and puts them into positions, which, if not impossible, would at least be thought very remarkable, and worthy of a leading article in every daily paper, if they had really been reported by a living witness."[13] Thus rather naively explicated, the term "modern-romantic" seems to imply much the same thing as the *Spectator's* "humorous fable"; yet the term is a useful one in suggesting elements of common ground in what had been to this point Hardy's extremely varied fictional output, and it also throws a suggestive light on the phrase "Utilitarian romance" which appears, entirely without context, at the back of one of Hardy's notebooks.[14] Nor was this to be Hardy's last "fable" in the "modern-romantic" manner: he did not by any means abandon the kind of methods and materials with which he had worked in *The Hand of Ethelberta* but returned to them, in one form or another, in *A Laodicean*, *Two on a Tower*, and *The Well-Beloved*. The general conception of Hardy's greatness as a novelist is primarily shaped by the major works of the late 1880s and early 1890s; *The Hand of Ethelberta* offers substantial evidence that he could conceivably have carved out for himself a career of notable if not major proportions along very different lines.

4

On Native Grounds:
Charles Kegan Paul and
William Barnes

Mr. Thomas Hardy's novels have been, on the whole, favourably received, and many of their merits recognised. Yet their most characteristic features have either been passed over in silence, or pronounced exaggerated, simply because very few of the readers are able to judge in these matters of his workmanship. Just as a gaping crowd, catalogue-armed, may stand before a great picture with vague, unintelligent admiration, while only those with special artistic training will be able to explain wherein its merit consists, so in Mr. Hardy's 'Rural Painting of the Dutch School,' and other studies, those can best appreciate his work who know the wolds and woods, the lanes and villages of his own Dorset, the speech and the thought of those who traverse and inhabit them.

* * *

'The Hand of Ethelberta,' again, is full of Dorset coast scenery, all recognisable, though distance between places is now and then, for artistic purposes, misstated. But Swanage, Corfe Castle, Bournemouth, Lulworth with its cove and castle, are all there, and the rustle of the beech trees and the scent of the fresh sea breathe from the pages and go far to neutralise the glare and noise of the hot London street in which we write.[1]

These extracts are from "The Wessex Labourer", that early

appreciative article in the *Examiner* which Hardy continued to value in later years. Its author, the Dorset man in London, was Charles Kegan Paul, as he himself revealed to Hardy in a letter of April 1877: "I reviewed you some time ago in the Examiner, and if you ever read my criticisms you will know that you have few more cordial admirers. Minto gave me the pleasure of your personal acquaintance at the Savile one evening, I have been always hoping it might be increased."[2] Kegan Paul was writing to Hardy in his capacity as literary adviser to the publishing house of Henry S. King & Co., which was about to publish a one-volume edition of *A Pair of Blue Eyes.* He had earlier (1862–1874) been vicar of the Dorset village of Sturminster Marshall; he subsequently became one of the founders of the firm of Kegan Paul, Trench, & Co. (successors to Henry S. King) and, later still, a notable convert to Roman Catholicism. In his autobiography, *Memories*, he recalled his friendship with Hardy and his long-standing admiration for Hardy's novels: "Living as I did in Dorsetshire, I was able perhaps to understand how absolutely true to life are the pictures in Hardy's early books."[3] Hardy once spoke of Kegan Paul as the only man who knew Dorsetshire better than himself,[4] and he must have taken a special satisfaction in Kegan Paul's informed endorsement of his own fictional portrayals of Dorset scenery, life, and speech.

Such endorsement must have been especially reassuring to Hardy during the difficult years when both his marriage and his professional career were still in an uncertain and uncrystallised state. According to *Early Life* (137), he felt "uneasy" at the realisation that he was now "committed by circumstances to novel-writing as a regular trade, as much as he had formerly been to architecture". At the time *The Hand of Ethelberta* was published, in April 1876, Hardy and his wife were living just outside Dorset, in the Somerset town of Yeovil, having moved into lodgings there "to facilitate", says *Early Life* (142), "their search for a little dwelling". The Hardys had now been married more than eighteen months, and if the poem "We Sat at the Window" (dating from July 1875)[5] reflects anything other than a temporary misunderstanding, their relationship must already have proved profoundly disappointing. Signs of restlessness on Hardy's part are detectable, indeed, even in advance of his wedding day. Quite apart from any feelings he may have had for his cousin, Tryphena Sparks, he seems to have been interested in a number of other women in the period between 1870 and 1874: he was friendly, for instance, with Leslie Stephen's sister-in-law, Annie Thackeray, and he was immediately attracted to Helen Paterson, the illustrator of *Far from the Madding Crowd*, when he met her early in 1874, his own marriage not taking place until after she had become the wife of William Allingham.[6] The second Mrs Hardy once told Miss Irene Cooper Willis that Hardy had been trapped into marrying Emma by the machinations of her sister, Mrs Holder; certainly the length of the engagement, the evidence (such as it is) of *A Pair of Blue Eyes* and of poems like "The Interloper", and the absence of Hardy's relatives from the wedding ceremony, all strengthen the impression that something was wrong, and known to be wrong, from the first.[7]

The situation cannot have been made easier by the nomadic life which the Hardys led during the first two years of their marriage. After the wedding trip to France they spent the winter of 1874–75 in Surbiton, moved in March to Westbourne Grove, went house-hunting in Dorset in June, and in July 1875, after a short period in Bournemouth, settled in Swanage until the move to Yeovil the following March. From Yeovil they made another trip to the Continent in May and June, and it was not until July 3, 1876, that they moved into more permanent quarters at Riverside Villa, Sturminster Newton.[8] *Early Life* (146) speaks of the criticism of relatives that Hardy and his wife were wandering about like tramps; that Emma herself felt dissatisfied with their manner of living is suggested by a note of June 1876 in her diary of the second continental tour: "Going back to England where we have no home and no chosen county."[9]

From Hardy's professional standpoint the wandering was more purposive. Much of the itinerary of his wedding trip to France was apparently determined by his desire (as he wrote to his brother the day after the wedding) to collect material for his "next story": at one stage in the planning of *The Hand of Ethelberta* the heroine was presumably to have carried out her plan to visit Paris with her brothers.[10] The choice of Swanage during the winter of 1875-76 seems to have been either cause or consequence of Hardy's decision to use the town as the major setting for the novel he was then completing. In the scene at Corvesgate Castle Hardy capitalised, perhaps too heavily, on a picnic visit which he had made to Corfe Castle with his wife and sisters in September 1875;[11] the geographical situation of Knollsea (Swanage) in relation to Sandbourne (Bournemouth) is used effectively as an element in ensuring the late arrival of those seeking to prevent Ethelberta's marriage; and the new building in progress at Swanage [12] provided him with ample warrant for the removal of Ethelberta from a sailor's cottage (such as the one in which he and Emma were living) to a new villa.

The journeyings in pursuit of settings and material must have confronted Emma rather abruptly with the practical implications of that professional status which she herself had encouraged Hardy to adopt. Despite the difficulties, her role was not without its compensations: it was apparently at Swanage that she herself began work on a novel, *The Maiden on the Shore*, described on its first page as "a story of fair passions, and bountiful pities, and loves without stain".[13] In the meantime, evidences of her husband's growing reputation were constantly forthcoming. He was beginning to be discussed in reviews and in general articles as a major literary figure, and even the least enthusiastic reviews of *The Hand of Ethelberta* had been fundamentally respectful. His first publication of a poem, "The Fire at Tranter Sweatley's", in 1875 was not followed by others at this period, but editors were certainly beginning to accept his short stories: "Destiny and a Blue Cloak" in 1874, the children's story "The Thieves Who Couldn't Help Sneezing" in 1877, and, in 1878, both "The Impulsive Lady of Croome Castle" (later incorporated, as "The Duchess of Hamptonshire", in *A Group of Noble Dames*) and "An Indiscretion in the Life of an Heiress".

"An Indiscretion" was solicited for the *New Quarterly Magazine* by Francis Hueffer;[14] in 1879 the editorship of the *New Quarterly* was taken over by Charles Kegan Paul, and during that and the following year Hardy published there two more short stories, "The Distracted Young Preacher" and "Fellow-Townsmen", and a review (the only review he was ever to write) of William Barnes's *Poems of Rural Life in the Dorset Dialect*. In 1880 Kegan Paul, Trench & Co., having already taken over the one-volume edition of *A Pair of Blue Eyes* from Henry S. King, brought out a one-volume edition of *The Return of the Native*. By this time Hardy and Kegan Paul had become friends: *Early Life* (159) recalls Hardy's presence at a dinner at Kegan Paul's in the summer of 1878 at which the other guests included T. H. Huxley and Lord Leighton's sister, Mrs Sutherland Orr. It was Mrs Orr who contributed to the *New Quarterly* the October 1879 article, "Mr. Hardy's Novels", which has sometimes been incorrectly attributed to Kegan Paul himself: "The writer is not a 'he' as you suggest," Kegan Paul wrote to Hardy on October 19, 1879, "but Mrs. Orr whom you may remember having sat next to at dinner at our house."[15] Kegan Paul did write the even more important article under the same title which appeared in the *British Quarterly Review* of April 1881, praising Hardy's work in strong and cogent terms, and confidently discussing him as the true successor to George Eliot and strong contender, since her death, for the title of greatest living English novelist. Characteristically, the article closes on a doubly propagandist note:

> That Mr. Hardy has taken his place in the true literature of England is to us beyond question. For his sake and for their own we trust the larger public will recognize the fact, and steep themselves in the fresh healthy air of Dorset, and come into contact with the kindly folk who dwell there, through these pages, and then test their truth, as they can, in summer visits to the wolds, hill-sides, and coasts, which their 'native' has described so well.[16]

Hardy, in a warm letter, gratefully acknowledged the article and spoke of the tendency of such appreciative criticism to stimulate a writer to his best work.[17] If he felt some reservations about the use of his work as a kind of tourist prospectus, an album of verbal snapshots of Dorset scenery, he no doubt bore in mind Kegan

Paul's earlier endeavours, in his own parish and through his writings, on behalf of the poorer classes of Dorset society, and especially the support he had given to Joseph Arch. In 1872, *Memories* records, Arch "carried his agitation into our neighbourhood with the aid of the Hon. Auberon Herbert. I threw myself into this movement with all my heart. Mr. Herbert and Mr. Arch spent some days with me, during which we visited many large meetings of labourers, and in spite of the opposition of farmers, squires, and clergy we had the satisfaction to know that we raised the rate of wages at least two shillings a week all round."[18] Hardy must also have appreciated that his friend's peroration had been chiefly designed to enhance the reputation of Dorset in the nation at large and to combat the accelerating effects of urbanisation. "Year by year masses of our people," the article had earlier observed, "and they our chief readers, see less and less of simple quiet country scenes. Bricks and mortar swallow up our lives..."[19] Kegan Paul's wish to bring city-dwellers to the Dorset countryside had, after all, its counterpart in Hardy's ambition to bring Dorset to an audience now (as Kegan Paul's references to "our chief readers" acknowledges) predominantly and increasingly urban.

Kegan Paul remained an enthusiastic admirer of Hardy's work and a constant friend.[20] He praised *The Mayor of Casterbridge* and *Tess of the d'Urbervilles*. Despite—or perhaps on account of—his ecclesiastical past, he thought it a "marvellously comic touch" that a bishop should have been made the victim of the marital deception in *Two on a Tower*.[21] When Hardy fell ill during the composition of *A Laodicean*, Kegan Paul concealed his dislike of the novel, passed on advice about doctors, and tracked down the correct name ("Wheatstone's A.B.C. Machine") of a particular telegraphic instrument which Hardy had apparently thought of introducing into his story.[22] In the early 1880s, as C. J. P. Beatty has shown, it was Kegan Paul who first involved Hardy in the activities of the Society for the Protection of Ancient Buildings, thus enabling him to put his architectural knowledge to practical use and make some restitution for those early acts of Church "restoration" he grieved to remember in later years. [23] But Kegan

Paul's most important contribution to Hardy's career was made at the time when Hardy was still trying to establish himself as a writer at once serious and professional. As a reviewer he praised Hardy's work and testified to its regional authenticity. As an editor he published some of Hardy's first short stories. As a publisher he was responsible for two of the earliest cheap editions of individual novels. If Kegan Paul did not possess the kind of power wielded by Leslie Stephen as editor of the *Cornhill*, he was nonetheless able, in a variety of ways, to give Hardy both the practical assistance and the personal reassurance he so urgently needed.

* * *

To the end of his life Kegan Paul's preference among Hardy's novels seems to have been for *The Return of the Native*: even *Tess*, though admittedly finer, seemed to him not so flawless.[24] Hardy apparently began work on what was to prove his second major novel early in 1877, about six months or so after he and Emma had moved into Riverside Villa, a house overlooking the River Stour at Sturminster Newton. Much has already been written of the "Sturminster Newton idyll", their "happiest time",[25] and nothing is more striking in the *Early Life* than the kind of energy and appetite for life which emerges from the diary and notebook entries attributed to this period. The Hardys made friends in Sturminster and took an eager interest in local activities; Hardy himself made copious notes of things he saw and heard, from a coroner's post-mortem examination to stories of poaching and an eye-witness recollection of the execution on Bincombe Down in 1801 which subsequently provided the basis for the story, "The Melancholy Hussar".

Apparently Hardy and Emma maintained a reasonably happy and stable relationship during this period, but Hardy's alert appreciativeness of the life he saw around him may also have owed a good deal to satisfaction with the progress of his new novel—if not with the negotiations for its publication. On February 13, 1877, Hardy wrote to the publishers of *Blackwood's Edinburgh Magazine* to ask if they would be interested in the possibility of serialising a rural story somewhat along the lines of *Far from the*

Madding Crowd; two months later, on April 12, he sent them fifteen chapters of the new story.[26] If, as is most likely, these were chapters of *The Return of the Native*, then it would seem that it was only after the rejection of the story by *Blackwood's* towards the end of April that he first submitted it to Leslie Stephen and the *Cornhill*—perhaps because he had anticipated Stephen's reaction that the story "might develop into something 'dangerous' for a family magazine".[27] Hardy seems to have tried at least one other magazine, *Temple Bar*, before coming to terms with Chatto and Windus for publication in *Belgravia* beginning with the issue of January 1878.[28]

One of the most interesting features of the three-volume first edition of *The Return of the Native*, when it appeared in November of that same year, was Hardy's own "sketch map of the scene of the story", included as a frontispiece.[29] The idea of the map seems to have owed something to John Hutton, brother of the *Spectator*'s editor, Richard H. Hutton. Although John Hutton had written the *Spectator* review of *Desperate Remedies* which caused Hardy such anguish, he greatly admired *Under the Greenwood Tree* and *A Pair of Blue Eyes* and reviewed the latter (again in the *Spectator*) in very favourable terms.[30] At this point the two men entered into an entirely friendly correspondence, and in one of his letters Hutton asked for some identification of the actual places under-lying the fictional names in Hardy's novels, adding: "I always want a *map* as a frontispiece to a good novel." [31] Although Hardy did not take up the suggestion immediately, the map he drew for *The Return of the Native* a few years later is a document of some importance in terms of his slowly developing conception of Wessex, and of even greater interest as a revelation of just how closely Hardy had modelled the setting of the novel upon the area of heath close to his own birthplace at Bockhampton. Clearly the map is not identical with the actual topography of Duddle Heath and its neighbourhood, but by looking at the map lengthways (instead of vertically, as it was published) its very substantial degree of correspondence with an identifiable landscape can readily be recognised. The position indicated for Bloom's End, for example, roughly approximates to that still occupied by

Hardy's birthplace; in a letter of 1900 Hardy said that Bloom's End embodied features of Bhompston Farmhouse (a mile to the south) but that its position had been "a little shifted".[32]

The map, like the title, makes it tempting to speculate on the possible implications of the novel for Hardy himself. Its story, after all, is that of a man diverted from his high purposes by an infatuation with an unusual woman living in a lonely place, and there are a number of specific hints (including the insistence in *Early Life* [154] that Clement was a Hardy family name and Hardy's statement to Sir Sidney Cockerell that Mrs Yeobright was based on his own mother)[33] to suggest some degree of auto-biographical relevance. Not the least remarkable feature of the novel, in this and other respects, is that Hardy's choice of setting involved a deliberate and uncharacteristic avoidance of his immediate surroundings. *Early Life* (154) itself acknowledges the oddity of Hardy's decision: "Strangely enough, the rich alluvial district of Sturminster Newton in which the author was now living was not used by him at this time as a setting for the story he was constructing there, but the heath country twenty miles off." Writing to Hardy in April 1877 Kegan Paul expressed the hope that he was again working on a Dorset story but confessed that he himself cared much less for the Vale of Blackmore, in which Sturminster Newton lies, than for the South Dorset settings of Hardy's previous novels.[34] It was a reasonable assumption on Paul's part that Hardy would once again be writing, as he had done in *Far from the Madding Crowd* and *The Hand of Ethelberta*, about the area in which he was currently living. And the Vale of Blackmore had the special attraction of its associations with William Barnes. The Dorset poet had been born near Sturminster more than three-quarters of a century earlier, and the surrounding countryside, so often evoked in his verse, might be expected to prove unusually rich in material and in allusive potential for a Dorset writer of a younger generation whose name had already been publicly linked with that of Barnes in Paul's *Examiner* article of 1876. Yet it may have been precisely Hardy's awareness of the area's associations with Barnes which drove him to seek elsewhere for the setting of *The Return of the Native*.

Hardy's great affection for Barnes emerges strongly from the obituary he wrote for the *Athenaeum* following Barnes's death in October 1886. He also expresses there his admiration for the old poet's many-sided achievement, especially in verse, philology, archaeology, and the study of folklore, and his gratitude for the opportunity of frequent intercourse with a mind "naturally imbued" with "now obsolete customs and beliefs", with "forgotten manners, words, and sentiments".[35]

Edmund Gosse—who had also known Barnes in his later years and described his appearance and personality in more than one lively letter—told Hardy: "Your account of Barnes is splendid—it puts all others in the shade. What a biographer was lost when nature stamped Novelist on your brow!"[36] But at the time of writing *The Return of the Native*, Hardy's feelings about Barnes must have been of a more ambiguous kind. Their friendship began in Dorchester in the late 1850s (when Barnes's "classical & mathematical school, South st." was next door to Hicks's office),[37] but it seems not to have become at all close until after the younger man had himself become established as an author. It was in 1876 that Barnes inscribed for Hardy ("With the author's kind regards and good wishes for his writings") a copy, not of one of his volumes of Dorset dialect verse, but of his 1868 collection, *Poems of Rural Life in Common English*.[38] The choice, whether made by Barnes or by Hardy, seems not inappropriate. Much as Hardy admired Barnes's dialect poems, as he later demonstrated by praising them in critical articles and editing them for the Clarendon Press, he must also have learned from Barnes's negative example, as from the positive example of George Eliot, that a writer seeking a national audience must avoid excessive localism. As he observed in his letter to the *Spectator* in October 1881:

> The rule of scrupulously preserving the local idiom, together with the words which have no synonym among those in general use, while printing in the ordinary way most of those local expressions which are but a modified articulation of words in use elsewhere, is the rule I usually follow; and it is, I believe,

[126]

generally recognised as the best, where every such rule must of necessity be a compromise, more or less unsatisfactory to lovers of form. It must, of course, be always a matter for regret that, in order to be understood, writers should be obliged thus slightingly to treat varieties of English which are intrinsically as genuine, grammatical, and worthy of the royal title as is the all-prevailing competitor which bears it; whose only fault was that they happened not to be central, and therefore were worsted in the struggle for existence, when a uniform tongue became a necessity among the advanced classes of the population.[39]

Though Hardy's practice differed so radically from that of Barnes, the final sentence of this letter constitutes an admirable summary of Barnes's views on Dorset speech as expressed in the prefatory dissertation to the original (1844) volume of *Poems of Rural Life, in the Dorset Dialect*: "The Dorset dialect is a broad and bold shape of the English language, as the Doric was of the Greek."[40] No doubt Hardy had read Barnes's writings on the subject, or even discussed it with Barnes himself. It seems quite possible, however, that some of Barnes's ideas may have reached Hardy through Horace Moule, who in 1862, in the course of a review article on "Dorset" in the *Quarterly Review*, had given high praise to Barnes's dialect poems and summarised at some length Barnes's philological conclusions about the dialect itself.[41] Barnes was on friendly terms with the Moule family—chiefly with Horace's distinguished father, the Rev. Henry Moule, Vicar of Fordington—and it was presumably at the instigation of Horace Moule, then an assistant master at the school, that in 1866 he was invited to give a poetry reading at Marlborough College, subsequently reported in *The Marlburian* (the school magazine) under the heading, "The Language of Wessex".[42]

Barnes was of course accustomed to speak of Wessex many years before the name appeared in the final serial instalment of *Far from the Madding Crowd*. In the prefatory dissertation to his 1844 volume, and even more notably in the revised dissertation of 1848, Barnes used Wessex in a specifically historical sense to denote the ancient kingdom of the West Saxons.[43] Horace Moule, who may have written the unsigned report in *The Marlburian*, also used Wessex as an historical expression in his *Quarterly Review* article of 1862.[44] But by 1868, in the preface to Barnes's *Poems of Rural Life in Common English* (the volume inscribed to Hardy), a more contemporary significance has crept into the word. "As I think," writes Barnes, "that some people, beyond the bounds of Wessex, would allow me the pleasure of believing that they have deemed the matter of my homely poems in our Dorset mother-speech to be worthy of their reading, I have written a few of a like kind, in common English."[45] A mild correction, clearly, needs to be made to Hardy's statement in the 1895 Preface to *Far from the Madding Crowd*: "But I believe I am correct in stating that, until the existence of this contemporaneous Wessex in place of the usual counties was announced in the present story, in 1874, it had never been heard of in fiction and current speech, if at all, and that the expression, 'a Wessex peasant,' or 'a Wessex custom,' would therefore have been taken to refer to nothing later in date than the Norman Conquest" (vii–viii).

Early Life (160–161) observes of Hardy's conception of Wessex that he grew "to forget the crossing of county boundaries within the ancient kingdom—in this respect being quite unlike the poet Barnes, who was 'Dorset' emphatically". The comment perhaps exaggerates the extent to which Hardy's fiction strays beyond the borders of Dorset, but it rightly emphasises the crucial difference between Hardy's regionalism and Barnes's intense localism. As Professor Samuel Hynes has observed of the two men, "Barnes was a provincial, Hardy was not"; where Barnes exploited the "unique qualities" of Dorset life, Hardy sought to draw upon it for "universally valid symbols".[46] In his 1879 review of the collected edition of Barnes's *Poems of Rural Life in the Dorset Dialect*, Hardy insisted that the poems belonged more specifically to Barnes's native Vale of Blackmore than to Dorset as a whole: "Though these poems are distinguished on the title-page by the name of the county generally from whose recesses their scenes and characters are derived, the more precise source of their inspiration is a limited district lying to the north and north-west

[128]

of Dorsetshire, and having marked characteristics of its own."[47]

This sentence is followed by the famous description of the Vale itself which Hardy was to use again, with only minor changes, in the second chapter of *Tess of the d'Urbervilles*. By the time he wrote *Tess* Hardy's own reputation was secure, and his choice of the Vale of Blackmore as Tess's home may have constituted, at least for his private satisfaction, an implicit rejection of the impression of life in the Vale which had been projected by a poet who, as Hardy said many years later, "held himself artistically aloof from the ugly side of things—or perhaps shunned it unconsciously".[48] The description of the Durbeyfields moving from their old home in Marlott reads like an ironic inversion of Barnes's "Leädy-Day an' Ridden House", while the course of Tess's own career soon marks her out from the "Blackmore Maidens" of that poem by Barnes which, in 1886, Hardy praised for its "blitheness".[49]

In the mid-1870s Hardy must still have felt unsure of himself and of his position. He must also have seen clearly that Barnes's way could not be his way, and that the need to establish for himself both a reputation and a territorial domain entirely independent of Barnes had become all the more imperative in the face of Kegan Paul's linking of the two names and of Richard Heath's presentation of Barnes's verse (in an article of 1872) as the characteristic voice of "Peasant Life in Dorset".[50] It seems extremely significant that Hardy's earliest letters to journals should have attempted to correct what he considered misrepresentations of his handling of dialect, [51] and that his review of 1879 should have stressed Barnes's almost exclusive use of north Dorset settings. Seen in this context, Hardy's decision, while living at Sturminster Newton, to write not about his immediate surroundings but about his own native countryside seems much more understandable. Hardy may have derived pleasure and even encouragement from the sense of living in Barnes country, but Barnes's pervasive presence was precisely what made the Vale of Blackmore forbidden fictional territory at this point in his career.

5

The Return of the Native

The new novel opened with a piece of scene setting and natural description far more ambitious than anything Hardy had previously attempted, and the early chapters made it abundantly clear that he was not only drawing more heavily upon more sources of imagery than ever before but deploying those images in a deliberate search for expressionistic and broadly symbolic effects. Hardy had by this time learned that there was much more to novels than characters and plots. He now realised that narrative and thematic statements could be made through setting, structure, symbolism, the conscious exploitation of pastoral and other conventions, and in *The Return of the Native* he set out to turn his discoveries to the fullest possible artistic advantage. Coming to the novel in the chronological sequence of Hardy's work, one senses that he felt the time had now come for him to aim beyond mere handiness at a serial, and to concern himself with "the proper artistic balance of the completed work".

In his study of the genesis of *The Return of the Native* John Paterson argues that the book may have been pastoral in its original conception, with the major characters little differentiated in class terms from the other inhabitants of Egdon, and that subsequent revision not only transformed Eustacia Vye from a witch to a romantic heroine but employed classical allusion and even technical features of the classical drama in an attempt to achieve "a formal and structural parallel with Greek tragedy". That attempt, Paterson believes, was not wholly successful; nevertheless, "by a virtually systematic accumulation of classical allusions, he evoked the atmosphere or background of Greek tragedy and, by so doing, framed and transfigured, as he had not done in *Far from the Madding Crowd* and as he would not do in *The Woodlanders*, his purely pastoral narrative".[1] It has recently been suggested that Paterson's account is both more confident and more dramatic than the evidence altogether justifies;[2] it might also be observed that Shakespeare seems in fact to be a stronger presence throughout the novel than either Aeschylus or Sophocles. The classical apparatus is, however, obvious and indeed obtrusive, the frame it provides both too heavy and too ornate. In *Far from the Madding Crowd* Hardy moderates the over-explicit pastoralism of the early scenes once he appreciates that what he is handling constitutes, in effect, authentic pastoral. In *The Woodlanders* he simply notes in the opening chapter the possibility of such rural fastnesses providing the setting for stories of Sophoclean grandeur. In *The Return of the Native* the allusions are sustained throughout, excessive in themselves and drawing attention to precisely those features in the novel which prove recalcitrant to analogical cross-referencing: the inappropriateness, for example, of any serious application of the term "Promethean" to the self-consuming passions of Eustacia Vye.

A similar ambitiousness marks Hardy's famous presentation of Egdon Heath in the opening chapters. He apparently saw in the heath not only a suitably bleak and open stage setting for the neo-Greek drama he proposed to unfold, but an opportunity to achieve an approximation to the classical unity of place.[3] The difficulty about Egdon is the way in which it perpetually threatens to move from background to foreground, to claim an importance and significance which, dramatically, it does not possess, but which— since the scenery and topography are based specifically on the heathlands close to Hardy's birthplace—may well derive from the importance and significance it held for Hardy personally. Hardy suggests in his 1912 Preface a link with the heath in *King Lear*;[4] a closer analogy would perhaps be with the moors in *Wuthering Heights*. But the moors in Emily Brontë's novel, though certainly no less powerfully realised, are kept in their inanimate place: they provide obstacles and problems, and characters may or may not have an affinity with them, yet even in so romantic a work they are not given the anthropomorphic elaboration of Egdon Heath.

Egdon provides, of course, a closed and isolated situation in which the action of the novel can be worked out as if in a laboratory, with little hope of escape for the inhabitants and the minimum of interference from outside. It also approximates to that "sort of poetic or fairy precinct" which Hawthorne found necessary to the writing of a romance.[5] As a place where paganism and witchcraft flourish and churchgoing is a rarity, the heath constitutes a kind of moral wilderness where the standards of value and behaviour adhered to by the major characters have to be imported from elsewhere. In the ensuing confrontation with the realities of the Egdon world it is all too often the alien values which are surrendered. Wildeve, Eustacia, and Mrs Yeobright all raise moral issues, to themselves or to others, only to contravene almost immediately the standards of what they know to be sensible, humane, and right. Similarly, Clym's account of his educational scheme is received by the Egdon folk with a scepticism which proves only too well founded:

> 'He'll never carry it out in the world,' said Fairway. 'In a few weeks he'll learn to see things otherwise.'
> "Tis good-hearted of the young man,' said another. 'But, for my part, I think he had better mind his business.' (202)

There remains a very important sense in which Hardy's initial creation of Egdon goes stubbornly against the grain of the novel as a whole. Both the allusions to Greek tragedy and the evocation of setting are presumably intended to elevate the central story, to project its narrative and thematic patterns as in some sense reflective or representative of permanent elements in human experience at all times and in all places. Yet just as Hardy's classical apparatus draws damaging attention to itself by its very explicitness, so in insisting upon Egdon's permanence he succeeds only in invoking an impression of its primitive strangeness: what is established in the early chapters is not the pastoral and pre-industrial world of *Far from the Madding Crowd* and *Under the Greenwood Tree* but a desert tract of pre-civilisation. To juxtapose against such a setting figures so strongly contrasted and so essentially of the nineteenth century as Clym, Eustacia, Wildeve, and Mrs Yeobright is to jar credulity and promote continuous unease, to establish not the representative character of the story but precisely its eccentricity.

Hardy's errors here are of proportion, of rhetorical decorum. Essentially, they derive from sheer ambition, a determination to thrust the novel towards literary distinction not only as a work of art but as in some degree, as he later suggested to the sculptor Thomas Woolner, a work about art.[6] More specifically they relate to a failure of technical sophistication, especially in the handling of point of view. In *Far from the Madding Crowd*, with its sweeping narrative, brilliant scenes, and rich social context, Hardy's failure to solve, or perhaps even to recognise, the problems of point of view had not been of major significance. In *The Return of the Native*, where the narrative is slow, the context meagre, the focus kept firmly upon the intense sexual and psychological interplay of the central characters, it becomes a serious weakness.

It becomes extremely difficult, for example, to distinguish Hardy's view of Eustacia from what is presumably intended to be Eustacia's view of herself. In the first sustained evocation of her personality, classical allusion and metaphorical identification—she combines the features of Sappho with those of Mrs Siddons and is associated with, among others, "Artemis, Athena, or Hera" (77)—are mingled with the stock paraphernalia of mid-nineteenth-century romanticism:

> Her presence brought memories of such things as Bourbon roses, rubies, and tropical midnights; her moods recalled lotus-eaters and the march in 'Athalie'; her motions, the ebb and flow of the sea; her voice, the viola. (76)

Other rich ingredients are added: her dark beauty, an ancestry stemming both from Greece and from the English aristocracy, her "smouldering rebelliousness" (77) and desire to be "loved to madness" (79). The description may be, technically speaking, that of the omniscient narrator, but what is being evoked appears to be largely the romantic self-dramatisation of a nineteen-year-old girl.[7] From the "Queen of the Night" chapter as a whole emerges not a portrait of Eustacia but a confused impression which subsequent dramatisation does not sufficiently resolve. The confusion focuses attention once again on the classical references —as the reader wonders whether in catching their precise nuances the key to Eustacia's personality might be found—and inevitably prompts the further reflection that the whole apparatus of allusion and symbolic landscape painting seems an unnecessarily ponderous method of establishing those central ironies in Eustacia's situation which arise from the fundamental disharmony between her ambitious personality and the setting in which she finds herself. On the one hand, her aura of romantic grandeur can shine only with "Haggard Egdon" (5) as a foil, her attitudes and ideas seem adventurous only "in relation to her situation among the very rereward of thinkers" (80). On the other, the restricted opportunities afforded by the heath force her to accommodations she would otherwise scorn:

> And so we see our Eustacia—for at times she was not altogether unlovable—arriving at that stage of enlightenment which feels that nothing is worth while, and filling up the spare hours of her existence by idealizing Wildeve for want of a better object. This was the sole reason of his ascendency: she knew it herself. At moments her pride rebelled against her passion for him, and she even had longed to be free. But there was only one circumstance which could dislodge him, and that was the advent of a greater man. (81–82)

This is the pathos and the irony of Eustacia's situation: that her aspirations are novelettish and impossibly grandiose does nothing to lessen the bitter sense of discrepancy between those aspirations and her actual opportunities. The Eustacia who finally gains the reader's sympathy is not a type of Promethean rebelliousness but a frightened, frustrated, and deeply disappointed woman, the sources of whose fear, frustration and disappointment are presented specifically and in intensely human terms: Clym's angry self-absorption; the denial of her femininity and of her social ambitions; her own appalled sense of being trapped in a hostile environment, with no alternative courses of action, no prospect of future amelioration.

This more concrete presentation of Eustacia depends largely upon what might almost be considered as an additional framing device, the sequence of folk rituals and festivals which mark the Egdon year. The stages of Eustacia's increasing desperation can almost be charted by the degree and nature of her involvement in such observances—if she exploits the heath fires she surrenders totally to the dance at East Egdon—and in these and other terms her participation in the mumming play of St George seems to have particular significance. As an element in the plot this play-within-a-novel has only minor importance; its function, like Gabriel Oak's view of Bathsheba in the first chapter of *Far from the Madding Crowd*, approximates to that of the Elizabethan dumb-show, symbolically establishing characters in their roles and foreshadowing the pattern of future events. John Paterson has suggested that the play enacts in miniature that "defeat of the pagan and the triumph of the Christian" which he sees as central to the novel as a whole;[8] more immediately, Eustacia's involvement demonstrates that mixture of impulsiveness and timidity which runs throughout her personality, while the mock-combat of rustic knights points parodically at the insubstantiality of her own romantic view of life.[9] The St George play, as Hardy well knew, embodied an ancient myth of the annual cycle of nature's death and renewal, and similar myths are specifically mentioned as providing the original impulse of such Egdon observances as the November bonfires and the Maypole dancing of early summer:

The instincts of merry England lingered on here with exceptional vitality, and the symbolic customs which tradition has attached to each season of the year were yet a reality on Egdon. Indeed, the impulses of all such outlandish hamlets are pagan still: in these spots homage to nature, self-adoration, frantic gaieties, fragments of Teutonic rites to divinities whose names are forgotten, seem in some way or other to have survived mediaeval doctrine. (459)

[135]

That the Maypole is specifically linked with Diggory Venn and with the renewal of life and hope in Thomasin seems to argue against too exclusive an identification between the paganism of Egdon and that of Eustacia herself. Such episodes as the mumming play and the wild dance at East Egdon suggest rather a source and pattern of ancient, instinctual vitality with which Diggory and Thomasin are in sympathy, to which Eustacia can respond, if only as to an artificial stimulant, but which Clym, for all his love of the heath, must as a puritan and as a reformer steadfastly oppose.[10]

"Take all the varying hates felt by Eustacia Vye towards the heath, and translate them into loves, and you have the heart of Clym" (205). It is characteristic of this highly calculated novel that Hardy's formulation of the fundamental opposition between Clym and Eustacia should be so absolute, and that it should invoke Egdon not so much as a touchstone but as a rock upon which their marriage will split. Although Eustacia is often thought of as the most remarkable character in the novel, the main focus is upon the returning native himself, and upon the implications and consequences of his homecoming. Born of a socially mismatched marriage between a farmer and the daughter of a curate—a pattern Swithin St Cleeve, in *Two on a Tower*, will later invert— he has become a successful Parisian jeweller through natural talents, good fortune, and the ambition of his widowed mother, who has been prepared to part with the son she so much loves in the interests of his education and advancement. Clym is, however, presented by Hardy as very much a modern and even a specifically Arnoldian type, who has "become acquainted" in Paris "with ethical systems popular at the time" (203). His sense of a profound disharmony between his beliefs and the "flashy" and "effeminate" (207) business by which he earns his living leads him to abandon Paris and his position and return to the Egdon Heath he has known and loved since infancy, there to become a "schoolmaster to the poor and ignorant, to teach them what nobody else will" (206).

Because Hardy wrote *The Return of the Native* in Dorset after the period of rather uncertain wandering which marked the first years of his marriage, and because the setting of the novel is so specifically Hardy's own native countryside, it is tempting to associate him in some way with Clym. Critics have often taken the view that to a greater or lesser degree Clym *is* Hardy in his moral earnestness and his gestures towards social reform, but this position seems not to take fully into account either the flimsiness of Clym's reformist pretensions or the essential negativity of his attitudes. Although Hardy at first presents Clym as a man of high ideals who is simply unfortunate in being ahead of his time, on the next page he is already stressing the essential impracticability of Clym's endeavour:

> To argue upon the possibility of culture before luxury to the bucolic world may be to argue truly, but it is an attempt to disturb a sequence to which humanity has been long accustomed. Yeobright preaching to the Egdon eremites that they might rise to a serene comprehensiveness without going through the process of enriching themselves, was not unlike arguing to ancient Chaldeans that in ascending from earth to the pure empyrean it was not necessary to pass first into the intervening heaven of ether. (204)

The Arnoldian idealism is not itself directly dismissed, but the self-defeating nature of Clym's educational ambitions for the heath folk is well emphasised by the statement that he "could not help indulging in a barbarous satisfaction at observing that, in some of the attempts at reclamation from the waste, tillage, after holding on for a year or two, had receded again in despair, the ferns and furze-tufts stubbornly reasserting themselves" (205).[11] But the natural wildness in which Clym delights finds its human embodiment in Susan Nunsuch, that practitioner of witchcraft; the heath he loves is absolutely at odds with civilisation and with his own ambitions as a reformer. In seeking to educate and uplift its inhabitants he can, at best, educate them *away* from the heath, as he himself had been educated earlier: the heath itself, as he learns, offers no employment other than furze-cutting. Mrs Yeobright makes the point sensibly enough:

'It is right that there should be schoolmasters, and mission-
aries, and all such men,' she replied. 'But it is right, too, that
I should try to lift you out of this life into something richer,
and that you should not come back again, and be as if I had not
tried at all.' (210)

There is no longer any proper place for Clym in the economy of
Egdon, and in returning there he is in effect rejecting his mother's
efforts while living off the money they have enabled him to amass.
The ironies in this situation are not the only ones Clym fails to
perceive. It is only after his mother's death that he seems finally
to understand that it is she and not Egdon or its people whom he
had really loved and for whom he had returned; in the extrava-
gance of his remorse he treats her memory with almost religious
devotion, her words with the sanctity of revealed truth. With the
death of Eustacia his specifically social reformism seems finally to
disappear, and he is last seen preaching his own private gospel in
which, to judge from his chosen text, maternal adoration plays a
large part.[12]

The ultimate unsoundness of Clym's position is revealed by the
readiness with which he distorts it. He has not the slightest
grounds for thinking that Eustacia would be interested in becoming a teacher, yet it is, pathetically, the furtherance of his
teaching scheme which he advances as the chief justification of his
marriage, while at the same time rapidly shifting his ambition
from running a school for the people of Egdon to the establishment of "a good private school for farmers' sons" (227). The
abandonment of the labouring in favour of the farming class seems
extremely significant here, especially as an index of the essential
futility of his ambitions, the naivety of his hope that on Egdon he
might at last escape "the chafing of social necessities" (230).

Clym's return, no matter how well intentioned, to a place where
he has no role to fulfil seems in social terms to be self-willed,
regressive, and almost a turning aside from life; his mother
certainly sees it thus. In human terms the return of the native
proves disastrous, as Eustacia observes:

She paused a few moments, and added, 'If you had never

returned to your native place, Clym, what a blessing it would have been for you! . . . [sic] It has altered the destinies of—'

'Three people.'

'Five,' Eustacia thought; but she kept that in. (325)

Primarily this is the consequence of Clym's utter self-absorption, and of that inflexibility in him which his idealism serves only to emphasise. It is not necessary to admire Eustacia's moral or mental qualities in order to feel that the initial and major responsibility for the breakdown of their marriage belongs to Clym rather than to her. Having defied and denied his mother in order to marry Eustacia, Clym forces his bride into a situation which blankly affronts not only her ambitions but her most fundamental sensitivities as a young and beautiful woman. His physical blindness becomes emblematic of his whole personality. By persisting in the work of a furze-cutter—financially dispensable, socially degrading in Eustacia's eyes, and physically exhausting—Clym prepares the ground for those characteristically impulsive actions of Eustacia's which drive the couple finally apart. Clym had been christened Clement, but after the "closed door" episode and his mother's death he ignores both the significance of his name and the lesson of forgiveness his relationship with his mother should have taught him in order to cultivate first his own guilt and then his anger against Eustacia with the obsessiveness of an Othello, a Coriolanus, a Lear.

Self-absorbed, isolated, humourless, Clym seems incapable of sympathetic communication with anyone outside himself. He marries Eustacia, as Angel Clare is later to marry Tess Durbeyfield, without attempting to see her as she really is, without confronting the fact of her yearning for Paris and entire revulsion from the heath to which he himself is so deeply attached .Although he is closest to his mother, he is consistently at odds with her: the scenes in which they quarrel are, in their bitter passion, among the most powerful in the book. And although the possibility of a marriage between Clym and Thomasin is often mentioned, it seems significant that nothing ever comes of it. Thomasin is presented, in extremely positive terms, as a girl of courage, good sense, and unusual charm. That no love develops between her and Clym, despite Mrs Yeobright's hopes and what Eustacia sees as their "inflammable proximity" (171), suggests that something may be missing in Clym's personality and emotional make-up. Since Thomasin does feel affection for Wildeve, he may conceivably possess in some degree what Clym lacks, and certainly Clym would never have been capable of the gentle consideration which Wildeve shows in omitting to tell Eustacia of his legacy at a moment when her own situation is so desperate. Nor, for better or worse, would Wildeve have been capable of Clym's stern resistance, at the moment of parting, to the appeal of Eustacia's beauty: "he turned his eyes aside, that he might not be tempted to softness" (393). Diggory Venn, too, in his self-effacing devotion to Thomasin, displays a kind of gallantry and sensitivity which Clym would have done well to emulate in his dealings with his mother, with Eustacia, and with Thomasin herself.

Early in 1878 Hardy told his illustrator: "Thomasin, as you have divined, is the *good* heroine, and she ultimately marries the reddleman, and lives happily. Eustacia is the wayward and erring heroine—She marries Yeobright, the son of Mrs Yeobright, is unhappy, and dies. The order of importance of the characters is as follows—1 Clym Yeobright 2 Eustacia 3 Thomasin and the reddleman 4 Wildeve 5 Mrs Yeobright."[13] The placing of Mrs Yeobright seems somewhat surprising—she is a strong character strongly presented—but Hardy is presumably thinking here in terms of the specifically narrative aspects of the serial version, and perhaps of the element of sub-plot which Diggory and Thomasin provide. Thomasin, as Hardy emphasises, is "the *good* heroine" and her moods of acceptance and endurance provide a contrast to Eustacia's rebellious impulsiveness even more striking than the opposition between Diggory and Clym. Diggory, by his well-meaning but unfortunate interventions in the central action, contributes largely to that recurrent pattern of thwarted or distorted intentions which John Hagan has analysed and which, with other inversions and reversals, R. W. Stallman posits as an element in the multi-level "hour-glass" structure which he perceives in the novel as a whole.[14] Stallman's account undoubtedly exaggerates the systematisation in Hardy's plotting, especially as it is actually experienced by the reader. At the same time, the apparatus of the opening chapters gives ample evidence of the degree of abstraction with which this particular novel was conceived, and Hardy may deliberately have used a sequence of misunderstandings, missed paths, delayed messages, and so on, as symbolic counterparts not so much of the malevolence of fate or circumstance but rather of the confused purposes of his characters, their loss of moral and emotional direction.

Throughout his career Hardy retained a fascination with inversions and reversals almost for their own sake, and in *The Return of the Native* he no doubt took pleasure in the gradual revelation of the man of courage and good sense who lay hidden beneath the grotesque reddleman exterior of Diggory Venn. The evolution is so successfully handled in the novel as it stands as to prompt certain doubts about the footnote to the end of the third chapter of Book Six which Hardy first introduced into the Wessex edition of 1912:

> The writer may state here that the original conception of the story did not design a marriage between Thomasin and Venn. He was to have retained his isolated and weird character to the last, and to have disappeared mysteriously from the heath, nobody knowing whither—Thomasin remaining a widow. But certain circumstances of serial publication led to a change of intent.
>
> Readers can therefore choose between the endings, and those with an austere artistic code can assume the more consistent conclusion to be the true one. (473)

The phrasing of the footnote seems extremely unfortunate. The obvious implication is that the "unhappy ending", with no marriage between Thomasin and Diggory, is the "more consistent" and hence the "true one". But Hardy does not in fact present the reader with a choice of alternative conclusions—as is done, for example, in some modern editions of *Great Expectations* —and the Wessex edition itself incorporates precisely the revisions by which Hardy sought to make a marriage between

Diggory and Thomasin seem entirely consistent. The present ending—as the chapter title "The Inevitable Movement Onwards" suggests—conforms to the quiet and characteristically "Shakespearean" pattern which Hardy had already adopted in *Far from the Madding Crowd* and which he would use again in *The Mayor of Casterbridge* and *Tess;* it has, in short, a "rightness" of its own which only Hardy's intrusive footnote disturbs.[15]

Paterson argues—largely, it would seem, on the basis of this footnote—that Hardy originally intended the novel to have only five books, corresponding to the classical five-act structure, and sought to maintain the unity of time at least to the extent of confining the action within the space of a year and a day.[16] The view certainly finds support in Hardy's comment, made late in life, that he had tried to observe the unities in *The Return of the Native*, and in such details as the title, "The Discovery", given to Book Fifth—in which Clym is both compared explicitly to Oedipus and presented as pursuing, in his persistent interrogation of Johnnie Nunsuch, the truth that will destroy him.[17] Less happily, perhaps, it seems possible that the relatively tangential material which now occupies much of Book Second may have been introduced precisely in order to make possible the creation of a separate book at this point and thus meet the demands of a self-imposed "five-act" pattern.

Even so, it is hard to imagine *The Return of the Native* without some version of its present concluding pages. Despite the late evocation of Clym as an Oedipus figure, there is a tendency for the classical imagery of the first half of the book, in which Eustacia is dominant, to give way to biblical imagery in the second half, where Clym is dominant. Eustacia, of course, is repeatedly evoked in terms of allusions to classical Greece, and she is actually of half Greek descent; she is also called a pagan and later finds one kind of apotheosis in what is specifically described as the paganism of the dance at East Egdon. Clym, on the other hand, is directly associated with what Hardy identifies as the modern displacement of "the Hellenic idea of life" (197); he is, in short, an anti-Greek, a non-Hellene. Critics have commented on the "Arnoldian" characteristics of Clym's views and of Clym himself,[18] and whether or not Hardy had specifically in mind Arnold's celebrated opposition, in *Culture and Anarchy*, between the Hellenic and Hebraic spirits there is no doubt that Clym becomes increasingly associated with biblical images. In explaining his abandonment of the diamond trade he quotes from St Paul; to Eustacia he is actually reminiscent "of the Apostle Paul" (334); at the very end of the novel he is deliberately evoked as a kind of Christ figure, a man whose "years" still number "less than thirty-three" (484) and who preaches from an outdoor eminence the first of "a series of moral lectures or Sermons on the Mount" (484).

The eminence is in fact Eustacia's Rainbarrow, and her replacement there by a Christ-like Clym seems, on the face of it, to suggest the triumph of Christianity over both the modern paganism of Eustacia and the more ancient paganism which Rainbarrow itself represents. But it seems clear that it is, at best, a triumph only in Swinburnian terms: "Thou hast conquered, O pale Galilean; the world has grown grey from Thy breath." If Clym is a Christ figure, he is one in a deliberately ironic sense. The very title of the novel, indeed, may well incorporate an ironic allusion to St Matthew 13.54–58, in which the description of Jesus upon coming "into his own country" prompts the observation about a prophet not being without honour except in his own country and in his own house. "And he did not many mighty works there because of their unbelief," the chapter concludes; of Clym's preaching we are told:

> Some believed him, and some believed not; some said that his words were commonplace, others complained of his want of theological doctrine; while others again remarked that it was well enough for a man to take to preaching who could not see to do anything else. (485)

In the final sentence of the novel the Oedipus pattern becomes dominant once more ("But everywhere he was kindly received, for the story of his life had become generally known"), and it would seem that Hardy does not so much pursue a detailed analogy between Clym and either Christ or Oedipus as draw upon both sets of associations—as upon others derived from works as diverse as *Pilgrim's Progress* and *Culture and Anarchy*—in establishing Clym as the apostle of a vaguely idealistic but austere and ultimately ineffectual world view.

When, at the very end of the novel, Clym is strongly, if ironically, evoked as a Christ figure, the imposition of this familiar pattern upon the pattern of Clym's life which the book itself has made familiar is sufficiently disturbing to compel a revaluation of his career as a whole. If nothing more, it forces the realisation that Eustacia judged correctly of the disastrousness of Clym's homecoming: the native cannot return and make over the world he once left into the kind of world he has learned to want. In that sense at least—and quite apart from anything that may be suggested by analogies with Oedipus and Lear and Jesus the man of Galilee—Clym discovers that, as Thomas Wolfe put it, you can't go home again.

Part Three
RECESSION

THE TRUMPET-MAJOR
Serial: January–December 1880
Published: October 1880

A LAODICEAN
Serial: December 1880–December 1881
Published: November 1881

TWO ON A TOWER
Serial: May–December 1882
Published: October 1882

I

The Trumpet-Major

On March 22, 1878, before *The Return of the Native* had been quite completed, Hardy and Emma moved into 1 Arundel Terrace, Trinity Road, Upper Tooting.[1] The second Mrs Hardy once suggested that the decision to leave Sturminster Newton was prompted by Emma's sensitivity to the scorn expressed by her brother at their living in a place so remote that a new species of bird on the lawn was an event.[2] According to *Early Life* (156), the new London location was adopted for professional purposes, Hardy having decided "that the practical side of his vocation of novelist demanded that he should have his headquarters in or near London". The next sentence adds a more sombre note ("The wisdom of his decision, considering the nature of his writing, he afterwards questioned"), and the years at Tooting were to prove happy neither for Hardy's work nor for his marriage. If Riverside Villa had witnessed a relatively idyllic period in his relationship with Emma, it was at 1 Arundel Terrace, *Early Life* (163) records, that "their troubles began".

Hardy did, however, take satisfaction in the enjoyment of his growing reputation, and in the opportunities he now had for extending his acquaintance, not only among publishers, editors, and men of letters, but also within the kind of social circle to which, as a young man, he could scarcely have ventured to aspire. His friendships with Lady Portsmouth and other members of the aristocracy seem to have begun in the mid-1880s, but while living at Tooting he was already attending Alexander Macmillan's garden parties, lunching with the Tennysons, meeting Sir Percy Shelley at W. O. Frith's studio, and dining in company with

Matthew Arnold and Henry James.[3] As a member of the Savile Club and of such convivial associations as the Rabelais Club and, later, the Omar Khayyam Club he also lingered in the smoke-filled rooms of that quasi-literary world of authorship presided over by such figures as Edmund Gosse, William Black, and Walter Besant. It was a world which a man like James could take in his social stride, as an occasional source of amusement and even of material, but which Hardy, less sure of his position and his values, ran the risk of taking too seriously. It is a little disturbing, for instance, that in *Early Life* (172–173) the founding of the Rabelais Club in December 1879 should be treated at some length and evident satisfaction derived from the statement—apparently inaccurate—that Henry James was excluded from membership because of the lack of virility in his writing.[4] Some of Hardy's own difficulties as a writer during the period may conceivably have derived, directly or indirectly, from the bad literary company he tended to keep: a wealth of dubious implication lies behind the bald statement in *Early Life* (159) that during the summer of 1878 he "by degrees fell into line as a London man again".

By this time he was thinking seriously about *The Trumpet-Major*. Notebook entries show that he was doing preparatory research at the British Museum on May 30, May 31, July 6, and July 27, 1878, and probably on other dates as well. Further notes were taken during another series of visits in the early summer of 1879,[5] and it seems to have been at about this time that sustained work on the final version of the novel was begun. Hardy had spoken in general terms about possible magazine publication of a new novel (apparently *The Trumpet-Major*) as early as August 1878,[6] but in February 1879 Leslie Stephen did not think the book far enough advanced for him to make a decision about its suitability for the *Cornhill*.[7] In June Hardy was offering the story to *Blackwood's*, and he may also have made an unsuccessful approach to *Macmillan's Magazine* before finally coming to terms with *Good Words*.[8] The editor of *Good Words*, Donald Macleod, sent him on June 20, 1879, a forceful definition of the scope permitted to the fiction published in the pages of the magazine:

it could, and should, be healthy, manly, and frank, but it must avoid "anything likely to offend the susceptibilities of honestly religious and domestic souls"—requirements which Hardy was at pains to meet in the serial version, at least to the extent of moderating the oaths and changing the day of Matilda Johnson's arrival from a Sunday to a Monday.[9]

Writing from Arundel Terrace on August 1, 1879, Hardy reported that he had been working regularly at the story and that the first two or three parts could be ready at any time.[10] Since proofs of the first four instalments (chapters 1–14) seem to have been printed by early September, Hardy had presumably submitted a substantial section of manuscript before going down to Dorset towards the end of August and taking his mother to visit some of the main scenes, including Weymouth, Portland, and Upwey.[11] Serialisation in *Good Words* began with the issue of January 1880 and ran through to December. Smith, Elder published the three-volume first edition, its cover designed by Hardy himself, in late October, 1880.[12]

It is helpful in approaching *The Trumpet-Major* to think in terms of a central domestic narrative, the story of Anne Garland and her suitors, unfolding within a framing narrative based upon actual events and historical personages. Quite apart from larger questions of historical authenticity, Hardy seems in the central narrative to have worked deliberately for a distinctive "period" flavour; Anne's quaint manners and quietly self-conscious gentility, indeed, are such as to prompt comparisons with the heroines of Jane Austen, while other aspects of the novel suggest specifically a condensation of major elements in *Sense and Sensibility*. Jane Austen's novels must have been almost inseparable from Hardy's sense of English society during the Napoleonic period—those "days of high-waisted and muslin-gowned women" (1) to which he refers in his opening sentence—and they may well have influenced the shaping of *The Trumpet-Major* into his nearest approximation to the classic English novel of manners.

The delicacy of the social discriminations in the novel is reflected in revisions still visible in the manuscript. The profession of Mrs Garland's late husband, for instance, has been changed from schoolmaster to landscape-painter, and that of the widow's elderly suitor from farmer to miller.[13] Certainly connected, these decisions may well have been simultaneous. The social position of a painter, hovering indeterminately between depths of bohemianism and heights of almost unlimited prosperity, was altogether more ambiguous than that of a schoolmaster. If the late Mr Garland had few pretensions and little actual success, his revised status nonetheless leaves his widow and daughter with some freedom (within the limits of their income) to choose the precise point on the social scale to which they will lay claim. In Anne's case, this freedom is much increased by her occupying, as a pretty girl of marriageable age, a position of maximum potential mobility. The change from farmer to miller had an opposite effect, for where the term "farmer" might reasonably be applied to men of quite different social and economic standing, from the upper ranks of the peasantry to the lower ranks of the squirearchy (e.g., the positions of Oak and Boldwood at the opening of *Far from the Madding Crowd*), the term "miller" serves to define much more precisely a man whose status, whatever his prosperity, is unmistakably "commercial" and lacking in the dignity conferred by the ownership of land. His son's army companions, significantly enough, are also tradesmen—skilled and intelligent, but of non-commissioned rank. The manuscript also shows revision of Loveday's mode of addressing Mrs Garland: where he once used her first name he now employs the much more respectful and social distancing "ma'am".[14] At some stage of composition Hardy seems to have gone through the manuscript systematically pointing up the "class" aspects of the book. Late insertions of this kind include many of the direct or indirect expressions of Anne's feeling that the Lovedays are socially her inferiors, as well as those opening paragraphs of chapter 2 which roundly declare the essential sturdiness of the Lovedays' unaristocratic pedigree.[15]

The main effect of such changes was to centre the action more firmly and consistently upon the choices open to the two unattached women, different as they are from each other in age, disposition, and sense of social propriety. In the early part of the book, where the emphasis on manners is strongest, much play is made with Anne's social anxieties. It is part of her "quaintness" and "old-fashionedness" that she should affect a seriousness and sense of responsibility going far beyond that of her relatively "girlish" mother, just as it is part of the book's irony that, for all her discretion, she should surrender at the end not merely to a Loveday but to the family's least reliable member—much as Marianne Dashwood in *Sense and Sensibility* finally marries the man she had at first refused even to consider.

There the irony is at the expense of "sensibility"; in *The Trumpet-Major* it is almost at the expense of "sense". Despite her eventual inheritance of Oxwell Hall—itself, perhaps, a dubious legacy—the prudential and prideful aspects of Anne's early gentility are certainly held up for implicit criticism, even if that criticism is to some extent qualified by the prevailing comic tone and by the stress on Anne's femininity and defencelessness. Unlike Fancy Day and Grace Melbury, those other charming but pro-voking heroines who prove less than worthy of the good men who love them, Anne can make little claim even to the justification of educational superiority. John Loveday is specifically portrayed as having been a promising pupil of Anne's father—originally in the role of schoolmaster, after revision in that of painter[16]—and by making him a trumpet-major Hardy presumably sought to suggest accomplishments and sensitivities which might otherwise seem improbable in a soldier of non-commissioned rank. Neither in this nor in any other respect, save that of physical courage, is Bob John's equal; the commission he eventually gains seems to have been at least partly the consequence of Anne's having mentioned his name to the King. Hardy offers no rational grounds for Anne's preference—except insofar as the early descriptions of camp life suggests the unlikelihood of Anne's ever marrying a regular soldier—and the novel exemplifies the power of simple sexuality just as surely as *The Return of the Native* or *Tess*.

Many readers early and late have found something quite gratuitously painful in the sufferings of John Loveday at the hands of Anne Garland and of his own scrupulosity, and there is cer-tainly reason to question the extent to which Hardy fulfilled his early promises that his heroine would be thoroughly "good" and that the novel as a whole would progress cheerfully and end happily.[17] Leslie Stephen seems to have felt that in so obviously choosing "the wrong man" Anne Garland had displayed a perversity beyond the limits permissible "in magazines", and while the *Pall Mall Gazette* reviewer defended Anne's choice he did so on somewhat unexpected grounds: "A novelist of the last century would have done poetical justice by giving Anne Garland to the steadfast and loyal soldier; not so Mr. Hardy, who so shows his sympathy with the discontent of an age that feels the prizes of life go, at least as often as not, to the weaker and the less true."[18] If a contemporary reviewer saw Anne's choice of Bob as an expression of the mid-Victorian *zeitgeist*, Guerard sees it—not so very differently, perhaps—as the consequence of John Loveday's unaggressiveness (characteristic of other Hardy heroes as well) and of the inability of Anne Garland, like Hardy's other "ingénues", to make "unsexed judgments".[19]

The action of the novel is aptly foreshadowed by the image of the ambiguously military weathervane as it appears both in Hardy's design for the cover of the first edition and in the second chapter of the book itself: "This revolving piece of statuary could not, however, be relied on as a vane, owing to a neighbouring hill, which formed variable currents in the wind" (12). But it is Bob who is the "weathercock"; for all the variable currents which flow through and from Anne Garland, it has to be said both in her defence and to her discredit that she remains true to an immature first love: "Youth is foolish; and does a woman often let her reasoning in favour of the worthier stand in the way of her perverse desire for the less worthy at such times as these?" (366). If the novel is concerned with education, it is chiefly in its demonstration of Anne's failure to learn from experience what she has had no opportunity to learn from precept. Whether by the end of the book she is genuinely weaned from her social pretensions or simply surrenders them seems an open question, but it is worth noting that Hardy lays some stress, in the title of chapter 39 as in the text, on Anne's susceptibility to Bob's appearance in officer's uniform:

He certainly was a splendid, gentlemanly, and gallant sailor from end to end of him; but then, what were a dashing present-ment, a naval rank, and telling scars, if a man was fickle-hearted? However, she peeped on till the fourth day, and then she did not peep. The window was open, she looked right out, and Bob knew that he had got a rise to his bait at last. (355)

The word "bait" precisely defines the character of Bob's cam-paign and the immaturity and conventionality of Anne's permit-ting herself to be thus caught. Nothing is more painful in the final paragraphs of the novel, and nothing (apart from the fore-warning of John's death) more ominous for the future, than the brutal coarseness and comprehensive insensitivity of Bob's farewell:

> 'It's all right, Jack, my dear fellow. After a coaxing that would have been enough to win three ordinary Englishwomen, five French, and ten Mulotters, she has to-day agreed to bestow her hand upon me at the end of six months. Good-bye, Jack, good-bye!' (374)

It is scarcely surprising that there should be a note of purposive-ness in the final statement that John "went off to blow his trumpet till silenced for ever upon one of the bloody battle-fields of Spain" (374).

The painful twist given to the reader's emotions by this allusion to John's forthcoming death carries important implica-tions for the relationship of the central narrative to the framing narrative of historical events. The book is named for the trumpet-major, and it is he who experiences and suffers most and for whom our sympathies are most consistently enlisted. The pivotal role, however, belongs to Anne. The novel opens with her, the action revolves upon her choice of a husband, the world of Overcombe is essentially the world she sees and inhabits:

> Immediately before her was the large, smooth mill-pond, over-full, and intruding into the hedge and into the road. The water, with its flowing leaves and spots of froth, was stealing away, like Time, under the dark arch, to tumble over the great

slimy wheel within. On the other side of the mill-pond was an open place called the Cross, because it was three-quarters of one, two lanes and a cattle-drive meeting there. It was the general rendezvous and arena of the surrounding village. Behind this a steep slope rose high into the sky, merging in a wide and open down, now littered with sheep newly shorn. The upland by its height completely sheltered the mill and village from north winds, making summers of springs, reducing winters to autumn temperatures, and permitting myrtle to flourish in the open air. (4)

Overcombe, as Anne sees it in the opening chapter, is an idyllic world: peaceful, isolated, protected, self-contained, and—as the mention of sheep suggests—essentially pastoral. But even as she sits watching the scene the sheep on the down take flight before the advancing soldiery, the pastoral world suffers the first of many invasions. The presence of John Loveday, already a member of Anne's and Overcombe's world, permits these first invaders to be at least temporarily domesticated and absorbed: as they accept cherries from the miller the soldiers are at one level (Anne's) incorporated into the idyll even while Hardy inserts, for the reader, a quiet warning about the future. The threat from Festus Derriman, because it comes from within Anne's world—as the miller tells Festus, "You'd look more natural with a spud in your hand, sir" (36)—is fairly comfortably repelled, but the outer world again begins to loom in chapters 11 and 12. The King passes nearby, subsequently to appear at the great review on the downs; as the titles of the chapters announce, "Our people are affected by the presence of royalty" and the review brings together "great and small" alike. The invasion by Matilda Johnson is specifically an urban one—much play is made with her mode of dress as well as with her manners—but her unfamiliarity with the countryside is treated with comic exaggeration which foreshadows her defeat and links her with Festus Derriman, her eventual husband. After the fear of an actual French invasion has swept over Overcombe, a press-gang pursues Bob into the heart of the mill itself, and the isolation of Anne's world from the world of war and great events

is finally shattered by Bob's decision to discard his miller's clothes
and return to sea and the service of his country. In the remaining
pages the historical framework presses in inexorably upon the
central narrative until, with Anne's anxiety for Bob's safety at
Trafalgar and John's departure for Spain, the two become
virtually indistinguishable.

Overcombe can thus be seen as a pastoral microcosm juxtaposed to, and eventually engulfed by, a macrocosmic world of
great events. Yet many of the interconnections seem at once less
direct than this and more subtle. The central narrative, despite
its insistence upon delicate social discriminations, is characterised
by the broad simplicity and familiarity of its dance-like pattern of
courtship and rivalry and by its profusion of stock characters: a
genteel widow and her marriageable daughter; a jolly miller and
his rival sons, one a soldier the other a sailor; a comic miser and
his *miles gloriosus* of a nephew. Rendered thus, the list of the
dramatis personae seems as time-honoured as that of any mummers' play, and there is a sense in which the emphatically domestic
and traditional quality of the sexual triangle and of the whole
Overcombe world projects a powerful assertion of human continuity, of the precious survival of man's most fundamental
experiences and rituals even during a period of revolutionary
events. At the same time, those experiences and rituals themselves
seem all the more poignant for the haunting awareness of violence
and danger close at hand. So Anne visits a Budmouth thrown into
high excitement by the presence of the King and the fear of an
invasion: "Anne now felt herself close to and looking into the
stream of recorded history, within whose banks the littlest things
are great, and outside which she and the general bulk of the
human race were content to live on as an unreckoned, unheeded
superfluity" (111). Happy in her obscurity, Anne fears that her
own world will be caught up and swept away. The reader knows
that her fears must inevitably be realised: John is a soldier, Bob a
sailor, and England is at war. That "stream of recorded history",
imaginatively linked with the early evocation of the mill-stream
"stealing away, like Time, under the dark arch", must draw the
world of Overcombe into the orbit of George III, Captain Hardy,

Trafalgar, and the Peninsular War. Time is personified on more than one occasion in *The Trumpet-Major*, and it is felt as a dominating presence throughout the novel, its implicit message, that of the Spirit Ironic, occasionally made explicit by Hardy in the tones of the Spirit of the Pities.[20]

2

The Uses of a Regional Past

Hardy's involvement with the Napoleonic era was remarked upon by T. E. Lawrence as late as 1923: "Napoleon is a real man to him, and the county of Dorsetshire echoes that name everywhere in Hardy's ears. He lives in his period, and thinks of it as the great war."[1] Such immersion came only with *The Dynasts*, and since the long evolution of that drama seems clearly to have begun prior to the composition of *The Trumpet-Major—Early Life* (140) preserves from 1875 an idea for a Napoleonic ballad-epic—it is tempting to regard the novel as no more than a preparatory foray, a minor by-product of the major work. But the success of *The Trumpet-Major* on its own terms and the position it occupies in the sequence of Hardy's career give a quite independent interest to its handling of time and history, its exploratory probing of the Wessex past.

Hardy had a long-standing fascination with things military. As he told a friend at the time of the Boer War, he was utterly opposed to war, yet once it had begun no one was more easily caught up by martial enthusiasm.[2] Dorchester's role as a garrison town gave its life a particular colour and excitement which Edmund Gosse noted when visiting Hardy in the early 1880s,[3] and it is precisely this quality, familiar to Hardy since childhood, which is captured in heightened form in the figure of Sergeant Troy. It was entirely characteristic both that Hardy should have introduced Troy's sword-exercises into *Far from the Madding Crowd* and that he should have taken care to ensure the technical accuracy of his representation by consulting the standard army handbook on sword drills.[4] Equally characteristic was Hardy's

special enthusiasm for the Napoleonic era, which not only saw
the bloodiest and most desperate foreign battles Britain had then
known but brought to her own shores the imminent threat of
invasion from across the Channel.

As Hardy explained in his Preface to *The Dynasts*, what gave
a peculiar excitement to events in his own county of Dorset was
the local expectation of a French landing combined with the
consequences of George III's fondness for Weymouth:

> It chanced that the writer was familiar with a part of England
> that lay within hail of the watering-place in which King
> George the Third had his favourite summer residence during
> the war with the first Napoléon, and where he was visited by
> ministers and others who bore the weight of English affairs on
> their more or less competent shoulders at that stressful time.
> Secondly, this district, being also near the coast which had
> echoed with rumours of invasion in their intensest form while
> the descent threatened, was formerly animated by memories
> and traditions of the desperate military preparations for that
> contingency. Thirdly, the same countryside happened to
> include the village which was the birthplace of Nelson's flag-
> captain at Trafalgar. (vii)

Dorset events of that period had already received occasional,
humorous treatment in the poems of William Barnes. His "Nanny
Gill", for example, describes a military review on the downs
behind Weymouth, one of many mounted during the early years
of the century to gratify the King's delight in such performances:

> Ah! they wer times, when Nanny Gill
> Went so'jerèn agëanst her will,
> Back when the King come down to view
> His ho'se an' voot, in red an' blue,
>   An' they did march in rows,
>   An' wheel in lines an' bows,
>   Below the King's own nose;
> An' guns did pwoint, an' swords did gleäre,
> A-fightèn foes that werden there.[5]

Stories of such reviews and of the many alarms and excursions in Dorset during the time of Napoleon must have been familiar to Hardy from boyhood, and in his 1895 Preface to *The Trumpet-Major*—as in the letters accompanying his presentation of copies of the novel to Queen Victoria and the Prince of Wales[6]—he emphasised his indebtedness to the direct testimony of old people and to local oral tradition, and spoke of the way in which tangible physical relics of the period had "brought to my imagination in early childhood the state of affairs at the date of the war more vividly than volumes of history could have done" (viii). Hardy was born in 1840, thirty-five years after Trafalgar, twenty-five after Waterloo; an almost identical time-lag occurs with Scott, born twenty-six years after the Jacobite rebellion of 1745, and with Faulkner, born thirty-two years after the end of the American Civil War. The common factor is clearly the stimulus to the future novelist's imagination given by youthful exposure to the first-hand recollections of survivors from an exciting moment in the local past.[7] Even for the first readers of *The Trumpet-Major* the period of Trafalgar and Waterloo was not so remote as to seem lost in oblivion; they were still in touch with it through palpable human links, so that a reviewer could remark that he himself might have known the characters in their old age.[8]

Because the main events of the Napoleonic period, especially Trafalgar and Waterloo, were so familiar to his readers, Hardy was able to use their knowledge of the war to control both emotional response and narrative suspense. The reader knows that Trafalgar will be won—but will Bob, like Nelson, be killed? Once Trafalgar is over, the reader is also aware that there remains little fighting to be done by sailors like Bob but that in the future of John and his friends loom the terrible land battles of the later stages of the war—as Hardy himself emphasises by referring, in chapter 5, to the coming deaths in such then unheard-of places as Albuera, Vittoria, and Waterloo of several of those sitting in the miller's living-room. At another level, the reader's awareness that Napoleon will not invade makes possible the creation of Festus Derriman and the militia in wholly comic terms—a fate similar to that which has overtaken the British Home Guard, untried during

the Second World War.[9] The idyllic world of Overcombe undergoes invasion by the world of great events; military occupation
results in sexual rivalries which offer an opportunity for the
exploitation, in terms of the action, of traditional analogies between
love and war. Bob's victory is linked with that of Nelson—himself
a notable lover, as the miller remarks (321)—and John's death
with his defeat in love. Festus loses his last chance to conquer
Anne just when the false invasion scare reminds the reader that
Napoleon is losing his last chance to sail against England. Not
only is the domestic narrative pervaded by images of attack and
defence—as Anne barricades herself against the besieging Festus,
puts the hedge between John and herself, suffers the invasion of
her room by Bob—but there is almost a sense in which England's
military beleaguerment becomes a metaphor for Anne's sexual
embattlement, and vice versa. What Hardy seems not to have
appreciated is the extent to which the assurance of an *historical*
happy ending would exacerbate the reader's disappointment at
the lack of an unequivocally happy ending to the central story.

The familiarity of the Napoleonic period had other implications
for Hardy's venture into historical fiction. The letter of February
17, 1879, in which Leslie Stephen wrote to him about *The
Trumpet-Major*, is partly quoted in *Early Life* (167); the quotation,
however, stops short of the point at which Stephen, by way of
illustrating what he means by a novel which has "a bit of history
in the background", instances Thackeray's handling of the
Waterloo scenes in *Vanity Fair*.[10] The omission seems significant.
Hardy was of course familiar with Thackeray's work, and his
avoidance of Waterloo, which had long fascinated him, may well
have been determined by a reluctance to challenge direct comparison with Thackeray. Even so, more or less unconscious
recollections of *Vanity Fair* seem to have coloured both the conception of *The Trumpet-Major* and a number of its characterisations: though the relationships are different, the John-Anne-Bob
triangle bears a marked resemblance to the Dobbin-Amelia-
George triangle, and more than a hint of Becky Sharp has gone
into the creation of Matilda Johnson.

The silent presence of *Vanity Fair* in the background of *The

Trumpet-Major inevitably prompts discussion of the latter as a specifically historical novel. Quite apart from the collection of reminiscences from those who still recalled the early years of the century, Hardy undertook a considerable amount of library research—much of it to be laid under contribution again during the writing of *The Dynasts*—in an effort to achieve accuracy and amplitude in his handling of the historical narrative and, at the same time, period authenticity in filling out the details of the central story. The notebook which preserves these materials shows the care and deliberateness with which he prepared himself to write the novel, and points up the kind of concern with details of dress, uniform, military procedure, and so on, which is reflected both in the actual text and in the sadly insipid serial illustrations prepared by John Collier under Hardy's direction.[11] At the same time, Hardy seems to have allowed himself a good deal of freedom in putting the results of his research to fictional use. His notebook contains references to several military reviews held outside Weymouth in the early years of the century, but none of them seems to have taken place on the particular date (August 15, 1804) to which he assigns the review in *The Trumpet-Major*;[12] a jotting elsewhere in the notebook shows that he felt himself at liberty to describe the panic at the false alarm of a French invasion as occurring either in 1803 or 1804.[13] Major historical events, such as Trafalgar and Ulm, could not be manipulated in this way, and these seem to be the only authentic dates in the book. Other specific dates supplied in the serial text were omitted from the first edition.[14]

The directly historical material in the novel can function to elevate the characters and themes through contact with famous people and great events: thus Bob is seen at his best in historical context, as a sailor on the *Victory*; Anne wins special sympathy as she watches the *Victory* sail down Channel to Trafalgar; even John's dignity is enlarged by that elegiac final sentence. But because the framework of *The Trumpet-Major* is so consistently historical—as that of *Vanity Fair* is not—and the historical events themselves of such importance, there is also a sense in which the characters and the central narrative are actually diminished by having to *share* the book with material drawn from such a momentous period. Nor does Hardy improve the situation by ignoring the reservations of Leslie Stephen about encountering historical personages "in full front":[15] both George III and Captain Hardy appear in conversation with characters who are wholly fictional creations. Hardy seems not to have thought out very clearly the implications of his adoption of an historical framework at once so obtrusive and so familiar, and although the characters of *The Trumpet-Major* are authentically dressed and housed, their lives impinged upon by the great events of the day, little in them as thinking and acting individuals could be said to mark them as belonging quintessentially to their period. Clearly, as Michael Edwards has argued in his thesis on the novel, *The Trumpet-Major* falls outside the category of historical fiction as practised by Scott and analysed by Georg Lukács.[16]

Hardy's researches into the Dorset past were perhaps not wholly free from self-indulgence. The book provided him with an opportunity, and perhaps with an excuse, to "get up" the Napoleonic period either for its own antiquarian sake or in furtherance of an already formed ambition to write the work which eventually became *The Dynasts*. It also gave him a chance to push back the temporal boundaries of Wessex. Although he had created his half-real, half-dream region some years before, he had not yet arrived at a very coherent conception of its fictional possibilities, and *The Trumpet-Major* should perhaps be seen as a "sounding", a survey operation deliberately undertaken by Hardy in order to establish the precise dimensions and limits of his usable past.

Elliott Felkin kept a record of some conversations with Hardy in 1919:

> Talking about time, he said that he always saw it stretch away in a long blue line like a railway line on the left (the past) and disappearing just round the crossing on his right. "It's like a railway line covered with a blue haze, and it goes uphill till 1900 and then it goes over the hill and disappears till about the middle of the century, and then it rises again up to about 1800, and then it disappears altogether."[17]

Hardy's historical imagination was apparently distinguished by elements of discontinuity and by a peculiar intensity of focus on the early years of the nineteenth century. Not only had the events of the Napoleonic era been of extraordinary magnitude, but the survival of witnesses of those events into Hardy's own lifetime had given him a special sense of the part played by history in shaping both his own region and the nation at large. Dorset/ Wessex as he knew it was the product not only of its geography and its climate but of its past. Yet the history of that region, unlike the history of the regions evoked by Scott and Faulkner, was associated not with defeat and tragedy but with victory and a fortunate escape from the threatened horrors of a war fought over its own soil. Though the troops stationed near Weymouth may eventually have fought and died overseas, their period in Dorset was itself one of relative safety and relaxation. William Barnes's "Nanny Gill" thus strikes a not inappropriate note, and within *The Trumpet-Major* itself the dragoons accept Miller Loveday's cherries during "a cheerful, careless, unpremeditated half-hour, which returned like the scent of a flower to the memories of some of those who enjoyed it, even at a distance of many years after, when they lay wounded and weak in foreign lands" (21).

Hardy's exploration of his regional past led, in fact, to the discovery that Dorset was largely devoid of public history, except insofar as it had become caught up in the fringes of great national events. Even in writing such a modest work as *The Trumpet-Major* he was forced to look beyond the resources of local oral tradition to the files of national newspapers and the shelves of the British Museum. Because of the lack of sufficiently specific and substantial local material his historical presentation tends to remain generalised and unfocused. He finds himself with the freedom, but also with the necessity, to evolve narrative patterns of his own. The action thus becomes exaggerated and highly coloured, the grouping and regrouping of characters almost balletic; the calculated juxtaposition of a world of pastoral "timelessness" with a world of specific yet thinly presented great events ultimately creates an effect which is the reverse of historical. Not only does Hardy fail or refuse to think himself and his

[163]

characters into a particular historical period, he actually uses the element of "quaintness", of fancy-dress, to achieve a generalised "period" flavour and remove the world of Overcombe out of any particularised time-scale into the idyllic limbo of "the past".

Hardy's own conception of history as a random sequence finds little reflection in the formal structuring of *The Trumpet-Major*, yet it is precisely in the way it incorporates large events and small in a single coherent pattern that the novel seems most obviously anticipatory of *The Dynasts*. It also represents much less of a departure from the characteristic features of Hardy's previous fiction than the choice of period might suggest. In its immediate predecessor, *The Return of the Native*, Granfer Cantle and the beacon fires already hint at a growing fascination with the Dorset of Napoleon's day, while Weymouth is given, under its half-disguise of Budmouth, a glamorous reputation more appropriate to its Georgian than to its Victorian status. Both novels approximate, in some important aspects, to the form of the "romance"—very much as understood and practised by Hawthorne—and if in *The Return of the Native* the tendency towards romance is constantly warring with the novelist's countervailing need to sustain credibility in terms of a narrative at least minimally realistic, in *The Trumpet-Major* the staging of what amounted to a costume-drama seems to have given Hardy a sense of relief from such restraints. The contribution of the novel to the development of Hardy's later fiction may well have been chiefly negative, in that he did not again work strenuously for a "period" flavour, nor attempt, except in occasional short stories, to move beyond the range of his own memory. More immediately, however, the partial relaxation of the demands of verisimilitude heralded a proliferation of romance elements not only in "The Romantic Adventures of a Milkmaid" but in such specifically contemporary works as *A Laodicean* and *Two on a Tower*.

3

A Laodicean

On July 27, 1880, while the serial parts of *The Trumpet-Major* were still appearing, the Hardys started out from Tooting on a visit to France. They were back in England by mid-August; in September Hardy was in Dorset; in October he and Emma spent a week in Cambridge. Immediately after his return to Tooting Hardy fell seriously ill. At that point, October 23, 1880, he had begun writing *A Laodicean* for serialisation in the European edition of *Harper's New Monthly Magazine* from December onwards, and had been working closely with his illustrator George Du Maurier—Helen Allingham having earlier declined his suggestion that she might illustrate the story.[1] But the task was far from finished, and it was only completed by Hardy's dictating the novel to Emma from his sickbed. It was, as Hardy recalled in a letter to Gosse in 1917, "an awful job".[2] He noted in Mrs Henniker's copy of the novel that "the original conception was but partially carried out",[3] and told the American scholar William Lyon Phelps that he had feared the illness would prove his last and, perhaps for that reason, put more of the facts of his own life into the book than into anything else he had written.[4] As his condition gradually improved the rate of composition seems to have accelerated, and *Early Life* (192) records the completion of a pencilled draft on May 1, 1881. The book appeared in December that same year, a one-volume American edition (in Harper's Franklin Square Library) preceding by about a week the three-volume English first edition published by Sampson Low.[5]

As Hardy's more patient admirers will know, Paula Power, the Laodicean of the title, is a very modern young woman living in the

ancient semi-ruin of Stancy Castle, once the home of the aristocratic family of de Stancy; her own father had been a *nouveau-
riche* railway contractor of strong Nonconformist views. The
evident incongruities of this juxtaposition are imaged early in the
novel in the discovery by George Somerset, the architect hero,
that a telegraph wire he has been following suddenly vanishes
through an arrow-slit in the castle keep; they are subsequently
sustained in terms of the divergent attitudes of the surviving de
Stancys. If Charlotte de Stancy claims Paula as her closest friend
and shows a fine disregard for her family's illustrious past, her
brother, Captain de Stancy, is persuaded by his illegitimate son,
the sinister William Dare, to try and regain possession of the
ancestral home by marrying Paula. Since both Paula and Charlotte have meanwhile fallen in love—the one undemonstratively,
the other secretly—with Somerset, the situation offers obvious
narrative and ironic potentialities which are exhaustively exploited
in terms of a story made heavily dependent upon Hardy's architectural experiences and upon visits he had made to the Continent.[6]

This tendency towards treatise and travelogue is to some extent
counteracted by the introduction of a series of melodramatic
incidents involving William Dare and Paula's scarcely less
sinister great-uncle, Abner Power; but these devices could not
prevent the book from becoming—by Hardy's own standards and
certainly in the opinion of most critics—a fairly disastrous failure.
Even Guerard, for example, can say little more for *A Laodicean*
than that its collapse after an excellent opening and its completion
in difficult circumstances help to "define what constituted for
Hardy the easy ways out".[7] Yet most of the main elements on
which Hardy relied were already present in the thirteen chapters
he is known to have completed before he fell ill,[8] and if the bulk
of the narrative is intolerably drawn out—inviting the application
to Paula of James Thurber's famous caption, "What do you want
to be inscrutable *for*, Marcia?"—enough of Hardy's original
conception emerges to give the book some credibility as the work
of a major novelist.

It has sometimes been objected of *A Laodicean* that the

apparent promise in the opening chapters of a stern and potentially tragic confrontation between old and new is not fulfilled in the
remainder of the novel. Yet the very passage which describes that
initial juxtaposition of the castle and the telegraph also establishes
precisely the limited and paradoxical terms in which the action of
the novel is to be played out:

> There was a certain unexpectedness in the fact that the hoary
> memorial of a stolid antagonism to the interchange of ideas, the
> monument of hard distinctions in blood and race, of deadly
> mistrust of one's neighbour in spite of the Church's teaching,
> and of a sublime unconsciousness of any other force than a
> brute one, should be the goal of a machine which beyond every-
> thing may be said to symbolize cosmopolitan views and the
> intellectual and moral kinship of all mankind. In that light the
> little buzzing wire had a far finer significance to the student
> Somerset than the vast walls which neighboured it. But the
> modern fever and fret which consumes people before they can
> grow old was also signified by the wire; and this aspect of to-day
> did not contrast well with the fairer side of feudalism—leisure,
> light-hearted generosity, intense friendships, hawks, hounds,
> rebels, healthy complexions, freedom from care, and such a
> living power in architectural art as the world may never again
> see. (22)

Like *The Hand of Ethelberta*, *A Laodicean* explores an extreme
instance of "the great modern fluctuations of classes and creeds"
(41): Paula's occupation of Stancy Castle, as an example of what
Hardy in his 1896 Preface calls the "changing of the old order in
country manors and mansions" (vii), is on the same pattern as
Ethelberta's dominance over Enckworth Court. That the exploration is again to be conducted chiefly in comic terms is made clear
by the imagery—Paula is early described as a "modern flower in
a mediaeval flower-pot" (41)—and by such episodes as Somerset's encounter with the inn-keeper whose prudential shifts of
religious allegiance rival those of the Vicar of Bray:

> 'As for yourself, you are a Churchman at present, I pre-
> sume?'

'Yes; not but I was a Methodist once—ay, for a length of time. 'Twas owing to my taking a house next door to a chapel; so that what with hearing the organ bizz like a bee through the wall, and what with finding it saved umbrellas on wet Zundays, I went over to that faith for two years—though I believe I dropped money by it—I wouldn't be the man to say so if I hadn't. Howsomever, when I moved into this house I turned back again to my old religion. Faith, I don't zee much difference: be you one, or be you t'other, you've got to get your living.' (42)

A threat of portentousness in the chapel scene in the second chapter is subsequently dispelled by Somerset's improbably taking up Mr Woodwell's "challenge" and entering into the theological lists in defence of the lady sitting in her "pavilion" (60)—an episode which Hardy perhaps intended to recall or even parody the Earl of Somerset's role in the famous quarrel scene in the first part of *Henry VI*. At the very end of the novel the sense of an achieved resolution is radically qualified by Paula's final remark: "I wish my castle wasn't burnt; and I wish you were a de Stancy!" (481) This piece of characteristic irony—or characteristic duplicity—on Hardy's part rounds out the essentially comic design inherent in the pattern of the novel from the opening chapters onwards.

If Hardy sought in *A Laodicean* to emulate *The Hand of Ethelberta*'s achievement of a "humorous fable" along "modern-romantic" lines,[9] he presumably saw the focus of his "Story of To-day" as an ideological struggle, fought out in specifically contemporary terms—intellectual, social, moral, aesthetic, religious, and economic—for the heart and mind of his heroine. Though he did not supply the novel with an epigraph he might appropriately have found one in the passage he marked in his copy of an English translation of Goethe's *Faust:* "What you term the spirit of the times is at bottom only your own spirit, in which the times are reflected".[10] Paula Power seems to be almost a constitutional Laodicean, irredeemably given to lukewarmness and prolonged hesitation between available alternatives, and if her abandonment of her father's Baptist beliefs provides one strand in the ideological pattern, its most significant contribution is the image of that baptismal pool in which she refuses to plunge: "The water looked so cold and dark and fearful, she said, that she could not do it to save her life" (35). Much of the novel revolves upon the question of whether Paula will eventually take a "plunge", make a firm commitment and, if so, to what?

The commitment comes in the final chapters. Immediately and primarily it is an emotional commitment to Somerset as her chosen husband, amusingly dramatised as an act of deliberate decision by her determined pursuit of the architect from one continental town to another. But the choice of Somerset also carries with it, as Ethelberta's bestowal of her hand had done, certain implications—blurred but not obscured by Paula's final speech—for those more abstract issues which have been at least falteringly and intermittently sustained throughout the novel. It implies above all the rejection of the opposing attitudes represented by the outmoded mediaevalism of Stancy Castle and by the aggressive, puritanical "modernism" of Paula's father, and the ratification, instead, of that commonsense eclecticism to which Paula has been instinctively drawn from the first, and which is consistently embodied in the figure of Somerset himself.

As a student of architecture, Somerset has suffered in the past from "the modern malady of unlimited appreciativeness" (9), and been forced by persistent shifts in stylistic fashion to conclude "that all styles were extinct, and with them all architecture as a living art" (6). A more recent realisation that the history of art has always shown such "shifts and compromises" (6) has encouraged him to pursue his own ideas and enthusiasms quite independently of "the general tide" (6) of taste and opinion, so that he can now engage in a belated study of English Gothic and conceive a marvellously simple solution to the problems involved in rebuilding Stancy Castle:

Its originality lay partly in the circumstance that Somerset had not attempted to adapt an old building to the wants of the new civilization. He had placed his new erection beside it as a slightly attached structure, harmonizing with the old; heightening and beautifying rather than subduing it. His work formed a palace, with a ruinous castle annexed as a curiosity. (157)

If the solution still seems "modern" in the middle of the twentieth century, that is perhaps because it represented, in the second half of the nineteenth century, a return to principles and practices common in the eighteenth.

Stancy Castle is not quite what Annie Macdonnell called it, the novel's most interesting character,[11] but it operates effectively enough as both physical and symbolic setting, permitting Hardy to exploit even more fully than he had done in *The Hand of Ethelberta* the potentialities of architecture as a source of moral and social criteria. The central issue here is that of restoration—a topic which much exercised Hardy in his days as a practising architect and, indeed, to the end of his life[12]—and it seems clear that his approval is given both to Paula's instinctive preference for "honest" restoration and to Somerset's solution to the whole problem of restoring Stancy Castle. Somerset's design is, in any case, a precise reflection of his own independence and eclecticism, as well as a direct anticipation of that final solution which he and Paula undertake—partly from choice, partly (and perhaps ironically) from necessity—after the castle has been burned down by William Dare:

> True, the main walls were still standing as firmly as ever; but there was a feeling common to both of them that it would be well to make an opportunity of a misfortune, and leaving the edifice in ruins start their married life in a mansion of independent construction hard by the old one, unencumbered with the ghosts of an unfortunate line. (480–481)

The burning down of Stancy Castle seems to be authorially endorsed as an appropriate exorcism of the "ghosts of an unfortunate line" (481). It is, at the same time, a standard item in the repertoire of Gothic melodrama, Hardy's favourite version of the "modern-romantic" manner, and the figure of William Dare himself seems largely derived from the same source. As J. O. Bailey pointed out, he is supplied with a profusion of Mephistophelian characteristics, some of which may have been directly drawn from Goethe's *Faust*,[13] and in view of the potentially allegorical element in the presentation of Dare and the presence of the "ghoul-like" (415) Abner Power and the virtuous and significantly named Mr Woodwell it is not inconceivable that Hardy once intended the battle for Paula's mind to take on something of a Faustian quality, with contending figures explicitly representative of good and evil. Yet William Dare's real affinity seems to be with the mischief-making scientists of such mid-century American writers as Poe and Hawthorne. Specifically, he suggests a malevolent version of Holgrave in *The House of the Seven Gables*, a novel Hardy knew well.[14] Dare is a photographer, Holgrave a daguerrotypist; both are men of many talents and obscure background. Both, too, play important roles in novels concerned with the working out of hereditary patterns, and what seems in terms of narrative suspense a wastefully early revelation of the secret of Dare's birth may have been determined by Hardy's concern to dramatise the decline of the house of de Stancy and foreshadow the collapse of all Captain de Stancy's pretensions to Paula's hand.

Hardy may have felt that such reassurance was proper to a comedy, and he may also have taken some pleasure—as he seems to have done in *The Hand of Ethelberta*—in the purely structural satisfaction to be derived from building in prefigurative devices. The account of the performance of *Loves' Labour's Lost*, for example, functions along the lines, if with little of the delicacy, of the *Lover's Vows* episode in *Mansfield Park*: like Edmund Bertram, Paula allows her moral standards to be subtly corrupted by influences she does not honestly recognise. It also provides one means among many for charting Paula's movement away from the values and principles for which her father had stood. At the same time, Hardy obviously intended to suggest a correspondence between the King of Navarre's vow to avoid the company of women and the similar vow taken by de Stancy, while a clear signalling of future developments appears in the repeated insistence that at the end of the play the Princess of France (the part taken by Paula) does not actually marry the King. Presumably

[171]

Hardy also perceived a similarity—emphasised later by Somerset's determination, in the face of Paula's neglect, to "accept no
return for his labours but the pleasure of presenting them to her
as a love-offering" (311)—between the Princess's tactics of discouragement and postponement and the behaviour of his own
heroine.

A firmer establishment of such correspondences within the
novel might have served to counterbalance the present lack of an
adequate explanation for Paula's reluctance to confess her love
for Somerset. It is true that the confirmation of her instinctive
choice of Somerset is precisely the outcome of that process of
self-discovery—externalised in the conflict of suitors and ideas—
which the novel offers to dramatise. In this as in so many aspects
of the book, however, Hardy's execution falls far short of his
conception, and the reader is given little guidance beyond an
occasional indication of Paula's extreme fastidiousness in sexual
matters: she has a "curious coyness" (90), nobody has ever kissed
her (136), and she displays an instinctive "habit of self-repression
at any new emotional impact" (246). Yet she has no hesitation in
demonstrating the intensity of her affection for Charlotte de
Stancy: as Somerset watches, "she clasped her fingers behind
Charlotte's neck, and smiled tenderly in her face" (92).

The action strikes Somerset as "quite unconsciously done" and
"very beautiful" (92), and, as Gordon S. Haight has recently
pointed out, it may be dangerous to obtrude a post-Freudian
awareness into the consideration of Victorian relationships.[15] It is
impossible, however, to take lightly what seems to be, from the
presented evidence, much the most powerful of Paula's emotional
attachments, or to ignore entirely that extraordinary scene in
which Paula, looking in her "pink doublet and hose" (196) like
"a lovely young youth and not a girl at all" (190), performs in the
gymnasium for the delectation of Charlotte and Mrs Goodman.
If it seems too much to suggest that Hardy saw Paula as a sexual
Laodicean, occupying an equivocal mid-way position between
male and female, it is none the less evident that here—as in the
presentation of Knight in *A Pair of Blue Eyes* and of the Miss
Aldclyffe-Cytherea-Manston triangle in *Desperate Remedies*—he

is not so much blundering in the pre-Freudian darkness as exploring, tentatively and with instinctive sensitivity, some of those areas of sexuality which lay beyond the stereotypes of Victorian fiction. Hardy's explorations reached a remarkable conclusion in the sustained portrayal of Sue Bridehead—whom Paula in her combination of fastidiousness, Hellenism, and rather aggressive modernism strikingly anticipates—and it is much to be regretted that in *A Laodicean* they remain only one of many fragmentary elements in a novel which Hardy began so ambitiously but completed in such weary despair.

4

Politics and Ideas:
Hardy's Laodiceanism

Some measure of Hardy's original ambitions in *A Laodicean* can
be gained from an examination of the background of one of the
novel's final paragraphs, in which Paula replies to Somerset's
forecast of her recovery from the "warping" effects of Stancy
Castle's mediaevalism:

> 'And be a perfect representative of "the modern spirit"?'
> she enquired; 'representing neither the senses and under-
> standing, nor the heart and imagination; but what a finished
> writer calls "the imaginative reason"?' (481)

The "finished writer" is of course Matthew Arnold, and the
immediate reference to a passage from his essay on "Pagan and
Mediaeval Religious Sentiment":

> The poetry of later paganism lived by the senses and under-
> standing; the poetry of mediaeval Christianity lived by the heart
> and imagination. But the main element of the modern spirit's
> life is neither the senses and understanding, nor the heart and
> imagination; it is the imaginative reason.[1]

Hardy had met Arnold for the first time in February 1880, and
his commonplace book shows that he had read extensively and
carefully both in *Essays in Criticism* and in *Mixed Essays* during
the years from 1878 onwards.[2] There is some reason, clearly, to
suspect that the obtrusive invocation of direct quotations from
"Pagan and Mediaeval Religious Sentiment"—at the end of a
novel which makes considerable, if somewhat casual, play both

with "paganism" and with "mediaevalism"—may point to a deliberate and sustained incorporation of Arnoldian themes in the book as a whole.

Early in the fourth book Somerset fears that Paula—whom he had first thought of as "a personification of the modern spirit, who had been dropped, like a seed from the bill of a bird, into a chink of mediaevalism" (305)—has become caught up by the spirit of romanticism: "Veneration for things old, not because of any merit in them, but because of their long continuance, had developed in her; and her modern spirit was taking to itself wings and flying away" (305). It seems necessary to relate this not only to one of Hardy's notes in the *Early Life* (189) but to a section of Arnold's essay on "Heinrich Heine" in which he describes how the "mystic and romantic school of Germany lost itself in the Middle Ages, was overwhelmed by their influence, came to ruin by its vain dreams of renewing them"; Heine, says Arnold, was able to escape because of his ability to "feel,—along with but above the power of the fascinating Middle Age itself,—the power of modern ideas".[3] This is precisely the danger Paula runs, and precisely the means of her escape, and it is tempting to speculate further that in his allusion on the last page of the novel to Arnold's definition of "the modern spirit" Hardy had in mind not only the essay on "Pagan and Mediaeval Religious Sentiment" but also the famous passage in the Heine essay in which Arnold defines the modern spirit in terms of "the sense of want of correspondence between the forms of modern Europe and its spirit, between the new wine of the eighteenth and nineteenth centuries, and the old bottles of the eleventh and twelfth centuries, or even of the sixteenth and seventeenth".[4] There seems no need of detailed analysis to demonstrate the extent to which this conception responds to the whole situation of *A Laodicean*, lays down, indeed, the lines of its central battle.

Since Hardy had also been reading *Mixed Essays* it is not surprising that in a novel centred upon the shifting relationships of classes as well as of creeds he should have drawn, as he seems to have done, upon Arnold's essay on "Equality", with its linking of "British non-conformity" and "British aristocracy"—the twin poles of Paula's initial dilemma—as two "great obstacles to our civilisation".[5] It was perhaps an instinct for irony which led Hardy to replace the Puritanical picture-burner of Arnold's essay by the aristocratic arsonist William Dare, but it was presumably an accident of his own autobiography which encouraged him to seize for fictional purposes upon Arnold's exemplification of Puritan dreariness in terms of a domestic debate on the issue of paedo-baptism.[6] *Early Life* (37–40) speaks of the arguments on this question which Hardy had with his fellow-pupils in Hicks's architectural office, although a long entry at the end of the "Trumpet-Major Notebook" shows that he found it necessary to brush up his own knowledge of theological niceties before bestowing it upon George Somerset.[7]

Hardy certainly drew on Arnold's ideas, but it seems impossible to discern any coherent pattern governing their incorporation. Arnoldian allusions tend to be clumsily introduced (the direct quotation on the final page, for instance), and they are often exploited in opportunistic fashion to serve wholly localised purposes. When Somerset speaks of Paula's modern spirit "taking to itself wings and flying away", the effective bearing of his observation appears only in the succeeding sentence: 'Whether his image was flying with the other was a question which moved him all the more deeply now that her silence gave him dread of an affirmative answer" (305). Nor must it be forgotten that any dramatisation of Arnold's ideas was necessarily contained, like everything else in the novel, within the comic and deflationary terms sustained throughout and confirmed in Paula's final remark. It is an interesting question whether Hardy, through hostility to Arnold, intended such an invidious placement, or whether he was, as a novelist, incapable of handling abstract ideas without in some way subjecting them to trivialisation or vulgarisation. Certainly his view of Arnold was far from uncritical—he objected to Arnold's "hair-splitting",[8] for example, and had handled with deliberate ambiguity the Arnoldian aspiration of Clym Yeobright—and it is perhaps significant that *A Laodicean* was written in the interval between Hardy's first meeting with Arnold in February 1880, when he seems to have found him unduly opinionated, and his second, in 1884, when he liked him much better.[9] Even so, Hardy knew Arnold's writings as well as those of any contemporary, and it is not clear that at this point of time he found them radically unsatisfactory. If, then, some allowance must be made for Hardy's temporary lack of sympathy with Arnold as a man, and still more for the conditions, so hostile to sustained intellectual effort, under which the novel was written, there still remains an unsatisfactory element in Hardy's handling of ideas in *A Laodicean* for which other explanations must be found.

Hardy noted in his commonplace book (probably in 1880) an observation of Henry James's that when Balzac attempts to deal with an abstraction "the presumption is always dead against him"; Hardy then added his own comment that this was equally true of many other novelists.[10] It seems a pity that he did not more fully appreciate the relevance of the observation to his own work. Hardy's sense of a profound involvement in the social and intellectual movements of his time, what he calls in *A Laodicean* the "great modern fluctuations of classes and creeds", makes itself felt not only in *Jude the Obscure* but in many of the earlier novels. Yet his mind, brooding rather than incisive, was not naturally equipped to move easily in realms of philosophical discourse. Certainly he received no formal philosophical training, nor (as we saw earlier) did he enjoy any form of higher education; and some sensitivity on precisely this score may have entered— more than a dozen years before the publication of *Jude*—into his feelings toward Matthew Arnold, whom he associated with Oxford and its values.

Hardy's social and intellectual insecurity was no doubt a factor in the equivocation and even obscurity which marks his treatment of philosophical and intellectual issues both within his fiction and elsewhere. It seems significant that the machinery of *The Dynasts* should have incorporated a multiplicity of viewpoints, none of them specifically endorsed by the author himself, and when in later years Hardy engaged in correspondence on philosophical topics he tended to disparage his own capacities for such specula- tion—"But I am a miserable reasoner," he told Galsworthy in 1916[11]—and to disclaim any personal commitment to a particular viewpoint: writing to Alfred Noyes in 1920 he mentioned "my sober opinion—so far as I have any definite one—of the Cause of Things".[12] Of particular interest is the letter he wrote to the philosopher J. McT. E. McTaggart on August 27, 1908:

> I am reading *The Relations of Time and Eternity* with much more interest than I expected from the title (with many thanks for the copy). I go quite with you in your argument. Sections 23, 24, 25, in which you grapple with ordinary experiences, are illuminating. 26 and 27 are as much as ever can be said for possibilities, I think. However I am not a trained philosopher as you are (though I do read *Mind* occasionally). As a mere empiricist I have the common-place feeling that the Timeless Reality knows no difference between what we call good and what we call evil, which are only apparent to the consciousness of organic nature generally—which consciousness is a sort of un-anticipated accident: so that no dignified philosophy can be built up out of the unworthy materials at our command.[13]

Here the self-deprecating comments ("However I am not a trained philosopher", "As a mere empiricist I have the common-place feeling") merge into a mild aggressiveness: having disclaimed any personal pretensions to competence in philosophy, Hardy goes on to challenge the pretensions of philosophy itself.

The double strategy seems essentially defensive, not unlike the self-protective attitude discernible in Hardy's rare political remarks: "I don't talk politics," he is reported to have said in 1920.[14] Notebook entries in *Early Life* reveal a profoundly conservative strain, and in particular a fear of the "proletarianisation" of art which Hardy shared with such friends as Edmund Gosse.[15] Assigned in *Early Life* to late April 1891—less than three months before serialisation of *Tess* was to begin—are Hardy's reflections during a visit to the British Museum:

> Crowds parading and gaily traipsing round the mummies, thinking to-day is for ever, and the girls casting sly glances at young men across the swathed dust of Mycerinus [?] [sic]. They pass with flippant comments the illuminated MSS.—the labours of years—and stand under Rameses the Great, joking.

[178]

Democratic government may be justice to man, but it will probably merge in proletarian, and when these people are our masters it will lead to more of this contempt, and possibly be the utter ruin of art and literature! . . . Looking, when I came out, at the Oxford Music Hall, an hour before the time of opening, there was already a queue.

The same theme, now linked with darker fears, occurs in a letter written to Galsworthy in 1921:

But England and Europe do not look particularly attractive in their political aspects. The extreme Party seems to forget that the opposite of error is error still—just as all the revolutionists of history have forgotten it. I suppose such is inevitable; you can't make a pendulum stop in the middle, except after infinite swinging. A friend of mine thinks the great danger is to art and literature, and that a new Dark Age is coming along, in which our books will be pulped to make newspaper for football and boxing journals and Cinema descriptions.[16]

Eighteen months earlier Hardy had used the same phrase about "the opposite of error" being "error still" in a brief published note on trade unionism in which he spoke in favour of "social re-adjustments rather than social subversions",[17] while in a letter to General J. H. Morgan of April 1921 he expressed the fear, prompted by the miners' strike then in progress, that the gradualist ideas of the more responsible Labour Party leaders might not be able to withstand the revolutionary pressures exerted by an illiterate working class.[18] Hardy's difficulty seems to have been that of reconciling an instinctive conservatism with an intellectual perception of the necessity for certain kinds of social and political change, a dilemma to which he had attempted to give a positive aspect in a note attributed in *Early Life* (268) to January 24, 1888:

January 24. I find that my politics really are neither Tory nor Radical. I may be called an Intrinsicalist. I am against privilege derived from accident of any kind, and am therefore equally opposed to aristocratic privilege and democratic privilege. (By the latter I mean the arrogant assumption that the only labour is hand-labour—a worse arrogance than that of the aristocrat, —the taxing of the worthy to help those masses of the population who will not help themselves when they might, etc.) Opportunity should be equal for all, but those who will not avail themselves of it should be cared for merely—not be a burden to, nor the rulers over, those who do avail themselves thereof.

It is clear from *Early Life*, as of course from the dramatised parliamentary debates in *The Dynasts*, that Hardy found British politics past and present an engrossing spectacle. He liked to sit in the gallery of the House of Commons and observe the battle from above. Gladstone's struggle for Irish Home Rule in the spring of 1886 seems especially to have excited him, and the page and a half devoted to this episode in *Early Life* conclude (234) in a statement of Hardy's view that Home Rule "was a staring dilemma, of which good policy and good philanthropy were the huge horns. Policy for England required that it should not be granted; humanity to Ireland that it should. Neither Liberals nor Conservatives would honestly own up to this opposition between two moralities, but speciously insisted that humanity and policy were both on one side—of course their own." Hardy's impatience with the narrowness of political partisanship and with the absorption of politicians in their own careers emerges later in *Early Life* (312) from an almost Trollopian comment on a social occasion at which "the talk was entirely political—of when the next election would be—of the probable Prime Minister—of ins and outs—of Lord This and the Duke of That—everything except the people for whose existence alone these politicians exist. Their welfare is never once thought of."

Not surprisingly, Hardy consistently refused to make any political commitment of a public kind. Although he was ready to cast his vote for his friend Robert Pearce-Edgecumbe, the Gladstonian candidate for South Dorset in the by-election of May 7, 1891, he explained in a letter to the candidate himself on April 23, 1891, that his position as an artist made it impossible for him to be politically active, and that he would not be casting a vote for either side had he not known and admired his correspondent as a man.[19] When Pearce-Edgecumbe again stood for election in the summer of 1892 Hardy declined on similar grounds to sign his nomination papers, telling the representative of the South Dorset Liberal Association that he had to remain politically neutral and in a position to "approach all classes of thinkers from an absolutely unpledged point".[20] Several years earlier, in 1883, he had declined to supplement his comments in "The Dorsetshire Labourer" by an article on the political aspects of the agricultural workers' movement;[21] in 1886 he told an interviewer that his political principles were "those of Bob Sawyer, a kind of plaid";[22] not long afterwards he noted down from the pages of the *Spectator* an observation by Max O'Rell that the literary man must of necessity be a political eclectic.[23] From *Early Life* (191) it appears that Hardy himself had come to this conclusion as early as 1881: "*February 17.* Conservatism is not estimable in itself, nor is Change, or Radicalism. To conserve the existing good, to supplant the existing bad by good, is to act on a true political principle, which is neither Conservative nor Radical."

This concept of political eclecticism is echoed within *A Laodicean*, on which Hardy was then working, in Somerset's aesthetic eclecticism and in his choice of a particular method of conducting building operations because, although generally regarded as old-fashioned, it seemed to him to be "the true one" (282). C. J. P. Beatty has argued that Somerset's modern "malady of unlimited appreciativeness" may have afflicted Hardy himself and influenced his decision to abandon architecture altogether. [24] But Hardy seems also to have been touched by the heroine's Laodiceanism. Paula's toying with ideas may reflect, like Somerset's aesthetic flirtations, the prevalent eclecticism of the day,[25] but it also suggests a profound shrinking from acts of choice and of decision, a willingness to rest in the placidity of irresolution, which it seems not unreasonable to link with Hardy's unsatisfactory handling of Arnoldian and other ideas within the novel itself and with his extreme anxiety to avoid any suggestion of political commitment. Hardy had perhaps learned only too well what he took to be the lesson of *The Poor Man and the Lady*; by 1888, certainly, he was expressing the view that "the didactic novel is so generally devoid of *vraisemblance* as to teach nothing but the impossibility of tampering with natural truth to advance dogmatic opinions".[26]

The decision to assume, as novelist and as public figure, a neutral, non-didactic stance is entirely consistent with Hardy's concern for personal privacy. In itself it seems a sensibly self-protective position for a serious artist to adopt, and Hardy himself clearly found it sufficient justification for his reluctance to make public statements on political questions or, indeed, on any topics not directly related to the profession of letters. But the work itself is by no means empty of contemporary issues and allusions, and the neutralist stance does not fully explain either the heavy-handedness and even obscurity with which such material is sometimes handled or the open-endedness of so much of Hardy's fiction—the tendency, evident in novels as widely separated in kind and in date as *Under the Greenwood Tree* and *Tess*—to end on a note of unresolved ambiguity. At its best, the effect is one of leashed implication, of a challenge thrown down to the reader as a test of his maturity. But too often one senses a fundamental hesitancy and even evasiveness—partly, no doubt, a product of successive encounters with editorial caution, but almost certainly related in some degree to Hardy's background and personality, to the failures of his personal life and to that incompleteness of his formal education which seems both to have drained his confidence and to have left him ill-equipped to operate within an intellectual climate dominated by abstract speculation.

5

Two on a Tower

After Hardy had recovered from his illness, he and Emma began
looking for a permanent home outside of London, and on June
25, 1881, they moved into a house in the small east Dorset town
of Wimborne. It was here that Hardy wrote *Two on a Tower*.[1]
Thomas Bailey Aldrich, the editor of the *Atlantic Monthly*, had
approached Hardy about a possible serial in late September, 1881,
but it was January, 1882, before a firm agreement was reached.[2]
Some of Hardy's time during the latter part of 1881 must have
been given to the completion of short stories,[3] but an indication
that he was working up material for *Two on a Tower* is provided
by his application to the Astronomer Royal on November 26,
1881, for permission to visit Greenwich Observatory.[4] Hardy
seems to have begun writing the novel early in 1882, and to have
completed it by September of the same year. He told Gosse that
it had been hastily written—"though the plan of the story was
carefully thought out, the actual writing was lamentably hurried"
—and later commented that the "backgrounds" had been more
lightly sketched in than was usual in his work.[5] The three-volume
first edition was published, by Sampson Low, in late October 1882.[6]

According to *Early Life* (195), Hardy chose the title of *Two on
a Tower* "off-hand" and subsequently disliked it. Yet it does
emphasise both the importance of the tower itself, that claustrophobic vestibule of space, and the persistent concentration on the
two central characters. At the first encounter between the languid
Lady Constantine and the young astronomer, Swithin St Cleeve,
the essential conditions of their relationship are immediately
established:

'What do you see?—something happening somewhere?'

'Yes, quite a catastrophe!' he automatically murmured without moving round.

'What?'

'A cyclone in the sun.'

The lady paused, as if to consider the weight of that event in the scale of terrene life.

'Will it make any difference to us here?' she asked. (7)

This is a fundamental opposition: Swithin's mind is focused on "higher" things, often to the detriment of human feelings and loyalties; Lady Constantine's concerns are earthly, but she proves capable of transcendent self-sacrifice. Swithin, says Hardy, "was a scientist, and took words literally. There is something in the inexorably simple logic of such men which partakes of the cruelty of the natural laws that are their study" (312). His mind is full of the horrors and "immensities" (35) of astronomical knowledge, Lady Constantine's of what she only half-ironically calls "such ephemeral trivialities as human tragedy" (36); his subject is "celestial", hers "lamentably human" (35). Yet when Lady Constantine suggests that "the less must give way to the greater" (35), she is not resolving but only raising, as Swithin's reply emphasises, that central issue which Hardy later formulated in his 1895 Preface:

This slightly-built romance was the outcome of a wish to set the emotional history of two infinitesimal lives against the stupendous background of the stellar universe, and to impart to readers the sentiment that of these contrasting magnitudes the smaller might be the greater to them as men. (vii)

The wisdom of Hardy's endeavour seems open to question, as indeed does its motive. "Mr. Hardy," wrote the *Athenaeum* reviewer, "may fairly claim for his last novel the credit of having added to the novelist's stock of 'properties' and 'business.' We have known military novels, sporting and dramatic novels, law and police novels, musical novels, but an astronomical novel never."[7] Following on the heels of *The Trumpet-Major*, with its historical detail, and *A Laodicean*, with its architectural technicalities, *Two on a Tower* seems very obviously "got up" (to use a term employed some years later by Henry James during a discussion of the "business novel"),[8] and although the evidence no longer survives, as it does for *The Trumpet-Major*, there is every indication that Hardy chiefly saw in astronomy a source of sufficient "properties" to carry him safely through to the conclusion of yet another serial, his seventh in ten years. The astronomical theme had nonetheless a certain appropriateness to a book—described by Hardy himself as a "slightly-built romance" and placed among the "Romances and Fantasies" in the Wessex Edition of 1912—which followed *The Hand of Ethelberta* and *A Laodicean* in their exemplification of a "modern-Romantic" manner.

Insofar as Hardy had clearly formulated conceptions of the romance as a literary form distinct from the novel, these seem originally to have derived from Scott and Ainsworth. In his essay on "The Science of Fiction" he also mentions the names of Dumas *père* and Mrs Radcliffe, and the composition of *Desperate Remedies* owed something to the sensational fiction of Wilkie Collins.[9] Yet none of these offers any substantial precedent for that curious juxtaposition of the ordinary and the extraordinary which Hardy introduced into such firmly contemporary novels as *Two on a Tower*, *A Laodicean*, and, to a lesser extent, *The Hand of Ethelberta*; nor is it easy to think of anything precisely similar in the work of other English novelists. The analogies which most strongly suggest themselves are with such novels of Hawthorne's as *The House of the Seven Gables* and *The Marble Faun*, both of which Hardy had read—the first by the time he wrote *The Hand of Ethelberta*, the other, as his commonplace book shows, by late 1879 or early 1880.[10] He also read Henry James's study of Hawthorne at this time, and copied out from it, with extensive underlining, the famous passage from the "Custom-House" introduction to *The Scarlet Letter* in which Hawthorne regrets not having made his everyday custom-house experiences the material of his fiction: "The wiser effort would have been, to diffuse thought and imagination through the opaque substance of to-day, and thus to make it a bright transparency."[11] Hardy, who tended to be sparing with his underlining, clearly found something unusually suggestive in these remarks, and perhaps in Hawthorne's whole example as a novelist. Much as Hawthorne in *The House of the Seven Gables* and *The Marble Faun* closes up the gaps between the present and the past, the actual and the unaccountable, so Hardy sought in *Two on a Tower* to make his contemporary narrative "of two infinitesimal lives" immediately responsive to that "stupendous background of the stellar universe" against which it was set.

Sending a copy of the book to Gosse, Hardy expressed the hope that he at least would appreciate the attempt to "make science, not the mere padding of a romance, but the actual vehicle of romance".[12] Gosse's warm and positive response did not disappoint him, but few published comments on the novel, then or since, have seen the astronomical elements as other than what the *Saturday Review* called "mere matters of episode".[13] Difficult as it is to argue against this latter view, there is nonetheless a sense in which Hardy achieves a more pervasive and more successful integration of astronomical material and imagery than the standard account would suggest. While stressing the scientific aspect of the book, Hardy did not forget that the night sky held, even in an age of science, "patterns stereotyped in history and legend" (297), that the stars were inescapably associated with ancient mythologies and with lingering and perhaps inextinguishable superstitions, that the heavenly bodies had always provided a rich source of imagery, especially for the poetry of love.

As Lady Constantine gazes down at the sleeping figure of Swithin, legend and science merge in her thoughts:

> Looking again at him her eyes became so sentimentally fixed on his face that it seemed as if she could not withdraw them. There lay, in the shape of an Antinous, no *amoroso*, no gallant, but a guileless philosopher. His parted lips were lips which spoke, not of love, but of millions of miles; those were eyes which habitually gazed not into the depths of other eyes, but into other worlds. Within his temples dwelt thoughts, not of woman's looks, but of stellar aspects and the configuration of constellations.

Thus, to his physical attractiveness was added the attractiveness of mental inaccessibility. The ennobling influence of scientific pursuits was demonstrated by the speculative purity which
expressed itself in his eyes whenever he looked at her in speaking,
and in the childlike faults of manner which arose from his
obtuseness to their difference of sex. He had never, since becoming a man, looked even so low as to the level of a Lady
Constantine. His heaven at present was truly in the skies, and
not in that only other place where they say it can be found, in
the eyes of some daughter of Eve. Would any Circe or Calypso
—and if so, what one?—ever check this pale-haired scientist's
nocturnal sailings into the interminable spaces overhead, and
hurl all his mighty calculations on cosmic force and stellar fire
into Limbo? O the pity of it, if such should be the case! (45–46)

It would be an exaggeration to argue that such passages operate
organically within patterns of imagery sustained throughout the
book. But some of the images do recur, the casting of Swithin as
a modern Odysseus has its appropriate point, and traditional
allusions are refreshed, here as elsewhere, by using an astronomer
as a central character and exploiting the knowledge of space made
available by contemporary science. Worn commonplaces about
the heaven in a mistress's eyes take on at least a fluttering life; the
Transit of Venus is invoked both as an actual occurrence and as
a source of ironic reflections on the human situation; a series of
references to double stars is initiated by the description of "two
stars in the Twins" looking down on Swithin and Lady Constantine
"as if those two persons could bear some sort of comparison with
them" (39). Such strenuous deployment of astronomical imagery—
heterogeneous as it is, and often of a painfully obvious, off-the-
peg kind—may simply represent Hardy's response to the contemporary scientific enthusiasm recently embodied in the title of
Richard A. Proctor's *The Poetry of Astronomy*, published in
1881.[14] It may also represent an attempt to "diffuse thought and
imagination through the opaque substance of to-day".

For the specific images of *Two on a Tower* Hardy seems to have
been largely indebted to Tennyson, and especially to the stanzas

about astronomy which were deleted from "The Palace of Art"
but retained as a footnote to the poem at the time of its first
publication:

> Hither, when all the deep unsounded skies
>> Shuddered with silent stars, she clomb,
> And as with optic glasses her keen eyes
>> Pierced thro' the mystic dome,
>
> Regions of lucid matter taking forms,
>> Brushes of fire, hazy gleams,
> Clusters and beds of worlds, and bee-like swarms
>> Of suns, and starry streams.
>
> She saw the snowy poles of moonless Mars,
>> That marvellous round of milky light
> Below Orion, and those double stars
>> Whereof the one more bright
> Is circled by the other, &c.[15]

Hardy's familiarity with these lines seems clear not only from the
whole conception of *Two on a Tower* but from his references to
double stars and from such passages as the description at the
beginning of chapter 41 of "suns of hybrid kind—fire-fogs,
floating nuclei, globes that flew in groups like swarms of bees"
(299). He also knew, of course, "The Palace of Art" itself, with
its allegorical presentation of the soul's growing sensitivity to
"the riddle of the painful earth" and eventual descent from her
"intellectual throne" on the "crag-platform" described in the
opening stanzas:

> The ranged ramparts bright
> From level meadow-bases of deep grass
>> Suddenly scaled the light.
> Thereon I built it firm. Of ledge or shelf
>> The rock rose clear, or winding stair,
> My soul would live alone unto herself
>> In her high palace there.
>
> And "while the world runs round and round," I said,
>> "Reign thou apart, a quiet king,

Still as, while Saturn whirls, his steadfast shade
Sleeps on his luminous ring."[16]

Tennyson did not include the deleted stanzas in subsequent
editions of his poems, and they were in 1881 relatively inaccessible; Hardy perhaps came upon them as the epigraph to another
work by Richard A. Proctor, *Essays on Astronomy* (1872), a book
which he owned and presumably used in writing *Two on a
Tower*.[17] From Tennyson's lines, especially as used for the epigraph to a book on astronomy, it must have been a relatively short
cut by way of the tower of Charborough Park (not far from Wimborne) and current interest in the Transit of Venus to the basic
conception of a novel with an astronomer hero.[18] Since, however,
"The Palace of Art" also adumbrates the pattern of Swithin's
moral career as he moves from scientific self-absorption to human
involvement, it could no doubt be argued that Hardy saw Swithin
—dedicated to his search, isolated on his lonely tower[19]—as a
figure representative not only of the scientist but of the artist,
perhaps even of the author of *Two on a Tower*. But if Hardy drew,
as always, upon what he knew, the sheer artificiality and moral
irresolution of the novel effectively discourage any search for
grave autobiographical or even allegorical significances.

Hardy seems to have been capable of pitching his work at quite
different levels of artistic seriousness. It is commonly said of
novels like *A Laodicean* and *Two on a Tower* that they begin well
but that there comes a point at which creative intensity suddenly
diminishes and Hardy surrenders to easy solutions, often in the
form of new characters or additional plot complications—the late
introduction of Abner Power in *A Laodicean*, for example, or of
Louis Glanville in *Two on a Tower*. Yet Hardy speaks of the plan
of the latter as having been "carefully thought out", and it seems
to have been his practice in writing for serial publication to work
out the plot in some detail, and even block out some of the
principal scenes, before beginning to write the opening chapters.
If Abner Power and Louis Glanville were present from the
beginning, not introduced as stop-gaps, the fault may lie as much
in poverty of conception as in hastiness of execution.

In *Two on a Tower*, as in so many of his novels, Hardy works largely in terms of schematised oppositions. Swithin and Lady Constantine are contrasted in terms not only of age but of physical and intellectual type. Swithin, the "scientific Adonis" (209), is beautiful, extremely fair, on a model variously described as Greek (183) or "early-Christian" (28). Lady Constantine is "of a totally opposite type" (6), extremely dark, with Romance blood in her veins (6), and—rather like Eustacia Vye—she is given "a warm and affectionate, perhaps slightly voluptuous temperament, languishing for want of something to do, cherish, or suffer for" (24).[20] Swithin's paganism, too, is set against Lady Constantine's religiosity—her temperament, as Hardy says, makes her "necessarily either lover or *dévote*" (157)—while his initiation of her into the mysteries of the universe balances her initiation of him into the realities of sexual passion.

Deliberate and almost diagrammatic manipulation of this kind extends to the handling of setting and the grouping of characters. Something more than convenience or picturesqueness has determined the topography of the novel, with its careful separation of three main areas: the Great House and its adjacent Church; the village in "the Bottom"; the tower, isolated from both worlds, not only by its height but also by its "insulating" (100) arable fields and the gloomy associations of its site. Corresponding to these dispositions, and projected by them, are the class-groupings: the inhabitants of Welland House and their guests; the villagers; and Swithin himself, offspring of a socially incongruous marriage between a curate and a farmer's daughter, and hence suspended between two worlds in a sense other than that suggested by his rapt study of the stars. Swithin's movements between Welland Bottom and Welland House dramatise those social dilemmas from which the tower offers him at least the illusion of escape; the gulf separating him from Lady Constantine is made tangible by his conversations with her suitor, the Bishop of Melchester, and by the readiness with which the local vicar cuts short a meeting of the village choir, assembled at some inconvenience in the cottage in which Swithin lives with his grandmother, in order to answer a casual summons from the great house.

That there is nothing accidental about this integration and schematisation of social and topographical elements is made clear by Hardy's observation upon the Vicar's arrival in Lady Constantine's presence: "His boots, which had seemed elegant in the farm-house, appeared rather clumsy here, and his coat, that was a model of tailoring when he stood amid the choir, now exhibited decidedly strained relations with his limbs" (24). The scene of the choir-practice itself is excellently done, and throughout the novel Hardy handles such village episodes with exceptional tact, showing compassion for the disadvantages of the labourers' lot and respect for their dignity as men, yet managing at the same time to keep the material amusing, reasonably brief, and continually relevant to the central action. As Ruth A. Firor pointed out, the villagers waiting outside the tower provide the listening Swithin with a very pungent summary of his relationship with Lady Constantine—"If they get up this tower ruling plannards together much longer, their plannards will soon rule them together, in my way o' thinking" (97)[21]—while Anthony Green's account of how he eventually married his pregnant Gloriana in conformity with "the custom of the country" (100) takes on specific as well as general significance in the light of the subsequent revelation that Lady Constantine herself had been chiefly responsible for ensuring that the conventions were observed.

The novel thus neatly sustains its patterns of contrast. The implications which flow from such contrasts, however, are much less surely handled. What, for instance, is the precise moral relationship between Lady Constantine's behaviour towards Anthony Green and the fact that she herself becomes pregnant by Swithin and fathers his son upon the unsuspecting Bishop of Melchester? How is the persistent irony with which both she and Swithin are presented reconcilable with those tragic aspects of her situation to which Hardy himself draws attention in his 1895 Preface? Does the Bishop's arrogance warrant the deception played upon him, or is it proper (if unepiscopal) that he should be finally "avenged"? Hardy's disgruntled Preface reveals—what is also evident from his letter answering the review of the novel in the *St James's Gazette* and from private letters written at the time[22]—

his extreme irritation at accusations of immorality and of hostility towards the established Church; in the original version of the Preface he quotes some of the "warm epithets" which the reviewers had used.[23] Much has been written of Hardy's difficulties with publishers and editors and with the haunting presence of Mrs Grundy, but on this occasion, as perhaps on others, the position he adopts seems scarcely defensible.

His Preface makes a strong assertion not only of the book's essential morality but of its propriety:

> I venture to think that those who care to read the story now will be quite astonished at the scrupulous propriety observed therein on the relations of the sexes; for though there may be frivolous, and even grotesque touches on occasion, there is hardly a single caress in the book outside legal matrimony, or what was intended so to be. (vii)

Though Hardy's phrasing ("hardly a single caress") maintains literal scrupulosity, it seems scarcely an adequate acknowledgment of the fact that the all-important caress during which Swithin's son is conceived occurs precisely at a moment when the marriage is known to be invalid: "O that last fatal evening with him!" laments Lady Constantine (281). Nor is Hardy's insistence that "the Bishop is every inch a gentleman" (viii) sufficient to dispel the brutal irony with which he is described as crediting to "the persuasive force of trained logical reasoning" a success in courtship which is in fact attributable to "a pleader on his side whom he knew little of " (291). That Hardy's defence, like the novel itself, seems partly tongue-in-cheek, does not make for reassurance. Much of the difficulty with the book is precisely its uncertainty of mode: if its tragic elements are unrealised, its comic elements are for the most part inconsistent, unfunny, and fundamentally unserious. Hardy quoted Launcelot Gobbo ("it is a wise father that knows his own child") in a letter to Gosse, [24] and he obviously enjoyed what might be called the Chaucerian aspects of Lady Constantine's *"coup d'audace"*—to borrow the term which he himself invoked in writing an advertisement for the novel.[25] But it was, at best, naive of him to ignore what must by any standards be considered the questionable morality of Lady Constantine's action—dwelt upon too much for its own sake to emerge simply as an act of forgivable desperation—or to fail to anticipate the response of reviewers. Most disturbing of all is his retreat under criticism to the most conventional of positions, challenging neither the premises nor the prejudices of his attackers but exculpating himself by somewhat specious claims to respectability, thereby implicitly acknowledging the validity of complaints against impropriety and the satirisation of bishops.

Several years later Hardy wrote to acknowledge the appearance in the *Daily Chronicle* of a "generous article" on *Tess of the d'Urbervilles*:

> Ever since I began to write—certainly ever since I wrote "Two on a Tower" in 1881—I have felt that the doll of English fiction must be demolished, if England is to have a school of fiction at all: and I think great honour is due to the D. Chronicle for frankly recognizing that the development of a more virile type of novel is not incompatible with sound morality.[26]

It seems impossible, however, to feel confidence in the soundness of the morality in *Two on a Tower*. The disingenuousness of Hardy's defence of the novel is anticipated in the ambiguity of the book itself, in the absence of firm resolutions of the questions inevitably prompted by the working out of the central narrative or by the concurrent sequence of juxtaposed contrasts. Not only do the patterns lack meaning, but the very consistency of their abstract design suggests that Hardy himself remained uninvolved, manipulating the story as a structural and thematic exercise of a thoroughly professional but essentially dispassionate kind.

Part Four
RENEWAL

THE MAYOR OF CASTERBRIDGE
Serial: January–May 1886
Published: May 1886

THE WOODLANDERS
Serial: May 1886–April 1887
Published: March 1887

I

Max Gate

Whereas earlier novels such as *Far from the Madding Crowd* and *The Return of the Native* had been independently serialised in England and in America, *Two on a Tower* and *A Laodicean* received single serialisations in American magazines circulating on both sides of the Atlantic. As Carl J. Weber showed in *Hardy in America*,[1] Hardy's work was popular in the United States, in both authorised and pirated editions, from a very early stage. The *New York Times* published his short story "Destiny and a Blue Cloak" in 1874; the American firm of Osgood, McIlvaine published the first collected edition of his novels in 1895–97. Hardy certainly did not find editors in Boston and New York any less cautious than their British counterparts. Some of his most radical bowdlerisations were made to the *Harper's* serial of *Jude*, and it was of *Two on a Tower* itself that Thomas Bailey Aldrich is said to have complained that in response to a request for "a family story" Hardy had given him "a story in the family way".[2] But in a period of personal difficulty and artistic uncertainty, when Hardy was entering into agreements with editors and publishers who had not previously handled his work, it would have been surprising if he had remained entirely unaffected by the impact then being made upon all aspects of the British literary scene by American magazines, American books, and American publishers. Journals like the *Atlantic* and the *Century* (of which Edmund Gosse was for some years the London editorial advisor)[3] achieved a very considerable popularity in England at this period, and *A Laodicean* was commissioned for serialisation in the initial volumes of the new European Edition of *Harper's Monthly*.[4]

Although *A Laodicean* and *Two on a Tower* are among Hardy's weakest books, there is no evidence that he consciously relaxed his standards because he was writing for American magazines: his illness largely explains the inadequacies of *A Laodicean*, while *Two on a Tower* he himself seems to have ranked among his better performances. But it is perhaps of some interest that both novels should have been in that "modern-romantic" mode of Hardy's which his reading of Hawthorne had perhaps led him to think of as characteristically American. It was with the historical romance *The Trumpet-Major*, and then with *A Laodicean* and *Two on a Tower*, that the pirating of Hardy's novels in the United States seems first to have gathered serious momentum; and while in England the fantastic little romance, "The Romantic Adventures of a Milkmaid", was not reprinted between its first magazine appearance in 1883 and its collection in *A Changed Man* in 1913, it was, as R. L. Purdy has remarked, "more frequently and cheaply reprinted in America through many years than perhaps any other work of Hardy's".[5]

Hardy sent off the "hastily written" manuscript of "The Romantic Adventures" on February 25, 1883.[6] Four months later, on June 25, it was published in the *Graphic;* on that same day Hardy dined at the Savile Club with Gosse and found himself in a large company of English and American men of letters, chief among them William Dean Howells.[7] Gosse and Howells had met and become friends during the summer of 1882, but this was Howells's first encounter with Hardy, whom he had earlier spoken of as the man in all England he most wanted to meet.[8] During the evening Howells told the story of Mark Twain's disastrous speech at the Whittier dinner, and Hardy responded with praise of *Life on the Mississippi* and admiration of Mark Twain himself as more than "merely a great humorist".[9] "What a charming night that was, last night!" Howells wrote to Gosse the following day. "Du Maurier and Hardy went most to my heart (you and Thornycroft were there already) but I felt that after all I had only shaken hands with Hardy across his threshold."[10] Hardy and Howells met again over the years, usually at long intervals, and Hardy wrote a congratulatory letter for publication in *Harper's Weekly* on the occasion of Howells's seventy-fifth birthday,[11] but their friendship does not seem to have been any closer than most of Hardy's other relationships with his literary contemporaries: years later Edith Wharton was to write of Hardy that "though he was as remote and uncommunicative as our most unsocial American men of letters, his silence seemed due to an unconquerable shyness rather than to the great man's disdain for humbler neighbours".[12]

As the leader of the American "realist" movement, and its chief spokesman in the transatlantic debate with the English advocates of romance (of whom Gosse was one of the most voluble), Howells had little sympathy with contemporary English writing. It may seem remarkable, therefore, that he should have so greatly admired the author of "The Romantic Adventures of a Milk-maid".[13] But Hardy was now producing work so varied in kind and in quality that he might have been claimed as the exemplar of any number of contemporary literary movements. The years 1881–1883 saw the publication not only of *A Laodicean*, *Two on a Tower*, and "The Romantic Adventures", but of stories as different from each other as "What the Shepherd Saw" (1881), "The Honourable Laura" (1881), "A Tradition of 1804" (1882), and "The Three Strangers" (1883); they also saw, in 1882, a performance of the dramatised version of *Far from the Madding Crowd* and, in 1883, the composition of the children's story "Our Exploits at West Poley" and the essay on "The Dorsetshire Labourer". Both in its range and in its quantity the list testifies to Hardy's thorough professionalism. But it hints, too, at a certain loss of direction, especially since Hardy appears at anything approaching his best only in "The Three Strangers" and, perhaps, "The Dorsetshire Labourer". That these were written during the latter stages of the brief Wimborne period perhaps indicates a growing realisation on Hardy's part that he was most successful, and most at ease, when dealing with Wessex scenes and subjects, and that the return from London to the countryside might prove beneficial to his work as well as to his health.

The June 1883 meeting at the Savile took place in the brief interval between the Hardys' vacation of their lodgings in Wimborne and their occupancy of new lodgings in Shire Hall Place, Dorchester. Two years later, on June 29, 1885, they moved again, into Max Gate—"Porta Maxima", as Hardy once jokingly rendered it in a letter to Gosse[14]—the house which Hardy had designed and built on the south-eastern outskirts of the town, out towards William Barnes's parish of Winterborne Came. These steps had been contemplated for some time—as early as April 1880 Hardy told his brother that he was looking for a plot of land in Dorchester, and in March 1882 he was enquiring about the possibility of acquiring a building site on Stinsford Hill[15]—but there is much evidence to suggest that they were often regretted: *Early Life* (231) records Hardy as already wondering, on the last evening of 1885, whether the building of the house had been "a wise expenditure of energy".

According to the same source (210), the Hardys "did not foresee" that Dorchester "was to be their country-quarters for the remainder of their lives". The avoidance of the word "home" was perhaps deliberate (the circumstances of Hardy's later life with Emma being such as to discourage suggestions of conventional domesticity), but the preferred term "country-quarters" needs to be read in the context of references within the same paragraph to the Hardys' annual practice of renting a house or apartment in London "for the season". Hardy never lost his fascination with London or with London society, never outgrew that reassuring sense of arrival and achievement which he seems to have received from his friendship with the rich, the aristocratic, and the powerful. Whatever his basic social sympathies, they seem not to have been of a kind to prevent him from sharing the traditional English love of a lord, and if the lord were, so to speak, a lady, the susceptibility was greater still. The influence of such attitudes can be detected throughout *Early Life* and *Later Years*, and in many of Hardy's letters: they undoubtedly created difficulties between himself and Emma, who cut a poor and even ridiculous figure in such circles, and they may have been the source of deprecating references to Max Gate as his "cottage", the place where he did his writing.[16]

The move to Dorchester and the building of Max Gate must

nonetheless be regarded not merely as acts of practical convenience but as symbolic gestures. Hardy said on a later occasion that
he had thought seriously of going to live in Winchester rather
than Dorchester,[17] and it is at least conceivable that the rich
historical associations of Winchester (capital of the historical
Wessex) and its excellent railway service to London may temporarily have recommended it to Hardy's attention. If the considerations determining the Hardys' choice had been of a purely
domestic kind, it might conceivably have devolved upon Winchester or even Salisbury, both larger and busier towns than
Dorchester, and closer to London. But in moving to Dorchester
Hardy was returning home. In building Max Gate he was setting
up as a gentleman in the place where, more than forty years
earlier, he had been born into the family of a stonemason and
where, as a youth of sixteen, he had been articled to a local architect.

If on his return to Dorchester Hardy obtained some satisfaction
from such things as his membership of local societies, the
acquaintance of members of the local gentry and, some years later,
his appointment to the bench of magistrates, he never entered at
all intimately into the essential life of the town. Though it is
dangerous to argue on the basis of what may be a wholly misleading selection, it seems significant that the notes ascribed in
Early Life to the middle and late 1880s tend on the whole to show
little of the eager recording enthusiasm of the years at Sturminster
Newton, where, as more recently at Wimborne, Hardy and Emma
seem to have become quickly and closely involved in the local life.
Hardy was of course getting older, and when he moved to Dorchester, and especially to Max Gate, the consciousness of being in
his own country may have prompted him to sustain with some
dignity and consistency his new status of independent gentleman.
For whatever reasons, Hardy's life at Max Gate, if not actually
reclusive, seems certainly to have been characterised by a strongly
evinced desire for personal privacy. Not surprisingly, he seems
never to have become popular among the local people, partly
because of his reputation for tight-fistedness, partly because of
Emma's eccentricities (for which he was sometimes blamed),

largely because his fellow-townsmen totally misunderstood both the artist's need for solitude and his lack of a "steady occupation".

Too much has perhaps been made of the walls and trees with which Hardy surrounded Max Gate. As can be seen from the illustration in *Early Life* (facing 226), the site was bare and windswept, rendering the need for shelter from the weather quite as urgent as any desire for seclusion from curious eyes. There seems no doubt, however, that Hardy saw such seclusion, enhanced by the comparative remoteness of Dorchester itself, as essential to his work. The *World* interview of February 17, 1886, reported: "When he has a story in hand, he begins writing immediately after breakfast, and remains indoors until he has finished for the day, even a very little time spent in the open air before beginning proving fatal to any work till after nightfall. When not dictating, a practice he indulges in occasionally, but not frequently, he prefers working alone, holding, moreover, with his friend Mr. Aubrey de Vere, that not only a solitary room, but an impregnable house, would be the most desirable place for complete literary performance."[18] Another interview, early in the 1890s, quoted Hardy as saying that he spent at Max Gate "at least six months of the year, seldom paying a visit anywhere, though I get a good many visitors. I find that in these six months I can do more work than I could in London all the year. Thus I am free to spend the remaining six months as I please—three or four months in London, a month or two at country-houses, in Scotland, or on the Continent."[19] The cutting of this interview in Hardy's "Personal" scrapbook bears the notation "largely faked"; even so, this particular passage seems to reflect accurately enough both Hardy's practice and the principles behind it. R. R. Bowker, who as London agent of *Harper's* had come to know Hardy well during the perilous composition of *A Laodicean*, had written as early as 1888 that Max Gate, despite its isolation, was in easy walking distance of the railway which could take Hardy to London "within four hours, so that he is more often in the bustling world than would be inferred from the seclusion of his 'writing-box', as he calls his house. Every spring, moreover, after he has put the finishing touches on his winter's work, he comes up to London for a long vacation (unless, by way of change, he flits off to the Continent), lives pleasantly there in temporary quarters, and receives with Mrs. Hardy on one day of the week, looks in at the Savile Club for letters and luncheon, and mixes freely in society."[20]

Clearly, the London visits had a recreative function for Hardy. They must also have played a part in the total economy of his life with Emma, although in later years she became reluctant to make the annual effort to find and maintain a London establishment. In a letter of February 3, 1928, J. M. Barrie suggested to Florence Hardy that the "biography" of Hardy, then still in typescript, was marred by "the intrusion of so many names of people in society he met in London. To my mind they are an excrescence on the book and get an importance in it, and so in his life, that is in false proportions. I believe it was a very fortunate thing for him that he had these holidays away from himself so to speak, they probably freshened his brain and spirits as nothing else could have done. But given so elaborately they don't belong, they would be misunderstood. Enough to my thinking to mention Lady Jeune and Mrs Henniker and that he visited in many houses. Of course I don't mean taking out any of the many fine jottings of his own or summing up that you record and that are probably as thick here as elsewhere. The man could not look out at a window without seeing something that had never been seen before."[21] Many of the names were in fact deleted,[22] but enough survived to give the impression Barrie feared. His comments provide, however, a useful corrective, and it may well have been that Hardy's lionisation by fashionable hostesses in London did a good deal to compensate for the lack of glamour at Max Gate and in his domestic life generally.

If Hardy at Max Gate looked outward to London for recreation and relief from domestic oppressiveness, he looked beyond contemporary Dorchester to the Dorchester of the past for the material of the first novel he wrote after coming to live in the town. From a specifically literary point of view, the chief significance of the move to Dorchester lies in its implicit confirmation of the centrality of Wessex to Hardy's imagination. Ten years before, he had told Leslie Stephen that he was finishing *Far from the Madding Crowd* at Bockhampton because he found it "a great advantage to be actually among the people described at the time of describing them".[23] Now, perhaps in a deliberate attempt to pick up lost Wessex threads, Hardy returned to his native countryside and to the town which supplied that countryside's focal point, bringing with him an antiquarian enthusiasm reinforced by his researches for *The Trumpet-Major* and his ambitions for *The Dynasts*.

While living in Wimborne Hardy had joined the Dorset Natural History and Antiquarian Field Club,[24] and poems like "The Levelled Churchyard" and "Copying Architecture in an Old Minster" reflect the beginning, during the Wimborne period, of his support for the Dorset activities of the Society for the Protection of Ancient Buildings.[25] It was at Wimborne, too, that he had written his essay, "The Dorsetshire Labourer", and discussed with H. J. Moule (one of Horace's brothers) the practicability of a book on Dorset to which Hardy would contribute the text and Moule the illustrations—an idea which seems to have originated with Emma and which was soon rejected by Hardy on the grounds that it would not pay.[26]

Removal to Dorchester brought Hardy into close touch again with William Barnes—within a month he had taken Gosse on a visit to Winterborne Came[27]—and gave him an opportunity to share more actively Barnes's enthusiasm for the Field Club and the Dorset County Museum. It was at a meeting at the Museum on May 13, 1884, that Hardy read to his fellow members of the Field Club a paper on some Romano-British remains discovered during the digging of the foundations for Max Gate. "It would be a worthy attempt," said Hardy in the final paragraph of his paper, "to rehabilitate, on paper, the living Durnovaria of fourteen or fifteen hundred years ago—as it actually appeared to the eyes of the then Dorchester men and women, and to the rays of the same morning and evening sun which rises and sets over it now."[28] In *The Mayor of Casterbridge*, still in its early stages in May 1884, Hardy was to incorporate, at the beginning of chapter 11, an extended reference to precisely the kind of burial described in his paper. But although "Casterbridge announced old Rome in every street, alley, and precinct" (80), the chief effort of Hardy's historical imagination was to be directed towards the creation of an authentic image of a Wessex country town in the middle of the nineteenth century, a fictional Casterbridge modelled not on the Roman Durnovaria nor even on the Dorchester to which he had just returned as a man in his early forties, but on the Dorchester he had known as a child.

2

"The Dorsetshire Labourer"

At almost precisely the moment in late June 1883 when Hardy and his wife were moving to Dorchester, "The Dorsetshire Labourer" was published in the July issue of *Longman's Magazine*.[1] Hardy must have been glad of the opportunity to appear in public as an authority on Dorset life, and his decision to write the essay should clearly be associated with his larger decision to return to his native countryside and establish himself as a gentleman of Dorset. At the same time, he can scarcely have been unaware that in publishing a signed article on such a topic he was venturing, somewhat uncharacteristically, on controversial ground.

The essay was one of a series dealing—as the editor, Charles J. Longman, explained to another contributor—with "the peasantry of the various parts of the kingdom, . . . their way of life, their surroundings, their hopes and fears, joys and griefs etc".[2] The specification was itself a reflection of current concern over the condition of the agricultural labourer. Royal commissions and private individuals had for some time been drawing attention to the low wages, poor diet, and insanitary housing prevalent in many rural areas, and although Joseph Arch's union had not long survived as an effective force it had attracted enormous public attention and achieved an increase in agricultural wages in several parts of the country. The most recent index of national interest in the labourer was the Liberal Party's commitment (made effective in 1884) to secure an extension of the franchise to workers in rural areas.

Hardy declined to write on the political aspects of the labourer's situation when invited to do so by the editor of the *Contemporary Review* a few years after the appearance of "The Dorsetshire Labourer".[3] Even so, it is not surprising that in the published essay there should be a tinge of cautious polemicism in Hardy's opening attack on the popular "Hodge" stereotype: "When we arrive at the farm-labouring community we find it to be seriously personified by the pitiable picture known as Hodge; not only so, but the community is assumed to be a uniform collection of concrete Hodges" (252). In his 1876 article on "The Wessex Labourer" Charles Kegan Paul had suggested that Hardy and Barnes, "both parts of that of which they write, ought to dissipate many popular fancies about their fair western county".[4] Consciously or not, Hardy now responded to Paul's appeal: by challenging the standard conception of "Hodge" he implicitly challenged the standard conception of Dorset—and even, perhaps, some damaging popular assumptions about the fictional world of Wessex. His opening paragraphs also established a particular attitude toward the subject of the essay: though not entirely free from condescension, they nevertheless entered a strong plea for the recognition of the labourer's fundamental humanity and individuality.

The term "Hodge" is at least as old as Chaucer, but Hardy must certainly have been aware of its recent use by Richard Jefferies in *Hodge and his Masters*, published in 1880; it is apparently to the final chapter of Jefferies' book[5] that Hardy refers when remarking that "to paraphrase the words of a recent writer on the labouring classes, in his [Hodge's] future there are only the workhouse and the grave". Hardy had met Jefferies in 1880[6] and presumably knew that he was to contribute an essay to the *Longman's* symposium; he must also have been aware of Jefferies' earlier agricultural essays as an important element in the overall context in which "The Dorsetshire Labourer" was being written and published. Jefferies' sympathies—in *Hodge and his Masters* and, more especially, in the letters on "Wiltshire Labourers" he had sent to *The Times* in 1872[7]—tended to be with the farmer rather than with the labourer; even so, he often reveals an understanding of the latter's situation at once more intimate and more evidently compassionate than anything in "The Dorsetshire Labourer". While it seems unlikely that in writing his own essay Hardy had any substantial sense of entering into competition or debate with Jefferies, either as a journalist or as the author of novels about a county adjacent to Dorset and well within the boundaries of Wessex, the fourteen paragraphs of his opening section are nonetheless rather nervously argumentative. Various detailed protestations are advanced—for example, about the danger of misinterpreting apparent squalor[8]—and these tend to blur the lines of the central argument that the class of agricultural labourers shows as much variety and individuality as any other, and that the labourer's day-to-day life, for all its privations, is less consistently gloomy than it has often been painted—if only because "A pure atmosphere and a pastoral environment are a very appreciable portion of the sustenance which tends to produce the sound mind and body, and thus much sustenance is, at least, the labourer's birthright" (255).

By the fifteenth paragraph the controversial promise of the opening has been dissipated, and the essay moves into the descriptive expansiveness of the central section, revolving upon the Hiring Fair and the Lady Day removals and other indications of the increasingly nomadic life of the Dorset labourer. This section contains the nub of what Hardy had to say about the labourer himself, and it is characteristic that it should consist not so much in reasoned arguments as in the recreation of particular scenes and incidents which his imagination had seized upon as at once enacting and symbolising an historic process of radical upheaval. Some of these scenes were to reappear in *The Mayor of Casterbridge* and in *Tess*, and at the time of writing "The Dorsetshire Labourer" Hardy may not have fully considered their implications. The description of the Lady Day removal, for example, is developed very much for its own sake, in a manner directly reminiscent of William Barnes's "Leǟdy-Day, an' Ridden House",[9] and with every suggestion of gaiety: "The day of removal, if fine, wears an aspect of jollity, and the whole proceeding is a blithe one" (261). The presentation is at odds with Hardy's general burden of regret at increasing agricultural mobility and discontinuity; his larger purpose, one feels, would have been better served by an adaptation of Jefferies' favourite technique (not, however, used in his own *Longman's* essay the following November) of approaching general topics by way of individualised examples handled in a lightly fictionalised manner—as in the last chapter of *Hodge and his Masters*, for example, or in "John Smith's Shanty", first published in 1874 and later collected, in abbreviated form, in *Toilers of the Field*.[10] Such particularisation characteristically gives point and life to Jefferies' themes, enriching them in ways beyond the range of his actual argument, and it might similarly have quickened the somewhat inert illustrative material of Hardy's essay, in which the novelist's hand is only fully evident in the brief episode of the old shepherd at the hiring fair.

Jefferies' method was perhaps at once too bold and too loose to recommend itself to Hardy as he struggled conscientiously within a stricter conception of the essay form. More importantly, Hardy's own attitude towards his material seems to have been too ambiguous to permit such deliberate selectivity and organisation. This fundamental uncertainty becomes more obvious in the final section of the essay (from paragraph 25 onwards), in which he attempts to weigh up the positive and negative aspects of recent changes in the countryside. Some changes he acknowledges as primarily aesthetic, aspects of "the old story that progress and picturesqueness do not harmonise": the labourers may be losing their distinctive features as a class, but "they are widening the range of their ideas, and gaining in freedom. It is too much to expect them to remain stagnant and old-fashioned for the pleasure of romantic spectators" (262–263). Other developments seem more serious: the interruption of the children's education, the disturbance of domestic stability, above all the loss of the old "intimate and kindly relation with the land". But the very context in which this last phrase occurs reveals the nature of the dilemma which confronted Hardy in his attempts to come to terms with this whole problem: "picturesqueness apart, a result of this increasing nomadic habit of the labourer is, naturally, a less intimate and kindly relation with the land he tills than existed before enlightenment enabled him to rise above the condition of a serf who lived and died on a particular plot like a tree" (263). It used to be "common enough", adds Hardy a little later, to hear farmers address their workers "with a contemptuousness which could not have been greatly exceeded in the days when the thralls of Cedric wore their collars of brass" (264). Much as he might dislike many of the by-products of recent developments, Hardy could not ignore their implications in terms of human dignity.

The conflict is partly one between intellectual progressivism and emotional conservatism, and as such it is directly related to Hardy's refusal to identify himself with either of the dominant political parties of the day. Partly, too, it reflects a scrupulous determination to eschew the kind of blinkered simplification essential to the politician or to the preacher, and to try instead to see and present things as they are or were, in all their dense and often confusing complexity. Hardy betrays, however, some descent from detachment in the two final paragraphs of the essay, where he suddenly turns his attention from the situation of the labourers to that of the village tradesman:

> Villages used to contain, in addition to the agricultural inhabitants, an interesting and better-informed class, ranking distinctly above those—the blacksmith, the carpenter, the shoemaker, the small higgler, the shopkeeper . . . together with nondescript-workers other than farm-labourers, who had remained in the houses where they were born for no especial reason beyond an instinct of association with the spot. (268)

Like the mobility of agricultural labour, the disappearance of such communities was, in 1883, already a well-established process, one which Hardy attributes exclusively to the landowners' policy (dramatised in *The Woodlanders* and elsewhere) of pulling down cottages as the old lifeholds fell in and thus forcing those occupants who once "formed the back-bone of village life" to "forsake the old nest" and "seek refuge in the boroughs" (269). The language here is much more emotionally charged than in earlier passages about the labourers' situation, and it is in relation to this class, not to the labourers, that Hardy makes his observation that the process of depopulation, "designated by statisticians as 'the tendency of the rural population towards the large towns,' is really the tendency of water to flow uphill when forced" (269).

It seems open to question whether, even taking into account the limitations of an immediately contemporary perspective, Hardy can really have believed that the pulling down of cottages in such circumstances was the only or even the most important cause of the decline in the numbers and fortunes of the village tradesmen. But the idea of such destruction carries a powerful emotional charge, and it is at least obvious that the fate of this section of the rural population moves him, involves him personally, as the fate of the labourers, for all his sympathy towards them, does not. The lifeholding class was, of course, the one into which Hardy himself was born, and his repeated emphasis on the strictness of the division between the "liviers" and the "work-folk" perhaps owed something to a firm inculcation of class-consciousness in his own childhood: according to one of his own annotations to Hedgecock's biographical study, "He knew the dialect but did not speak it.—it [sic] was not spoken in his mother's house, but only when necessary to the cottagers, & by his father to his workmen— some six or a dozen."[11] This sensitivity to questions of class and status within the village community is perhaps excessive and, as such, responsible for some of the ambiguities and strenuous impartialities of "The Dorsetshire Labourer". In economic terms, however, such divisions were unquestionably real and deep, and Hardy had sound historical as well as personal grounds for selecting them as focal points of his Wessex fiction.

During the first half of the nineteenth century, the labourer and the village tradesman were separated by an economic gulf between something little better than serfdom and, on the other side, at least a minimal sense of human dignity, at least some degree of economic independence and some prospect of rising a little in the world. If Hardy's instinctive feeling for the tradesman and lifeholding class sprang inevitably from his upbringing, it was at the same time a major source of his strength as a novelist. For a writer whose gifts were so largely narrative and dramatic the life of the agricultural labourer could have provided little material.[12] If the labourer had almost no prospect of rising out of his class, he could scarcely fall below it—except (in times of un-employment, infirmity, or old age) into the workhouse. This was a point forcefully made by William Barnes, in a submission to the 1867 Royal Commission, when he spoke of the labourer's need of a " 'rung' in the ladder of rural life, by which he may hope to raise himself by his industry towards a higher position. He cannot now hope ever to step from day labour to farming."[13] The situation of the village tradesman, on the other hand, was full of potential drama. Not only was this class, as Hardy says, "better-informed" than the labouring class, it had much greater prospects of mobility, up or down, and much greater opportunity for independent action of every kind. In Hardy's fiction it is the class of Tranter Dewy and most of the other members of the Mellstock choir; the class—though their membership, their tenure precisely, is often insecure—of Gabriel Oak, Giles Winterborne, and Tess Durbey-field; the class of such phenomena of social mobility as Fancy Day, Stephen Smith, and Grace Melbury. The characteristic situation in Hardy's fiction—and it is one of perpetual crisis—is that of the cottager who aspires to social and economic advance-ment but remains perpetually haunted by the abyss of economic failure into which misfortune or misjudgment could so easily plunge him. So Oak loses his sheep; so the death of his horse brings disaster upon John Durbeyfield's haggling business; so Henchard rides the wheel of rural fortune full circle.

Most fully explored is the situation of Giles Winterborne in *The Woodlanders*. Forestry and coppice work once played an important part in the economy of the particular area of Dorset in which the novel is set. At least one fairly substantial timber yard still survives there (at Middlemarsh) and, as Barbara Kerr has recently pointed out, in the middle of the nineteenth century the renting of a few acres of coppice offered (like the renting of a few cows) one of the few opportunities for a labouring man to begin raising himself to a higher economic and social level: "The man who rented coppice was responsible for cutting the rods, poles and brushwood. These he sold or had made into spars, sheep cribs and hurdles; the profits were small but a man was launched as his own master." She instances the Gould family of Thornford, two and a half miles south-west of Sherborne (Hardy's Sherton), who by renting coppice achieved "the formidable task in the 1830s of lifting themselves back to the tenant-farming class from which they had sunk to labourers earlier in the century".[14] When Giles loses his cottages, his inherited position of minimal independence turns out to be desperately insecure; his subsequent success in regaining lost ground is assisted by an unexpected piece of good fortune and no doubt facilitated—like similar advances made by Gabriel Oak and Michael Henchard—by his freedom from the encumbrance of a wife and family.

In an interview published in 1892 Hardy agreed that he was sometimes called the novelist of the agricultural labourer, but added: "That is not inclusive, I think." Not only had he written novels like *A Laodicean*, but in his books dealing specifically with rural life he had endeavoured "to describe the village community generally" and "to write from the point of view of the village people themselves instead of from that of the Hall or the Parsonage. I chose them because there appeared to be much more dramatic interest in their lives."[15] Clearly Hardy does not mean that he identified himself as a novelist with any specific class within the village community, but rather that he deliberately focused his attention upon that narrow segment of rural society in which mobility, and hence "dramatic interest", was at a maximum. The same restriction of the available social context can be seen in Hardy's presentation of the more urban setting of *The Mayor of Casterbridge*, the first novel he wrote following the publication of "The Dorsetshire Labourer". Dorchester, the original of the fictional Casterbridge, must have been in the middle of the nineteenth century a town dominated by commerce and by commercial men. It had no major industry, and hence no industrial magnates; no cathedral, and no cathedral clergy. It was a county town and an assize town, but it had no "season" and offered no competition to Bath or even to Weymouth as a centre of fashionable life. Unlike the Fleeceborough of *Hodge and his Masters*, it was not dominated by a great local landowner; the Mayor of Dorchester, it would appear, was *ex officio* Lord of the Manor.[16]

Hardy seems, however, to have deliberately exceeded his model in so entirely omitting the clergy, the gentry, and the landed aristocracy not merely as characters but even as subjects of conversation. His intention was unquestionably to emphasise or invent a social structure in which, above a certain minimum level, movement was possible and the determination of rank depended less upon birth than upon achieved financial success. It is thus that a Michael Henchard, starting from humble (though by no means unskilled) beginnings, can gradually raise himself to become, as Solomon Longways puts it, not merely "a pillar of the town" but "the powerfullest member of the Town Council, and quite a principal man in the county round besides" (39).

* * *

Because it was the only occasion during his career as a novelist on which Hardy addressed himself at length to the question of actual conditions in the Dorset countryside, "The Dorsetshire Labourer" has become a crucial document for those who see Hardy's concern with agricultural depression and rural depopulation as absolutely central to his whole endeavour and achievement as a novelist. Yet it remains, in its determined impartiality, curiously unsatisfactory as an index of Hardy's attitudes: he might well have said of it, as he did later of *Tess*, that it was "intended to be neither didactic nor aggressive, but in the scenic parts to be representative simply, and in the contemplative to be oftener charged with impressions than with convictions" (xviii). It is obvious from the essay that Hardy knows the countryside well; it is much less clear that he has any intimate knowledge of the labourers themselves. He shows himself sympathetic to their situation, but the very judiciousness of his comments adumbrates the limits of that sympathy. He gives no real sense of the hardships of the labourers' working lives, nor of the appalling housing conditions they were too often forced to accept for themselves and their families.[17] A few years later, when their economic situation began to show some improvement, he seems to have stopped thinking of them as an exploited class: he could confidently remark in 1892 that "the young labourer is as happy as any man—the happiest in the community, indeed".[18]

Hardy's emphasis on class-divisions within village society—his rigid separation of the labourers from the village tradesmen—makes it difficult to speak, as some critics have done, of his deliberately dramatising the fate of the "peasantry", the "defeat" of the agricultural community as a consequence of nineteenth-century industrialisation, urbanisation, and agricultural depression. Raymond Williams, indeed, in an important article, has called the whole concept of the "peasant" in Hardy's fiction "absurdly misleading: the actual social relationships, of the rural England Hardy describes, are those of rent and trade. The class system is not something that comes from outside, into an otherwise unchanging rural scene. The rural scene, rather, is a class system, of a kind determined by the development of the society as a whole."[19] Williams perhaps makes insufficient allowance for Hardy's tendency to write not about the immediate present but about periods somewhat vaguely located in the recent past, and proponents of the "decline of the peasantry" view would no doubt argue, with some justice, that the invasion of the countryside by urban and crudely commercial values, by "the new money-making industrialism",[20] is precisely the historical process charted in novels like *The Mayor of Casterbridge* and *Tess of the d'Urbervilles*. It is one thing, however, to insist on the intimacy between the Wessex novels and actual conditions in rural England during the second half of the nineteenth century, and quite another to present Hardy as being, above all else, the compassionate observer and passionate chronicler of an English "agricultural tragedy".

Most discussions of the agricultural theme in Hardy's work seem to have taken more or less for granted the classic analysis of nineteenth-century agricultural history presented in Lord Ernle's *English Farming Past and Present* (1912) and substantially adopted by such historians as Halévy and G. M. Trevelyan.[21] According to this interpretation, a "golden age" of agricultural prosperity in the 1850s and 1860s, the heyday of "high" (or high input) farming, was followed by a steep decline into a disastrous depression, provoked primarily by the bad weather of the late 1870s and by that ever-increasing flow of wheat and other foodstuffs from abroad, especially North America, made possible by the repeal of the Corn Laws. A number of recent studies, however, have suggested that this standard account is at once too dramatic and too lacking in discrimination; that the depression was less profound than has normally been assumed, and subject to greater local variations; and that Lord Ernle's concentration on wheat production led him to underestimate the importance of the often very different trends in livestock.

T. W. Fletcher, for example, argues that the decline of wheat was accompanied by a general shift to livestock production, and that what really occurred during the years of the "Great Depression" was not the ruin of agriculture but the accomplishment of "an important internal revolution", in which the real suffering was undergone not so much by the industry as a whole as by the large corn-growers.[22] E. L. Jones, noting that persistent disagreement among historians in dating the onset of the depression suggests that it must have been a gradual rather than a sudden change, argues that even in the years of evident prosperity during the 1850s and 1860s "profits from livestock rather than grain had become increasingly the basis of agricultural prosperity".[23] The closing years of the century saw, of course, not only the massive importation of foreign wheat but also, with the development of steamships and refrigeration, much higher imports of meat and dairy products. But the effect of such imports on British agriculture was cushioned in various ways. As the price of cereals went down so did the cost of winter feed for livestock, while the persistent growth both in the size of the population and in the general standard of living resulted not only in a constantly expanding market but also in a greater demand for protein as against starch—a situation summed up in 1899 in the remark that "the sort of man who had bread and cheese for his dinner 40 years ago now demands a chop".[24] These are trends which Lord Ernle clearly recognised, but which he tended to date much later —in the years immediately preceding the First World War.[25]

Such recent adjustments in the thinking of economic historians about late nineteenth-century British agriculture may not, in themselves, carry any very radical implications for the study of the relationship between Hardy's work and contemporary developments in the life of rural England. They do, however, offer a warning against exaggerated views of the economic badness of the times—a warning especially relevant to the situation in Dorset itself.

Dorset was included among the predominantly arable counties in the broad division, originally suggested by James Caird, between the "grazing" counties of the north and west and the "corn" counties of the east and south.[26] But the line drawn by Caird actually passes between Dorset and Somerset, thus placing Dorset on the borderline of a division which never pretended to be more than approximate, and all accounts of Dorset agriculture during the nineteenth century lay stress on the dairying in the Frome and Blackmore valleys—Hardy's vales of the Great and the Little Dairies—and on the primacy of sheep in the thinking of so many Dorset farmers. An important essay of 1872 provides evidence to suggest that in Dorset the shift to livestock had indeed begun ahead of the depression years,[27] while Royal Commission reports prepared in 1882 and 1895 show clearly that the overall diversity of agriculture in the county and an increased reliance on livestock (despite a fall in the numbers of sheep, which had been an important element in the pattern of high farming) were enabling local farmers to weather a period of economic stress rather better than those in many other counties.[28]

In Dorset, as in most of the country, the labour-glut on the land during the first half of the nineteenth century was gradually reduced by the attraction of urban industry and overseas emigration. By the late 1860s shortage of labour seems to have become a general complaint, and the account of Dorset farming published in 1872 speaks of the introduction of machinery as having been in part encouraged by "the greater scarcity of hands".[29] The demand, however, seems chiefly to have been for skilled labour to perform specifically mechanical jobs. When such labour could not be found locally it had to be imported from elsewhere, and the northern mechanic thus became a familiar figure in southern fields, his appearance as the attendant of the threshing-machine in *Tess of the d'Urbervilles* anticipated by Richard Jefferies' description of the "village factory" in *Hodge and his Masters*: "Busy workmen pass to and fro, lithe men, quick of step and motion, who come from Leeds, or some similar manufacturing town, and whose very step distinguishes them in a moment from the agricultural labourer."[30]

The high premium on mechanical skills produced among employers and workers alike a more positive attitude towards education—especially following the 1870 Education Act—and a diminished tendency to force children out into the fields at an early age to provide cheap labour for the farmer and a desperately needed supplement to the total family income. Even so, the economic situation of the workers who remained on the land only began to improve once they realised the leverage available to them through a demonstrated readiness to move elsewhere. Joseph Arch preached what many labourers had begun to practise—the refusal to enter into long-term binding contracts—and the whole eruption of union agitation in 1872 seems to have been not so much the action of hopeless and desperate men as of men already sensing, however dimly, the possibility of shifting the balance of economic power.[31] Hardy himself, in "The Dorsetshire Labourer", recognises both the necessity and the inevitability of the labourer's discovering in organisation a means of breaking free from old oppressions, reflecting that "if a farmer can afford to pay thirty per cent more wages in times of agricultural depression than he paid in times of agricultural prosperity, and yet live, and keep a carriage, while the landlord still thrives on the reduced rent which has resulted, the labourer must have been greatly wronged in those prosperous times" (265–266).

Whatever his later views may have been, Hardy in 1883 saw the depression as less than ruinous for farmer and landlord, and as a period of increased prosperity for the labourer. That he also recognised the nomadic habits of the labourer as already well established is suggested by his reference elsewhere in the essay to a period of stability "down to twenty or thirty years ago, before the power of unlimited migration had been clearly realised" (263). Apparently, Hardy saw the process of disruption as having begun towards the end of the 1850s, a time when, in purely economic terms, English agriculture was about to enter on its "Golden Age". Questions of literary interpretation cannot ultimately be resolved, one way or another, in terms of extrinsic evidence, but it seems at least to be clear that any attempts to establish direct correlations between the fate of the English countryside and the destinies of Hardy's characters must take very carefully into account the precise historical situation prevailing at the time when Hardy was writing—and at the time of which he was writing: J. C. Maxwell, for example, has recently demonstrated some of the flaws in the historical argument incorporated in Douglas Brown's brilliant analyses of *The Mayor of Casterbridge*.[32]

Hardy's profound awareness of the larger movements of social and economic change—greatly increased physical and social mobility, enhanced educational opportunities, the growth of cities and the decline of agriculture—is evident throughout his work. Speaking in the Preface to *Far from the Madding Crowd* of the anachronism of the name Wessex as used in a nineteenth-century context, he stressed precisely those elements making for change in the countryside: railways, the penny post, mowing and reaping machines, labourers who could read and write. Various pronouncements, outside his fiction, on rural matters all reflect an instinctive emotional and aesthetic conservatism in matters pertaining to the countryside, especially to the countryside of his native Dorset. He saw—he could not but see—that the pattern of rural life had changed radically and irreversibly in his lifetime. He believed that most of the changes had been ultimately for the worse, tending to the penetration of the rural by the urban—Dorchester, he observed in 1910, had already become "almost a London suburb"[33]—and to the breakdown of that rural stability which had been fundamental both to the oral transmission of rural history, folklore, and tradition, and to the existence of the virtually self-sufficient rural community.

In his later years Hardy's statements on these matters are obviously bound up with a simple but not the less powerful regret for a world which had vanished with his own vanished youth—for the "Dorchester that I knew best" which can now only be found

[219]

in the local churchyard[34]—and even with a desire, as in the 1906 address, "Memories of Church Restoration", to make confession of past infidelities to beliefs now passionately held. But although he profoundly regrets the isolated, static, integrated rural life that he once knew, he is by no means the impassioned advocate of a return to a Golden Age. He realises not only that the pressures making for change are inexorable—wiser in this, perhaps, than more recent writers who have felt that the nineteenth-century process of urbanisation and of rural depopulation could somehow have been prevented or arrested—but that the changes themselves are not without their beneficial aspects. The present life of the labourers, he wrote to Rider Haggard in 1902, "is almost without exception one of comfort, if the most ordinary thrift be observed. I could take you to the cottage of a shepherd not many miles from here that has a carpet and brass-rods to the staircase, and from the open door of which you hear a piano strumming within." He adds: "The son of another labourer I know takes dancing lessons at a quadrille-class in the neighbouring town. Well, why not?"[35] For the agricultural labourer, as Hardy well knew, there had never been a Golden Age, and if that final rhetorical question—apparently very much of an afterthought[36]—betrays a lingering uncertainty as to the implications of such developments, it at least proclaims an intellectual willingness to accept the inevitability of change. As he remarked of the threatened suburbanisation of Dorchester in 1910: "Though some of us may regret this, it has to be."[37]

3

The Mayor of Casterbridge

Hardy wrote *The Mayor of Casterbridge* in the house in Shire Hall Place, during the building of Max Gate. According to *Early Life* (223) the manuscript was finished on April 17, 1885, after more than a year of intermittent work.[1] Publication in the *Graphic* did not begin until January 2, 1886, but Hardy seems not to have taken advantage of the interval to reconsider his serial text.[2] He did, however, revise the *Graphic* text before Smith, Elder brought out the two-volume first edition on May 10, 1886, and although he later complained that he "could not get thoroughly into it after the interval", the changes were nonetheless substantial, and of particular interest as representing his first comprehensive revision of a serial text prior to volume publication.[3]

What is in question here is genuine revision, not—as with *Tess* and *Jude*—the reinstatement of passages and incidents present in the manuscript but deliberately deleted from the serial out of fearful respect for Mrs Grundy. The book version does show rather more sexual frankness, but far more striking is the improvement in narrative cogency, and—as appears from Mary Ellen Chase's account,[4] somewhat confused though it is and marred by minor inaccuracies of transcription—this seems to have been the chief direction of Hardy's changes. In the serial Henchard marries Lucetta out of a sense of obligation and in the sincere belief that Susan is dead; this, at any rate, is the story he tells Farfrae, adding: "Odd as it may seem to you, I've always liked Susan in my heart, and like her best now."[5] Odd it undoubtedly was, and complicated indeed were the ensuing contortions of the narrative: they involved, for example, Farfrae's delivering to

Lucetta at Budmouth a letter in which Henchard (apparently unconscious of any possibility of bigamy proceedings) announced Susan's return and the consequent setting aside of the more recent marriage. The first edition's presentation of Lucetta as Henchard's mistress unquestionably makes for greater plausibility, greater narrative coherence, and a more consistent characterisation of Lucetta herself.

There are many other changes of a less radical nature, and the fact that Hardy had for the first time found, or given himself, such an opportunity for reflection marks a new stage in his development as an artist. When *The Mayor of Casterbridge* was published, more than three and a half years had passed since the appearance of the first edition of *Two on a Tower* in October 1882. Though stories and other minor pieces had been written and published during these years, the interval, quite unprecedented at this point in his career, provided Hardy with an opportunity virtually to reconstruct himself as a novelist upon a new basis. The semi-romances of the early 1880s were now left sternly behind; the idea of Wessex, hitherto only vaguely perceived, became clear and concrete; and Hardy emerged in *The Mayor of Casterbridge* as a conscious artist with an altogether richer conception of the novel form and a firmer grasp of its techniques.

As its title suggests, *The Mayor of Casterbridge* is securely centred upon the changing fortunes and continuing life of a particular town, and upon the career and personality of its chief magistrate. The basic physical layout of Casterbridge is carefully described, and individual buildings—Henchard's house, Jopp's cottage, High Place Hall, the various inns—are fitted into place. But Hardy's chief concern is not so much to enumerate the town's visual features—topographical, architectural, archaeological—as to evoke the precise texture of its social and economic life. He thus insists upon the intimate connection between Casterbridge and the surrounding countryside, and while it is a relationship in itself picturesque—as butterflies fly along the High Street on their way from one field to another—it is at the same time absolutely fundamental to the economy of the town, and to the action of the novel. It is upon the growing and marketing of hay and corn—upon the quality of the harvest and the prevailing conditions of supply and demand—that the livelihood of Casterbridge chiefly depends. Agriculture provides the reason for the town's existence, the procession of the seasons dominates the pattern of its life.

Since Henchard and Farfrae are both in the corn and fodder business, Casterbridge market-place acts as the natural focus for that rivalry between them which dominates the novel, and which both extends outwards to the men in their employ—as in the clash by moonlight between the two waggons—and draws in upon itself the attention of all classes of the population. When Susan and Elizabeth-Jane first arrive in Casterbridge they see Henchard presiding at a dinner attended by the dignitaries of the town, the men of wealth and position whose equal—and indeed superior— he has through ambition and unaided effort become. But ominous voices already make themselves heard from among those members of the lower orders whose participation in the dinner is confined to observation of the proceedings from a position outside and below, and as the novel proceeds these early indications of class division and class hostility are confirmed and amplified. If the "gentle-people and such like leading volk" (36) meet in the King's Arms, those of the next rank frequent the Three Mariners a little further down the street. Here are to be found "a secondary set of worthies, of a grade somewhat below that of the diners at the King's Arms" (46), and, in less privileged positions away from the bow-window, "an inferior set" (57) among whom Elizabeth-Jane notices "some of those personages who had stood outside the windows of the King's Arms" (58).

Hardy keeps Casterbridge constantly before the reader's attention by spacing his descriptive passages throughout the length of the novel. It is only in chapter 36 that he fills in the part of the map called Mixen Lane, whose relationship to the polite face of the town is somewhat analogous to that between the sinister rear of High Place Hall and its dignified front elevation. The focal point of the area—its "church", as Hardy remarks, with perhaps an ironic allusion to the actual St Peter's Church which stands at the central cross-roads of Dorchester—is Peter's Finger, an inn bearing "about the same social relation to the Three

Mariners as the latter bore to the King's Arms" (295)—though, Hardy adds, "the lowest fringe of the Mariner's party touched the crest of Peter's at points" (296). The skimmity-ride which originates in Peter's Finger derives immediately from Jopp's animosity towards Henchard, Farfrae, and Lucetta, and from Henchard's poor judgment in trusting him with confidential matters. Fundamentally, however, it has its roots in that more generalised class hostility already evident among the crowd outside the King's Arms: it is Nance Mockridge, the woman who complained of Henchard's "unprincipled bread" (33), who first suggests the skimmity-ride, motivated, as Farfrae himself recognises, by the "tempting prospect of putting to the blush people who stand at the head of affairs—that supreme and piquant enjoyment of those who writhe under the heel of the same" (346).

Early Life (137) records Hardy's sense of being interested not "in manners, but in the substance of life only". But if his notation of manners (as most English novelists have understood that term) is a little sparse, there is no lack either of fullness or of assurance in his evocation of towns, villages, and hamlets as vital social organisms. The comprehensive social knowledge and understanding displayed in *The Mayor of Casterbridge* obviously owe something to childhood memories of the actual Dorchester, to continuing daily experience of the town, and to deliberate research; but everything that Hardy draws from these sources is merged and transmuted in the creation of a specifically fictional Casterbridge, the product of an informed imagination.

That the mayor of Casterbridge should be annually elected to the headship of its affairs provides an element in the novel which has prompted discussion of available analogies with ancient myths and rituals of priesthood and kingship.[6] More immediately it serves as a means of dramatising both Henchard's initial achievement as a self-made man and his subsequent supersession by Farfrae, the man he has helped to make. In Casterbridge, as Hardy recognises, the symbols of power gravitate inevitably in directions determined by the realities of power, and the first hint of Farfrae's accession to the mayoralty follows immediately upon a description of Henchard working as a day labourer in the yard that had once been his, watching "with the other men in the yard Donald Farfrae going in and out the green door that led to the garden, and the big house, and Lucetta" (264). Sexual rivalry mingles with economic rivalry in the struggle between Henchard and Farfrae, with the emphasis consistently on possession and owner-ship, and on the benefits in terms of status and reputation which possession and ownership carry with them. So the downward path of Henchard's career is charted by the different houses in which he lives, while Farfrae's rise can be measured by his successive acquisitions—themselves implicitly evoking the stages of that earlier rise of Henchard's which Hardy, with great structural tact, displays only at the moment when it has reached its apex.

The gap of eighteen undocumented years in Henchard's career fails to disturb the structural flow of this most shapely of Hardy's major novels. The first chapter—splendidly evoked by Douglas Brown in his detailed study of the book—contains the most successful of those prefigurative fore-scenes of which Hardy was so fond. The opening offers precise descriptions of the family group of man, woman, and child, and seems to promise an early revelation of their past history and present preoccupations. But the anticipated close-up is withheld; Hardy maintains his and the reader's distance, and the figures in a landscape remain essentially that for most of the chapter. The setting, too, is described with some specificity—the vegetation has "entered the blackened-green stage of colour that the doomed leaves pass through on their way to dingy, and yellow, and red" (3)—but Hardy emphasises that the scene might be almost anywhere in England at this time of year, and that the only sound, "the voice of a weak bird", might have been heard "with the self-same trills, quavers, and breves, at any sunset of that season for centuries untold" (3). The initial impulse towards particularisation is again checked and even reversed: both the figures and their landscape become less indi-vidual than they promised to be—and more representative. The novel thus strikes very early what is to be one of its most charac-teristic notes, the constant balance and even co-existence of the individual and the representative, the concrete and the general, the actual and the symbolic. The action throughout has immense concrete strength and particularity, yet it asserts scarcely less forcefully its representative functions. The fair at Weydon Priors is both quite specifically itself and at the same time another in the long line of fairs—Jonson's Bartholomew Fair, for instance, and the Vanity Fairs of both Bunyan and Thackeray—which have served in literature and fable as images of man's vanity and folly. However individual Henchard becomes, he rema ns in some measure the figure of the opening chapter. As the invocation of biblical and dramatic analogies suggests, he is a type of the "self-alienated man" (380), of all men pursued by the sins of their past; he may also be, as some critics have argued, a semi-allegorical figure embodying values intimately associated with the rural way of life.[7]

We do not learn Henchard's surname until the moment when he makes that vow of abstinence which—together, it must be said, with his new freedom from the encumbrance of a family—will provide the foundation of his subsequent rise. The vow will find its counterpart at the end of the novel in the bleak abnegation of his testament, and even before that point is reached the sense of coming full circle will have been stressed by his departure from Casterbridge dressed and equipped as in these first two chapters. But this opening movement is not simply concerned with setting up patterns of circularity. Instead of narrating Henchard's rise, or introducing him immediately as the sober and respected mayor, Hardy presents an initial image of a man capable of the impulsiveness, irresponsibility, and violent self-will sufficient to drive or permit him to sell his wife on the whim of a moment. This disturbing awareness remains throughout the novel, even at the times of Henchard's greatest prosperity: a sense of foreboding prepared for by the *Life and Death* of the title, established by the powerfully realised violence of the opening chapter, confirmed by Henchard's recurrent acts of rejection—of Farfrae, of Elizabeth-Jane, and, finally, of himself. It is in this novel that Hardy directly invokes the concept that "Character is Fate" (131), and Henchard, as the title again suggests in its reference to a *Man of Character*, is more than any other the man whose fate is implicit in his character—and implicit, by that token, in the action of the

[226]

opening chapter. Shifting violently from passionate anger and affection to equally passionate disappointment and frustration, he becomes a huge inarticulate animal at bay—like the bull which pursues Lucetta and Elizabeth-Jane and which Henchard himself reduces to impotence through the ingenious man-made cruelty of the nose-ring and the pole. In his agony Henchard condemns some mysterious fate or malignant influence which he believes to be working against him, never recognising that his downfall and his friendlessness derive directly from his own actions, or that these proceed in turn from his whole personality. Self-made, Henchard is also self-destroyed; if he feels pursued, it is essentially himself that he cannot escape.

Yet Hardy nonetheless compels us to recognise in Henchard a man of almost superhuman grandeur, of great if uncontrollable passions, a tragic hero whom it is not ludicrous to compare with Captain Ahab, or even with King Lear. The presentation is powerful in itself, but demands as its corollary an unflattering treatment of the deliberately contrasted figure of Farfrae. Like Henchard himself, the reader is initially attracted to Farfrae by his practical competence, his friendliness, his possession of those ordinary pleasant qualities of politeness and charm in which Henchard is so signally lacking. It is only gradually that the essential shallowness of Farfrae's character becomes fully apparent: in his sentimentality about a homeland he has left deliberately enough; in his skill in disguising impurities in wheat rather than making them good; in the attitudes revealed by his first courtship of Elizabeth-Jane—"who so pleasing, thrifty, and satisfactory in every way as Elizabeth-Jane?" (181)—and by the nature of his attraction to Lucetta. Finally, he argues cannily against continuing the search for Henchard overnight, since that would "make a hole in a sovereign" (381).[8] Farfrae sympathises with Abel Whittle when Henchard forces him out into the world without his trousers, but his action betrays considerable prudishness, and in raising the issue in front of Henchard's men he undoubtedly offers, as Henchard complains, a direct and unwarranted challenge to his employer's authority. The subsequent revelation that Henchard has shown great consideration to Whittle's

[227]

mother in her poverty is perhaps one of several examples of
Hardy's explicit fairness to Farfrae being compromised by an
implicit hostility, and although Whittle later testifies to his preference for Farfrae as an employer, despite a substantial reduction
in wages, this is more than counterbalanced by Whittle's devotion
to Henchard in the days of his destitution and lonely death.

The book ends, however, not with Henchard but with Elizabeth-
Jane—married, and with every appearance of contentment if not
of ecstasy, to Farfrae. Quiet and unobtrusive though she is,
Elizabeth-Jane's role is an extraordinarily interesting one, without
a close parallel elsewhere in Hardy's work. In the early chapters
there may seem something irritating in her insistence on respec-
ability, in her primness, but as the novel progresses what is
revealed is precisely the process of her self-education. If her
conscious effort is towards the kind of education contained in and
symbolised by books, her more substantial and more significant
progress is towards the kind of education in the business of living
which is usually called wisdom. Elizabeth-Jane sits quietly,
suffers quietly, watches, and learns. Like the Fanny Price of
Mansfield Park she is, though not especially sympathetic,
absolutely a person, essentially right-thinking, and very much to
be taken seriously. Because of her position of onlooker, and because of her good sense, she gradually establishes herself for the
reader as much the most acute and reliable intelligence within the
novel, the one whose judgments are most to be trusted. In a real
sense, she becomes the reader's representative within the novel's
world, and it is perhaps significant that she should be so often on
the scene when there is no absolute necessity for her presence.
She stands at the point of intersection of all the social and
emotional ties within the group of major characters—she is
Henchard's step-daughter and long believes herself to be his
actual daughter; she is Lucetta's chosen friend and confidante;
she is early courted by Farfrae and later marries him—and the
action revolves about her almost as its central pivot.

The role of Elizabeth-Jane prompts certain questions about
Hardy's handling of point of view in *The Mayor of Casterbridge*.
No more than in earlier novels is there any apparent awareness of

[228]

the rich technical possibilities described and exploited by Henry James; nor does Hardy display any particular rigour in accepting, with whatever degree of deliberateness, the freedoms available to the omniscient narrator. What is noticeable is a recurrent, though by no means consistent, tendency to present action and description as seen by one of the participants or by an isolated observer, often an unseen witness or eavesdropper.[9] In *Far from the Madding Crowd* Gabriel Oak shows an almost voyeuristic talent for finding himself in positions from which he can observe Bathsheba unseen; in *The Hand of Ethelberta* polite society is viewed from the servants' hall; in *The Return of the Native* Diggory Venn becomes almost an ubiquitous seeing eye. In *The Mayor of Casterbridge*, particularly the first two-thirds, Hardy repeatedly uses Elizabeth-Jane as the point from which events are viewed. Wherever she happens to be living, she seems always to be in a position to overlook significant meetings and activities. It is she, technically speaking, who observes Henchard's dining-room (76-77), the grim back entrance of High Place Hall, and much of the detail of Casterbridge life (68-70); she looks on at the Three Mariners when Farfrae first wins the hearts of the patrons with his sentimental songs; she is present, though often silent and ignored, at many encounters involving permutations of the Henchard-Lucetta-Farfrae triangle.

Elizabeth-Jane is thus kept constantly before the reader even during stretches of the action in which she has no substantial part to play. Sometimes, too, her presence as the observer—for example, in the scenes of Farfrae's courtship of Lucetta—lends poignancy to what might otherwise be a rather conventional or even ludicrous episode. When the viewpoint is temporarily shifted to another character it is often for a quite specific reason: Lucetta's first impression of Farfrae both dramatises his impact upon her and gives the reader a fresh view of Farfrae at a moment when his fortunes are on the rise; the implications which flow from the superiority of Farfrae's entertainment over Henchard's are emphasised as much by the presentation of Farfrae's "pavilion" through Henchard's eyes as by the explicit comments of bystanders. Yet it is not always possible to justify Hardy's manipulation of viewpoint in such positive terms. His approach to the problem is technically very limited, comparable to the interest of an artist in perspective, a theatrical producer in sight lines, a film director in camera angles. His need is apparently to visualise quite specifically, to think himself into, the precise point within the world of the novel from which each scene is being observed. His concern is not so much with the quality of the observer's response as with the visual and auditory possibilities of the vantage point he occupies.

Hardy's observers can thus scarcely be said to mediate between the author and his created world in the manner of such figures as Conrad's Marlow or even James's Strether. Characteristically, the observers perceive but rarely comment. What their eyes and ears report is absorbed directly into the narrative fabric, not filtered through a unique consciousness or isolated as "objective" dramatisation. They function not as surrogates for the author but rather as a distancing device. Even when no specific observer is introduced Hardy often writes as if one were present. At the beginning of chapter 5, the progress of Susan Henchard and her daughter is described with a heavy use of the passive voice and the implication of watching eyes: "Change was only to be observed in details" (20); "A glance was sufficient to inform the eye that this was Susan Henchard's grown-up daughter" (20); "it could be perceived that this was the act of simple affection" (21). It is almost as though Hardy shrank from the responsibilities of omniscience, from the necessity for moral judgments and firm intellectual commitments, and found a certain security in adopting—usually quite inconsistently and on a scene-to-scene basis—the limited but essentially human perspectives available to particular characters.

Both the tendency to delimitation and the urgent need for visualisation find their ideal correlative in the incorporation within the structure of the novel of patterns and techniques essentially theatrical. At the beginning of chapter 24 Hardy explains why Elizabeth-Jane—again it is her view that is primarily invoked— takes pleasure in the prospect of remaining at High Place Hall:

For in addition to Lucetta's house being a home, that raking

view of the market-place which it afforded had as much attraction for her as for Lucetta. The *carrefour* was like the regulation
Open Place in spectacular dramas, where the incidents that
occur always happen to bear on the lives of the adjoining resi-
dents. Farmers, merchants, dairymen, quacks, hawkers,
appeared there from week to week, and disappeared as the
afternoon wasted away. It was the node of all orbits. (190)

Lucetta and Elizabeth-Jane are so positioned as to be able to look
down upon the market-place, chief setting for the rivalry of
Henchard and Farfrae, as if from a pavilion overlooking a jousting
field. Specifically, they are, at the window of High Place Hall,
spectators of a weekly performance conducted as if for their
benefit. From the same vantage point they observe the collision
of the two waggons, as well as the final disastrous performance of
the skimmity ride itself, which achieves despite its garishness a
deadly realism:

> 'My—why—'tis dressed just as *she* was dressed when she
> sat in the front seat at the time the play-actors came to the
> Town Hall!' (320)

There is a momentary suggestion here of a receding perspective
of plays-within-plays-within-plays. Hardy does not pursue, perhaps does not wholly recognise, this hint, yet he certainly
exploits the grotesque and quasi-magical aspects of the primitive
ritual which is being enacted, incorporating them very powerfully
(and with touches reminiscent of Hawthorne's story "My
Kinsman, Major Molineux") in the scene in which Henchard,
the following day, is deterred from suicide by the appearance in
the water of a figure which seems to be "*himself*. Not a man somewhat resembling him, but one in all respects his counterpart, his
actual double" (342). Several other episodes in the novel seem
deliberately theatrical: the melting away of the crowd at the end
of the first chapter until Henchard is left alone with his guilt; the
scene in which Lucetta, expecting Henchard, suddenly finds
Farfrae before her for the first time; Henchard's highly melodramatic rescue of Lucetta from the menacing bull. There are, too,

the encounters in the Ring—in secret, yet oppressed and virtually overlooked by that sense of the long and dubious history of the spot which Hardy has earlier evoked in terms of the ghosts of Hadrian's "gazing" (82) soldiery and of the ten thousand spectators who watched the execution of a woman there—and the description of Farfrae drawing everyone at the Three Mariners inwards towards the sound of his voice.

In this last scene, as elsewhere in the novel, the rustics like Solomon Longways, Mother Cuxsom, and Christopher Coney perform a modest choral function, and if the members of this group are often reminiscent of the lively, disenchanted figures who populate the low-life world of Shakespeare's history plays, Hardy seems nonetheless to have precedents from Greek literature chiefly in mind. The novel as a whole resumes with more sophistication and less obtrusiveness the attempt earlier made in *The Return of the Native* to recapture certain aspects of the techniques and experience of tragic drama. Certainly the focus on Casterbridge provides a unified sense of place at least as consistent as the Egdon setting in *The Return of the Native*, and if there is no attempt to achieve technical unity of time—any more, indeed, than in *The Return of the Native* in its published form—time is to some extent shaped and vitalised by Henchard's vow in chapter 2 to "avoid all strong liquors for the space of twenty-one years to come, being a year for every year that I have lived" (18).

Although the action of *The Mayor of Casterbridge* is diversified by reversals and discoveries of the kind so richly strewn throughout the earlier novel, the controlling image is that of fortune's wheel: "Small as the police-court incident had been in itself, it formed the edge or turn in the incline of Henchard's fortunes. On that day—almost at that minute—he passed the ridge of prosperity and honour, and began to descend rapidly on the other side" (251). This hint of a "morality" structure implicit in the sequence of Henchard's rise and fall is further stressed in the full title of the novel—*The Life and Death of the Mayor of Casterbridge: A Story of a Man of Character*[10]—with its deliberate echo of such allegorical works as Bunyan's *The Life and Death of Mr Badman*. But it is unnecessary to debate the precise ancestry of the dramatic patterns incorporated within *The Mayor of Casterbridge* in order to insist on the presence of unmistakably tragic elements in the story of Henchard's life or in the manner of his death, as he shares with Othello a determination to "extenuate nothing" (380) and echoes in his dying testament the bitter epitaph found on "the rude tomb" of Timon of Athens.

It is only at the very end of the novel that it becomes possible to appreciate the full importance of the central if unspectacular position occupied by Elizabeth-Jane. Henchard's retention of the reader's sympathy in the final chapters is largely dependent upon his now unequivocal love for Elizabeth-Jane, and upon the revival of her love and compassion for him. Equally, however, it is our now developed responsiveness to Elizabeth-Jane's good sense and good judgment which ensures that in our surrender to the power of Henchard we do not utterly reject the man who, next to Henchard himself, is most responsible for his downfall. Farfrae has real if limited virtues, and Elizabeth-Jane's acceptance of him in marriage ensures that we remember these. The ending of the novel is quiet, low-keyed, like the ending of a Shakespearean tragedy: the central figure has been removed by death and the lesser ones who formerly stood in his shadow are left to pick up the pieces and restore order as best they can. So Elizabeth-Jane is left with Donald Farfrae, accommodating herself patiently to his limitations and to the knowledge that she is his second choice. Because of her, because of what she has learned, because she is in a real sense Henchard's heir even if not his actual daughter, the book ends on a note of quiet hopefulness which we recognise as essentially hers, the impress of her character as we have come to know it. In her marriage with Farfrae we perhaps glimpse the possibility which E. M. Forster later pursued in *Howards End*, that efficiency *can* be combined with humanity, that the commercial life need not necessarily imply insensitivity to the natural affections or to the natural world itself. Henchard is dead, and something profoundly valuable—something which connected him with the land, the seasons, and with the rural way of life— seems to have died with him. But that death, Hardy seems to suggest, was perhaps necessary. Although Henchard experienced it as defeat it may be the part of wisdom to temper regret with realism and to recognise the inevitability of change as old ways, dating from the "days of the Heptarchy" (191), necessarily yield to more modern methods. And so the novel ends not on Henchard's bitter cry of despair but upon Elizabeth-Jane's note of quiet acceptance. Implicit in that acceptance, however, is the sense of having lived on into a world from which a kind of greatness has disappeared, and perhaps for ever.

4

The Evolution of Wessex

The manuscript of *Under the Greenwood Tree* already contains some of the disguised place names which Hardy was to employ throughout his later work, and it was in this novel that he established the basic topographical framework of Mellstock (with Yalbury Wood), Casterbridge, and Budmouth. *Far from the Madding Crowd* developed the presentation of Casterbridge and Budmouth, introduced a number of minor settings, created the village of Weatherbury in all the rich variety of its agricultural life, and introduced the name Wessex into Hardy's fiction for the first time. In his 1895 Preface to *Far from the Madding Crowd* Hardy recalled: "The series of novels I projected being mainly of the kind called local, they seemed to require a territorial definition of some sort to lend unity to their scene. Finding that the area of a single county did not afford a canvas large enough for this purpose, and that there were objections to an invented name, I disinterred the old one." (vii) It is hard to believe that Hardy, by the autumn of 1874, had in fact gone much beyond a rather general recognition of the attractions and advantages of choosing the settings of future novels from a fairly limited geographical area. Despite *The Trumpet-Major* and the sketch-map of Egdon Heath drawn for the first edition of *The Return of the Native*, he seems to have retained throughout the 1870s a fairly limited conception of Wessex and of its potentialities for development, and the publication of *A Laodicean* and *Two on a Tower* in the early 1880s suggests that he remained fundamentally uncertain as to the kind of novel, of setting, and of period most appropriate to his talents.

It was only with *The Mayor of Casterbridge* that Hardy achieved a full realisation of the Wessex concept, a realisation which depended on the establishment of Casterbridge itself (significantly insisted upon in the novel's title) as the central point, the economic, administrative, and social capital, of a whole region. Critics have long noticed the allusions in *The Mayor of Casterbridge* to the world of *Far from the Madding Crowd*,[1] and W. J. Keith has more recently pointed to the way in which the novel incorporates other references which seem deliberately designed to draw into its orbit places which provide the setting for other novels and stories: Hardy describes, for example, the carriers' vans which travelled to Casterbridge "from Mellstock, Weatherbury, The Hintocks, Sherton-Abbas, Kingsbere, Overcombe, and many other towns and villages round" (68).[2] Budmouth, Shottsford, and Melchester are all mentioned; the appearance of a church choir, with "bass-viols, fiddles, and flutes under their arms" (266), provides a specific reminiscence of the Mellstock world; Mixen Lane is not simply an appendage to Casterbridge itself but "the Adullam of all the surrounding villages" (293). The whole structure of the novel, with its emphasis on arrivals and departures—Susan Henchard's, Farfrae's, Lucetta's, Newson's, Henchard's—serves to strengthen the impression of Casterbridge as a focal point, and the role played in the central action by the hay and corn trade and by the market-place itself, the town's physical and symbolic heart, works consistently to reinforce the importance of Casterbridge as what the novel itself calls "the pole, focus, or nerve-knot of the surrounding country life" (70).

It seems reasonable to suggest that this reassertion of the Wessex pattern was directly related to Hardy's desire, after wandering to and fro between various parts of Dorset and various sections of London, to settle down permanently in Dorchester—the original of Casterbridge, the actual nerve-knot of his own native countryside—and build himself a house. From the moment of thus firming his roots back into his native soil Hardy's handling of Wessex settings became both more frequent and more confident. He wrote to his publishers to recommend a more consistent use of the terms Wessex and Wessex Novels in their advertisements of his books, and when in 1895–96 he was preparing the first collected edition of his novels he took the opportunity of revising the place-names, distances, and descriptions in the various volumes in order to bring them into line with each other and with his developed conception of the Wessex world.[3]

It was apparently in March 1884, some nine months after his return to Dorchester, that Hardy began reading systematically through back files of the local weekly newspaper, the *Dorset County Chronicle and Somersetshire Gazette*. He seems to have begun with the issues of January 1826, and the memoranda in his "Facts" notebook suggest that by the summer of 1884 he had read through to the issues for late 1829 or early 1830. During this long and peculiarly intimate exposure to a particular period in the past of the county town and the surrounding countryside he came across several items which he was able to incorporate, more or less directly, into the novel on which he was then beginning work.

In the early decades of the nineteenth century the *Dorset County Chronicle*, like most other newspapers in London and the provinces, was largely filled with reports of crimes, accidents, and sensational legal proceedings. Hardy duly summarised a number of such reports, including one of the murder of Maria Marten. The contemporary conception of "human interest" also extended to extraordinary events of the "believe it or not" variety, including inexplicable suicides and disappearances, astounding reappearances by people long presumed dead, and coincidences far more bizarre than anything to be found in Hardy's own fiction. As might have been expected, Hardy noted down a good many items of the kind: the young man, for instance, who tapped at night on his fiancée's window and was stabbed and killed through the glass by the girl's father, who thought he was a burglar; the man who returned to his native village after twenty-seven years of absence, found his wife married to a second husband, and simply settled down again to live by himself in the same village.[4]

But Hardy was no less interested in items which spoke directly and unsensationally of their period: descriptions of current fashions in dress; the names and times of the stage-coaches leaving the King's Arms, Dorchester, in late 1827; stories of injuries and deaths caused by spring-guns; an account of the

Yeovil glove trade and the opportunities it provided for the wives and children of farm labourers to supplement the family income; a report, copied out by Hardy at some length, of speeches made at an election meeting in Ilchester in 1826.[5] In the issue of December 4, 1828, Hardy found a long account of the Dorchester Tradesmen's Dinner for that year, held in the King's Arms. The report mentions the special tribute paid to Major Garland, a native of the town who had fought at Waterloo, describes the actual dinner (including "a noble baron of beef"), disclaims completeness for its list of twenty-three toasts drunk during the dinner, and concludes:

> Several excellent songs were sung in very superior style in the course of the evening, and on the Chairman's quitting the Chair, about nine o'clock, it was taken by Major Garland, and the festivities of the day were continued to a late hour, when the company departed highly delighted with the enjoyment of the convivial and harmonious meeting of which they had partaken.[6]

Hardy may originally have noted and summarised this report simply for its reference to Waterloo and for its general "period" flavour. But at some point, clearly, he drew upon it for the description of the dinner at the King's Arms over which Henchard presides in *The Mayor of Casterbridge*.

In the issue of April 27, 1826, Hardy discovered, and summarised in his notebook, the following item:

> On Wednesday se'nnight a meeting of the Commissioners under the bankruptcy of Mr. Harvey of Launceston, banker, took place at the White Hart Inn there, for the purpose of his final examination. At the close of the proceedings Mr. Harvey laid his gold watch and pocket-money on the table; but they were immediately returned by the unanimous vote of the creditors present. The senior Commissioner, Mr. Tonkin, addressed Mr. Harvey, and said he had been a commissioner for a number of years, but in all his experience he had never yet found a bankrupt who had acted more honorably and honestly; his balance sheet was the most satisfactory that he had seen on any similar occasion, and his creditors—a great number of whom were

present—ought to feel perfectly well satisfied with his conduct. The other commissioners, Mr. Bird and Mr. R. K. Frost, perfectly coincided in the opinion expressed by Mr. Tonkin, and only one feeling appeared to pervade the meeting—that of sympathy with Mr. Harvey.[7]

Bankruptcies are of course common enough, and in a letter of January 1903 Hardy was to recall that not long after the publication of *The Mayor of Casterbridge* a "leading member of the Town Council here, in the *same business* as the Mayor, became bankrupt just as he did".[8] But there can be little doubt of Hardy's indebtedness to this passage for the scene in which Henchard produced his gold watch and purse in precisely similar circumstances:

'Well,' said the senior Commissioner, addressing Henchard, 'though the case is a desperate one, I am bound to admit that I have never met a debtor who behaved more fairly. I've proved the balance-sheet to be as honestly made out as it could possibly be; we have had no trouble; there have been no evasions and no concealments. The rashness of dealing which led to this unhappy situation is obvious enough; but as far as I can see every attempt has been made to avoid wronging anybody.' (253)

If this item provided an opportunity for showing Henchard at his best, the scene in which he bullies Abel Whittle was perhaps suggested by a story (in the issue of September 14, 1826) about a soldier who shot himself after having been marched through the streets of Kilkenny without shirt, stockings, or shoes.[9] From the *Dorset County Chronicle* of July 9, 1829, Hardy noted an item, headed "Sobriety and its beneficial consequences", about a man who had raised himself from a "common nuisance" to a "respectable tradesman" by deciding "to *swear* that for *seven years* he would not taste of any liquid stronger than tea. This oath he kept most inviolably, and by his regularity obtained a friend who put him into business. In November last the term of his oath expired, and he anxiously looked forward to the day, that he might enjoy himself without infringing upon his conscience. In fact he did get as much intoxicated as he ever had been, but on the next day renewed his oath for *twelve years*, since which he has gone on in the steady money-getting way in which he had passed the last seven years."[10]

Once again, the relevance to the story of Henchard seems plain, and it is perhaps of some significance that an attempt has been made, presumably by Hardy himself, to render the notebook entry illegible. Other notes have been more effectively scored through or scraped away, and some have been removed altogether. It is, of course, impossible to make a positive identification of material excised in this way, but in some instances it is at least possible to determine the issue of the *Dorset County Chronicle* from which the note must originally have been taken. In one such issue, that of April 17, 1826, appears the following report:

Phoebe Hooper, aged about 50, and apparently a respectable woman, was indicted for feloniously marrying Jonathan Puxtone, her former husband, Wm. Hooper, being living.

The object of the prosecution did not appear, nor was it suggested that any injury had been sustained by any person in consequence of the alleged offence of the prisoner.

It was proved that a marriage had taken place in 1810, between a man named Hooper, and a female supposed to be the prisoner, by her maiden name of Holloway; but the witness, the parish clerk, who was called to prove this fact, said he was not certain of the prisoner's identity. She appeared to be the the same woman; but she was, if the same, very much altered in appearance. The second marriage with one Puxtone, a farmer, in the present year, (as well as the prisoner's identity with regard to this marriage,) was clearly proved. This took place in April in the present year. To clear up the fact as to the identity of the prisoner on the first marriage, the constable who apprehended her was called. She was living with her second husband, farmer Puxtone, at the time. When told there was a warrant against her for bigamy, she said it was impossible, as there had been an agreement between "them"—an agreement prepared by a lawyer; and therefore she, at first, could not be made to believe that there could be any legal charge against her. The meaning of the expression "them" would be clearly made out as referring to the two husbands, if the conversation on the same subject, at the same time, but occurring while the prisoner was dressing herself, in order to go to prison, could be made legal evidence against her; but as it took place in her absence, it was not admitted in evidence. Upon this defect in the case on the part of the prosecution, the learned Judge directed an acquittal, because, although it had been proved that there had been a marriage between two persons in the year 1819, it was not proved, either by evidence, or by the prisoner's confession, that she was one of them.

The Jury accordingly acquitted her. The prisoner, from her appearance and manner, as well as from her deportment through the trial, excited the sympathy of every person in court. Nothing was alleged against her character in any respect whatever.[11]

It is tempting to see in this passage the basis not only of important plot elements in *The Mayor of Casterbridge* but of much of the actual characterisation of Susan Henchard. The legal nicety about a conversation which took place in the prisoner's "absence"— apparently because she was dressing herself out of sight of the officers arresting her—may also have suggested to Hardy the furmity-woman's courtroom quibble: "I was not capable enough to hear what I said, and what is said out of my hearing is not evidence" (231).

For the story of wife-selling Hardy had no need to go to the files of the *Dorset County Chronicle*. The existence of such practices was well known, and a long entry on the subject appears in John Timbs's *Things Not Generally Known, Faithfully Explained* (1856), a book of miscellaneous information which Hardy owned, probably from childhood.[12] He did, however, jot down at least three instances of wife-selling from the pages of the *Dorset County Chronicle*, and one such note, attributed to the issue of December 6, 1827, is of particular interest:

Selling *wife*. At Buckland, nr. Frome, a labring [sic] man named Charles Pearce sold wife to shoemaker named Elton for £5, & delivered her in a halter in the public street. She seemed very willing. Bells rang.[13]

[241]

The sum mentioned here closely corresponds to the five guineas which Newson pays in *The Mayor of Casterbridge*; in other reports the payment is sometimes no more than the price of a few drinks. What seems more important is that the scene of the transaction, though outside Dorset, is well within the boundaries of "Wessex". Both the Somersetshire setting of the Buckland wife-selling and its date in the late 1820s—"before the nineteenth century had reached one-third of its span" (1)—suggest, in fact, that this may have been the specific incident to which Hardy referred in his 1895 Preface to *The Mayor of Casterbridge*:

> The incidents narrated arise mainly out of three events, which chanced to range themselves in the order and at or about the intervals of time here given, in the real history of the town called Casterbridge and the neighbouring country. They were the sale of a wife by her husband, the uncertain harvests which immediately preceded the repeal of the Corn Laws, and the visit of a Royal personage to the aforesaid part of England. (vii)

It is clear from chapter 37 that the "Royal personage" must have been Prince Albert, who passed through Dorchester in July 1849 on his way to Weymouth, "for the purpose", as the *Dorset County Chronicle* put it, "of laying the foundation stone of that highly important national work, the Portland Breakwater". In the novel the royal visitor leaves Casterbridge by "the Budmouth Road" (308) to "inaugurate an immense engineering work out that way" (302). The newspaper report continued:

> His Royal Highness's condescending goodness in undertaking the journey to Portland for this purpose was fully appreciated by the loyal inhabitants of Portland, Weymouth, and Dorchester. Every possible means of demonstrating the loyal and excellent feelings of the public in this county was had recourse to. On the auspicious day the bells of St. Peter's, Dorchester, rang merry peals, and a band of music was untiring in its efforts to give expression to the lively pleasure with which all persons seemed to be animated. The railway terminus was very tastefully decorated, and a pretty triumphal arch was erected between the trees at the entrance to the drive up to the

station. Further on the Weymouth road was a remarkably handsome arch of boughs and flowers erected opposite the toll gate at Monckton, being surrounded with a crown, and having the inscription in the arch "Welcome, Prince Albert".[14]

The reference to the Dorchester railway station, opened two years before the Prince Consort's visit, points to at least one way in which the novel diverges from strict historical accuracy: "The railway had stretched out an arm towards Casterbridge at this time, but had not reached it by several miles as yet; so that the intervening distance, as well as the remainder of the journey, was to be traversed by road in the old fashion" (305). But if Hardy deliberately kept Casterbridge, however tenuously, beyond the reach of the invading railway, the report in the *Dorchester County Chronicle* provides ample evidence for the authenticity of his allusions to the ringing of bells, the presentation of an illuminated address, and the erection of "green arches" (311) over the royal route.[15] Hardy no doubt turned to such reports before writing chapter 37 of *The Mayor of Casterbridge*. He may also have witnessed the Dorchester ceremonies himself, as a child of nine, and drawn directly, thirty-five years later, upon his own memories of the Prince's visit, while his source for the episode of Henchard's ludicrous and pathetic gesture of welcome may well have been the Reverend Henry Moule's story, preserved by Handley C. G. Moule in *Memories of a Vicarage*, of how the Mayor of Dorchester "was so much moved by the royal presence that he dropped on *both* knees to read his address".[16]

In the General Preface to the Wessex Edition Hardy wrote:

At the dates represented in the various narrations things were like that in Wessex: the inhabitants lived in certain ways, engaged in certain occupations, kept alive certain customs, just as they are shown doing in these pages. And in particularising such I have often been reminded of Boswell's remarks on the trouble to which he was put and the pilgrimages he was obliged to make to authenticate some detail, though the labour was one which would bring him no praise. Unlike his achievement, however, on which an error would as he says have brought

[243]

discredit, if these country customs and vocations, obsolete and obsolescent, had been detailed wrongly, nobody would have discovered such errors to the end of Time. Yet I have instituted inquiries to correct tricks of memory, and striven against temptations to exaggerate, in order to preserve for my own satisfaction a fairly true record of a vanishing life.[17]

The particular terms of this claim suggest how much of the Victorian antiquary there was in Hardy—delver into the back files of local newspapers, amateur archaeologist and dialectologist, friend and editor of William Barnes, member of the Dorset Natural History and Antiquarian Field Club and contributor to its published *Proceedings*. When Hardy speaks of having pursued accuracy of historical detail for his own satisfaction, he seems to recognise that such precision was, in a strict sense, gratuitous, in excess of the demands of that novelistic verisimilitude which depends not so much upon a delineation of the world as it is or was as upon a compelling image of a world, past or present, in which the reader can believe. But Hardy wanted nonetheless to record the Wessex world as it actually *was*. As evidence of his fidelity to regional topography there survives in the Dorset County Museum a printed map of Dorset on which he had marked in red pencil the route of Tess's wanderings.[18] His own Wessex maps closely correspond, apart from the names, to contemporary maps of southern England;[19] the comments and photographs of Hermann Lea, checked and approved by Hardy, demonstrate a high degree of identification between the fictional Wessex and the actual buildings and scenery of Dorset.[20] The definitive statements on the relationship between the world of Hardy's imagination and the actual region on which it is based are to be found in the 1895 Preface to *Tess*, the General Preface to the Wessex Edition, and the sentences which Hardy specifically recommended to Hermann Lea for inclusion in his original Wessex handbook of 1905:

It may be wise to state clearly at the outset that the author has never admitted more than that the places named fictitiously were *suggested* by such and such real places. But assuming these places of fiction and verse to be idealizations, there is little difficulty in recognizing the majority of them in substance. And the natural features, as distinct from the towns, villages, &c., are described in a way that makes identification almost an easy matter, even where they have not received their real names, as they have in many cases.[21]

Hardy consistently needed the stimulus and reassurance of the known, the seen, the verifiably authentic. Even so, fact is never allowed to become tyrannical but must always yield to the novelist's convenience: so the town-plan of Dorchester undergoes some modification in the process of its transformation into Casterbridge; so Puddletown/Weatherbury gains a great barn, itself a composite of actual barns at Abbotsbury and Cerne Abbas.[22]

It was Carl J. Weber's view—one still widely accepted—that Hardy deliberately chose both the settings and the periods of his novels in order to build up a comprehensive account of nineteenth-century Wessex as both a geographical and an historical fact. In an article of 1938 Weber wrote that Hardy "surveyed the entire nineteenth century with a view to making his historical study as accurate as were his topographical observations".[23] In the revised (1965) edition of *Hardy of Wessex*, Weber adjusted the dating of *The Woodlanders* from the 1875–78 of his original article to 1876–79;[24] he apparently had no other second thoughts during the intervening years, and his account of the periods and internal chronologies of the novels has remained largely unchallenged.[25] All his datings can, however, be questioned on points of detail, and some of them seem to be radically in error as to the very period of the action. His attempt to establish a precise chronology for *The Mayor of Casterbridge* founders on a failure to realise that the Dorchester Candlemas Fair was held not on February 2 but on *Old* Candlemas Day, February 14.[26] His assignment of *Two on a Tower* to 1858–63 ignores the frequent references to the Transit of Venus which occurred, for the first time since the eighteenth century, in December 1874.[27] His dating of *The Woodlanders* depends, in both instances, upon the allusions to the South Carolinian gentleman who had left the United States "on the failure of the Southern cause" (181), yet other references firmly suggest that Hardy's knowledge of American history must have been at fault (unless the South Carolinian had been a supporter of John C. Calhoun rather than of Jefferson Davis) and that he conceived of the action as taking place at an earlier period. Certainly the reference to the new divorce law is absolutely precise—"twenty and twenty-one Vic., cap. eighty-five" (326), the Divorce Act of 1857, came into force on January 1, 1858[28]—and the railway which prompted the rebuilding of the Earl of Wessex Hotel in Sherton presumably corresponds to the line to Sherborne which was opened, with much celebration, in May 1860.[29]

Hardy's handling of time shows precisely the same flexibility as his handling of place. When he speaks in the General Preface of "the dates represented in the various narrations" his phrasing prompts more questions than it solves. He certainly comments in the prefaces of a few novels on the period at which the action is to be imagined as taking place, and several books seem both to follow a strictly calculated chronology and to offer internal evidence of specific dating. On closer inspection, however, the chronologies tend to break down and the evidence, whether external or internal, all too often proves imprecise or even self-contradictory. In *The Return of the Native*, for example, unquestionably one of the most carefully plotted of Hardy's novels, a detailed calendar is invoked by the insistence that November 5 is a Saturday. Yet Christmas that same year is apparently made to fall on a Monday, whereas the calendar would inexorably require December 25 to be a Sunday. Hardy, it is true, does not actually say that Christmas Day is a Monday, but that is the day of the mumming at the Yeobrights' (146, 153), which is itself two days after December 23 (141, 149, 152). Even in *The Trumpet-Major*, where the central narrative moves within a framework of resounding historical events, the chronology becomes confused in the later chapters, and in revising the novel for volume publication Hardy omitted the dates he had supplied in the serial version.[30] When carrying out research for the novel he had recorded in his notebook that "June 30. 1801, was a Tuesday":[31] both this note and the jumbled chronology of so deliberately historical a novel seem to carry a clear warning against assuming too readily that Hardy used a perpetual calendar or that he was at all consistent in using a specific calendar in working out the plots of individual novels.

The effect of Weber's work has been to foster the impression of Hardy as a highly schematic writer and of the world of Wessex as having been self-consciously parcelled out among the various novels both as to location and as to time. The title of "Historian of Wessex" was deserved, Weber argued, "not only because Hardy knew his land like a surveyor, but knew his time, too, with all the accuracy of an almanac-maker".[32] Clearly this is to overstate the accuracy of Hardy's chronology; it is also to misrepresent the whole character of Wessex itself. Even the precise historical references in the Preface to *The Mayor of Casterbridge* prove to be suggestive of general period rather than definitive of a specific time-span, and if the novels appear to cover between them much of the nineteenth century they do so only in the broadest terms, evocative rather of a sense of pastness than of identifiable moments in time. Hardy was, after all, a nineteenth-century novelist, and in several of his books (for instance, *Desperate Remedies*, *A Pair of Blue Eyes*, *The Hand of Ethelberta*, *A Laodicean*, *Two on a Tower*) he was writing of a world that was immediately contemporary, or only a very few years in the past. Apart from the special case of *The Trumpet-Major*, the novels which can be said to incorporate a significant element of historical reconstruction are *Under the Greenwood Tree*, *Far from the Madding Crowd*, *The Return of the Native*, *The Mayor of Casterbridge*, *The Woodlanders*, and perhaps *Tess*. Not surprisingly, Hardy's imagination tended to move forward more or less in step with his own life: in the early 1870s he looked back thirty years to the world of *Under the Greenwood Tree*; by the early 1880s he was re-creating the county town he had known at mid-century.

These retrospective novels of Hardy's—it seems excessive to call them historical—are also those which establish the chief landmarks of Wessex and contribute substantially to its progressive creation as a comprehensive fictional world. Together with *Jude the Obscure*, they also constitute the roll-call of Hardy's major fiction. The stimulation of his deepest creative instincts—in fiction, poetry, and drama—seems to have been inseparable from a profound brooding upon the past and upon the practical and philosophical implications of time's passage. That consciousness of mortality which gives unexpected emotional force to the conclusion of *The Trumpet-Major* also informs, less obviously but no less surely, all of Hardy's best work, finally emerging into explicitness in the pages of *The Well-Beloved* and the prefaces to the Osgood, McIlvaine edition. Rather like the agrarian myth which haunted the nineteenth-century American imagination, Hardy's Wessex was located somewhere in a vague, unspecifiable past, seeming all the more elusive of historical definition because of the very success with which it evoked a remote and almost timeless rural world in which "three or four score years were included in the mere present, and nothing less than a century set a mark on its face or tone".[33]

Hardy pursued his researches into the history of his region in the British Museum, in the files of the *Dorset County Chronicle*, in the pages of Hutchins's *History and Antiquities of Dorset*, and no doubt elsewhere; he also jotted down in diaries and notebooks instances of old customs and beliefs which had survived into his own day. But just as in writing *The Trumpet-Major* he amalgamated details of several historical reviews into a single fictional event which was itself unhistorical, so in writing his other Wessex novels Hardy had no hesitation in transferring to later in the century incidents and episodes which he found in the *Dorset County Chronicle* of the 1820s and 1830s, in shifting to Wessex settings events which had taken place in other parts of the kingdom, or in blending such material with rural anecdotes, ballads, superstitions, and folklore, and with the widest possible range of agricultural, architectural, and social detail. This composite image of the regional past answers closely to Hardy's formulation of Wessex as a "partly real, partly dream-country".[34] Sufficiently real to project a strong impression of authenticity, Wessex is sufficiently the stuff of imagination to meet all of Hardy's creative needs. His world remains essentially fictional, infinitely flexible within broad self-imposed limits of time and place, susceptible to comparison with an actual geographical area but on no account to be confused with it: as he himself wrote on one of his own maps, "This is an imaginative Wessex only."[35]

5

The Woodlanders

When *The Woodlanders* was published by Macmillan in March 1887 a review in the *World* spoke of it as "a story of vulgar intrigue, and nothing more".[1] Unacceptable as this characterisation may seem, it does point to the novel's profusion of mysteries, liaisons, infidelities, secret meetings, and mistaken identities, and to the unexpectedness of such plot devices in a work written so late in Hardy's career. A possible clue to their ancestry appears in the phrase "desperate remedies" (328), here applied to the divorce laws, and in other similarities of phrase and situation between *The Woodlanders* and Hardy's first published novel. In both books a handsome unmarried woman inhabiting the great house of the neighbourhood attracts to her, and is attracted by, a beautiful young girl of lesser sophistication and lower social class (Cytherea, Grace); she also has a secret relationship with the girl's lover (Manston, Fitzpiers), a stranger to the community and seemingly possessed of mysterious powers. In both novels a strict insistence on the letter of the leases of a group of cottages brings economic disaster to the former tenant, while the scene in *The Woodlanders* in which Grace and Mrs Charmond cling to each other for mutual warmth and comfort seems a muted echo of the extraordinary "lesbian" episode in *Desperate Remedies*.

Other contemporary reviewers suggested that the new novel was, in certain respects, a reworking of *Far from the Madding Crowd*,[2] and such analogies with the early fiction perhaps have some bearing upon the statement in *Early Life* (230) that when Hardy began writing *The Woodlanders* in November 1885 he went back to his "original plot". If, as seems possible, that plot dated from as far back as 1874 or early 1875 when—again according to *Early Life* (135)—he put aside "a woodland story he had thought of" in order to write *The Hand of Ethelberta*, then it would not only account for features otherwise surprising in a novel published between *The Mayor of Casterbridge* and *Tess of the d'Urbervilles* but allow the story to be thought of as combining the pastoral material and intricate plotting characteristic of the early novels with the greater maturity of technique and tone which marks the later works.

Within a setting chosen principally for its rural remoteness and claustrophobic isolation—Hintock, says one of the characters, bottles up emotions "till one can no longer hold them" (228)—Hardy presents, almost in the manner of a *"roman expérimental"*, a small group of central characters, carefully selected and differentiated as to birth, education, wealth, and class, divided quite specifically into the two basic groups of woodlanders and ex-urbanites, and deliberately subjected to a wide range of the misfortunes which nature, society, sexual drive, human folly, and simple accident can bring. Working with the established human ecology—men and women trained by the inheritance of generations to live in these particular circumstances—Hardy transplants exotic growths (Mrs Charmond and Fitzpiers) from elsewhere. He also takes one promising plant (Grace Melbury) from its natural soil, forces it in hothouse conditions, and then transplants it back to its place of origin. Such metaphors seem justifiable in discussing a novel in which the relationship between man and nature is of such pervasive importance. In a famous passage Hardy speaks of the woodlands displaying the same "Unfulfilled Intention" (59) as is visible in any city slum, and the "Darwinian" point is made even more forcefully in his poem, "In a Wood": the woods seem to promise "sylvan peace" and "a soft release/ From men's unrest", but on closer view "Great growths and small/ Show them to men akin—/Combatants all!"[3] As one of the early reviewers remarked, the country of *The Woodlanders* is "no Arcadia";[4] the woods may be beautiful, but they can also be terrifying, nor are the woodlanders themselves exempt from the fight for survival. Little Hintock becomes not a haven of "sylvan peace" but the microcosm of a world in which the struggle for existence is everywhere the chief condition of existence. It is not simply a question of the struggle in nature mirroring the struggle in human society: nature and society are engaged in the same struggle, interconnected by a myriad strands. The woods yield a living to the woodlanders but they yield it only at a price—Melbury's injuries and aches, Marty's life of labour—and they are always ready to take their toll: this, indeed, seems to be one of the chief significances of John South's obsession with what H. J. Moule, in a letter to Hardy, called the "elm-tree totem".[5]

The presentation of the woods themselves as setting and as conditioning environment involves an abundant but not excessive particularisation of seasonal sights, sounds, and smells. It also evokes and defines a whole way of life, as in the description of an oak tree being stripped of its bark:

> As soon as it had fallen the barkers attacked it like locusts, and in a short time not a particle of rind was left on the trunk and larger limbs. Marty South was an adept at peeling the upper parts; and there she stood encaged amid the mass of twigs and buds like a great bird, running her ripping-tool into the smallest branches, beyond the further points to which the skill and patience of the men enabled them to proceed—branches which, in their lifetime, had swayed high above the bulk of the wood, and caught the earliest rays of the sun and moon while the lower part of the forest was still in darkness.
>
> 'You seem to have a better instrument than they, Marty,' said Fitzpiers.
>
> 'No, sir,' she said, holding up the tool, a horse's leg-bone fitted into a handle and filed to an edge; ''tis only that they've less patience with the twigs, because their time is worth more than mine.'
>
> A little shed had been constructed on the spot, of thatched hurdles and boughs, and in front of it was a fire, over which a kettle sang. Fitzpiers sat down inside the shelter and went on with his reading, except when he looked up to observe the scene and the actors.(160)

What to Fitzpiers is a pleasant scene for aesthetic contemplation is to Marty a matter of hard economic reality. Giles may appear, to a Grace beginning to appreciate his true worth, in the poetic guise of "Autumn's very brother" (246), but he remains throughout the novel a man with a living to make. He, Melbury, Marty, and the workfolk are all firmly created in their occupational roles, and the pattern of the woodman's year is evoked in brief but vivid vignettes distributed throughout the novel, pacing its narrative movement by the movement of the seasons. It is scarcely surprising that Alfred Austin, inscribing one of his own books to Hardy, should refer to *The Woodlanders* as one of Hardy's "Prose Georgics".[6]

Critics such as Douglas Brown have, for these and other reasons, read *The Woodlanders* as a kind of companion or counterpart to George Sturt's *The Wheelwright's Shop*, and they have had little difficulty in arguing that a high moral valuation is placed on intimacy with the woods and the life of the woods and on skill in the woodland crafts—as in the scene in which Giles and Marty South are planting trees together. By the same token, a negative judgment seems to be implicit in revelations of unfamiliarity with trees and with rural life: Felice Charmond hates the woods, and Fitzpiers is a poor horseman. Yet the kind of expertise displayed by Giles and Marty is valued less as the embodiment of fidelity to a disappearing way of life—little in the novel itself suggests that the woodland crafts and trades are falling into disuse—than as an index of other, more universal qualities. For Hardy's sympathetic characters, life is a serious and ultimately intractable business: people like Mrs Charmond and Fitzpiers don't treat it as such but rather as a stage for their own posturings. Like Manston's feckless first wife in *Desperate Remedies*, Mrs Charmond has been an actress, a student of "cross-loves and crooked passions" (274), while Fitzpiers, often "theatrical" (154) in his manner, is presented as something of a shabby Faust, dabbling in occult knowledge and transcendental philosophy. Fitzpiers's very decision to establish himself in the heart of the country seems a whim so arbitrary as to be the mark of an aesthete. His studies and speculations emphasise his remoteness from reality, and it is his peculiar self-deceptive talent to mould life into the shape of his changing desires—his courtship of Grace is a triumph of self-persuasion.

Marty South and Giles Winterborne, the two figures set off against Felice Charmond and Edred Fitzpiers, are both utter realists: they accept the world for what it is and get on with the world's work. Hardy does not insist that Giles's inherited country-man's skill with trees is inherently superior to Fitzpiers's educated skill in medicine; what he does stress is that while Giles uses his skill both consistently and creatively, Fitzpiers employs his potentially greater powers (Giles, after all, can merely make trees grow straight, not human beings) only intermittently, arbitrarily, and with little concern for what they may or may not achieve. Fitzpiers's undoubted talents as a doctor are compromised by a lack of human sympathy for his poorer patients, such as John South and Grammer Oliver, and by the frittering away of his time and energy in casual and highly unprofessional seductions and in idle speculations unrelated to everyday realities.

Fitzpiers's interest in transcendental philosophy is treated with obvious irony, his "idealism" implicitly contrasted with the quality of imagination and sensibility revealed in the vulgar theatricality of his declaration to Grace—"The design is for once carried out. Nature has at last recovered her lost union with the Idea!" (154)—and in his susceptibility to the sexual artifice of Felice Charmond:

> He was shown into a room at the top of the staircase, cosily and femininely draped, where by the light of the shaded lamp he saw a woman of elegant figure reclining upon a couch in such a position as not to disturb a pile of magnificent hair on the crown of her head. A deep purple dressing-gown formed an admirable foil to the peculiarly rich brown of her hair-plaits; her left arm, which was naked nearly up to the shoulder, was thrown upwards, and between the fingers of her right hand she held a cigarette, while she idly breathed from her delicately curled lips a thin stream of smoke towards the ceiling. (224)

Hardy has been criticised for taking his portraits of Fitzpiers and Mrs Charmond from "a vulgar fashion plate",[7] yet in this passage the impression of self-conscious quasi-fashionable vulgarity seems precisely relevant. The pose is artificial—it shortly appears

[253]

that Mrs Charmond is as yet only "learning" to smoke (225)—
and its centrepiece, the not-to-be-disturbed "pile of magnificent
hair", has been obtained from poor "deflowered" (20) Marty. In
question here is not simply the quality of Fitzpiers's sensibility, or
of Mrs Charmond's, but a deliberate opposition between the ideal
and the actual, the real and the unreal, the false and the true. Entries in Hardy's notebooks at the time he was writing *The Woodlanders* show him to have been much occupied with the problem
of the nature of reality,[8] especially as it affected the work of the
creative artist, and there are indications of a growing sense of dissatisfaction with the capacity of the novel to encompass the kind of
expressionistic presentation to which he was now feeling his way.

Among several important notes assigned in *Early Life* (232) to
March 4, 1886, is the following:

> Novel-writing as an art cannot go backward. Having reached
> the analytic stage it must transcend it by going still further in
> the same direction. Why not by rendering as visible essences,
> spectres, etc. the abstract thoughts of the analytic school?

Hardy adds that this conception eventually found its realisation
not in his fiction but "through the much more appropriate
medium of poetry", especially in *The Dynasts*. It closely corresponds, however, to the passage in *The Woodlanders* in which
Hardy attempts to educe the real tensions underlying the polite
conversational surface on the occasion of Fitzpiers's first visit to
the Melburys as Grace's acknowledged suitor:

> Whenever the chat over the tea sank into pleasant desultori-
> ness Mr. Melbury broke in with speeches of laboured precision
> on very remote topics, as if he feared to let Fitzpiers's mind dwell
> critically on the subject nearest the hearts of all. In truth a con-
> strained manner was natural enough in Melbury just now, for
> the greatest interest of his life was reaching its crisis. Could the
> real have been beheld instead of the corporeal merely, the
> corner of the room in which he sat would have been filled with
> a form typical of anxious suspense, large-eyed, tight-lipped,
> awaiting the issue. (194–195)

In the image presented here, and in the use of the word "typical", it seems possible to glimpse what Hardy meant by making visible the fundamental truth of a given situation, what another note of March 4, 1886, referred to as "the true realities of life, hitherto called abstractions".[9] Conception and realisation are essentially visual and even pictorial, as in an allegorical or emblematic painting, and it seems once again to be his obsession with visualisation which compels Hardy to approach with disabling literalness a limited problem in technique of the kind which Henry James—in a novel like *The Portrait of a Lady*, written and published a year or so earlier than *The Woodlanders*—could regard as precisely the sort of challenge it was the novelist's business and glory to meet and overcome.

If Hardy was impelled in the direction of *The Dynasts* by a genuine sense of the limitations of the novel form, his long-standing ambition to write poetic drama may have led him to exaggerate the difficulties he encountered in writing fiction. There are, at all events, other anticipations of *The Dynasts* in the pages of *The Woodlanders*. Near the end of the third chapter, in a passage suggestive of the microcosmic function of the Hintock world, the isolation of Winterborne and Marty is described as more apparent than real: "And yet their lonely courses formed no detached design at all, but were part of the pattern in the great web of human doings then weaving in both hemispheres from the White Sea to Cape Horn" (21). The obvious link with *The Dynasts* can perhaps be best made by way of a further note assigned in *Early Life* (232) to March 4, 1886: "The human race to be shown as one great network or tissue which quivers in every part when one point is shaken, like a spider's web if touched." The next sentence of the note—"Abstract realisms to be in the form of Spirits, Spectral figures, etc."—points to the moment at the very end of the novel when Marty speaks her lament for Giles:

As this solitary and silent girl stood there in the moonlight, a straight slim figure, clothed in a plaitless gown, the contours of womanhood so undeveloped as to be scarcely perceptible in her, the marks of poverty and toil effaced by the misty hour, she touched sublimity at points, and looked almost like a being who had rejected with indifference the attribute of sex for the loftier quality of abstract humanism. (443)

If Marty stands out quite explicitly at the last as the representative of "abstract humanism", there is a sense in which she has been throughout the novel not so much a character as a static and symbolic figure resembling the Good and Bad Angels of *Dr Faustus*—or the Spirits of *The Dynasts*.

Marty's role is, of course, crucial to the question of point of view, or of reference, within *The Woodlanders* as a whole. In chapter 3 it is she who overhears the conversation between Melbury and his wife which reveals the likelihood of marriage between Grace Melbury and Giles Winterborne. The dialogue is in itself clumsy, improbably recapitulative of information which might more happily have been dramatised or handled in authorial summary. As in similar episodes in *The Mayor of Casterbridge*, however, Hardy has multiple objectives: he has information to convey about the previous relationship between the Melburys and the Winterbornes; by presenting it through dialogue he can emphasise Melbury's obsession with his daughter and his responsibility, past and present, for the shaping of her life; by making Marty an involuntary eavesdropper he can evoke her suffering at the recognition of the hopelessness of her own position and the consequent mood of abnegation which prompts her to cut off her hair—an action richly symbolic in itself and rich in consequences for the eventual outcome of the novel. Rather like Elizabeth-Jane in *The Mayor of Casterbridge*, Marty is the observer of other scenes in which she is herself emotionally but not actually involved—for instance, the first encounter between Giles and Grace in the market-place at Sherton—and she becomes, again like Elizabeth-Jane, a kind of moral touchstone of her world. Because she is so essentially an observer, because she functions as a chorus figure of a non-comic kind (distinguished thus from the rustics of earlier novels), and because her somewhat delphic utterances seem to carry the stamp of authorial approval, the reader quite naturally accepts Marty's viewpoint, and with it all its implications of distance and spectatorship.

He accepts it the more readily since there is in this novel—unlike its predecessor and its successor—no character with whom he can easily identify, no one who compels attention and sympathy so consistently and so powerfully as do Henchard and Tess. But if the reader stands aside with Marty to watch the working out of the pattern created by the interaction of the four central characters, what is it precisely that Hardy wishes him to observe? What is the work "about"? Because the 1895 Preface deals chiefly with the issue of divorce as it arises in the story, *The Woodlanders* has sometimes been thought of as a prototype social novel, the "purposeful" forerunner of *Tess* and, more especially, *Jude*. It is hard, however, to detect in the novel any great weight of protest against the divorce laws as such, apart from the hint that the rich have always had access to escape-routes closed to the poor. Grace can scarcely be reckoned a victim in her relationship with Fitzpiers. She chooses him under considerable pressure, no doubt, but still with some degree of freedom, and even had she been able to obtain a divorce her life with Giles might not have been an easy one. The combined effect of her birth and her upbringing is to suspend her somewhere between Giles and Fitzpiers, "in mid-air between two storeys of society" (260). If Grace discovers too late that Giles would have been the wiser choice, that is not a social judgment but a realisation under the most immediate kind of stress that Giles is the better man.

Hardy seems to direct his main thrust not against social institutions but towards the manipulation of a tragi-comedy of social and sexual mismatching. *Early Life* (230) records that soon after completing his outline of the plot of *The Woodlanders* Hardy noted in his diary: "a tragedy exhibits a state of things in the life of an individual which unavoidably causes some natural aim or desire of his to end in a catastrophe when carried out." Within *The Woodlanders* itself the comment is relevant to Melbury's desire to educate his daughter for social advancement and to the physical passions which move Fitzpiers; it prompts, however, the question as to whether "tragedy" is not altogether too portentous a term to invoke in this context. If Giles's fate is a sombre one, his final act of self-sacrifice has often been regarded as excessive, as almost comic in its strict observation of the proprieties, and certainly as undercut by Grace's eventual return to Fitzpiers. Yet awareness of the ironies surrounding Giles's death—ironies perceived and emphasised by Hardy himself—should not prevent it from being recognised as an extraordinary act of courage, loyalty, and love.

All the actions which shape Giles's career—not least those which lead to the loss of his cottages—flow inevitably from his character and his economic situation. In *The Woodlanders*, as in *Far from the Madding Crowd*, the persistent emphasis upon social mobility suggests that the hero's economic insecurity and actual business failure may contribute more than has usually been appreciated to the lack of sexual force displayed in his courtship of the heroine. Giles's self-sacrifice is absolutely of a piece with his sense of social inferiority, his remorse at having failed to reveal to Grace his knowledge that she cannot be divorced, and those fundamental inhibitions of character at which Hardy may deliberately have hinted in his surname. "Winterborne" may intrinsically suggest an ill-starred birth, but it is also a common Dorset place-name derived (as Hardy must have known) from the phenomenon of streams which dry up in summer but whose "fountains periodically well up, or 'break', as it is termed, in the winter. The bursting of these springs is, however, always delayed until the occurrence of a gale of wind, however wet the season."[10]

Much of the final chapter, however, is concerned not with contemplation of Giles's death but with speculation about the future married life of Grace and Fitzpiers. Not only here but throughout the novel it could be argued that if that element of the story which centres on Giles is ultimately tragic, that which centres on Fitzpiers is ultimately comic. Fitzpiers is, after all, a somewhat improbable figure. Apart from the gentleman from South Carolina (who seems lost in time as well as space), he is the one real intruder in terms of the novel's setting: the big houses of the countryside must have their inhabitants and Mrs Charmond is reasonably credible in such a role. The convenience of Fitzpiers is that, once his presence is accepted, he becomes a ready instrument for bringing into juxtaposition and interaction the two elements of rural simplicity and urban sophistication. Precisely because Fitzpiers is the odd man out, it is he who precipitates the more violent and striking actions, and it seems worth noting that Hardy once suggested "Fitzpiers at Hintock" as an alternative title for the novel.[11]

Any overall conception of the novel must thus absorb as best it can the occasional episodes of situation comedy and even of what is commonly called "French" farce—notably the "Wives all" scene, in which Grace thinks of Suke Damson and Mrs Charmond as "Petticoat the First and Petticoat the Second of her *Bien-aimé*" (314)—and the rising comic tide which mounts with the stages of the final "reconciliation" between Grace and Fitzpiers. Several of these closing scenes are reminiscent of stage comedy, and the air is heavy with dramatic irony. In one exchange Grace deflates Fitzpiers by catching him in a quotation from *Measure for Measure*, yet goes on a sentence or two later to strike her own pose in a similarly unacknowledged borrowing from *Julius Caesar*: "My heart is in the grave with Giles" (411). Like Antony she is not insincere, yet she manages, as Antony does, to be self-regarding. The scene subtly suggests the degree to which Grace and Fitzpiers are on a level and even of a type: this kind of banter would have been far above the head of poor Giles himself. In a scene of potential horror dissolved into comedy, it is the mantrap which extorts the overheard declaration from Fitzpiers and returns him to the arms of a Grace temporarily bereft of her skirt. Their abrupt departure for Sherton prompts in its turn the conversation in the Sherton public house, a splendidly comic scene whose chief function is to raise conjectures, left deliberately unresolved, as to the character of future relationships between Fitzpiers and Grace.[12]

There is plenty of earthy wisdom on the subject of husbands and wives, some sharp and telling comment about Grace and Fitzpiers themselves, and a strong suggestion that Fitzpiers will soon be unfaithful again. But Mrs Charmond is dead, Suke Damson has left, and there are indications that Grace may now be at least a match for Fitzpiers: her experiences have made her tougher and chastened her feelings for Fitzpiers to perfectly manageable proportions. And so Grace drifts off—inevitably, as it now seems— into the class orbit represented by Fitzpiers and into another part of England, leaving Marty South quite alone to cherish the memory of Giles and those values for which he stood, and to sound a final note of stoical resignation grounded in a despairing estimate of the human condition. In assessing her own condition Marty surely has reasons for despair. She can be self-denying, self-sacrificing, and self-effacing largely because that "self" is so little valued, either by her or by others. Even Giles, who alone treats her with consideration, fails to notice her devotion or even, at times, her very presence. By the end of the novel she has become the repository, the residuary legatee, of all the sorrows of the Hintock world—almost a scapegoat figure (though left behind rather than driven out) whose acceptance of the burden facilitates a renewal of love, however equivocal its terms, on the part of Grace and Fitzpiers.

The ending is tragi-comic. Rather, it is tragic and comic, in contrastive juxtaposition. Hardy seems deliberately to have conceived of both the structure and the meaning of the novel in just such terms. Several years later he told Edmund Gosse that he had envisaged *Jude the Obscure* as composed of a pattern of multiple contrasts,[13] and in *The Woodlanders* he seems already to have been moving in that direction. Within the broad contrast of the comic and the tragic many subordinate contrasts can be picked out: the reviewer in the *Pall Mall Gazette* saw the novel as essentially a "struggle between modern life and old-world customs";[14] other oppositions are those between country and town, poverty and wealth, simplicity and sophistication, truth and dissimulation, devotion and fickleness, inherited wisdom and educated knowledge, skills used and skills unused, the local and the exotic. The novel revolves upon questions of class distinction and division, and upon the contrast between the responsible though inhibiting realism of Giles and the irresponsible, self-indulgent "idealism" of Fitzpiers. These oppositions are well balanced and obviously intentional. At the same time they combine with the open-endedness of the final chapter to confirm the tendency in Hardy's work towards moral ambiguity and narrative irresolution—a tendency perhaps exacerbated at this advanced point in his career by a sense of the conflict between his continuing economic need to write for a magazine public and the growing urgency of his need as an artist to embody comprehensively in works of literature his disturbing vision of the human condition.

Part Five

FULFILMENT

TESS OF THE D'URBERVILLES
Serial: July–December 1891
Published: November 1891

THE WELL-BELOVED
Serial: October–December 1892
Published: March 1897

JUDE THE OBSCURE
Serial: December 1894–November 1895
Published: November 1895

I

Tess of the d'Urbervilles

"Fulfilment" is the title Hardy gave to the last "phase" of *Tess of the d'Urbervilles*, and it seems appropriate to apply it also to the last, most distinguished stage of his own career as a novelist. At no period in that career was Hardy more numerously, variously, or richly productive than during the three years which intervened between the commencement of work on *Tess* in the autumn of 1888 and book publication of the novel in November 1891, and it seems significant both that his most incisive critical essay, "The Science of Fiction", was published in April 1891, and that he told John Lane in June of that year that he had only recently begun to feel confidence in his work.[1] Quite apart from *Tess* itself, unmistakably his finest novel, and two important essays ("Candour in English Fiction" was published in January 1890), Hardy wrote at this time most of the stories subsequently collected in *Life's Little Ironies* (1893); he also collected together and published the volume called *A Group of Noble Dames* (1891).

It seems clear that Hardy liked to conceive of his volumes of stories—and, later, of poems—not as miscellaneous assemblages but as possessing some degree of integration. The stories in *Life's Little Ironies* are linked—if somewhat tenuously—by similarities of theme; those in Hardy's first collection, *Wessex Tales* (1888), have at least their Wessex setting in common; while *A Group of Noble Dames* is organised around the core provided by a meeting of the "South-Wessex Field and Antiquarian Club" (51), at which the stormbound members take turns in telling tales drawn from local "legends and traditions of gentle and noble dames" (50). With a characteristic glance towards the actual, Hardy based the

[263]

club upon the Dorset Natural History and Antiquarian Field Club, of which he was himself a member, and its museum meeting-place upon the Dorset County Museum in Dorchester. Presumably the fact that he had himself delivered a paper before the society modified to some extent the impact of the book's unflattering allusions to the usual topics discussed at such gatherings; that his relations, even so, with some of his fellow-members were not of the happiest kind is suggested by the curious delay in the publication of Hardy's own paper on "Some Romano-British Relics Found at Max Gate, Dorchester", by his refusal to write for the Club an obituary of William Barnes, and by his story "A Tryst at an Ancient Earthwork", said by R. L. Purdy to have been prompted by the activities of a local archaeologist.[2]

But whatever his differences with the committee or with individual members, Hardy's interest in the Club helps both to emphasise and to focus the extent to which he drew in much of his work—in *The Trumpet-Major*, *The Mayor of Casterbridge*, the stories collected in *Wessex Tales*, and now *Tess of the d'Urbervilles*—upon local history and tradition. When, on June 3, 1885, the Club met at Bindon Abbey and went on to visit the Manor House at Wool, Hardy's friend H. J. Moule gave a paper in which he spoke not only of the Turberville connection with Wool Manor (the Wellbridge Manor of *Tess*) but mentioned the legend of the Turberville coach: "none can see the ghostly coach of the Turbervilles but those who have Turberville blood in their veins."[3] A paper on "Dorsetshire Folk-Speech and Superstitions relating to Natural History" by J. S. Udal, another friend and correspondent of Hardy's, was read at a meeting of the Club held in the Dorset County Museum on February 13, 1889; it spoke of the decline of old beliefs "under the civilising influence of compulsory education and the unsympathetic attitude of the Board Schools", and listed many characteristic Dorset superstitions, among them the belief that an afternoon cockcrow (such as occurs when Tess and Angel leave Talbothays) heralded impending sickness or death.[4]

Hardy may, of course, have intended the cockcrow in Tess to carry a sexual connotation, and he may already have known the story of Wool Manor and the Turberville coach.[5] It is not even certain that he attended these particular meetings of the Club—though he could, in any case, have read full reports in the local newspaper and, later, in the Club's printed *Proceedings*. But that *Tess* was largely constructed out of specifically local material there can be no doubt. The opening incident of the novel, Hardy told Norman MacColl, "occurred under my own eyes. I was standing at the street corner of a little town in this county when a tipsy man swaggered past me singing '*I've-got a-great family vault-over at-*' (&c., as in the novel). I enquired of some bystanders, & learnt that all he had sung was quite true—& that he represented one of the oldest of our Norman families. The story grew up from this, supplemented by other facts."[6] Remarkably enough, two of the most sensational episodes in *Tess*—the death of Prince, the Durbeyfield horse, and that other blood-drenched moment when Mrs Brooks of "The Herons" sees the spreading stain on her ceiling—both originated in newspaper reports of actual incidents. Hardy's "Facts" notebook records no less than three stories of night collisions found in old copies of the *Dorset County Chronicle*, and in one of these (imperfectly deleted by Hardy) a waggoner is asleep when the shaft of his vehicle pierces the breast of the lead horse of an oncoming coach.[7] The blood dripping from the ceiling was suggested by a more recent report in the same newspaper of the suicide of an Army officer in an inn on Dartmoor: the cutting, dated in what seems to be Hardy's hand, is glued into a copy of the novel which he presented to Florence Emily Dugdale in 1911.[8] In *The Woodlanders* the accident to Mrs Charmond's carriage as a direct result of the destruction of Giles Winterborne's cottage similarly had its source in a court case of the 1820s which Hardy noted as he read through back files of the local newspaper.[9]

Hardy liked a good story, and his newspaper reading—especially those deliberate forays into the reportage of distant decades which had preceded the writing of *The Trumpet-Major* and *The Mayor of Casterbridge*—must quickly have taught him where to find ready gratification of his taste for the extraordinary, the melodramatic, and even the macabre. He seems always to have believed that fiction must depend largely upon narrative excitement for any claims it might make upon the reader's attention. "A story must be exceptional enough to justify its telling," *Later Years* (15–16) reports him as observing in 1893. "We tale-tellers are all Ancient Mariners, and none of us is warranted in stopping Wedding Guests (in other words, the hurrying public) unless he has something more unusual to relate than the ordinary experience of every average man and woman."[10] At the same time, he liked to insist that a novel like *Tess* was grounded in fact, and he seems to have gone to some trouble to visit or revisit the settings of his novels before re-creating them in fictional form.[11] This was not simply the result of discovering that truth could indeed be stranger than fiction: like Theodore Dreiser after him, he seems to have found a certain reassurance in the verifiability of material drawn directly from the actual world.

No more for Hardy than for Dreiser, however, was reliance on the actual a guarantee of success. In *A Group of Noble Dames* the deliberate recourse to antiquarian sources—specifically, Hutchins's *History and Antiquities of the County of Dorset*[12]—results in stories at best undistinguished, at worst distasteful. What is remarkable in *Tess* is the process by which antiquarian items, newspaper reports, scraps of folk-lore—many of them still identifiable within the fiction—become transmuted into the quintessential material of Hardy's greatest novel. David Lodge has described the book's narrative voice as that of the local historian, speaking of people and events still within living memory,[13] and there are curious hints in the book of information having been collected from such people as Mrs Brooks and the cottager who happened to see Angel and Tess walking desolately in the dark: "It was only on account of his preoccupation with his own affairs, and the illness in his house, that he did not bear in mind the curious incident, which, however, he recalled a long while after" (298). Whether or not it is appropriate to think of the brooding, investigating presence as Hardy himself, it is certainly possible to detect the pressure of a directly personal commitment both in the novel itself—in the reference, for example, to the quality of Tess's voice "which will never be forgotten by those who knew her" (120)—and in Hardy's own comments about it: "I am glad you like Tess [he told a correspondent in October 1891]—though I have not been able to put on paper all that she is, or was, to me."[14] It is hard to know what to make of such remarks. In describing Tess's appearance Hardy seems chiefly to have had in mind the woman he thought the most beautiful in England, the wife of the sculptor Hamo Thornycroft, but it is clear both that his acquaintance with Mrs Thornycroft was of a purely social kind and that his use of her as the inspiration for Tess was an act of idealisation.[15]

The roots of *Tess* lie deeper. Early experiences such as his presence at the execution of Martha Brown[16] may well have made their contribution, and much of the intense compassionateness of the novel can certainly be linked with his own sympathy for the innocently victimised. He once spoke of the profound effect made upon him by his father's story of a boy hanged during the 1830 agricultural riots simply for being near the scene of a rick-burning,[17] and a letter he wrote in 1904 to the Rev. S. W. Key is sufficiently eloquent of his horror of blood-sports:

> I am not sufficiently acquainted with the many varieties of sport to pronounce which is, quantitatively, the most cruel. I can only say generally that the prevalence of those sports which consist in the pleasure of watching a fellow-creature, weaker or less favoured than ourselves, in its struggles, by Nature's poor resources only, to escape the death-agony we mean to inflict by the treacherous contrivances of science, seems one of the many convincing proofs that we have not yet emerged from barbarism.[18]

On November 8, 1891, Hardy wrote to Sir George Douglas: "My neighbours here who own preserves have called to lecture me about the chapter on the *battue* in Tess. Two can lecture about that, however."[19] Hardy had confidence in his facts as well as in his moral position. Indeed, the description of a *battue* which he got from a gamekeeper in January 1882 offers a rare opportunity of seeing his novelist's imagination actually at work upon the raw material of experience: "Can see the night scene [Hardy's note ends]—moon—fluttering and gasping birds as the hours go on— the place being now deserted of humankind."[20] Here, clearly, is the source of the incident in which Tess takes shelter beneath a tree full of pheasants, injured by gunfire and silently dying, and although the scene functions directly within the novel as an image of Tess's situation, the strength of Hardy's feelings about blood-sports almost makes it possible to speak of Tess's plight as dramatising that of the birds.

The theme of Tess's victimisation is enforced throughout the book in terms of scenes and images wholly integrated into the narrative sequence—the cornered animals in the hayfield, the rats in the corn rick, the dying pheasants overhead—and of Tess's geographical wanderings across the face of Wessex, flying like a hunted animal from one refuge to another almost always less satisfactory and safe.[21] At Flintcomb Ash she is surrounded not only by cruelty and oppression, human and climatic, but by people who know different parts of her past and thus represent to her a conscious or unconscious threat. Even in the idyllic days of Angel's courtship Tess is aware of dangers prowling just beyond the circle of light in which she seems so magically to move, and Hardy goes so far as to introduce implicit comparisons with Christ, especially in the analogies between the scene at Stonehenge and the story of Gethsemane.

Such imagery of victimisation forms a central element in what can only be described as Hardy's advocacy of Tess's cause. Elliott Felkin recorded in 1919: "Hardy said of course in writing one had to keep up the immense illusion. In one's heart of hearts one did not of course *really* think one's heroine was as good and pure as all that, but then one was making out a case for her before the world."[22] Hardy apparently learned to regret the sub-title, *A Pure Woman*, which he had added to the first edition of *Tess*: "*Melius fuerat non scribere*," he remarked in the 1912 Preface. Yet he continued, "But there it stands" (xxi). What Hardy regretted was the open declaration of interest, the invitation to controversy, not the interest and advocacy itself. Nothing is more remarkable in the novel than the extraordinary passion with which Tess is described and justified, and the "pure woman" formulation only serves to make explicit what is everywhere implicit—that Tess's personality makes it impossible to accommodate her within any of the conventional categories suggested by the crude facts of her situation and story: the helpless female victim of stage melodrama, the betrayed maiden of the popular moral tract, the seduced country girl of innumerable ballads and anecdotes of oral tradition—like Hardy's ballad of "The Bride-Night Fire" or the story of Jack Dollop within the novel itself.[23]

But if none of these categories proves adequate to contain Tess, none of them is wholly rejected. Like the various economic roles she occupies from time to time—milkmaid, field-hand, family bread-winner, kept woman—they contribute to that multiplicity of lightly invoked frames and patterns against which her situation and conduct are successively measured and evaluated, and to that wider range of referents—mythological, biblical, and literary as well as historical and sociological—by which the implications of her story are at once defined and drawn out. Less obtrusively but more powerfully than in earlier novels, *Tess* resonates with allusions to larger, more universal patterns which lie beyond its own world. Although the account of the Trantridge dance lacks in the novel the title, "Saturday Night in Arcady", under which it was originally published,[24] the couples at the hay-trusser's dance are still described as "satyrs clasping nymphs—a multiplicity of Pans whirling a multiplicity of Syrinxes; Lotis attempting to elude Priapus, and always failing" (77); meanwhile various "Sileni of the throng" (78) sit on benches and hay-trusses nearby. In the vibrant harvest scene of chapter 14 Tess's method of binding corn is evoked with a precision which serves not only to describe the actual conditions of work for "field-women"[25] but also to celebrate Tess herself as the performer of actions at once so ancient, so skilful, so suggestive of natural fecundity—and so precisely suited to her name, said in the standard Victorian work on Christian names to mean "carrying ears of corn" or "the reaper".[26]

The whole scene of sunshine and harvest and productive work —of women who merge perfectly with their setting to become "part and parcel of outdoor nature" (111)—presents a striking image of personal and agricultural health, one which stands contrastively in the background of the dark scene in chapter 47 in which Tess unties the sheaves to feed that "Plutonic" (415)

monster, the threshing machine. The note is struck immediately
by the opening description of the sunrise:

> It was a hazy sunrise in August. The denser nocturnal vap-
> ours, attacked by the warm beams, were dividing and shrinking
> into isolated fleeces within hollows and coverts, where they
> waited till they should be dried away to nothing.
>
> The sun, on account of the mist, had a curious sentient, per-
> sonal look, demanding the masculine pronoun for its adequate
> expression. His present aspect, coupled with the lack of all
> human forms in the scene, explained the old-time heliolatries in
> a moment. One could feel that a saner religion had never pre-
> vailed under the sky. The luminary was a golden-haired,
> beaming, mild-eyed, God-like creature, gazing down in the
> vigour and intentness of youth upon an earth that was brimming
> with interest for him.
>
> His light, a little later, broke through chinks of cottage shut-
> ters, throwing stripes like red-hot pokers upon cupboards,
> chests of drawers, and other furniture within; and awakening
> harvesters who were not already astir. (109)

This invocation of a God-like sun, actively calling country ants to
harvest offices, obviously has its immediate relevance to the rural
episode which follows and to the process of recovery for Tess
which it so powerfully initiates. It stresses the lesson which Tess
herself is learning: "Meanwhile the trees were just as green as
before; the birds sang and the sun shone as clearly now as ever.
The familiar surroundings had not darkened because of her grief,
nor sickened because of her pain" (115). Beyond that, the very
strength and positiveness of the scene, the elaboration of Hardy's
description of the sun, and his deliberate reference to solar myths[27]
("the old-time heliolatries"), all seem to invite consideration in
terms of a larger pattern—as offering, for instance, a specific basis
for that instinctual paganism of Tess's which is opposed in later
stages of the novel to both the crude amoralism of Alec d'Urberville and the cold agnosticism of Angel Clare.

Yet elsewhere in the novel the "Wordsworthian" concept of
nature's healing power is explicitly rejected. Of the helplessness

of the Durbeyfield children Hardy remarks that "some people would like to know whence the poet whose philosophy is in these days deemed as profound and trustworthy as his song is breezy and pure, gets his authority for speaking of 'Nature's holy plan'" (24). Critics from Lionel Johnson onwards have remarked on the inconsistency of the philosophical positions advanced in *Tess*, apparently with authorial authority, and Robert C. Schweik has pointed to the disturbing juxtaposition—in the final paragraphs of chapter 13, immediately preceding the sunrise of chapter 14—of a quasi-Berkeleyan assertion that "the world is only a psychological phenomenon" with the apparently antithetical comment that Tess's sense of guilt was "out of harmony with the actual world" (108).[28] It seems clear, in fact, that Hardy's philosophical formulations—like his allusions, however elaborate, and his "set-piece" descriptions, however extended—are not to be regarded as focal points of the novel, as encapsulated moments of vision which radiate clarification into remote corners of the fiction. They are not, that is to say, genuinely thematic, integrated elements in an articulated pattern of statement and implication, but serve rather as notations of the immediate context, pointing up and intensifying, in a quite limited way, the effects being sought in a particular scene or chapter.

They operate, in fact, rather in the manner of Hardy's famous coincidences—almost as metaphors for the emotions or motivations of the characters. When Tess pushes her letter to Angel under the door it is both credible and characteristic—of Tess as of Hardy—that it should go beneath the carpet: it is "in her haste" (269) that she has so thrust it, and if any aspect in the presentation of Tess has been insisted upon throughout the novel it is that "slight incautiousness of character inherited from her race" (114) ominously referred to even amidst the hopeful surroundings of the harvest field. The hand of fate, destiny, or even of the President of the Immortals does not seem unduly heavy here, any more than in the accident with the mail cart which kills Prince: though shocking in its violence and in its results, the collision itself—given the darkness, Tess's natural weariness, and the mail cart's rubber wheels—is explicable enough. The careers of Hardy's characters, indeed, the accidents that befall them, are rarely if ever a product of the random inexplicable intrusion of fate but rather the inevitable—or at least, credible—outcome of the immediate narrative context and of their own personalities as conditioned and limited by the forces of heredity and environment.[29] It was in *The Mayor of Casterbridge* that Hardy specifically evoked the concept of character as fate, but it seems no less valid for his other mature fiction.

Tess, it has often been pointed out, is not a psychological novel in the sense understood and practised by George Eliot and Henry James. It does offer, however, a continuous and remarkably precise record of Tess's mental condition, and a sharp if less developed sense of the thoughts and feelings of other characters, at least at the moment when their lives impinge most nearly upon Tess's own career. This perception of internal states is only partly achieved by direct analysis, or even by the dramatised revelations of dialogue. More important and more powerful than either of these is the externalisation of emotional states in terms of the particular colouring given to the accounts of the places Tess inhabits, the work she does, the people she encounters, the treatment she receives, the natural and climatic conditions she experiences. The emotional is evoked and recorded in terms of the sensory. The constant disturbance of the narrative surface reflects the intensity of Tess's own internal life.

Ian Gregor, in a fine essay on *Tess*, speaks of the way in which "at every stage of the tale interior states are visualized in terms of landscape".[30] Irving Howe has more recently compared the novel to *Pilgrim's Progress* in that its structure is "that of a journey in which each place of rest becomes a test for the soul and the function of plot is largely to serve as an agency for transporting the central figure from one point to another".[31] Both insights are relevant: the chief locations of the novel serve both as testing places for Tess and as expressions of her states of mind. Even the names of places—Marlott, the Valley of the Great Dairies, Flintcomb Ash—seem freighted with significances both experiential and moral. Alec d'Urberville's home, "The Slopes", is aggressively modern and bright: "Everything looked like money—like the last coin issued from the Mint" (43).[32] It is clear from maps he drew that Hardy was extremely conscious of the journeying aspects of Tess's career, and not only do possible allusions to *Pilgrim's Progress* occur in the course of the novel—Dairyman Crick's wife is called Christiana, for example, the Trantridge villagers on their visit to the fair and market at Chaseborough are referred to as "pilgrims" (76)—but a pattern of pilgrimage seems to govern the book as a whole. As in *Pilgrim's Progress* the physical experience of walking through the countryside is very faithfully evoked, and like Christian (or Christiana) Tess encounters and re-encounters many other pedestrians who both relate immediately to her and yet possess a more generalised significance: the text-painter, the man who knows of her Trantridge past, the change-able shape of Alec d'Urberville himself.

Tess's tragedy is that her pilgrimage has no possible goal. It is true that some of the profuse paradisal imagery creates a sense of Tess herself as an earthly paradise capable of surviving the discovery of the tree of knowledge, and such a feeling certainly pervades the Talbothays chapters and the heavily charged and almost magical atmosphere of the days spent with Angel in the empty house. Yet despite that eventual satisfaction of the "appetite for joy" (244) and the sacrificial apotheosis at Stonehenge, Tess's terrestrial journey ends on the scaffold, and in the final pages images from *Pilgrim's Progress* blend with others from *Paradise Lost* as Angel and Liza-Lu emerge "through a narrow barred wicket" (506) and set off, with bowed heads and joined hands, as if on a fresh attempt to arrive at the Celestial City. *Tess* is not allegory. Its allusions, like its philosophical formulations, are unlikely to carry relevance for more than their immediate context. At the same time, the allegorical landscape of Bunyan's work and its population of moral types seem not impossibly remote from symbolic landscapes such as those of Talbothays, Flintcomb Ash, and Stonehenge, or from characters called Mercy Chant, Sorrow, and Angel Clare—"who but Hardy," asks Dorothy Van Ghent, "would have dared to give him the name Angel, and a harp too?"[33]

As in *Pilgrim's Progress* so in *Tess*, the significance embodied in places and in people emerges all the more powerfully and believably from their location within a concretely realised fictional world. Indeed, the richness and sheer solidity of Hardy's creation both of this rural setting and of Tess's situation—her controlling environment of work and social victimisation, of agricultural economics and the English class system—enables him to venture upon further expressionistic techniques. Despite the heavy rurality of her surname (Durbeyfield) and the deliberately "pastoral" Christian names (John and Joan) of her parents, Tess's immediate family situation is fairly consistently presented in realistic terms, with a conscientious concern for the actual conditions of rural life and for the precise quality of the human relationships involved: the character and attitudes of Joan Durbeyfield, for example, are developed with some amplitude and given an important role in the novel as a whole. But Hardy does not hesitate to exaggerate the characterisation of the members of Angel Clare's family circle, while Alec d'Urberville and his mother are often treated with a degree of caricature which verges on the grotesque. To some extent such distortion may image Tess's own view of people and manners previously outside her experience, and there is also the obvious element of contrast between those examples of emotional rigidity—even Angel Clare's parents cannot accept with natural spontaneity the gifts sent by Mrs Crick—and the atmosphere of uncritical acceptance which pervades Tess's own background. But the Durbeyfield household—in its casual irresponsibility and general fecklessness a doubtful representative of "the agricultural community"—is itself portrayed in highly critical terms, and one aspect of the novel is clearly its concern with the failure of human relationships within all the family groups and with the repeated efforts of Tess herself to create and sustain a basic family unit of a more viable kind. In view of Tess's remarks shortly before her capture, the closing description of Angel hand in hand with Liza-Lu can be seen as representing her final gesture, and perhaps achievement, in this direction.

When Tess is living with Alec, at Trantridge and Sandbourne, the emphasis is on luxurious artificiality: the villa at Sandbourne, indeed, that "Mediterranean lounging-place on the English Channel" (480), bears a striking resemblance to the white Mediterranean villa with which Rochester tries to tempt Jane Eyre to a similar surrender. Tess's marriage with Angel, on the other hand, is associated with sterility and unnaturalness. The honeymoon becomes funereal, the mistletoe bough withers unused, the symbols of domesticity lose all their positive force:

> But the complexion even of external things seemed to suffer transmutation as her announcement progressed. The fire in the grate looked impish—demoniacally funny, as if it did not care in the least about her strait. The fender grinned idly, as if it too did not care. The light from the water-bottle was merely engaged in a chromatic problem. All material objects around announced their irresponsibility with terrible iteration. (291)

If Tess is trapped by the fatalities of her heredity and environment,[34] she is equally caught between the contrasted personalities of the two men—both superior to her in class, wealth, and education—who dominate her life. If Alec now and then suggests the unchastened Rochester, Angel sometimes echoes the principled inhumanity of St John Rivers—though it is Alec, ironically enough, during the period of his conversion, who begs Tess to become his partner in a missionary enterprise, while Angel permits himself to make a brutally frank proposal to Izz Huett. Hardy probably did not have *Jane Eyre* specifically in mind, but the double inversion of role for Alec and Angel is deliberate enough, constituting one element in a pattern of opposition which runs throughout the novel.

The basic norms from which Alec and Angel thus momentarily depart can perhaps be crudely identified in terms of the polar opposites of "Paganism" and "Paulinism" which Hardy invokes in his description of Alec's conversion (390). Alec adopts Paulinism for a while, but his basic creed is closer to "animalism" (390). Angel affects to have revolted against the Paulinism of his temperament and upbringing, but at the crisis of his relationship with Tess he proves to be still its slave. Soon after Tess's revelation to Angel she is presented as a personification of "Apostolic Charity" who "sought not her own; was not provoked; thought no evil of his treatment of her" (308-309).[35] The ironic allusion is to St Paul's own words in the thirteenth chapter of the first epistle to the Corinthians, and Hardy may well have intended to prompt recollection of the famous opening verse of that chapter: "Though I speak with the tongues of men and of angels, and have not charity, I am become as sounding brass, or a tinkling cymbal." It is Angel himself—quoting the first epistle to Timothy (4.12)— who first invokes the word "charity" just before the exchange of confessions with Tess (286), yet in practice he proves to be, even in a conventional sense, much less charitable than Alec himself, who does at least take pains to improve the material circumstances of Tess and her family.

Angel's rigidity and lack of charity constitute the terrible flaw in a man who seems—if only because Tess loves him with such unquestioning fervency—to possess unusual potentialities for goodness and right action. Little enough can be expected of Alec after his first introduction as the typical villain of melodrama, and in some ways he turns out better than anticipated. Angel, for all his obvious superiority to Alec, does even greater damage to Tess, and it is made clear—from the emphasis on his resolute and un-natural resistance to Tess's beauty—that he could have done with a little of Alec's unreflecting animality:

> Tess stole a glance at her husband. He was pale, even trem-ulous; but, as before, she was appalled by the determination revealed in the depths of this gentle being she had married— the will to subdue the grosser to the subtler emotion, the sub-stance to the conception, the flesh to the spirit. Propensities, tendencies, habits, were as dead leaves upon the tyrannous wind of his imaginative ascendency. (313)

If Alec sacrifices Tess to his lust, Angel sacrifices her to his theory of womanly purity. The one obeys a natural law, the other a social law, and Hardy has no hesitation in assigning to the latter the greater blame. Angel is saved from utter condemnation by the quasi-redemptive effect of his own sufferings in Brazil and by the transforming power of Tess's love during their brief period of ecstasy, made magical by Tess's serenity and by their strange sus-pension within a kind of social and moral vacuum, itself directly symbolised by the empty house. Even at this point in the novel, however, when the moral Angel has abandoned himself to the power of Tess's love and will—despite the knowledge that she is now adultress and murderer as well as maiden seduced—he still cannot free himself from dogma: when Tess urges him to marry Liza-Lu, he can only object that she is his sister-in-law; when Tess, like Hester Prynne in *The Scarlet Letter*, begs to be allowed to hope for the reunion of lovers after death, he, like Dimmesdale, remains silent. Angel's humanity fails him in these passages, and it receives a proper rebuke in those final words of Tess herself which reveal a love so profound as to comprehend a clear-sighted recognition of the beloved's inadequacies and of what must inevitably have followed a descent from magical suspension into social actuality:[36]

'What is it, Angel?' she said, starting up. 'Have they come for me?'

'Yes, dearest,' he said. 'They have come.'

'It is as it should be,' she murmured. 'Angel, I am almost glad—yes, glad! This happiness could not have lasted. It was too much. I have had enough; and now I shall not live for you to despise me!'

She stood up, shook herself, and went forward, neither of the men having moved.

'I am ready,' she said quietly. (505)

Alec and Angel between them leave Tess so devastated in mind and spirit that Angel, returning "too late" to find her installed in the lodging house as Alec's mistress, realises "that his original Tess had spiritually ceased to recognize the body before him as hers—allowing it to drift, like a corpse upon the current, in a direction dissociated from its living will" (484). The moment has been prepared for by Tess's earlier talk of separating soul from body. Coming at this point in the novel it serves as a moving image of Tess's whole tragedy—the recalcitrance of circumstance to the most refined aspirations of the human spirit, the most passionate imperatives of the human emotions. Against the coarse animalism of Alec and the sterile intellectualism of Angel—alike inhuman, life-denying, destructive of the individual—Tess can muster only the forces of that generous and spontaneous "naturalism" so richly evoked in the harvest episode and elsewhere. She can offer, in fact, only the passive defence which comes from sheer instinctual resilience, a quality akin to that "endurance" which Faulkner attributed to his rural poor.

There are many aspects of *Tess* which seem to look forward to Faulkner, and particularly to what Cleanth Brooks has described as the nature poetry of *The Hamlet*:[37] the idyllic aspects of Ike's love for the cow, for example, might well have been suggested by the lush summer evocation of Angel's courtship of Tess in the meadows near Talbothays dairy. Faulkner also resembles Hardy in his readiness to exploit literary and legendary allusions for local rather than structural purposes, and in his capacity to retain, even during the most ecstatic merging of natural description with emotional fervour, a firm grasp on actuality, on the irreducible conditions of rural existence. In Lawrence—whose debt to Hardy and especially to *Tess* he himself was only the first to remark— there is a tendency for the world of tangible objects to become progressively swept away by the rising emotional tide: in the scene in *The Rainbow* in which Will and Anna stook the sheaves of wheat the rhythm of their work becomes, is absorbed wholly into, the rhythm of their sexual passion. In Hardy, as in Faulkner, the merging never becomes quite so complete. His novels constitute a kind of peaceable kingdom of the imagination, capable of accommodating as discrete yet interconnected elements both the emotion and the natural or climatic phenomenon which prompts or reflects it, the emblem and the concrete presentation, the narrative quirk and the thread of the thematic pattern. His method is not to blend together the disparate constituents of the fiction but to leave them—individual, identifiable—in permanent suspension. If there is incongruity, Hardy himself is not disturbed by it. He takes, indeed, a curious satisfaction in touches of the macabre, in inversions of situation or role, in life's little ironies. In *Tess*, because the unity of the work radiates so strongly from the profoundly apprehended and powerfully created central figure, and from a richly evoked sense of the Wessex world in which she moves, the fictional structure can accommodate an extraordinary diversity of narrative and descriptive modes, from the theatrical to the poetic, without danger of fragmentation.

This technique of multiple juxtaposition produces unusual richness of texture. It also permits Hardy to establish a pattern of constant reverberation to and fro within the world of the novel. This is not merely a question of "prefigurations" such as the death of Prince and Tess's pricked chin, or of early thematic statements—such as Parson Tringham's "our impulses are too strong for our judgment sometimes" (5)—whose full force is only appreciated at a later stage. It is rather a method of constantly recalling crucial moments of the action in such a way as to keep those moments alive in the reader's mind. The sight of Tess on the altar at Stonehenge looks back to Alec on the d'Urberville tomb and beyond that to Angel laying Tess in the abbot's tomb. Angel finding Tess in her dressing-gown at Sandbourne recalls the time, equally rich in sexual overtones, when he returned to Talbothays to meet her descending fresh from sleep. The recollection twists the knife of regret, of what might have been. Moments of prefiguration become, at a later stage in the narrative, points for retrospective reference, heightening the emotional intensity of each successive crisis, keeping the past continuously alive for the reader as it is always so cruelly alive for Tess herself. At the time of her marriage to Angel, the signs of ill omen—occasions for recalling the bitter past, allusions to d'Urberville family history—build up like a tidal wave about to sweep her away. The anguish inseparable from any sympathetic reading of the novel is largely extorted by this acute and immediate sense of the pressures bearing so relentlessly upon Tess at each of her moments of decision—pressures almost physical in their immediacy, as if she were always on the threshing machine. We see her determined not to give in, yet knowing—as we also know and feel—that in the end she must, that there will come a point where further resistance is unbearable.

Tess may be essentially the victim, and we may from an early stage feel that she is doomed, if only because of what myths and ballads and melodramas have taught us to anticipate as the life pattern of seduced country maidens. But Hardy makes clear that

Tess herself has choices to make, even though they can only lead her into worse difficulties. She is not entirely helpless in the grip of a mechanistic universe, and a less passive, more self-confident character might have found avenues of escape not discovered by Tess herself. In handling the question of Tess's ultimate responsibility for her most decisive acts—the sexual surrender to Alec, the failure to confess to Angel, the second surrender to Alec, the murder—Hardy achieves an entirely valid ambiguity. He nowhere suggests that Tess is *right* to do these things, and he metes out to her, in terms of mental suffering and the final legalised execution, punishment enough to satisfy the sternest moralist. Yet his compassionate presentation of Tess makes it impossible to make attribution of responsibility co-extensive with assignment of blame, especially since the avoidance of analysis in favour of dramatic and expressionistic techniques forces the reader to an extraordinary degree of participation in Tess's career.

With a restraint that is eloquent of artistic maturity, Hardy does not present the actual moments of surrender or crisis: the seduction on the Chase, the subsequent period of co-habitation, the telling of her story to Angel, the murder at "The Herons". Faulkner once said of *The Sound and the Fury* that it seemed more "passionate" not to present his heroine directly;[38] in *Tess* the important elements in Tess's crises are precisely the pressures she experiences, and once we see these as irresistible we need see no more. It is, in this respect, a marvellous touch of Hardy's to present the murder as if through the uninvolved, commonplace eyes of Mrs Brooks, the Sandbourne landlady, and in terms which suggest a lurid newspaper report, or evidence given at Tess's trial. Tess's career, so Hardy seems to insist, can be made to fit many stereotypes, from ballad maiden-no-more and melodrama victim-heroine to "the woman" in a sordid domestic "tragedy"; yet she evades all such restrictive social classifications to emerge at the end of the novel as a figure at once representative and individual whose evident sexuality in no way compromises that triumphant purity which Hardy's sub-title so properly, if polemically, asserts.

2

Candour in English Fiction

In June 1891, less than six months before the appearance of *Tess of the d'Urbervilles*, Hardy published what is perhaps the least engaging of his books, the volume of connected short stories called *A Group of Noble Dames*. Interest in the work has particularly centred on that grotesque narrative of mutilation, "Barbara of the House of Grebe", much criticised by contemporary reviewers[1] and subsequently made the subject of hostile comment by George Moore (in *Conversations in Ebury Street*) and T. S. Eliot (in *After Strange Gods*). Yet when Hardy had his difficulties with the *Graphic* prior to publication of six of the "Noble Dames" in its Christmas Number for 1890, it was not to this story that objection seems to have been made but to two stories which revolved upon the illegitimate offspring of members of the aristocracy: the issue was joined not on a question of taste or (to use Eliot's terminology) of wholesomeness[2] but on a technical point of conventional morality. It is perhaps not surprising that the manuscript of one of the offending stories, "Squire Petrick's Lady", should still preserve Hardy's angry references to deletions made "solely on account of the tyranny of Mrs. Grundy", or that Hardy, who seems most to have cherished what others had most criticised, should have particularly recommended "Squire Petrick's Lady" when sending a copy of the book to his friend Edward Clodd.[3]

Hardy's irritation with the baleful presence he identified as Grundyism had earlier found overt expression in the essay, "Candour in English Fiction", published in the *New Review* for January 1890:

It is in the self-consciousness engendered by interference with spontaneity, and in aims at a compromise to square with circumstances, that the real secret lies of the charlatanry pervading so much of English fiction. It may be urged that abundance of great and profound novels might be written which should require no compromising, contain not an episode deemed questionable by prudes. This I venture to doubt. In a ramification of the profounder passions the treatment of which makes the great style, something "unsuitable" is sure to arise; and then comes the struggle with the literary conscience. The opening scenes of the would-be great story may, in a rash moment, have been printed in some popular magazine before the remainder is written; as it advances month by month the situations develop, and the writer asks himself, what will his characters do next? What would probably happen to them, given such beginnings? On his life and conscience, though he had not foreseen the thing, only one event could possibly happen, and that therefore he should narrate, as he calls himself a faithful artist. But, though pointing a fine moral, it is just one of those issues which are not to be mentioned in respectable magazines and select libraries. The dilemma then confronts him, he must either whip and scourge those characters into doing something contrary to their natures, to produce the spurious effect of their being in harmony with social forms and ordinances, or, by leaving them too alone to act as they will, he must bring down the thunders of respectability upon his head, not to say ruin his editor, his publisher, and himself.

What he often does, indeed can scarcely help doing in such a strait, is, belie his literary conscience, do despite to his best imaginative instincts by arranging a *dénouement* which he knows to be indescribably unreal and meretricious, but dear to the Grundyist and subscriber. If the true artist ever weeps it probably is then, when he first discovers the fearful price that he has to pay for the privilege of writing in the English language— no less a price than the complete extinction, in the mind of every mature and penetrating reader, of sympathetic belief in his personages.[4]

This is an argument to which objections might be made both in general and in detail, not least because it addresses itself entirely to the case of the serial story whose development has been inadequately planned in advance of publication of the first instalment. Even so, neither Hardy's sense of persecution nor his decision to protest were without justification. He had encountered difficulties with *Two on a Tower* and even with *Far from the Madding Crowd*. Leslie Stephen had balked at *The Return of the Native*, whose conclusion, so Hardy later claimed, had been weakened to conform with contemporary taste. Even a story like "The Distracted Preacher" had been given a respectable ending at odds with both artistic and literal truth,[5] while a note (dated 1927) in Hardy's own copy of *A Changed Man* suggests that a somewhat similar fate had befallen "The Romantic Adventures of a Milkmaid":

> Note: The foregoing finish of the Milkmaid's adventures by a re-union with her husband was adopted to suit the requirements of the summer number of a periodical in which the story was first printed. But it is well to inform readers that the ending originally sketched was a different one, Margery, instead of returning to Jim, disappearing with the Baron in his yacht at Idmouth after his final proposal to her, & being no more heard of in England.[6]

Especially frustrating had been his recent series of encounters with editors during the long pre-publication history of *Tess of the d'Urbervilles*. *Tess* was originally intended for publication by Tillotson's newspaper syndicate, but after Hardy had submitted about half of the story in late August 1889 he received a request for deletions and revisions more drastic than he was prepared to contemplate. The agreement with Tillotson's was eventually cancelled, in circumstances fully documented by R. L. Purdy, and Hardy was forced to look for another publisher.[7] He sent the manuscript first to *Murray's Magazine*, but the editor, Edward Arnold, rejected it in a letter of November 15, 1889:

> I have now finished the perusal of the M.S. you sent me, and have also consulted Mr. Murray on the subject, and we are

agreed that the story, powerful though it be, is not, in our opinion, well adapted for publication in this Magazine.

When I had the pleasure of seeing you here some time ago, I told you my views about publishing stories where the plot involves frequent and detailed reference to immoral situations; I know well enough that these tragedies are being played out every day in our midst, but I believe the less publicity they have the better, and that it is quite possible and very desirable for women to grow up & pass through life without the knowledge of them. I know your views are different, and I honour your motive which is, as you told me, to spare many girls the misery of unhappy marriages made in ignorance of how wicked men can be. But since I dissent from that view, I feel bound to take my own course in regard to the Magazine.[8]

Arnold's letter, though scarcely satisfactory to Hardy, was nonetheless an honest and entirely straightforward statement of a particular point of view. Hardy's exchanges with Mowbray Morris, the editor of *Macmillan's Magazine*, were both more complex and less congenial.

Hardy and Morris had encountered each other three years earlier, when Morris had insisted upon a number of minor bowdlerisations being made to the serial text of *The Woodlanders*, then appearing in *Macmillan's*;[9] now, on November 25, 1889, he refused altogether to accept *Tess* for serialisation. His letter, like Arnold's, deserves quotation as a characteristic document of its period:

I have now read your manuscript—read it always with interest & often with pleasure. The rural scenes seem to me particularly good—more so than the "entirely modern bearings" &c. I cannot think there should be any theological offence in it. The amateur baptism might perhaps startle some good souls; but there is nothing that can in reason be called irreverent, for poor Tess was obviously in very sober earnestness.

But there are other things which might give offence, &, as I must frankly own to think, not altogether unreasonably. Of course, you will understand that I write only of the fitness of the story for my magazine, beyond which I have neither the right nor the wish to go. My objection is of the same nature as I found myself obliged, you may remember, to make occasionally to the Woodlanders. It is not easy for me to frame it in precise words, as it is general rather than particular. Perhaps an instance or two may explain my meaning. It is obvious from the first page what is to be Tess's fate at Trantridge; it is apparently obvious also to the mother, who does not seem to mind, consoling herself with the somewhat cynical reflection that she may be made a lady *after* if not *before*. All the first part therefore is a sort of prologue to the girl's seduction which is hardly ever, & can hardly ever be out of the reader's mind. Even Angel Clare, who seems inclined to "make an honest woman" of Tess, has not as yet got beyond a purely sensuous admiration for her person. Tess herself does not appear to have any feelings of this sort about her; but her capacity for stirring & by implication for gratifying these feelings for others is pressed rather more frequently & elaborately than strikes me as altogether convenient, at any rate for my magazine. You use the word *succulent* more than once to describe the general appearance & condition of the Frome Valley. Perhaps I might say that the general impression left on me by reading your story—so far as it has gone —is one of rather too much succulence. All this, I know, makes the story "entirely modern", & will therefore, I have no doubt, bring it plenty of praise. I must confess, however, to being rather too old-fashioned—as I suppose I must call it—to quite relish the entirely modern style of fiction.

There is one other criticism I am tempted to make. It seems to me that a story dealing almost entirely with country life & people is the better served by being written in as simple, clear, straightforward a style as possible. There are some passages in your manuscript where neither the thought nor the language is very clear to me; & words sometimes of which I am not sure that I understand the meaning. This you will doubtless say, & possibly with justice, is my stupidity. But you also sometimes use words which do not seem to me English at all. *Venust*, for example, on p.214. The meaning is clear enough, of course;

but surely the word is no English one. Surely one might as well say of a brave man that he was *fort*, or of a learned man that he was *doct*, as of a pretty woman that she was *venust*.

I hope that I shall not seem to have said too much, or to have said it discourteously. You asked for my frank opinion, & I have tried to give it with no unnecessary frankness, but yet to give it.

I make no doubt that your story will find many admirers, & certainly noone can deny its cleverness; but I have also no doubt that it would be unwise for me to publish it in my magazine.[10]

Morris's profound revulsion from the book's sexuality is evident throughout: in objecting to "venust" on etymological grounds he is implicitly protesting against everything it implies, especially in terms of what Tess herself is and represents. It must, however, be said for Morris here that his objections to the novel are acknowledged as personal, not blamed entirely on the readership of *Macmillan's Magazine* as they had been in an earlier letter about *The Woodlanders*: "I am not afraid (as you may imagine) for my own morals: but we have, I fancy, rather a queer public: pious Scottish souls who take offence wondrous easily. Already, in my short editorial career, I have received a Round Robin concerning some offence against morality that had been smelled out in our pages! . . . Of course it is very annoying to have to reckon for such asses; still, I can't help it; an editor must be commercial as well as literary; and the magazine has scarcely so abundant a sale that I can afford to disregard any section of its readers."[11] According to *Early Life* (290–291), it was following Morris's rejection of *Tess* that Hardy determined to remove entirely from the novel those sections most likely to give offence, carry out a thorough bowdlerisation of the remainder, and offer it for serial publication in that emasculated form. It was thus accepted by the *Graphic* for weekly serialisation between June and December 1891, while two deleted sections, "The Midnight Baptism" and "Saturday Night in Arcady", were separately published in other journals in May and November 1891.[12]

Hardy had not, however, heard the last of Mowbray Morris. In February 1890 he contributed to *Macmillan's* an editorial strongly attacking the views which Hardy had expressed in his "Candour in English Fiction" article the previous month.[13] Two years later, in April 1892, he wrote an anonymous and peculiarly offensive review of *Tess* for the *Quarterly Review*, not only condemning the book itself as "this clumsy sordid tale of boorish brutality and lust" but returning to Hardy's arguments in "Candour in English Fiction" in order to dismiss them as "pure cant", quite inadequate to justify "a novelist who, in his own interests, has gratuitously chosen to tell a coarse and disagreeable story in a coarse and disagreeable manner". Some of the objections he had made in his letter to Hardy now reappear, and in less delicate form: Hardy is too fond "of making experiments in a form of language which he does not seem clearly to understand, and in a style for which he was assuredly not born"; "Poor Tess's sensual qualifications for the part of heroine are paraded over and over again with a persistence like that of a horse-dealer egging on some wavering customer to a deal, or a slave-dealer appraising his wares to some full-blooded pasha. . . . From first to last his book recalls the terrible sentence passed by Wordsworth on 'Wilhelm Meister': 'It is like the crossing of flies in the air.' "[4]

It was, in the circumstances, a particularly savage stroke of Morris's to mock the "queer manner" in which the story had been published following Hardy's dismemberment of his manuscript: "Putting the sense of the ridiculous and the sense of self-respect out of the question, one might have thought that a writer who entertains such grandiose views of the mission of the novelist would see something derogatory in this hole-and-corner form of publication."[15] Hardy could only have fully appreciated the bitter irony of this had he been able to discover who had written the review. But his reaction was, in any case, strong and predictable. As *Later Years* (7) makes clear, it was the review in the *Quarterly*, read on Good Friday, 1891, which prompted Hardy to remark: "Well, if this sort of thing continues no more novel-writing for me. A man must be a fool to deliberately stand up to be shot at." It appears from the surviving typescript of the "Life" that the brief published comments on the article ("it is easy to be smart and amusing if a man will forgo veracity and sincerity") were at one time supplemented by more than a paragraph of sardonic commentary on critics in general and the *Quarterly* critic in particular.[16] These and similar deletions from *Later Years* were judiciously made. Hardy's reputation could not have benefited from further exposure of his sensitivity and insecurity in the face of obviously misrepresentational criticism, and if it is impossible not to feel sympathy with the sense of opposition and even persecution he must have felt, it is equally difficult not to feel that he protests too much, even in the considered paragraphs of "Candour in English Fiction".

Victorian editors may have been excessively cautious, but, as Leslie Stephen had told Hardy long before, their situation was not without its difficulties.[17] Mowbray Morris had no doubt received just such a "Round Robin" as he mentioned to Hardy, and he could probably have pointed to letters of protest about *The Woodlanders* itself besides the one received from The Vicarage, Crewkerne, in April 1887:

> I fear you will think I am taking a liberty, but I cannot forbear expressing the regret felt by myself and other mothers that you should have admitted such a story as *The Woodlanders* into your *Magazine*. We have hitherto felt that *Macmillan's* might be put without any hesitation into the hands of our daughters, and it has been with both surprise and sorrow that I have seen such a story in it. I feel sure that it must have been through some oversight that this has happened.
>
> A story which can hinge on conjugal infidelity, can describe coarse flirtations, and can end in pronouncing a married woman's avowed lover to be a 'good man who did good things', is certainly not fit to be printed in a high-toned periodical and to be put into the hands of pure-minded English girls. I regret much having to make this protest but I cannot apologize for doing so.[18]

It seems nonetheless remarkable that Hardy should have experienced his greatest difficulties—including the radical recasting for serialisation of both *Tess* and *Jude*—at a moment when, as Joseph Warren Beach long ago pointed out, such authors as Ibsen, George Moore, and Oscar Wilde had already begun to make their various impacts, and when Meredith was "treating, with a cool assurance far from puritan, situations very far from 'proper' ".[19]

It is extraordinarily difficult to determine Hardy's precise position in relation to either the notoriously restrictive conditions of serial publication or the possibilities of greater freedom inherent in changing tastes and attitudes, at least among the *avant-garde*. His statements on such questions tend to be curiously evasive— perhaps deliberately so, perhaps because he remained genuinely incapable of anticipating the effect of his writings on readers less "advanced" than himself. In July 1890, for example, he wrote to protest against the review of *A Group of Noble Dames* in the *Pall Mall Gazette*, and especially against its objections to "Barbara of the House of Grebe":

On reading your notice of "A Group of Noble Dames," I confess to a feeling of surprise that the critic of a paper which I had imagined to possess a certain virility should be shocked at the mere tale of a mutilated piece of marble, seeing what we have had of late years in mutilations and bloody bones, both fictitious and real. I have almost concluded that the *Pall Mall* reviewer must be a highly sensitive and beautiful young lady, who herself nourishes an unhappy attachment to a gentleman in some such circumstances as those of the story. If so, I admit that I have treated her ready imagination rudely; if not so, there must be something unusual in the telling of the story. This can hardly be the case, since to guard against the infliction of "a hideous and hateful fantasy," as you call it, the action is thrown back into a second plane or middle distance, being described by a character to characters, and not point-blank by author to reader. But supposing "Barbara of the House of Grebe" to be indeed a grisly narrative. A good horror has its place in art. Shall we, for instance, condemn "Alonzo the Brave"? For my part I would not give up a single worm of his skull. With respect to the dames generally, I can assure you that these tales were fairly tested before they were offered to the genteel public. They have been read aloud by me, or told in drawing-rooms to ladies whose names, if I were to give them, would be a sufficient guarantee of their trustworthiness in ethical judgments; and the listeners were unanimous in recognizing no harm. To a modest query of my own concerning possible criticism they replied brusquely, "Critics don't know." I hope that opinion may be true for once of the *Pall Mall* critic in his estimate of "Barbara"—the particular dame's history censured.[20]

The jocularity of tone is apparently strategic rather than intrinsic, and Hardy's arguments deserve examination. Unfortunately—as the reviewer had no difficulty in demonstrating in a lively reply published on the same page—they are of a somewhat specious kind. The appeal to the friendly judgment of (to quote the 1896 Preface to the book) "several bright-eyed Noble Dames yet in the flesh" (vii) seems both affected and inept, an embarrassing attempt to "pull rank". And although it may be of considerable technical interest that Hardy should speak of the action of "Barbara of the House of Grebe" as being "thrown back into a second plane or middle distance" by the formal intervention of a secondary narrator, it is difficult to refute the reviewer's argument that this "aesthetic nicety" does little if anything to modify the impact of the story's horrific details: "If Mr. Hardy suggests a hateful picture to the imagination, it is none the less hateful because the machinery he uses happens to be more or less old-fashioned and inartistic." Nor does the invocation of *Alonzo the Brave* entirely remove one's sense of discomfort at the peculiar perversity, not to say perversion, of Hardy's tale.

Hardy's disingenuousness in countering charges of plagiarism has been noted by Carl J. Weber, while R. L. Purdy has similarly commented on a public statement Hardy made about the reasons for Tillotson's rejection of *Tess*.[21] Reference has already been made within the present study to Hardy's questionable response to criticisms of *Two on a Tower*, and it is notable that in his letter of protest to the *St James's Gazette* he employed an evasive tactic comparable to the invocation of drawing-room opinion in justification of *A Group of Noble Dames*: "Purely artistic conditions necessitated an episcopal position for the character alluded to, as will be apparent to those readers who are at all experienced in the story-telling trade."²² Nor, if Aldrich's complaint about "a story in the family way" is anything to go by, does Hardy seem to have been entirely straightforward in representing forthcoming novels to prospective editors. Although he offered to withdraw *Jude* from *Harper's Monthly* after it had led him into "unexpected fields", it is hard to believe that the novel had ever been, as Hardy had declared to the publishers, "a tale that could not offend the most fastidious maiden".²³ Most remarkable of all, perhaps, is his insistence, early and late, that *The Well-Beloved* was a story every word of which, as he told his editor, "can be circulated freely in schools and families—ay in nurseries".²⁴

If Hardy created difficulties for himself by his own failures of candour, this is not necessarily to say that his misrepresentations were deliberately calculated to deceive. They apparently derived from a failure, quite simply, to recognise the essential character of the material he was handling and the issues he was raising—a refusal or an incapacity to see his own work with the eyes of his readers. He seems never to have faced up to the full implications of his position. Until the moment when he abandoned novel-writing entirely, he was not prepared to forgo the financial rewards of the serial, to step outside the current system of publishing fiction and cast himself specifically in the role of a revolutionary. Nor, on the other hand, was he prepared to accommodate himself completely to the prevailing conditions of serialisation, to accept without struggle or protest the rulings of Mrs Grundy. The course he pursued was, as the product of such conflicting inclinations, inevitably an oblique one. With each new novel he seems to have been capable of persuading both his editor and himself that the story envisaged would not actually transgress (though it might well skirt) the unwritten conventions governing the tone and subject-matter of English family magazines during the last quarter of the nineteenth century. Yet as each new story took shape it proved to dwell not incidentally but centrally upon questions of sexuality and technical immorality almost certain to provoke criticism and complaint. It was little wonder that Aldrich, writing to Hardy in December 1885 about the possibility of his contributing another serial to the *Atlantic Monthly*, should insist upon having the complete text in his hands before publishing the first instalment.[25] Hardy seems persistently to have entertained an obscure hope, perhaps never consciously formulated, that *this* time he would break through the editorial barriers which sealed him off from the magazine audience. It is conceivable, too, that the particular bitterness with which he responded to hostile reviews of books such as *Two on a Tower*, *A Group of Noble Dames*, *Tess*, and *Jude*, which had earlier run into difficulties at the stage of magazine publication, was provoked precisely by his dismay at discovering that the editorial barriers at which he had directed his efforts were not in fact the ultimate strongholds of Grundyism but only its outworks.

Hardy's peculiar difficulties with his editors were largely the product of his own indecision, of a characteristic reluctance to take firm positions; as such, they turned upon no clear issues of principle and now seem to have been for the most part unnecessary. There is no doubt, however, that Hardy could scarcely have avoided giving offence to many late-Victorian readers, not so much by his choice of plot and subject-matter as by that almost näive directness and explicitness of treatment which is fundamental to his whole stance as a novelist—above all, by that unusually frank and even polemical acknowledgment of sexuality as a powerful determinant in human affairs. In so far as Hardy anticipated Lawrence he could scarcely fail to be, in some measure, at odds with his own time. Edward Arnold had rejected *Tess*, as *Early Life* (290) acknowledges, "virtually on the score of its improper explicitness"; Mowbray Morris complained of "rather too much succulence". And although Hardy continued to protest in private letters at the stifling of progress in English fiction by the activities of obtuse critics and the obstructive presence of the "Young Person",[26] he was capable of acknowledging from the remoter and perhaps serener standpoint of 1912 that his critics, if misguided, were not entirely to be blamed: "When *Jude* comes out at the end of this month in the new series," he told Sir Sydney Cockerell, "and you read the Preface and Postscript you will say to yourself (as I did to myself when I passed the proof for press) 'How very natural, and even commendable, it is for old fashioned cautious people to shy at a man who could write that!' "[27]

3

The Well-Beloved

Although *The Well-Beloved* did not appear in volume form until March 1897, it was written in late 1891 and early 1892 and published as a weekly serial in the *Illustrated London News* from October to December 1892.[1] It was the heavily revised book version that Hardy referred to (in a letter to Sir George Douglas) as a "fanciful, tragi-comic, half allegorical tale of a poor Visionary pursuing a Vision".[2] Fanciful it certainly is. Of his central character, the sculptor Jocelyn Pierston, Hardy writes in the second chapter:

> To his Well-Beloved he had always been faithful; but she had had many embodiments. Each individuality known as Lucy, Jane, Flora, Evangeline, or what-not, had been merely a transient condition of her. He did not recognize this as an excuse or as a defence, but as a fact simply. Essentially she was perhaps of no tangible substance; a spirit, a dream, a frenzy, a conception, an aroma, an epitomized sex, a light of the eye, a parting of the lips. God only knew what she really was; Pierston did not. She was indescribable. (10–11)

In a letter written in response to a review of the novel in the *Academy*, Hardy spoke of Pierston's situation as an exemplification of "the Platonic Idea", adding: "There is, of course, underlying the fantasy followed by the visionary artist the truth that all men are pursuing a shadow, the Unattainable."[3] Despite this invocation of Plato and "the visionary artist", the apparent insubstantiality of Hardy's theme and of the book as a whole has led *The Well-Beloved*, although interestingly located in the sequence of Hardy's novels, to be largely ignored by recent critics. Where

[293]

not ignored, it has generally been dismissed as a casual fantasy written in response to a request from Tillotson's for "something light" for serialisation; even Guerard, who praises the novel for its "simple and unmannered prose", concludes that "it is not the worst book ever published by a major writer. But it is certainly one of the most trivial".[4] Contemporary reviewers, however, were generally favourable, and while this response may be attributed in part to a respect for Hardy's established reputation it nonetheless produced a number of perceptive comments.

Hardy, observed the reviewer in the *Academy*:

> . . . has taken, after his wont in his recent books, the extreme case, and has presented it with the perfection of directness, himself retreating into the dimmest shadow of the background while the events follow each other with the certainty of sunset after sunrise. Extreme though the case is, Mr. Hardy has proved it. We believe unhesitatingly, when we lay down this record, that there was once a sculptor, who, at the age of twenty, loved, but did not marry, a girl called Avice; that, at the age of forty, he returned to love, but did not marry, her daughter, Avice the second; that, at the age of sixty, he loved once again, but again did not marry, the daughter of this daughter, Avice the third. It is almost to state that Mr. Hardy has succeeded in his perilous task when we say that never at any moment does the narrative verge on the ludicrous, comic though the scheme of it is in the abstract.[5]

Not all readers have found the narrative so convincing, its comic aspect so easy to overlook. The latter, indeed, seem to be implicitly acknowledged at one point within the novel itself:

> 'Your mother's and your grandmother's young man,' he repeated.
>
> 'And were you my great-grandmother's too?' she asked, with an expectant interest in his case as a drama that overcame her personal considerations for a moment.
>
> 'No—not your great-grandmother's. Your imagination beats even my confessions! . . . But I am *very* old, as you see.' (177)

The chief interest of the *Academy* review, however, lies in its stress on Hardy's choice of the extreme case and his skill in avoiding the obtrusion of an authorial voice or personality. *The Well-Beloved* is, formally, among the most "objective" of his books: the imposition of a largely abstract pattern, emphasised by the division into three parts, works together with the choice of a new and overtly "romantic" setting both to distance the book from Hardy himself and to set it apart from the rest of his work as a kind of composite fable and romance. These features are perhaps more evident in the book version than in the original serial, where Pearston (as his name is there given) marries both Marcia Bencomb, the girl whose attractions make him disloyal to the first Avice, and Avice the third. The first of these marriages ends in disaster for reasons of family hostility, representing an extension of that inverted *Romeo and Juliet* theme which Hardy had conceived several years earlier[6] and which he retained in the final version. The second marriage is made intolerable by the disparity in age between the sixty-year-old Pearston and his twenty-year-old bride, and Pearston eventually attempts suicide as a way of releasing Avice from a union she finds physically repugnant. As the authors of *Providence and Mr Hardy* point out,[7] this latter marriage anticipates in certain limited respects Phillotson's marriage with Sue in *Jude the Obscure*, which was published in the interval between the serial and book versions of *The Well-Beloved*; in revising the earlier novel Hardy may have deleted this material to avoid the appearance of repetition, or simply to forestall a fresh outbreak of the kind of hysterical attack which *Jude* had received from some quarters.

An attack did nevertheless come—from the reviewer in the *World*, who wrote that "Of all forms of sex-mania in fiction we have no hesitation in pronouncing the most unpleasant to be the Wessex-mania of Mr. Thomas Hardy".[8] It appears from a passage deleted from *Later Years* that Hardy believed *The Well-Beloved* had simply been made the pretext for a pre-determined onslaught: "It made him say, naturally enough, 'What foul cess-pits some men's minds must be, and what a Night-cart would be required to empty them!'"[9] Yet, as on previous occasions, Hardy's outbursts of angry astonishment seem somewhat excessive. Despite his emphasis—in the prospectus he prepared for Tillotson's and in private letters[10]—upon the absolute innocuousness of the tale, it is hard to believe that he could have expected no Victorian eyebrows to be raised at a story which, even in its revised version, treats of extra-marital intercourse and of an elderly man seeking to obtain a bride only one-third his age by exploiting his wealth and his influence with the girl's mother. Hardy insists upon Pierston's pursuit of an ideal, but it needs only the mildest scepticism about platonic love, as here presented, to see the sculptor's idealism as little different from that of Humbert Humbert: indeed, the *Saturday Review*, while praising the book for its "preoccupation with beauty", suggested that it might be renamed "the Tragicomedy of a Nympholet".[11]

The removal of the two marriage episodes from the book version gave Hardy an opportunity to introduce an ending which, while still painful, at least held more hint of reconciliation than the final paragraph of the serial, in which Pearston—finding himself married not to the beautiful young Avice but to the "parchment-coloured skull" that is the elderly Marcia—breaks into uncontrollable laughter: " 'I—I—it is too, too droll—this ending to my would-be romantic history!' Ho-ho-ho!"[12] The revised plotline also permitted Hardy to shape much more firmly the outline of his three-stage progression, and to develop what his letter to Douglas calls the novel's "half allegorical" aspects—at least to the extent of indulging in repeated invocations of Aphrodite under names so various as to suggest a possible influence from his recent reading of Frazer's *The Golden Bough*.[13] Hardy had already dispensed, and quite deliberately, with the conventions of realism. In August 1890, when he may already have been thinking about *The Well-Beloved*, he went with the painter Alfred Parsons to Weymouth, and quite possibly to the adjoining Isle of Portland, the original of his fictional Isle of Slingers; a note jotted down a few days earlier is preserved in *Early Life* (299):

Art is a disproportioning—(*i.e.*, distorting, throwing out of proportion)—of realities, to show more clearly the features that matter in those realities, which, if merely copied or reported inventorially, might possibly be observed but would more probably be overlooked. Hence 'realism' is not Art.

The relevance of these observations to *The Well-Beloved* is emphasised by a passage in the 1912 Preface which explains that because "the interest aimed at is of an ideal or subjective nature, and frankly imaginative, verisimilitude in the sequence of events has been subordinated to the said aim" (viii).

Hardy seems to have in mind here the way he had manipulated plot, setting, and characterisation in order to permit the fullest possible development of the central theme—to stress repeatedly, for example, the contrast between the sophistication of the London world of art and fashionable society in which Pierston moves as a successful sculptor and, on the other hand, the primitive and almost unchanging world of the Isle where he was born and to which he repeatedly returns. The opposition is brought out by references to the bleakness and wildness of the island scenery and weather and—especially in the chapter specifically entitled "Juxtapositions"—by the occasional intrusion there of such quintessentially urban characters as Somers and Mrs Pine-Avon. Pierston's own revisitations take on something of the quality of a return to his innermost self, a revelation of his most fundamental needs and desires, and while the Freudian implications that suggest themselves should not be pursued too far, Hardy seems certainly to have thought of the Isle as in some sense representing the essential Pierston lying somewhere beneath the urban veneer.

When, however, Hardy speaks of abandoning, in the interests of thematic statement, "verisimilitude in the sequence of events", he presumably refers not simply to the basic improbabilities of Pierston's multi-stage love affair with the Caro family but also to the more detailed narrative intricacies involved in the constant shuttling between the London and Island settings and in the various complications by which Pierston's designs are repeatedly frustrated. Once again Hardy has chosen a setting which precisely suits his purposes. Not only is (or was) Portland a curiously isolated and backward part of England, but its limited area, sharply defined by sea and cliffs, made it easier for him to devise those repetitions and coincidences which are so central to his pattern. We become familiar with a limited range of settings—Red King Castle, Sylvania Castle, the Pebble Bank, the house of the Caros, Pierston's own birthplace—and the way in which they recur over the years serves to emphasise the element of repetition in Pierston's own career.

The pattern of recurrent settings and situations, of the persistence of physical characteristics through several generations, is played off, deliberately and bitterly, against the inevitable and irreversible progression of Pierston himself towards old age and eventual death. If Pierston's history tends to repeat itself, it never does so exactly, and with increasing age the hope of recovering the past, of redeeming a lost opportunity, becomes more and more elusive. There is, indeed, a sense in which *The Well-Beloved* incorporates within the framework of fable that counterpoint of seasonal and racial recurrence against the transitoriness of the individual life and experience which lies close to the heart of Hardy's greatest novels. And the main "statement" of the fable is precisely that this counterpoint exists, a source of perpetual bitterness and of what Hardy himself calls "tragi-comedy".

What is ostensibly the central concept of the book—the theory, as it is expressed in *Later Years* (59), "of the transmigration of the ideal beloved one, who only exists in the lover, from material woman to material woman"—can perhaps be best seen as structural rather than thematic. In the serial, it is true, invocation of the theory allowed Hardy the opportunity for exploration of the harsh possibilities implicit in contemporary attitudes to marriage, but in the novel as revised this element almost disappears: following the death of the first Avice the "pursuit" of the ideal modulates almost imperceptibly into the attempted recovery of the past, of those opportunities for happiness once slighted and now so desperately regretted, and it seems significant that in revising the novel Hardy shortened its title from *The Pursuit of the Well-Beloved* to *The Well-Beloved*.

Both versions, however, carry the sub-title "A Sketch of a Temperament". That it was intended specifically as a sketch of

[298]

the artistic temperament is suggested by Hardy's own remark in a letter to Swinburne of April 1, 1897, about the novel being "a fanciful exhibition of the artistic nature" and having, as such, "some little foundation in fact".[14] It has been interestingly argued that Hardy designed *The Well-Beloved* specifically as his farewell to fiction,[15] and certainly the end of the book, and especially Pierston's abandonment of sculpture, does have about it a suggestion of a Prospero-like book-burning. But what Pierston has lost, along with his idealism, is precisely his whole sensitivity as an artist and even as a human being: he is now capable of closing the ancient wells of the Isle and pulling down old houses of the kind to which Hardy makes affectionate reference in his Preface. Hardy himself, on the other hand, already knew by late 1896, when the revisions to *The Well-Beloved* were made, that he was about to move forward, as he himself undoubtedly saw it, to a new career as a poet.[16]

In so far as Hardy's conception of the artistic temperament is to be identified with Pierston's restless search for a Shelleyan ideal it is, as Guerard observes,[17] a sadly limited one, nor does Hardy ever seem to have identified any factual foundation for Pierston's obsession other than the remark of a sculptor that he had often pursued across London not so much a beautiful woman as a beautiful feature—an ear, a nose, or whatever it might be.[18] There are, however, many indications that Hardy himself had, at the very least, a propensity for taking careful note of such feminine features as and when he encountered them.[19] He also confesses to delayed emotional maturity,[20] and we know something of his susceptibility in middle age to handsome women, especially those encountered in London society. *Early Life* and *Later Years* are full of references to such women, particularly in the period of the late 1880s and early 1890s, and some of the passages excised from the typescript are even franker in their comments: "Miss Amélie Rives," reads a deleted note of July 1889, "was the pretty woman of the party—a fair, pink, golden-haired creature, but not quite ethereal enough, suggesting a flesh-surface too palpably. A girlish, almost childish laugh, showing beautiful young teeth."[21] R. L. Purdy has outlined the course of Hardy's relationship with Mrs

Henniker from 1893 onwards, while in the poem "Concerning Agnes" Hardy spoke of his meeting with Lady Grove in his fifty-eighth year as "That old romance" and revealed how they sat "After the dance/The while I held her hand".[22] It does not seem inconceivable that Hardy wrote in all earnestness of symptoms identified within himself, finding in the poems of Shelley and Swinburne—both of whom are quoted several times within the novel—not only a diagnostic terminology but grounds for projecting the disease as a restless idealism endemic to the artistic temperament.

The novel certainly incorporates elements of personal experience. Hardy's notes preserved in *Early Life* (305)—"Presently Ellen Terry arrived—diaphanous—a sort of balsam or sea-anemone, without shadow. . . . Ellen Terry was like a machine in which, if you press a spring, all the works fly open"—leave no doubt as to the original of the "leading actress" described in chapter 2 of Part Second of *The Well-Beloved*: "a creature in airy clothing, translucent, like a balsam or sea-anemone, without shadows, and in movement as responsive as some highly lubricated, many-wired machine, which if one presses a particular spring, flies open and reveals its works" (70). But there are other, if remoter, resemblances between the description in *Early Life* (305) of the January 1891 dinner (a letter of Hardy's makes clear that it was at Mrs Jeune's)[23] and the novel's description of the dinner-party at Lady Iris Speedwell's. The fictional "representative of Family" who speaks "as if shouting down a vista of five hundred years from the Feudal past" (70) may owe something to Evelyn Ashley and his loud laugh, while the novel's reference to the wife of a "Lord Justice of Appeal" (70) may obliquely correspond to the mention in *Early Life* (305) of a Judge of the Supreme Court.

Further details in this and the preceding chapter of the novel may conceivably have some basis in Hardy's experience. The "past Prime Minister" (59), for instance, may well have been suggested by Lord Salisbury, whom Hardy had first met in 1885,[24] while Lady Portsmouth—directly described in a note of 1888 in *Early Life* (275) as looking "more like a model countess than ever I have seen her do before"—may have contributed a good deal to the creation of the suggestively-named Lady Channelcliffe. Again, the "kindly young lady of the house, his hostess's relation", with her "sky-blue dress" (59–60) seems directly reminiscent of Lady Portsmouth's niece, Lady Winifred Herbert, described in *Early Life* (242) as "friendly" and in a letter of Hardy's as wearing "divine blue";[25] in the novel, moreover, the young lady's glance strays repeatedly towards a young man "of military appearance" (60), conceivably a reflection of Lady Winifred Herbert's marriage to Captain the Hon. Alfred Byng in January 1887.[26] Another reference in the novel, to "the Lady Mabella Buttermead, who appeared in a cloud of muslin and was going on to a ball" (61), corresponds precisely to a note for May 16, 1887, still preserved in the typescript of *Early Life*: "Lady Marge W— looked pretty in gauzy muslin—going to a ball she told me."[27] It also seems possible that Alfred Somers, the painter in the novel, may have been based in some degree upon Hardy's friend, the painter Alfred Parsons,[28] while the eccentricity of some of the other names—Mrs Pine-Avon, the Honourable Mrs Brightwalton—suggests further possibilities of half-hidden allusion.

The precise function of these allusions (if such they are) is not easy to determine. The names may have been designed simply for satirical effect; the correspondences to actuality may be, in a sense, accidental—the result of Hardy leafing through his notebooks and diaries in a search for "society" material.[29] It is, of course, abundantly clear that he took great satisfaction, if of a somewhat complicated kind, in his friendships with the great, the fashionable, and the aristocratic, and he always showed particular sensitivity—perhaps because his own acceptance in such circles was on the basis not of birth but acquired fame—to criticisms which questioned the authenticity of his fictional portrayals of London society. It is not inconceivable, then, that he sought to demonstrate in *The Well-Beloved*, at least to those in a position to judge, that his portraiture was from the life. References to women for whom he felt affection—Lady Portsmouth and her niece, for instance—may have been intended as a private tribute or joke: *Early Life* (242) records that Lady Winifred Herbert had begged Hardy to name the heroine of *The Woodlanders* after her. It may even have been

that Hardy was acknowledging, with perhaps questionable delicacy, the attraction he himself had felt towards particular women
encountered in such circles. In using the name Avice he may have
been conscious of a punning allusion to *The Bird-Bride*, the title of
a volume of poems by "Graham R. Tomson", the pseudonym of
Rosamund Tomson, wife of the landscape painter Arthur Graham
Tomson.[30] Mrs Tomson—described in 1890 as being a "tall,
slight, brown-haired woman, with large gray eyes, that at times
seemed to be a deep hazel, and a striking individuality pervading
her carriage, manner, and dress, the artistic largely dominating
the latter"[31]—may, indeed, have been a model for Mrs Nichola
Pine-Avon, that "intellectual woman" with "sound rather than
current opinions on the plastic arts" (63), who eventually marries
Somers, the painter: she has "chestnut hair" (65), her "grey"
(117) eyes are "round, inquiring, luminous" (65), her figure is
like "a sylph" (116), and it is by her striking dress that she first
catches Pierston's attention across Lady Channelcliffe's drawing-
room. It was Mrs Tomson whom Hardy had in mind when recalling to Mrs Henniker, in July 1893, an earlier experience with an
apparently enfranchised woman who proved to be interested only
in enrolling him among her train of admirers;[32] if, then, Mrs Pine-
Avon was in some sense Mrs Tomson's representative, Hardy
may have taken a certain satisfaction in Pierston's rejection of her
advances.

There is some evidence that the presentation of Mrs Pine-Avon
was a kind of composite portrait to which more than one of
Hardy's elegant friends made their contribution—a note deleted
from *Early Life* records of one of Lady Portsmouth's daughters
that she had "round luminous enquiring eyes"[33]—and the same
is no doubt true of other figures in the novel. It is rather as if
Hardy were practising as an author the kind of connoisseurship he
attributed to the sculptor friend who collected individual features
from various sources. But even if the book is something of a
roman à clef, this aspect of it seems to be minor and confined
almost entirely to the scenes of London society which occupy the
first two chapters of Part Second. It has generally been felt that
these chapters stand somewhat apart from the rest of the book,

and the *Academy* reviewer particularly criticised the relaxation of control at this point which allowed the reader to see the author "angered by quite harmless artificialities of society, which other men are content to take for granted".[34] The reviewer had in mind such passages as this description of Pierston amid a fashionable throng:

> After ten minutes given to a preoccupied regard of shoulder-blades, back hair, glittering headgear, neck-napes, moles, hair-pins, pearl-powder, pimples, minerals cut into facets of many-coloured rays, necklace-clasps, fans, stays, the seven styles of elbow and arm, the thirteen varieties of ear; and by using the toes of his dress-boots as coulters with which he ploughed his way and that of Lady Mabella in the direction they were aiming at, he drew near to Mrs. Pine-Avon, who was drinking a cup of tea in the back drawing-room. (62)

The observation is unoriginal, the technique ponderous, the satirical tone all too obviously willed and factitious—almost as if Hardy were attempting to disguise a fundamental approval of such scenes. The satirical element, often curiously reminiscent of the ineptitudes of *A Pair of Blue Eyes*, seems unduly obtrusive at this point in the novel, and certainly in excess of what is needed to provide a background of London artificiality against which the rural simplicity and directness of the first Avice can be seen in its proper light and at a proper evaluation. The two chapters can indeed be best regarded as a largely self-contained unit, designed to achieve limited and perhaps private ends, and it seems significant that they were scarcely touched during the revision of the serial text for book publication: although Hardy transferred them from the end of Part First to the beginning of Part Second he made only minor alterations to the text itself.

The overall structure and theme still prompt questions as to the extent to which the novel can be said to reflect Hardy's backward glance over his own life from the vantage point of his sixth decade. In his letter to the *Academy* he stressed that *The Well-Beloved* had been sketched "many years" before the publication of the serial, when he was "comparatively a young man",[35] and it is certainly true that he had long been interested in Shelley and in Shelleyan adaptations of the idea of platonic love. The "One shape of many names" invoked on the title page of *The Well-Beloved* had already been somewhat inauspiciously associated in *The Woodlanders* with the character of Fitzpiers (a name suggestively close to that of Pierston), whose claim to be pursuing an ideal vision resolves itself into little more than philanderer's double-talk.[36] Technically, too, *The Well-Beloved* demands to be grouped, as it is in the Wessex edition, with earlier "Romances and Fantasies" such as *A Pair of Blue Eyes* and *Two on a Tower*. Yet the edgy bitterness and weary ambiguity of the novel suggest the work of a middle-aged rather than of a young man, and Hardy's comment about a much earlier conception date—though presumably not without some foundation—may have been yet another of the ways in which he sought, as it were, to put a safe distance between the story and himself. For much the same reason, no doubt, he portrayed in Pierston a man considerably older than himself, especially at the time of serial publication, and chose, in Portland, a setting with which—despite its location near the centre of Wessex—he could not be readily associated.

If these were indeed Hardy's intentions, they were to some extent frustrated by the illustrator of the serial, who gave Pearston a marked physical resemblance to Hardy himself[37]—a comparison facilitated by the full-page portrait of Hardy which accompanied the first number.[38] And although Hardy's links with Portland may be hard to pin down, he certainly had many associations with the adjoining town of Weymouth, the Budmouth of so many of the novels. In view of Hardy's familiarity with Weymouth, indeed, his references within the novel to the dating of the events in the opening chapters raise some curious questions. Both the serial, published in 1892, and the book, published in 1897, insist that the action of Part First had occurred more than forty years previously, as they must necessarily have done for Pierston to reach his sixties in the final pages. Yet Hardy mentions, during the account of Pierston's "elopement" with Marcia, that the railway to Budmouth "had only recently been opened, as if on purpose for this event" (29); he also notes that at this point in time the Budmouth station formed the terminus of the line. Neither of these comments seems required by the story itself, and their presence is the more remarkable in that Hardy must have known very well that the line from Dorchester to Weymouth was not opened until 1857, with the extension to Portland completed in 1865.[39]

Hardy would have been seventeen in 1857, and it is tempting to associate this "factual" dating of the novel, somewhat at odds with the ostensible dating, with his own visits to Weymouth at about this time in vain pursuit of Louisa Harding, to whom he refers in *Early Life* (33–34) and in the poems "Louie", "To Louisa in the Lane", and "The Passer-by".[40] There appears to be specific evidence of such a visit on August 21, 1859,[41] and what is known of Louisa Harding's personality seems perfectly compatible with the description of the first Avice.[42] The point is perhaps not worth pursuing very far, but it is at least interesting, in view of Hardy's reference to "a poor Visionary pursuing a Vision", to find *Early Life* (34) remarking that Hardy's "vision" of Louisa remained permanently with him. It has, of course, been suggested that all three Avices "are" Tryphena Sparks[43]—a statement manifestly absurd, and based upon an argument of extreme tenuousness. That the first Avice owes something to Tryphena Sparks seems plausible enough, but here as elsewhere it is almost impossible to break down into their individual constituents those "familiar compound" ghosts which haunt Hardy's later work, the verse even more than the prose. What seems crucial is that sense— powerfully expressed both in the poems to Louisa Harding and in "Thoughts of Phena"[44]—of poignant regret at the contemplation of years long vanished, of lamentation for opportunities not properly appreciated and now irrecoverably lost. It seems regrettable that recent attempts to establish Tryphena Sparks as a major influence on Hardy's life and work have compromised their potential usefulness by indulgence in irresponsible speculations of an almost entirely unsupported kind.[45] Hardy's poems to the memory of Louisa Harding express his yearning regret at his failure to love her then as he has learned to love her since, and in the few poems that can convincingly be associated with Tryphena Sparks she too is seen as a woman slighted in her girlhood, never fully loved or appreciated, but now seen as an epitomisation of what might have been.

Within *The Well-Beloved* itself it would no doubt be possible to posit a fairly elaborate autobiographical pattern in which an engagement with Avice I/Tryphena–Louisa, lightly entered into, is suspended by a sudden and passionate involvement with Marcia/ Emma Lavinia, who later becomes the time-worn figure, ugly and old, with whom Pierston/Hardy must end his days. Something of the class and family hostility which entered into Hardy's own marriage may indeed be reflected in the rapid breakdown of the original relationship between Pierston and Marcia, and in the serial, where the relationship becomes a marriage, the definition of their relative social positions seems particularly relevant to Hardy's own situation:

> In birth the pair were about equal, but Marcia's family had gained a start in the accumulation of wealth and in the initiation of social distinction, which lent a colour to the feeling that the advantages of the match had been mainly on one side. Nevertheless, Pearston was a sculptor rising to fame by fairly rapid strides; and potentially the marriage was not a bad one for a woman who, beyond being the probable successor to a stone-merchant's considerable fortune, had no exceptional opportunities.

As in *Jude*, personal experience no doubt contributed to statements such as the following:

> A legal marriage it was, but not a true marriage. In the night they heard sardonic voices and laughter in the wind at the ludicrous facility afforded them by events for taking a step in two days which they could not retrace in a lifetime, despite their mutual desire as the two persons solely concerned.[46]

Conceivably, too, the shift from the bitter conclusion of the serial to the final resignation of the novel had something to do with the fading of the early fervour of Hardy's relationship with Mrs Henniker and perhaps even with an attempt to reach a *modus vivendi* with Emma; in his volume of Matthew Arnold's *Poetical Works*

Hardy wrote alongside "Dover Beach": "Sept—1896—/T.H./ E.L.H."⁴⁷ The "old natural fountains" (217) closed by Pierston at the end of the novel may even—if they "represent" anything at all—carry a sexual rather than an artistic connotation.

But to say that a novel incorporates elements of personal experience and even the shadowy outlines of autobiographical episodes is not necessarily to say that it is, in any consistent sense, an inadequately camouflaged record of the author's life and loves. In *The Well-Beloved*, in particular, any search for sustained point-by-point correspondences is effectively baffled by the highly patterned structure of the novel, itself as effective a distancing agent as the use of Portland or of more or less fortuitous plot elements. *The Well-Beloved*, it seems clear, is not fictionalised autobiography but a carefully wrought fable which is both relevant to Hardy's own experience and largely written out of that experience. Its statements, essentially, are the familiar ones of transcience and mutability to be found in such poems as "The Well-Beloved", with its suggestion that love itself is an ungraspable spectre,⁴⁸ and the bitter "I look into my glass":

> But Time, to make me grieve,
> Part steals, lets part abide;
> And shakes this fragile frame at eve
> With throbbings of noontide.⁴⁹

4

Hardy and the Theatre

The spring of 1893 brought two important events in Hardy's life and career, the beginning of his friendship with Florence Henniker and the revival of his active interest in the drama. In May of that year Hardy and his wife accepted an invitation to stay at the Viceregal Lodge in Dublin, where Hardy met, apparently for the first time, the Lord-Lieutenant's sister, the charming, attractive, talented Mrs Arthur Henniker, daughter of Lord Houghton.[1] The contrast with Emma—who had characteristically chosen to wear at the Viceregal Lodge an absurdly youthful outfit of muslin and blue ribbon[2]—could scarcely have been greater, and a friendship began between Hardy (then fifty-two) and Mrs Henniker (then thirty-eight) which, as R. L. Purdy observes, "meant much to him at a dark and embittered time".[3] The earliest, and most intense, phase of that friendship closely coincided with Hardy's new theatrical activity. His earliest surviving letter to Mrs Henniker was written on June 3, 1893, the date of the first performance of his one-act play, *The Three Wayfarers*—which, he told her, had taken up a great deal of his time during the previous week—and later that same month he went with Mrs Henniker and some of her relatives to see Ibsen's *The Master Builder*.[4]

Hardy's apparent enthusiasm for the theatre at this period is, on the face of it, somewhat surprising. On August 31, 1892, he had contributed to the *Pall Mall Gazette* symposium "Why I Don't Write Plays", explaining his own concentration on the novel on the grounds that the latter "affords scope for getting nearer to the heart and meaning of things than does the play", and that the contemporary theatre was preoccupied with elaborate staging "to

[308]

the neglect of the principle that the material stage should be a conventional or figurative arena, in which accessories are kept down to the plane of mere suggestions of place and time, so as not to interfere with the required high-relief of the action and emotions".[5] He had expressed similar views before, most fully in a letter of 1889 published in the magazine *Weekly Comedy*, which had solicited his opinions on a proposal for the foundation of a British "Free Stage" on the model of a "*Théatre Libre*" recently established in France. Hardy concludes his letter:

> Could not something be done to weed away the intolerable masses of scenery and costume? A good many hundred people would travel a good many miles to see a play performed in the following manner:— The ordinary pit boarded over to make a stage, so that the theatre would approach in arrangement the form of an old Roman amphitheatre; the scenery being simply a painted canvas hung in place of the present curtain, the actors performing in front of it, and disappearing behind it when they go off the stage; a horizontal canvas for sky or ceiling; few moveable articles of furniture or trees in boxes, as the case may be indoors or out; the present stage being the green room. The costumes to be suggestive of the time and situation, and not exclusively suggestive of what they cost. Spectators would then, sitting to a great extent round the actors, see the *play* as it was seen in old times, but as they do not see it now for its accessories.[6]

As Harold Orel has remarked, Hardy here suggests something not unlike the modern theatre-in-the-round,[7] and it is clear that he was essentially in sympathy with the more advanced dramatic theorists and practitioners of his day. A similar approach appears in the stage-directions to *The Queen of Cornwall* (1923), his only work originally conceived and written for theatrical performance: "The Stage is any large room; round or at the end of which the audience sit." He goes on to recommend that "curtains, screens or chairs" be used to represent various elements in a scene—conceding, however, that "should the performance take place in an ordinary theatre, the aforesaid imaginary surroundings may be supplied by imitative scenery" (220).

The originators of the proposal for a British *"Théâtre Libre"*, J. T. Grein and C. W. Jarvis, explained in their opening statement in the *Weekly Comedy* that they had approached Hardy as one of a number of novelists "whose romances reveal great dramatic ability".[8] Since they had recently been collaborating in a dramatisation of *The Woodlanders* they could speak with some authority.[9] Whatever the technical success of that adaptation may have been, its eventual fate was of a kind to confirm Hardy's scepticism about the contemporary theatre: according to *Early Life* (289), "nothing arose out of the dramatization, it becoming obvious that no English manager at this date would venture to defy the formalities to such an extent as was required by the novel, in which some of the situations were approximately of the kind afterwards introduced to English playgoers by translations from Ibsen". Florence Hardy suggested in a letter of July 17, 1926, to St John Ervine that Henry Irving was attracted by the play but turned it down because it offered him no adequate starring role.[10] If this was indeed the difficulty—and it is certainly true that Irving read the play[11]—it was to recur in Hardy's experience: on February 17, 1909, he told William Archer that the stage version of *Tess* had not been performed because "there was no hero in it, that the manager cd. personate, and bring down the gallery. A manager owned it to me."[12]

Hardy's estimate of the theatre seems to have changed little over the years. When, on January 9, 1909, he complained to Archer of the tendency for a situation regarded "as a stale thing in a novel or dramatic poem" to be praised for its "dazzling originality" when later used in a stage production,[13] he was echoing what he had been quoted as saying in an interview of March 1894:

In my opinion the drama is an inferior form of art, although there are, it is true, greater possibilities in it in one sense, appealing as it does so powerfully and directly to the feelings and emotions. But on the stage you can take such liberties with your characters, bringing about sudden changes in their

[310]

temperaments and motives as would be ridiculous in a novel; while, on the other hand, you are seriously embarrassed by limitations of time and space. A play which the papers praise as really first-rate ranks in point of art, and, above all, character-drawing, no higher than a second or third-rate novel.[14]

Though Hardy has cast doubts on the interview's authenticity, the accents of the particular passage seem to be his: he had made precisely the same point in a letter to Mrs Henniker of December 1, 1893, instancing *The Second Mrs Tanqueray* as an example of a play which would have made a very inferior novel.[15] In the same interview he is quoted as replying somewhat negatively to a question as to whether he would write a successor to *The Three Wayfarers;* the larger question which inevitably suggests itself is why, within nine months of explaining "Why I don't write plays", Hardy should have agreed at all to Barrie's suggestion (of April 19, 1893) that he should write a dramatisation of his story, "The Three Strangers".[16]

Yet what emerges most strikingly, if paradoxically, from "Why I Don't Write Plays" and especially from the comments on a British *"Théâtre Libre"* is an underlying enthusiasm for the drama itself, as distinct from its contemporary manifestations on the London stage. Despite that early, and somewhat juvenile, disgust with "stage realities" which is reflected in his poem "A Victorian Rehearsal"[17] and to which *Early Life* (72) ascribes his abandonment in 1867 of a scheme to get practical stage experience as a preparation for writing blank-verse drama—despite, too, his generally unhappy experience with the various play versions of *Far from the Madding Crowd*[18]—Hardy had clearly not abandoned all thoughts of seeing his own work on the stage. It is true that the composition of *The Three Wayfarers* was prompted by a friend's invitation to produce a play for immediate and conceivably profitable performance—though in the event the programme of five plays ran for only a week[19]—but Hardy went on in subsequent years to write a stage version of *Tess*, prepare schemes for a possible dramatisation of *Jude*, write and publish *The Dynasts*, and co-operate (though to a limited extent) in the productions of the

[311]

Dorchester Debating and Dramatic Society, subsequently known as "The Hardy Players". In the last years of his life he not only completed *The Queen of Cornwall* but devoted an astonishing amount of time and energy to the various productions of *Tess*, especially that at the Barnes Theatre in 1925.[20]

W. R. Rutland has suggested[21] that Hardy's resumption of active interest in the drama in the early 1890s should be linked with the arrival in England of the plays of Ibsen, in whose cause two friends of Hardy's, Edmund Gosse and William Archer, were particularly active—though not always harmoniously so, as Archer's review of Gosse's translation of *Hedda Gabler* sufficiently demonstrates.[22] *Later Years* (20) mentions visits to Ibsen productions in 1893, and in May 1890 Hardy summarised in one of his notebooks part of Havelock Ellis's account, in *The New Spirit*, of Ibsen's *The Lady From the Sea*:

> At length the mysterious "stranger" turns up again, resolved, if she [Ellida] wishes, to carry her off in spite of everything. She feels that she must be free—free to go or free to stay. The husband, naturally, refuses to hear of this, proposes to send the man about his business. At length he consents to allow her to choose as she will. Then at once she feels able to decide against the "stranger", who leaps over the wall and disappears. The charm is broken for ever, and she has the chance to make something of her life. The moral is evident: without freedom of choice there can be no real emancipation or development.[23]

The relevance to *Jude*, and especially to Sue's separation from Phillotson, is obvious, and it is certainly possible to argue, as Rutland does, that Ibsen was an important influence upon this last and most polemical of Hardy's novels. One of Hardy's schemes for dramatising *Jude* was tentatively given such titles as "The New Woman" and "A Woman with Ideas",[24] and he evidently saw posibilities for reworking the novel into what would be, quite specifically, a "problem" play. Though none of the schemes materialised, Hardy preserved them, and in 1926 Florence Hardy forwarded them on her husband's behalf to St John Ervine.[25] In a letter of September 9, 1926, Hardy himself wrote to Ervine, giving formal authorisation for him to make a dramatisation of *Jude* and offering specific suggestions as to the way the problem might be handled.[26]

Marguerite Roberts, the chronicler of Hardy's long involvement with various stage versions of *Tess*, has suggested that "Hardy's gifts were essentially dramatic" and that the novels themselves contain elements of plot and melodramatic action which seem readily adaptable to stage presentation.[27] Certainly *Jude* itself is strongly theatrical in many of its aspects, eschewing the rich tonal qualities of *Tess* in favour of simplicity of outline and directness—at times stridency—of action and statement. Other novels tend towards the theatrical: *Far from the Madding Crowd*, with its broad sweep of action and its range of sharply differentiated characters; *The Hand of Ethelberta*, that "comedy in chapters"; *The Mayor of Casterbridge*, with its demonstration, somewhat in the manner of *The Scarlet Letter*, of the rich symbolic and dramatic possibilities inherent in the use of quasi-theatrical settings and devices. And Alexander Fischler has recently pointed to the profusion of theatrical techniques in Hardy's shorter fiction.[28] The element of exaggeration, of heightened coloration, inherent in the theatrical—especially as it was understood and practised in the Victorian period—answered immediately to Hardy's propensity for seeing scenes and characters slightly larger than life, and to that desire for an expressionist art which he had voiced in notes ascribed in *Early Life* (231–232) to January 3, 1886, the day following the appearance of the first serial part of *The Mayor of Casterbridge*: "My art is to intensify the expression of things, as is done by Crivelli, Bellini, etc., so that the heart and inner meaning is made vividly visible."

In writing his major fiction Hardy seems to have turned for precedents not only to his predecessors and contemporaries in fiction (of whom, indeed, he speaks remarkably little) but to the dramatists—to Shakespeare, the Jacobeans, the Greeks, and finally to Ibsen. It is to the drama that one must often look for the models and techniques, even the terminology, most appropriate to the discussion of particular aspects of Hardy's fiction, and he himself repeatedly defines his aims and achievements in images

[313]

from the theatre. In the 1895 Preface to *A Pair of Blue Eyes* he speaks of "those convenient corners wherein I have ventured to erect my theatre for these imperfect dramas of country life and passions" (vii–viii). In the General Preface to the Wessex Edition allusions to the "circumscribed scene" of the Wessex novels and to "the geographical limits of the stage here trodden" are picked up in terms of a specific analogy with the Greek drama, which "found sufficient room for a large proportion of its action in an extent of their country not much larger than . . . Wessex"; a contrast is also drawn with his own verse, "the dramatic part especially having a very broad theatre of action".[29]

Hardy has *The Dynasts* particularly in mind here, and his comment is suggestive of the position occupied by that work in relation to the volumes of fiction which precede it. Barker Fairley has argued that *The Dynasts* "shares and in a sense combines" not only the tradition of epic, of Shakespearean historical drama, and of the "philosophical dramas" of Aeschylus, Goethe, and Shelley, but also the tradition of the novel, and especially of the Wessex novels themselves:

> . . . the relation of *The Dynasts* to the novel is at once close and remote; close in substance, remote in form. It would not be difficult to recast mentally any of the greater novels in the intricate mould of *The Dynasts* or to fuse *The Dynasts* into the compacted masses of the novels. Thus, the Spirit Sinister speaks the closing comment in the best-known of the tales, "the President of the Immortals (in Aeschylean phrase) had ended his sport with Tess." Similarly the Spirit Ironic closes *Two on a Tower*, "The Bishop was avenged"; the Years pronounce through the mouthpiece of Arabella the fearful epilogue of *Jude the Obscure*; whilst in *The Return of the Native*, as in *The Dynasts* itself, the Pities strike the final and deepest chord: "But everywhere he was kindly received, for the story of his life had become generally known."[30]

It is not necessary to accept all the particular emphases of this analysis in order to appreciate its force. There is, indeed, a further sense in which *The Dynasts* is the natural culmination of the fiction, the point of confluence of its most persistent tendencies, both technical and thematic. It was suggested earlier that the machinery of the Spirits provided Hardy with a means of offering comment while avoiding the limitations and dangers of a specific commitment. It now seems clear that the same machinery of ubiquitous invisible presences offered a solution to that technical problem of point of view which Hardy seems habitually to have regarded in narrowly visual terms: at the same time, the choice of verse drama as the vehicle of the main action not only released those poetic impulses which had been partly (though by no means entirely) stifled during the years of novel-writing but gave him freedom to exercise to the full his *penchant* for the theatrical. Even that "dumbshow" effect achieved at the beginning of several novels (including *Far from the Madding Crowd*, *The Mayor of Casterbridge*, and, as Fairley suggests,[31] *The Return of the Native*) now found its formal apotheosis.

Best of all, as Hardy insists in his Preface, *The Dynasts* was "intended simply for mental performance, and not for the stage" (x–xi); it ran no risk, therefore, of exposure to the contamination of the contemporary theatre. With a characteristic recourse to the traditions of Wessex and the memories of childhood, Hardy suggests that if a performance were to be attempted it might perhaps take the shape of "a monotonic delivery of speeches, with dreamy conventional gestures, something in the manner traditionally maintained by the old Christmas mummers, the curiously hypnotizing impressiveness of whose automatic style—that of persons who spoke by no will of their own—may be remembered by all who experienced it. Gauzes or screens to blur outlines might still further shut off the actual, as has, indeed, already been done in exceptional cases. But with this branch of the subject we are not concerned here" (xii). Characteristically again, the statement of unconcern is juxtaposed with evidence of the intensest interest. Similarly, when scenes from *The Dynasts* were in fact staged by Harley Granville-Barker in 1914, Hardy's decision not to "interfere" in the details of the production did not prevent him from voicing criticism of it afterwards.[32]

Vast, ungainly, and unassimilable although it may sometimes

appear, *The Dynasts* is absolutely of a piece with Hardy's other work and with the pattern of his whole career. Portentous both in form and in statement, it nonetheless represents a kind of sublimated fusion of his hitherto divergent impulses towards fiction, poetry, and the drama. And if it is in a real sense the culminating point of Hardy's major fiction, it is also the fullest embodiment of those historical and regional enthusiasms which produced *The Trumpet-Major*, and the most coherent expression, despite the invocation of far wider scenes, of Hardy's developed concept of Wessex. It is pleasant to think, indeed, that in writing *The Dynasts* Hardy may even have drawn a measure of inspiration from the example of the obscure Dorsetshire writer, J. F. Pennie of Lulworth, author (among other volumes) of an autobiography which Hardy was reading in the early 1880s[33] and of *Britain's Historical Drama; a Series of National Tragedies* (1832), a work whose ambition was amply set forth in the opening paragraph of its preface:

> The following Tragedies are intended to form a portion of a National Dramatic Work; not merely devoted to the purposes of illustrating certain particular events, which stand like lofty and isolated rocks amid the downward rolling stream of British history, but also to display a faithful picture of the manners, customs, and religious observances of those various nations that have successively obtained the possession and dominion of this island.[34]

Hardy's scope was not quite so grand as this, yet he too might justifiably have said of *The Dynasts* what Pennie could so confidently proclaim of *Britain's Historical Drama*: "As far as I have any acquaintance with dramatic writings, no similar work has ever yet been published."[35]

5

Jude the Obscure

On October 22, 1893, Hardy concluded a letter to Mrs Henniker —identified by Florence Hardy as one of the models for Sue Bridehead—by asking her what he should call the heroine of his new novel.[1] It appears from the letter that he had not yet begun work on the actual writing of the book, and evidence of other literary activity during the autumn of 1893, the period of his collaboration with Mrs Henniker on the story "The Spectre of the Real",[2] serves to cast further doubt on the statement in the Preface to the first edition of *Jude* that the manuscript was written "at full length" from August 1893 onwards, on the basis of an outline completed the previous spring (vii). Clearly, however, the book was very much in Hardy's mind, and although on December 1, 1893, he told Mrs Henniker that he was reluctant to go on with it, by January 15, 1894, he was becoming enthusiastic about his heroine; by April 7 the story had carried him into such "unexpected fields" that he wrote to Harper & Brothers suggesting cancellation of their agreement with him.[3] In the event, Hardy prepared a heavily bowdlerised serial version of the novel for *Harper's New Monthly Magazine* and then restored the original text for the first edition, published by Osgood, McIlvaine in November 1895.[4]

The serialisation of *Jude* in an American magazine prompts speculation as to the kind of analysis it might by now have received if Hardy had been an American author. It is, after all, the General Epistle of Jude in the New Testament which contains the famous phrase about "the blackness of darkness", and within the novel itself the "predestinate Jude" (48) is not only designated "the Obscure" but caught up in dramas of sin and guilt, determinism and free will, whose configurations are plotted in terms as much theological as psychological, and with a heavy reliance on prefigurative and emblematic devices. Points of similarity between Hardy and Hawthorne have been mentioned in earlier chapters, and there may even be some virtue in viewing Hardy's work in relation to that tendency towards romance forms and symbolic techniques often identified as the American "tradition" of the novel, rather than in an exclusive context of nineteenth-century English fiction.

But although Jude himself is of "dark complexion", with "dark harmonizing eyes", a "black beard" and a "great mass of black curly hair" (89), Hardy clearly intended the "obscure" of his title to carry—as it does whenever it occurs within the text of the novel—the exclusive sense of "to Fame unknown". Remote as the novel may seem from the pastoral world of *Far from the Madding Crowd*, the presence of Gray's *Elegy* can still be felt: Jude comes from an "obscure home" (93), he identifies Sue and himself as "poor obscure people" (310); the theme of education denied which runs throughout the novel glances at the fate not only of Jude himself but of countless others who remained "mute" and "inglorious", their potentialities unrecognised and unfulfilled. Yet it is only one of the novel's proliferating ironies that Jude should, within a limited sphere, be neither silent nor unknown. He achieves a kind of fame not only in Marygreen but in Christminster itself. People notice and remember him; he is "nicknamed Tutor of St. Slums" (392) and recognised by several among the Christminster crowd which listens so attentively to his story of his life. His relationship with Sue has continually brought them under public scrutiny, and Father Time's act of murder and suicide adds only the final appalling increment to the burden of notoriety: "Accounts in the newspapers had brought to the spot curious idlers, who stood apparently counting the window-panes and the stones of the walls. Doubt of the real relations of the couple added zest to their curiosity" (409–410). The reputation of the house itself threatens to be so damaged that the landlord consults with the owner as to the possibility of getting its number changed.

Jude's relationship with Sue represents nothing more, and nothing less, than an attempt to lead a private life—an attempt embarked upon with full and almost unreflecting confidence in the possibility of such a life for people so circumstanced.[5] For all their moral and intellectual anxieties, Jude and Sue give an impression of almost Dostoievskean simplicity and innocence, and their childlikeness, specifically reflected in Hardy's abandoned title, "The Simpletons",[6] is emphasised throughout. The opening presentation of Jude as a boy is extended and powerful, lingering in the mind until it is reinforced by Aunt Drusilla's reminiscences of Sue as a child. The subsequent reappearances of Aunt Drusilla and the Widow Edlin help to keep alive an awareness of both Jude and Sue in childhood: in the presence of these grandmotherly figures the pair remain—to them and in some measure to us—the children they once were. They never wholly grasp what social pressures they are likely to encounter, the effect they will have upon other people, the amount of attention their way of life must inevitably attract: they are slow to recognise, for example, that there could be any inappropriateness in their contracting to re-paint the Ten Commandments in the church near Aldbrickham. Phillotson seems to anticipate Sue's quoting of "Epipsychidion" (294), and to speak to some extent for Hardy himself, when defining their "extraordinary affinity, or sympathy" (278) in terms not so much platonic as "Shelleyan": "They remind me of—what are their names—Laon and Cythna" (279). As David J. DeLaura has pointed out,[7] and as the contrasted treatment of Fitzpiers and Pierston would itself suggest, Hardy's feelings about Shelleyan idealism seem to have been of a somewhat ambivalent kind; the allusion to *The Revolt of Islam* seems, however, sufficiently appropriate as a means of evoking the spiritual affinity and illusory self-isolation of Jude and Sue.

At the beginning of their life together Jude is able to accept with fairly good grace Sue's denial of sexual intimacy:

He laughed. 'Never mind!' he said. 'So that I am near you, I am comparatively happy. It is more than this earthly wretch called Me deserves—you spirit, you disembodied creature, you dear, sweet, tantalizing phantom—hardly flesh at all; so that when I put my arms round you I almost expect them to pass through you as through air! Forgive me for being gross, as you call it!' (294)

Though Jude's love for Sue demands physical expression, it is strong enough to comprehend Shelleyan modes of thought and feeling. The sympathy between them is real, and the sense of their "comradeship" casts an extraordinary glow over such episodes as the visit to the Great Wessex Agricultural Show. For Sue, however, the Shelleyan position becomes a defensive redoubt which she refuses to abandon, an intellectual counterpart of her policy of permitting the exchange of endearments only at times when she is beyond the range of immediate sexual assault: Jude cannot forbear complaining that "you are often not so nice in your real presence as you are in your letters!" (197) On more than one occasion she addresses him from the security of a window, and if Jude thus finds himself in a position of suppliance traditional to complaining lovers, his attempts to win Sue from coyness are as prolonged and as painful as legend or literary convention could demand: the "bride" in Sue is fatally inhibited by the "head", by intellectuality and a revulsion from the physical.[8] Jude is always rescuing her from actual or symbolic prisons—Miss Fontover's, the Melchester Normal School, Phillotson's home in Shaston, that "city of a dream" (239)—but his kiss fails to awaken her sleeping sexuality.

The character of Sue, at first sight one of the most innovatory aspects of the book, is in some respects only a more extreme, much franker treatment of a type Hardy had portrayed many times before. He told Gosse: "Sue is a type of woman which has always had an attraction for me, but the difficulty of drawing the type has kept me from attempting it till now."[9] Yet as early as 1881 Charles Kegan Paul could offer the following generalisation about Hardy's women, whom he calls "Undines of the earth":

They are all charming; they are all flirts from their cradle; they are all in love with more than one man at once; they seldom, if they marry at all, marry the right man; and while well conducted for the most part, are somewhat lacking in moral sense, and have only rudimentary souls.[10]

This is not by any means a portrait of Sue, but it does suggest the degree to which Sue's wilfulness and elusiveness are qualities which Hardy had dwelt upon in previous books. The article was, moreover, written before the appearance of *A Laodicean* and of its heroine Paula Power, a "modern" girl who quotes Arnold (as Sue quotes Mill) and appears to be something of a "Laodicean"—lukewarm, fastidious, and even slightly ambiguous—in sexual as in other matters. Sue herself, as Hardy remarks in his 1912 Preface, was quickly seized upon as a type of the "New Woman", and it seems useful, up to a point, to consider her in such a light. Yet she is by no means the exclusive product of a particular period. In her immaturity, her combination of a tendency to flirt with a basic fear of sexuality, Sue—as Robert B. Heilman has demonstrated—is a recognisable and not especially uncommon type: as Hardy insisted in writing to Gosse, the sexual instinct in her is "healthy as far as it goes, but unusually weak and fastidious".[11] Her intellectual "paganism", what makes her specifically of her time, serves to exacerbate her fundamental tendencies by providing her with a series of rational, or at least rationalised, justifications for acting as she perhaps must—converting her instinctive actions into elements in a programme. Hardy seems to have been at some pains to indicate the extent to which in earlier years she has been starved both emotionally and intellectually by her lack of formal education and the absence of a secure family environment. Precisely the same could be said of Jude, of course, and this is one of the ways in which it appears from an early stage that he and Sue have more than their cousinship in common.

In letters written after the publication of *Jude* Hardy made a good deal of what he called "the tragic issues of two bad marriages, owing in the main to a doom or curse of hereditary temperament peculiar to the family of the parties".[12] "The Fawleys were not made for wedlock," declares Aunt Drusilla: "It never seemed to sit well upon us" (81). But if it is their cousinship which first brings Jude and Sue together, the family curse has otherwise little

direct bearing on the development or outcome of their relationship. Like so much else in the novel, it seems emblematic and
prefigurative of the central action rather than integral to it. This,
at least, appears to be the principal function of a passage such as
the following, in which Jude, before he has ever spoken to Sue,
sums up the arguments against falling in love with her:

> The first reason was that he was married, and it would be
> wrong. The second was that they were cousins. It was not well
> for cousins to fall in love even when circumstances seemed to
> favour the passion. The third: even were he free, in a family
> like his own where marriage usually meant a tragic sadness,
> marriage with a blood-relation would duplicate the adverse
> conditions, and a tragic sadness might be intensified to a tragic
> horror. (105)

The profusion of such signals in *Jude the Obscure* is reminiscent of
the heavy incidence of prophecies and omens in *The Bride of
Lammermoor*—praised by Hardy in 1888 as "an almost perfect
specimen of form", of "the well-knit interdependence of parts"[13]
—while Aunt Drusilla's role perhaps has something in common
with that of Scott's prophetess, Blind Alice.

Jude, like *The Bride of Lammermoor*, certainly incorporates
inversions, oppositions, reversals, ironies of all kinds, and the
deliberateness with which such contrastive patterning is built
into the novel was from the beginning acknowledged and even
proclaimed by Hardy himself:

> Of course the book is all contrasts—or was meant to be in its
> original conception. Alas, what a miserable accomplishment it
> is, when I compare it with what I meant to make it!—*e.g.* Sue
> and her heathen gods set against Jude's reading the Greek
> Testament; Christminster academical, Christminster in the
> slums; Jude the Saint, Jude the sinner; Sue the Pagan, Sue the
> saint; marriage, no marriage; &c., &c.[14]

The method has its limitations, but it is the source of such
moments as the final bitter juxtaposition of Jude's dying recitation

of the Book of Job with the cheers of the crowd at the Remembrance games. It was in late 1882 or early 1883 that Hardy had entered into one of his commonplace books the following from an unidentified article in the *Athenaeum*:

In certain temperaments the eternal incongruities between man's mind & the scheme of the universe produce, no doubt, the pessimism of Schopenhauer and Novalis; but to other temperaments—to a Rabelais or Sterne for instance—the apprehension of them turns the cosmos into disorder, turns it into something like [a] [sic] boisterous joke.[15]

A similar conception of the monstrous absurdity of things may have influenced the composition of *Jude*.

Fernand Lagarde has recently analysed Hardy's exhaustive pursuit of symmetry in the novel and related it to the contemporary phenomenon of the well-made play. He concludes:

Comme dans une salle de spectacle un rôle est imparti au public. L'auteur a dépouillé la tragédie des excroissances habituelles; il a simplifié les données, souligné les redites, grossi les accidents. Le meilleur exemple des simplifications que s'est imposées le romancier est sans conteste la suppression quasi totale des dialogues d'amoureux dans un livre consacré à l'amour; seuls demeurent les dialogues qui mettent en relief la construction ou qui font avancer l'action.[16]

It might perhaps be objected that Sue and Jude do indeed talk of love in their own somewhat eccentric terms; but that the dialogue throughout is economical and directly functional there can be no question. Hardy, as we have seen, was by no means oblivious of the potentialities of the drama, and even before the novel was published he had prepared at least one scheme for its adaptation to the stage.[17] Like a solidly constructed play, *Jude* focuses on a few important figures, all of them firmly characterised. Even a relatively minor figure like the Widow Edlin is very palpably "there", and—with the arguable exception of Father Time—the novel displays none of those weak links (such as Lucetta and Fitzpiers) which mar even the finest of the previous books. Arabella herself, with her sexuality, her vulgarity, her instinct for

survival, is richly imagined and created, and her role is deliberately played off against Sue's in a manner reminiscent of the
oppositions between Alec and Angel in *Tess* and between Grace
and Marty in *The Woodlanders*.

In the 1912 Postscript to the original Preface Hardy observed
that the theme of the marriage that had become "a cruelty" to one
of the parties, and hence "essentially and morally no marriage",
had "seemed a good foundation for the fable of a tragedy, told for
its own sake as a presentation of particulars containing a good deal
that was universal, and not without a hope that certain cathartic,
Aristotelian qualities might be found therein" (x). Within the
novel itself, Sue speaks at one point of a "tragic doom" over-
hanging the Fawleys "as it did the house of Atreus" (341), and it
becomes clear that Hardy is again deliberately invoking, as earlier
in *The Return of the Native*, images, analogies, and even structural
patterns derived ultimately from Greek drama. Aunt Drusilla and
the Widow Edlin have something of the role of a chorus; Jude
quotes from the *Antigone* (475) and from the *Agamemnon* (409);
the book ends with a prophecy by Arabella—"She's never found
peace since she left his arms, and never will again till she's as he
is now!"—which seems strikingly similar to the famous conclusion
of *Oedipus Tyrannus*, rendered, in the translation which Hardy
used, as "call no man happy, ere he shall have crossed the bound-
ary of life, the sufferer of nought painful".[18] If it seems excessive
to suggest that in calling Jude "the Obscure" Hardy may have
had in mind an ironic allusion to such titles as Oedipus "the
King", it is at least conceivable that in writing *Jude* he had the
career of Oedipus very much in mind.

The introduction to the translation of Sophocles which Hardy
owned praised *Oedipus Rex* as "the most complicated and artfully
sustained of extant Greek plays", one in which "we are continually kept in alternate doubt, fear, and hope".[19] In the highly self-
conscious patterning of *Jude* the steadily downward curve of the
tragedy is repeatedly delayed or disguised by moments of "alternate doubt, fear, and hope", even as its inexorability is repeatedly
confirmed by instances of inversion, reversal, and *peripeteia*—
seen at its bitterest in the outcome of Jude's last visit to Sue. The

apparently excessive suffering of Jude and Sue in the final chapters has caused difficulty to readers and critics alike, and has perhaps cast a kind of retrospective pall over earlier novels of Hardy's in which the outcome is in fact much less desperate and unrelieved. Edmund Gosse voiced such feelings in his review of *Jude* in the *St James's Gazette*:

> It is a very gloomy, it is even a grimy, story that Mr. Hardy has at last presented to his admirers. . . . We do not presume to blame him for the tone he has chosen to adopt, nor for the sordid phases of failure through which he drags us. The genius of this writer is too widely acknowledged to permit us to question his right to take us into what scenes he pleases; but, of course, we are at liberty to say whether we enjoy them or no. Plainly, we do not enjoy them. We think the fortunes, even of the poorest, are more variegated with pleasures, or at least with alleviations, than Mr. Hardy chooses to admit. . . . But in his new book Mr. Hardy concentrates his observation on the sordid and painful side of life and nature. We rise from the perusal of it stunned with a sense of the hollowness of existence.[20]

This represents a kind of charge against Hardy, and specifically against *Jude*, which it is perhaps impossible to refute as completely as one might wish. There does seem to be something gratuitous about Jude's sufferings, the death of Father Time and the other children, the violence of Sue's abnegation and self-flagellation. In view, however, of the Greek precedents Hardy seems to have had in mind, such turns of the screw can perhaps be explained, if not entirely justified, in terms of a deliberate determination to leave the reader precisely "stunned with a sense of the hollowness of existence".

Hardy responded warmly to Gosse's review in a series of letters on which Gosse drew, in turn, in writing a second and more extended review of the novel for the first issue of the international literary journal, *Cosmopolis*.[21] That some of Gosse's remarks rankled, however, is clear from the postscript to the first of these letters:

One thing I did not answer. The "grimy" features of the story go to show the contrast between the ideal life a man wished to lead, and the squalid real life he was fated to lead. The throwing of the pizzle, at the supreme moment of his young dream, is to sharply initiate this contrast. But I must have lamentably failed, as I feel I have, if this requires explanation and is not self-evident. The idea was meant to run all through the novel. It is, in fact, to be discovered in *everybody's* life, though it lies less on the surface perhaps than it does in my poor puppet's.[22]

What Gosse so gratingly characterised as the "grimy" episodes in *Jude* were crucial to Hardy's whole conception, though it is significant of Hardy's sensitivity to criticism even at this late stage of his career that in revising the novel in 1903 he should have reduced the explicitness of Jude's first encounter with Arabella[23] —a scene deplored, of course, by other reviewers besides Gosse himself.

But if his revision removed the visual grotesquerie of Jude and Arabella engaging in amorous dalliance with the pig's pizzle dangling between them, Hardy retained a strong comic element in the scene, introducing, for example, a reference to Arabella's "novel artillery". To the schoolroom battle at Shaston, another scene to which objection had been made when the book first appeared, Hardy in his 1912 revision for the Wessex Edition added the farcical detail of the church warden being "dealt such a topper with the map of Palestine that his head went right through Samaria" (299).[24] Such scenes, Hardy had observed to Gosse on November 20, 1895, might more appropriately be compared to Fielding, to whom he himself "felt akin locally", than to Zola, in whom he was "very little" read,[25] and there seems no doubt that he saw them as primarily comic both in form and function.

One remarkable feature of *Jude* is the lightness of the opening manner: the early pages offer few hints of the way the story is to end. If the tone here is scarcely comic, it is often humorous, and Jude himself tends to be viewed with affectionate amusement.

While we may sympathise with his compassion for the birds he is supposed to be scaring away, we also smile at his lack of practical good sense. His entrapment into marriage is a disaster, but the tricks used by Arabella Donn (that arable bella donna) are of a kind which would, in a slightly different context, make Jude into a butt for time-honoured mirth. Comic irony is everywhere implicit in the vanity of Jude's ambitions, a soaring superstructure based on frail foundations; in his manner of listing the vast un-done as if, somehow, it was as good as accomplished; in the disrup-tion of this train of thought by the arrival of Arabella's outrageous missile. The first hint of interruption coincides with the mention of Aristophanes in the recital of authors he has yet to read; the pizzle itself arrives just as he has made a virtual godhead of Christminster and a Christ of himself: "Yes, Christminster shall be my Alma Mater; and I'll be her beloved son, in whom she shall be well pleased" (41).

The irony, emphatic yet controlled, serves several purposes. Not only is the relative lightness at the beginning a necessary starting-point for the story's subsequent decline into disaster and death, but the occasional presentation of Jude in a humorous light helps to establish a sense of his normality, his human fallibi-lity, and thus to prevent his appearing as an offensive prig. The juxtaposition of Jude's dogged Anglicanism with Sue's frank paganism—his assumption, for example, that Miss Fontover must have destroyed Sue's statues because they were "too Catholic-apostolic for her" (120)—is one of several ways in which the note of comedy is kept alive, and with it our sense of Jude as a potentially comic figure. The commentary provided by Aunt Drusilla and the Widow Edlin also incorporates comic elements, while even Phillotson, in his moment of abnegation, is made to cut a ludicrous figure in the world's eyes and given a central role in the outright comedy of the brawl at the public enquiry.

As the example of Phillotson would suggest, the alternation of "doubt, fear, and hope" runs throughout the novel. Although the course of events is persistently downward, the descent into utter disaster following the fatal return to Christminster in pursuit of Jude's obsession is both late and sudden. Only a few chapters earlier, in the scene at the Great Wessex Agricultural Show, Jude and Sue have been seen at their happiest, and the positive aspects of their comradeship have received their strongest celebration:

> Sue, in her new summer clothes, flexible and light as a bird, her little thumb stuck up by the stem of her white cotton sunshade, went along as if she hardly touched ground, and as if a moderately strong puff of wind would float her over the hedge into the next field. Jude, in his light grey holiday-suit, was really proud of her companionship, not more for her external attractiveness than for her sympathetic words and ways. That complete mutual understanding, in which every glance and movement was as effectual as speech for conveying intelligence between them, made them almost the two parts of a single whole. (352)

The momentary upward movement is skilfully held in check by the looming background presence of a scornful yet envious Arabella, appearing here, as so often in the novel, as a figure of ill omen. If the promise of what might yet be is strong, so is the blighting threat of what must be.

The pattern of *Jude* cannot be spoken of as a fall from "great estate", except in so far as the central figure does exemplify—in all aspects of his emotional, intellectual, and spiritual life—the gradual, relentless atrophy of hope, the one thing in which he had been rich when the novel opened. Hardy spoke in his original Preface of "the tragedy of unfulfilled aims" (viii), and if this is understood as applying not merely to the educational theme but to the whole of Jude's experience it sufficiently points to the degree of waste and agony involved. It is, indeed, tempting to reflect on the possible association of Jude's name with that of Judas Iscariot, and on the theme of betrayal as it appears in the novel. Jude in the latter stages of the book speaks of himself, in self-dramatising fashion, as Sue's "seducer", but if he technically betrays Sue, this is far outweighed by her eventual betrayal of their achieved relationship when she returns to Phillotson, who himself betrays by his final surrender to selfishness and repressiveness the altruism and open-mindedness he had originally shown in letting Sue go. Jude's most serious betrayal is surely of his own dream, as he abandons the pursuit of education and self-advancement at the first contact with Arabella's sexuality, while dominating the whole book is the sense of Christminster's betrayal of Jude, his efforts, and his ambitions.

This larger treachery has itself to be evaluated in terms of our cumulative awareness of the ultimate self-betrayal of Christminster itself and, by implication, of the society and civilisation of which it is the fine flower. As the book proceeds, it becomes increasingly clear not merely that Christminster is impregnable to such as Jude, but that the values the college walls protect are themselves hypocritical and debased. The point is heavily underlined by the incident in which the cab-driver kicks his horse in the belly: 'If that can be done,' said Jude, 'at college gates in the most religious and educational city in the world, what shall we say as to how far we've got?' " (395) Christminster, though "religious and educational", is not enlightened. Jude on his first visit to the city had recalled the enthusiastic words of Matthew Arnold:

> 'Beautiful city! so venerable, so lovely, so unravaged by the fierce intellectual life of our century, so serene! . . . Her ineffable charm keeps ever calling us to the true goal of all of us, to the ideal, to perfection.' (94-95)

Although Jude, Hardy notes, had forgotten that Arnold also "mourned Christminster as 'the home of lost causes'" (94), his subsequent experiences conspire to teach him that what Christminster represents and teaches is far from synonymous with sweetness and light. Yet the fascination with Christminster remains, as obsessive, as illusory, and, for Jude and those dear to him, as dangerous as Sue's rigid adherence to shifting principles and her propensity for "impulsive penances" (436). The dream gains the upper hand, indeed, just at the moment when human and economic needs are greatest, becoming a nightmare as Jude insists on watching the Remembrance Day procession, ignoring both the rain which is to lead eventually to his own death and the lack of lodgings which is to lead immediately to the death of his children.

Ultimately, perhaps, Jude's obsession with Christminster

should be seen in terms of its relationship to deeper, obscurer needs. What he carves on the milestone is not "Christminster" but "Thither" (85). Hardy at one point suggests that Jude's obsession goes absolutely against the grain of his background, his training, and his own best instincts. When Jude first seeks work in Christminster he goes to a busy stone-mason's yard:

> For a moment there fell on Jude a true illumination; that here in the stone yard was a centre of effort as worthy as that digni-fied by the name of scholarly study within the noblest of the colleges. But he lost it under stress of his old idea. He would accept any employment which might be offered him on the strength of his late employer's recommendation; but he would accept it as a provisional thing only. This was his form of the modern vice of unrest. (98)

Hardy places a high value on Jude's skill, and on the dignity of craftsmanship; he also establishes here the ironies implicit in Jude's quest, in his rejection of that valuable possession his crafts-manship for the sake of a false grail.[26] Clearly, there is a bitter sense in which the Master of Biblioll College is right to advise Jude that the best chances of success lie in "remaining in your own sphere and sticking to your trade" (138). Characteristically, how-ever, Hardy undercuts this position by pointing out that the work being done in the yard was "at best only copying, patching and imitating", and that the mediaevalism in which Jude (like Hardy himself) had been trained was "as dead as a fern-leaf in a lump of coal" (98–99). The paragraph quoted nonetheless illustrates Hardy's skill in drawing out and sustaining all the ironies implicit in his material and in his story, and in manipulating the occupa-tion of his protagonist as an element integral to the total pattern. It is not simply that Hardy uses developments in architectural decoration to suggest much broader historical movements, or that the craftsmanship involved in stone-masonry is established as an alternative ideal to the one which Jude actually pursues; even more important is the way in which Jude's trade is one which ties him to old buildings, churches, and graveyards—to the restoration of the past and the perpetuation of precisely those influences and traditions which bar his educational and social aspirations and menace the privacy of his life with Sue. Jude and Sue are necessarily at war with dogma, with regulations, with rules of conduct, and their dismissal from the task of restoring the lettering of the Ten Commandments develops into a kind of savage pun on the novel's epigraph, "The letter killeth".

The allusive device is entirely characteristic of a novel in which points are driven home with the firmness and almost the explicitness of the marginal commentary in the *Pilgrim's Progress*. For none of the characters in *Jude* does Hardy offer anything approaching an extended psychological analysis: his people are made to reveal themselves in action and in dialogue. Even fundamentally unreflective characters like Arabella are required to indulge in verbalised self-analysis, and the novel moves through a series of moments not so much of vision as of revelation, with the central characters defining their mingled affinity and opposition through direct intellectual or emotional confrontation, or in terms of their differing responses to people, objects, or institutions wholly external to themselves and their immediate relationship. So Jude and Arabella clash over the killing of the pig, Jude and Sue disagree over Christminster and react differently to the pictures at Wardour Castle:

> They reached the Park and Castle and wandered through the picture-galleries, Jude stopping by preference in front of the devotional pictures by Del Sarto, Guido Reni, Spagnoletto, Sassoferrato, Carlo Dolci, and others. Sue paused patiently beside him, and stole critical looks into his face as, regarding the Virgins, Holy Families, and Saints, it grew reverent and abstracted. When she had thoroughly estimated him at this, she would move on and wait for him before a Lely or Reynolds. It was evident that her cousin deeply interested her, as one might be interested in a man puzzling out his way along a labyrinth from which one had one's self escaped. (163)

As so often in Hardy, the points of external reference are not merely concrete but authentic. Wardour Castle, an actual place, contained just such paintings as Hardy specifies. Similarly,

Shaston is the old name for Shaftesbury, and the town is described in phrases taken in part from Hutchins's *History and Antiquities of Dorset*. To all intents and purposes Christminster *is* Oxford, Melchester Salisbury. *Jude* is crowded with place-names, often thinly disguised adaptations of the real names of substantial towns in and near the Thames Valley—places, that is to say, well-known to many of his readers, not remote Dorset hamlets but precisely the kind of "raw towns that we believe and die in". Movement from place to place is persistent throughout the novel, its importance emphasised by the heading given to the various parts: "At Marygreen", "At Christminster", and so on. Yet *Jude* is a novel curiously deficient in the sense of place. Apart from Christminster and Shaston, the places visited by Sue and Jude remain, by comparison with the places in Hardy's other novels, singularly devoid of individuality, atmosphere, associations. Gosse, in his *Cosmopolis* review, attributed this to the quality of the actual landscape:

> Berkshire is an unpoetical county, "meanly utilitarian," as Mr. Hardy confesses; the imagination hates its concave, loamy cornfields and dreary, hedgeless highways. The local history has been singularly tampered with in Berkshire; it is useless to speak to us of ancient records where the past is all obliterated, and the thatched and dormered houses replaced by modern cottages. In choosing North Wessex as the scene of a novel Mr. Hardy wilfully deprives himself of a great element of his strength. Where there are no prehistoric monuments, no ancient buildings, no mossed and immemorial woodlands, he is Sampson shorn. In Berkshire, the change which is coming over England so rapidly, the resignation of the old dreamy elements of beauty, has proceeded further than anywhere else in Wessex. Pastoral loveliness is to be discovered only here and there, while in Dorsetshire it still remains the master-element.[27]

The criticism is an unwitting acknowledgment of Hardy's success. Like the prophecies, the sudden violent events, and the clamorous ironies, the multiple settings of *Jude* serve to throw into relief at once the sequence and the patterning of the central action. The story is full of arrivals and departures, new beginnings attempted and old paths inadvertently re-entered. The featureless towns and villages of North Wessex—Ald*brick*ham, Stoke-*Bare*hills, and the rest—answer precisely to the rootlessness of the nomadic life to which Jude and Sue are progressively reduced. They also perhaps serve, like the stages of Tess's pilgrimage, as Bunyanesque testing-places of the soul and as externalisations of internal states. W. J. Keith has argued, indeed, that the landscape of the novel is in effect the creation of Jude's own vision and intellect and functions less as background or setting than as "symbolic commentary".[28]

The narrative itself follows these journeyings with unusual closeness. Instead of moving all aspects of the story forward concurrently, at more or less the same pace, Hardy tends to push ahead quickly on a narrow front, following the history of a particular character or group of characters and leaving other contemporary aspects of the story to be covered at a later stage. Thus we are kept, with Jude, in ignorance of Arabella's return from Australia until she suddenly materialises behind the bar in Christminster. When Sue leaves Phillotson we find she has gone to meet Jude by previous arrangement, though there had been no firm indication of this before her departure. At the simplest, of course, this method brings to the narrative an element of surprise and even of suspense. More generally, and perhaps more importantly, it contributes to the experience of restlessness and discontinuity, to the way in which good intentions are unexpectedly thwarted, ideals abruptly shattered, the best-laid plans turned suddenly awry.

The characteristic restlessness of the novel operates as an image, a dramatic reflection, of "the modern vice of unrest" (98). Hardy apparently comprehends in this term not only the breakdown in traditional patterns of rural life and the greater ease of physical mobility brought about by those railways which play such an important part in *Jude*, but also the spiritual and intellectual disruption of the time, Matthew Arnold's "strange disease of modern life". Jude is perhaps in some sense ironically identified with the hero of "The Scholar Gypsy", whom the narrator—himself seated on a hill-top, whence his eye, like Jude's from the Brown House, "travels down to Oxford's towers"—imagines as wandering in solitude, cherishing "the unconquerable hope" with a tenacity impossible to a more sophisticated world. The urgent warning to the Scholar Gypsy embodies a prediction which closely matches Jude's own case:

> "But fly our paths, our feverish contact fly!
> For strong the infection of our mental strife,
>   Which, though it gives no bliss, yet spoils for rest;
> And we should win thee from thy own fair life,
>   Like us distracted, and like us unblest,
>   Soon, soon thy cheer would die,
> Thy hopes grow timorous, and unfix'd thy powers,
>   And thy clear aims be cross and shifting made;
> And then thy glad perennial youth would fade,
> Fade, and grow old at last, and die like ours."[29]

Jude does not escape the infection. Christminster beckons him; the echoes of the Tractarian movement have reached even his little village; neither his faith nor Sue's unbelief proves sufficient to withstand the strains put upon them. As in *The Return of the Native* and *A Laodicean*, both of which anticipate important aspects of *Jude*, there are suggestions of a deliberate rejection of Arnoldian ideas. No more than in those earlier novels, however, does Hardy offer a resolution of the intellectual and social dilemmas which his characters confront. "Like former productions of this pen," observes the 1895 Preface, "*Jude the Obscure* is simply an endeavour to give shape and coherence to a series of seemings, or personal impressions, the question of their consistency or their discordance, of their permanence or their transitoriness, being regarded as not of the first moment" (viii). If the intellectual concepts embodied in *Jude* do not cohere, that is perhaps because they were never intended to do so, because Hardy conceived and composed his last novel as a comprehensive image of intellectual and social chaos. If the wandering Jude is permitted visions of a promised land, he is himself forbidden to enter it, and Hardy closes the book—and, with it, his career as a novelist—on a scene of despair, bitterness and death, of mankind still languishing in the wilderness. Hardy can scarcely have expected such a novel to be universally welcomed, and the crucial paragraph of his original Preface not only summarised the book's central themes and hinted at their relative importance but sounded an unmistakable note of conscious challenge:

> For a novel addressed by a man to men and women of full age; which attempts to deal unaffectedly with the fret and fever, derision and disaster, that may press in the wake of the strongest passion known to humanity; to tell, without a mincing of words, of a deadly war waged between flesh and spirit; and to point the tragedy of unfulfilled aims, I am not aware that there is anything in the handling to which exception can be taken. (viii)

Afterword
THE END OF PROSE

The End of Prose

Hardy seems to have been much more communicative about *Jude* in his private correspondence than about any of his earlier novels. At the same time as he was writing the letters to Gosse published in *Later Years* (40-43), he was expressing precisely similar views to some of his other friends: on November 10, 1895, for example, he wrote not only to Gosse but to Mrs Henniker and Edward Clodd, stressing again and again, as he was to do in subsequent letters, that although he regarded *Jude* as a work which "makes for morality", it was not a manifesto upon the marriage question, nor did it advocate a programme of any kind.[1] As he told Sir George Douglas ten days later: "The marriage question was made the vehicle of the tragedy, in one part, but I did not intend to argue it at all on its merits. I feel that a bad marriage is one of the direst things on earth, & one of the cruellest things, but beyond that my opinions on the subject are vague enough."[2]

Hardy's insistence on these points was a response to the early reviews, some of which had recoiled in mingled revulsion and incomprehension. "Did you see that the *World* nearly fainted away, & *Pall Mall* went into fits over the story?" he asked Douglas, in a reference to the pieces respectively entitled "Hardy the Degenerate" and "Jude the Obscene".[3] In his November 10 letter to Mrs Henniker, Hardy had declared himself to be somewhat indifferent to the opinions of the reviewers, and he told Douglas two months later:

I have really not been much upset by the missiles heaved at the poor book—not nearly so much as by my own opinion on its shortcomings. Somehow I feel that the critics are not sincere: everybody knows that silence is the remedy in the case of immoral works. But they advertise it with sensational headings, because that advertises their newspapers—a far more important matter with them than so-called immorality.[4]

Although the reviews were less uniformly hostile than the account in *Later Years* (39) might suggest, much of the comment was gratuitously and often grossly offensive. Supporters and denigrators of the novel also wrote directly to Hardy himself, as he reported to Mrs Henniker on November 30, 1895, and he had even to experience the betrayal of friends: in a letter to Gosse of July 1909 he recalled how angry he had been years before when Gosse spoke to his face of the extreme indecency of *Jude*.[5] To Hardy, with his sensitivity to criticism, the whole affair must have been thoroughly distasteful. That it was also hurtful, despite the bold face he presented to his friends, passages deleted from the *Later Years* typescript sufficiently demonstrate; at one point, it appears, he collected notes for an article in reply, "the criticisms being outrageously personal, unfair, and untrue".[6] It is by no means clear, however, that the attacks on *Jude* were the cause of his abandonment of fiction.[7]

The very violence of the response to *Jude* was an index of the position Hardy had achieved. "None but a writer of exceptional talent indeed," concluded the reviewer in the *World*, "could have produced so gruesome and gloomy a book; but that is the mischief of it. *Corruptio optimi pessima*."[8] Since the publication of *Tess*, Hardy had been widely acknowledged not just as a major novelist, but as the leading English novelist of his day. The first published attempt to map his fictional Wessex was made in the London *Bookman* in October 1891, during the serialisation of *Tess*;[9] after the novel's publication the incidence of interviews with "the author of *Tess*" greatly increased, and in 1894 the first two book-length studies of Hardy made their appearance. "Both Lionel Johnsons [sic] book & another on my novels by Miss Macdonell were unauthorized by me, as you will suppose," Hardy reported to Douglas. "While he is too pedantic, & hers too knowing, & both are too laudatory, they are not in bad taste on the whole, if one concedes that they had to be written, which I do not quite. Indeed I rather dreaded their appearance."[10]

Hardy's reputation now seemed secure, and he could regard with some satisfaction the shelf of novels and short stories he had written and the financial security he had won. His new publishers, Osgood, McIlvaine, had begun in April 1895 the publication in monthly volumes of the first complete collected edition of "The Wessex Novels"—Sampson Low had brought out several of the novels in a matching format some years earlier—and it was as the eighth volume of the Osgood, McIlvaine edition that *Jude* made its appearance. It must have seemed to Hardy a highly propitious moment for his long-contemplated return to poetry. Direct evidence is lacking, but the crucial decision almost certainly preceded the publication of *Jude*, and perhaps even its composition. In a note attributed in *Early Life* (302) to Christmas Day, 1890, Hardy recorded: "While thinking of resuming 'the viewless wings of poesy' before dawn this morning, new horizons seemed to open, and worrying pettiness to disappear." In preparing his novels for the Osgood, McIlvaine edition he not only revised the texts and regularised the Wessex names and descriptions but wrote a series of prefaces casting a retrospective and suspiciously valedictory glance—self-critical yet far from apologetic—over his past career as a writer of fiction. In *Jude* itself the very forcefulness of the social criticism suggests that he knew the novel was to be his last and deliberately incorporated views and feelings which had been largely suppressed since the time of *The Poor Man and the Lady*.

Whenever Hardy may have decided upon it, the shift from fiction to poetry became effective following the completion of the revisions to *The Well-Beloved*: on June 3, 1897, he told Mrs Henniker that since correcting *The Well-Beloved* he had given novels no thought whatsoever.[11] He did subsequently publish three short stories, the last of them, "A Changed Man", as late as April 1900, but he seems not to have contemplated embarking upon another novel. And while *Wessex Poems* did not appear until the end of December 1898, Hardy's first reference to it serves to dramatise what *Later Years*(1) calls "the end of prose" in a more immediate way. The Preface to the first edition of *The Well-Beloved* is dated "January 1897"; against the date February 4, 1897, *Later Years* (58) records: "Title: 'Wessex Poems: with Sketches of their Scenes by the Author'."

* * *

If the shift from prose to poetry was to prove both complete and final, the title of the first volume of verse nonetheless pointed to the presence of a strong element of continuity. Quite apart from *Wessex Poems*, indeed, the titles of such subsequent volumes as *Time's Laughingstocks*, *Satires of Circumstance*, *Moments of Vision*, and *Winter Words* are themselves evocative of moods and narrative patterns made familiar by Hardy's fiction, and it has already been suggested that *The Dynasts* represents both the logical outcome of tendencies evident throughout the novels and one of the most comprehensive expressions of his matured conception of Wessex. But if Hardy's creation of Wessex held for him an imaginative scope and relevance extending far beyond the limits of his career as a novelist, it was as a specifically fictional, novelistic world that Wessex was first evolved and given its richest and most directly functional development.

In July 1889, in the interval between *The Woodlanders* and *Tess of the d'Urbervilles*, J. M. Barrie published an article in the *Contemporary Review* entitled "Thomas Hardy: The Historian of Wessex". Though he found *The Woodlanders* itself disappointing, Barrie was deeply sympathetic to the other novels with Wessex settings and spoke of Hardy as "the only realist to be considered, so far as life in country parts is concerned": "he knows the common as Mr. Jefferies knew it; but he knows the inhabitants, as well as the common".[12] But the accuracy of Hardy's descriptions, both of the countryside and of country people, has sometimes been called in doubt. After a visit to Max Gate in September 1895, George Gissing wrote to his brother:

There is a deplorable inclination in Thomas to fashionable society; his talk is much of lords & dignitaries. This, I think, is greatly due to his wife's influence. But other things surprised me. I find that he does not know the flowers of the field! And it is plain that he does not read much. On the whole, he is a very difficult man to understand, & I suspect that his own home is *not* the best place for getting to know him.[13]

Despite its evident exaggerations, Gissing's letter usefully counterbalances Barrie's remarks and serves as a reminder that Hardy, for good or ill, lacked that preoccupation with minutely discriminated rural detail which distinguishes the work of Richard Jefferies.

As a working journalist, Jefferies wrote too much too fast. That his essays on nature and the countryside survive is largely a tribute to the strength they derive from their author's instinct for the specific, and from his apparently inexhaustible reservoir of recollected observation. Hardy's strengths lie elsewhere. The naturalist in him, though certainly present, never becomes highly developed, and there are few passages in his work comparable to the meticulous, if somewhat miscellaneous, perceptions of books like *The Gamekeeper at Home* and *The Amateur Poacher*. At a period when the precise description of natural detail had become almost *de rigueur* for poets and artists alike—inducing urban painters to get up their botany and short-sighted poets to peer intently at horse-chestnut buds—most of Hardy's references to flora and fauna are made in very general terms.[14] In the famous opening chapters of *The Return of the Native* there is scarcely a specific allusion other than those to thorn, furze, and the dried heath-bells. In the lushest descriptions of Tess's sojourn at Talbothays hardly a plant receives a name, apart from the garlic which has to be rooted up, and from the flocks of birds and waterfowl only the heron is singled out. Even in a poem like "Afterwards" the actual references to natural phenomena tend to be somewhat imprecise ("glad green leaves", "dewfall-hawk", "mothy"), and it seems characteristic that most of the stanzas should deal with darkness rather than with daylight, and with animals rather than plants.[15] The poem offers not so much natural observation of and for itself, but the experience of such observation—the sense of what it feels like to stand exposed to the life of nature at particular times and places. Hardy's response is to the active life of nature as it impinges upon the life of men. His passages of natural description are almost always mediated by a human presence, actual or implied—for example, the furze-cutter, the rambler, the "dwellers in a wood" invoked in the opening pages of, respectively, *The Return of the Native*, *The Woodlanders*, and *Under the Greenwood Tree*. Nature chiefly concerns him not as a spectacle but as the environment which determines the infinitely variable conditions of existence for those who live on and by the land.

Hardy's presentation of rural society has itself been called into question by E. W. Martin, an historian of the English countryside. Martin argued in 1949 that Hardy was too isolated from the rural labourer—by his own class-assumptions and by his reputation for godlessness—to fully understand either the man or the manual work he performed. For all his "genuine sympathy and insight", Hardy remained no more than "a knowledgeable stranger, a foreigner and an outsider to whom no labourer would talk freely"; countryman though he was, "as a novelist Hardy was forced by circumstances to rely upon a study of records and documents, upon observations of manners and customs, and not sufficiently upon the actual living human being".[16] The evidence of "The Dorsetshire Labourer" would seem to lend substantial support to such views. Yet no more than the question of the historical and regional authenticity of the Wessex novels are such considerations really relevant to an assessment of Hardy's achievement as a novelist. What matters in the fiction is not the literal accuracy or inaccuracy of Hardy's observations of man and nature but his capacity to project a convincing image of characters in their setting. John F. Lynen has said of Robert Frost, often praised for the "realism" of his evocations of the people and landscape of New England, that what his poems in fact present is not reality itself but a symbolic picture expressive of the essence of that reality.[17] George Gissing perhaps had a similar conception in mind when he spoke of Hardy as being not a realist but the author of "fantasias on the rural theme".[18]

That Hardy did not think of himself as a realist is clear from various comments recorded in *Early Life* and from the perceptive critique of literary realism which he contributed to the *New Review* symposium, "The Science of Fiction", in 1891. Yet his definition of realism on that occasion—"an artificiality distilled from the fruits of closest observation"[19]—might well stand as a definition of Wessex. Though firmly grounded in reality, Wessex remains essentially fictional, "an imaginative Wessex only". It is an artificiality, a deliberately created fictional world. Certainly less comprehensive and systematic than Balzac's world in the *Comédie humaine*, it yet offers a regional image richer than Trollope's, more ambitious than Arnold Bennett's or Willa Cather's. The closest parallel, at least among novelists writing in English, would seem to be with William Faulkner, the creater of Yoknapatawpha County.

"Beginning with *Sartoris*," said Faulkner, in his most explicit and most famous statement about the origins of Yoknapatawpha, "I discovered that my own little postage stamp of native soil was worth writing about and that I would never live long enough to exhaust it, and that by sublimating the actual into apocryphal I would have complete liberty to use whatever talent I might have to its absolute top. It opened up a gold mine of other peoples, so I created a cosmos of my own. I can move these people around like God, not only in space but in time too."[20] In answer to another question about the creation of Yoknapatawpha, Faulkner recalled:

> I think it was because about that time I realized there was a great deal of writing I wanted to do, had to do, and I could simplify, economize, by picking out one country and putting enough people in it to keep me busy. And save myself trouble, time—that was probably a reason. Or it may have been the same reason that is responsible for the long clumsy sentences and paragraphs. I was still trying to reduce my one individual experience of the world into one compact thing which could be picked up and held in the hands at one time.[21]

Faulkner's world was thus fluid but organic. It was also microcosmic—the individual experience reduced to one compact thing —and quite self-consciously an artefact: something deliberately created and capable of being held in the hand, contemplated from all sides like a Grecian urn or a jar in Tennessee, like the "intact world" he so much admired in Balzac.[22]

There are at least superficial resemblances between such statements of Faulkner's and some of Hardy's remarks in the General Preface to the Wessex Edition:

> I would state that the geographical limits of the stage here trodden were not absolutely forced upon the writer by circumstances; he forced them upon himself from judgment. I considered that our magnificent heritage from the Greeks in dramatic literature found sufficient room for a large proportion of its action in an extent of their country not much larger than the half-dozen counties here reunited under the old name of Wessex, that the domestic emotions have throbbed in Wessex nooks with as much intensity as in the palaces of Europe, and that, anyhow, there was quite enough human nature in Wessex for one man's literary purpose.[23]

Recognising that his own native soil would be ground and space enough for all his purposes, Hardy succeeded, like Faulkner, in "sublimating the actual into apocryphal". In both writers this fundamental rootedness is a source of immense strength. Something comparable, again, to Faulkner's sense of the need for a microcosmic world seems to be implicit in Hardy's allusions to Greek literature, especially when these are associated with his interest in the dramatic unities (most notably in *The Return of the Native*) and with his famous remark early in *The Woodlanders* about "those sequestered spots outside the gates of the world" in which "from time to time, dramas of a grandeur and unity truly Sophoclean are enacted in the real, by virtue of the concentrated passions and closely-knit interdependence of the lives therein" (4–5). What Hardy sought in book after book was precisely the sense of isolation in individual towns, villages, and hamlets, the absence of alternatives, the claustrophobic pressures of the close-knit community, the violent disruption that could be produced by the incursion of a newcomer from the world beyond—the kind of dramatic ingredients, indeed, which Conrad found on ships and islands. It was in response to such inner and outer pressures—Hardy's needs as a novelist and the actual conditions of his chosen region—that Wessex took its shape. Despite the centrality of Casterbridge, Wessex remains essentially a world of separate communities—Mellstock, Egdon, Weatherbury, Little Hintock—each tightly closed upon itself.

Hardy's procedure as a regionalist was thus to scrutinise microcosmic samples, to blow up particular segments of the map into much larger scale, to insist upon the particular rather than upon the whole. Historically the method was entirely appropriate: as Charles Kegan Paul observed in 1876, "Dorset was the very last county in England whose sacred soil was broken by a railroad, and those which now traverse it leave the very heart of the shire untouched."[24] At the same time, the general lack of movement and the scarcity of cross-references—from one place to another, or from one novel to another—suggest that Hardy simply did not conceive of Wessex as Faulkner did of Yoknapatawpha: organically, comprehensively, centripetally. The microcosmic concern displayed itself in a sequence of separate exemplars, not in the creation of a single world so tightly integrated that it was capable of being held in the hand.

It is clearly crucial to both worlds that the setting should be rural. Though neither writer is in any important sense a naturalist, both are extraordinarily sensitive to natural phenomena: it is instructive, for instance, to compare Hardy's description in *Tess* (166) of the difference in the quality of light at dawn and dusk with Faulkner's elaboration of a similar perception in *The Hamlet*.[25] Both see rural life somewhat in the terms of the Preface to the *Lyrical Ballads*—a work whose influence Hardy himself acknowledged[26]—and of Wordsworth's insistence upon the directness with which human passions reveal themselves in the simpler context of rural life. In his essay, "The Profitable Reading of Fiction", Hardy argued that "social refinement operates upon character in a way which is oftener than not prejudicial to vigorous portraiture, by making the exteriors of men their screen rather than their index, as with untutored mankind".[27] In 1892 he used specifically Wordsworthian terminology in explaining that he had chosen to write of country people because "their passions are franker, for one thing".[28] Cleanth Brooks, demonstrating Faulkner's affinity with Wordsworth, speaks of his creation of an isolated and culturally backward rural society in which "human nature operates without the refinements and restraints that we associate with a modern urban world, but also without its inhibitions and disguises".[29]

When Brooks identifies such presentation as belonging essentially to the pastoral mode,[30] his perception seems relevant also to some of Hardy's Wessex fiction. What is in question here is not so much the particular convention of English pastoral poetry—as invoked by Robert Y. Drake, Jr, in his analysis of *The Woodlanders* as "traditional pastoral"[31]—but rather the essential strategy embodied in all pastoral literature. John F. Lynen sees the pastoral stance as deriving from the perennial impulse of those living in complex urban societies to evaluate their own world in terms of the standards of a simpler rural world.[32] It is not to be identified with self-conscious ruralism, back-to-naturism, or the agrarian myth. Though the subject-matter is rural, it is always viewed with implicit reference to the dominant culture, the more complex and sophisticated world of experience shared by the author and his reader. The author is engaged not in an accurate portrayal of a particular region for its own sake, but rather in drawing selectively upon the actual features of that region in the deliberate creation of a world essentially his own—symbolic, isolated, unique. In presenting this world the author is in effect inviting his audience in nineteenth-century London or twentieth-century New York to contemplate another and simpler world than the one he and they inhabit, a world characterised by values and standards of conduct which they in their sophistication have lost sight of.

Raymond Williams has argued that Hardy's fiction must not be viewed "in the sentimental terms of a pastoral: the contrast between country and town",[33] and it is certainly true that rural Wessex is by no means exempt from the characteristic dilemmas —social, economic, intellectual, moral—of Victorianism. Yet it is

clearly of the first importance that the characters and their situations belong not to the town but to the countryside, often the
remote countryside, and that the resulting culture-lag should be
further exaggerated by the choice of a vague but specifically non-
contemporary location in time. Williams, clearly, is thinking
chiefly in terms of traditional pastoral stereotypes—he refers to
the "pastoral convention of the countryman as an age-old figure"
—rather than of the pastoral strategy in its larger and more
general sense: elsewhere in the article, indeed, he himself makes
the point that Hardy was writing of a rural world for an essentially
urban reading public, dealing in simplicity for the sophisticated.[34]

To think of Hardy and Faulkner as in some sense exponents of
the pastoral mode does at least help to make sense of their curious
situation as artists living in backward rural areas and in cultural
isolation but necessarily addressing themselves to an audience of
city-dwellers. In "The Profitable Reading of Fiction" Hardy
spoke first of all of the simplest kind of pleasure to be got from
reading and of its dependence upon a sudden shift of scene: "The
town man finds what he seeks in novels of the country, the
countryman in novels of society, the indoor class generally in outdoor novels, the villager in novels of the mansion, the aristocrat
in novels of the cottage."[35] Hardy saw it as part of his job as a
novelist to satisfy this kind of reading pleasure, among others, and
since his own books might fairly be described as outdoor novels of
the country and the cottage it could reasonably be concluded that
he expected to find his audience among town men, the aristocracy,
and "the indoor class generally". Obviously, however, neither he
nor Faulkner is writing escapist fiction. Both, on the contrary, are
profoundly moral writers, treating of human experience in general
—what Faulkner called "the old verities and truths of the heart"[36]
—and one aspect of their moral statement emerges precisely in the
creation of a symbolic rural world implicitly available for juxtaposition and contrast with the urban world of their readers. It
emerges too in the high valuation assigned in Hardy's fiction to
such characters as Gabriel Oak and Giles Winterborne, and in the
central significance to Faulkner's Snopes trilogy of V. K. Ratliff.
It is not so much that Oak and Winterborne and Ratliff are "close

to nature"—though they may be that in certain ways—but rather that they express a sane, normative, and profoundly moral viewpoint in specifically regional and perceptibly dialectal speech: they represent the rural voice at its best.

In both novelists the pastoral impulse is largely sustained through the exploitation of elements drawn from rural and traditional sources—tall tales, ballads, folk-songs, country crafts, customs, and superstitions. *Under the Greenwood Tree*, *Far from the Madding Crowd*, and *The Woodlanders*, the most specifically pastoral of Hardy's novels, are especially rich in such material, and the latter contains Hardy's most explicit statement of what it meant to live in an immemorially stable and isolated community:

> Winter in a solitary house in the country, without society, is tolerable, nay, even enjoyable and delightful, given certain conditions; but these are not the conditions which attach to the life of a professional man who drops down into such a place by mere accident. They were present to the lives of Winterborne, Melbury, and Grace; but not to the doctor's. They are old association—an almost exhaustive biographical or historical acquaintance with every object, animate and inanimate, within the observer's horizon. He must know all about those invisible ones of the days gone by, whose feet have traversed the fields which look so grey from his windows; recall whose creaking plough has turned those sods from time to time; whose hands planted the trees that form a crest to the opposite hill; whose horses and hounds have torn through that underwood; what birds affect that particular brake; what bygone domestic dramas of love, jealousy, revenge, or disappointment have been enacted in the cottages, the mansion, the street or on the green. The spot may have beauty, grandeur, salubrity, convenience; but if it lack memories it will ultimately pall upon him who settles there without opportunity of intercourse with his kind. (145–146)

Asked in 1892 how he had become a novelist, Hardy replied: "I suppose the impressions which all unconsciously I had been gathering of rural life during my youth in Dorsetshire recurred to me, and the theme—in fiction—seemed to have absolute freshness."[37] By 1892 Hardy knew his strengths as a novelist and recognised their source—that plot of native soil, narrow in area, infinite in possibilities, which he had come to know, during a childhood and youth spent in one isolated spot, with the kind of total intimacy of which he spoke in *The Woodlanders*. It was an all-sufficient setting and source of material, and Hardy made of it a world of perfect imaginative freedom.

"I may say, once for all," Hardy told Edward Clodd in 1894, "that every superstition, custom, &c., described in my novels may be depended on as true records of the same (whatever merit in folklorists [sic] eyes they may have as such)—& not inventions of mine."[38] As "The Historian of Wessex", Hardy's achievement was not to reconstruct authentic representations of specific moments in the past of his region, but rather, as Barrie rightly insisted, to record the features of a vanishing way of life: "The closing years of the nineteenth century see the end of many things in country parts, of the peasantry who never go beyond their own parish, of quaint manners and customs, of local modes of speech and ways of looking at existence. . . . Thus, the shepherds and thatchers and farmers and villagers, who were, will soon be no more, and if their likeness is not taken now it will be lost for ever."[39] To Hardy's achievement as the *novelist* of Wessex his recording role is significant only insofar as it reflects the immense security of the foundations upon which he erected his fictional world. What is crucial about Wessex is precisely that it *is* fictional, Hardy's own world, entirely available for his manipulation. Hardy perhaps did not perceive as clearly as Faulkner the full importance of such an invention. But if Wessex lacks the organic unity of Yoknapatawpha, it nonetheless emerges as an autonomous world essentially outside of time and space, pastoral in its setting and in its implications, permanently eloquent of permanent truths.

* * *

Once he had presented himself to the world as a poet, Hardy consistently insisted that his verse was "the more individual part of my literary fruitage", and that his prose, written out of necessity merely, was relatively inessential.[40] He apparently saw literature in hierarchical terms, with poetic drama at the top, lyric poetry a little lower down, prose fiction lower still, and prose drama (at least as practised in his own day) firmly at the bottom. He certainly took particular pride in *The Dynasts* and in his successive volumes of verse, and always regretted that his achievement as a poet seemed permanently overshadowed by his reputation as a novelist. He wrote to Gosse in February 1918: "For the relief of my necessities, as the Prayer Book puts it, I began writing novels, & made a sort of trade of it; but last night I found that I had spent more years in verse-writing than at prose-writing! (prose 25½ yrs. —verse 26 years.) Yet my my [sic] verses will always be considered a bye-product, I suppose, owing to this odd accident of the printing press."[41]

Hardy did not, however, hold his fiction in contempt. As his letter to Gosse suggests, his dismissive comments upon it were largely designed to challenge the reluctance of critics and readers to take him seriously as a poet. While reading proof for the Macmillan Wessex edition in October 1912 he expressed to Edward Clodd a wish that half of what he had written could be destroyed;[42] even assuming the comment to have been seriously made, what seems infinitely more significant is the fact of the Wessex edition itself. Quite apart from earlier revisions to individual books, Hardy had in 1895–96 revised all his novels and short story volumes for Osgood, McIlvaine; in 1902 he made minor corrections and alterations to this edition when the plates were taken over by Macmillan;[43] in 1912, for the Wessex edition, he undertook a second major revision of all his work. Nor did the process end there: he made a few more corrections, chiefly to *A Pair of Blue Eyes*, for the Mellstock edition of 1919–20, and in 1920 he supplied Macmillan with still further corrections for incorporation in later printings from the Wessex edition plates.[44] Hardy's set of the Wessex edition in the Dorset County Museum has been marked to show a few additional corrections, some of them made as late as September 1926; the note on the ending of "The Romantic Adventures of a Milkmaid" is dated 1927.[45]

Though constantly refining the texts of his novels and short stories, Hardy made little attempt to weed any of them out. His low opinion of the stories collected in *A Changed Man* did not prevent him from publishing the volume in 1913, although he complained to Douglas that his hand had been forced by the circulation of pirated American editions.[46] Despite his remark to Clodd about destroying half of what he had written, it was he who in 1894 had pressed for the inclusion of *Desperate Remedies* in Macmillan's Colonial edition, recommending it as a book which always sold well.[47] Hardy's quickness in noting the omission from the list his publishers had prepared was very much in character. He read his contracts meticulously, and his correspondence with Macmillan[48] shows very strikingly his development, after the early experiences with Tinsley Brothers, into a shrewd manager of his own affairs. He had a sharp awareness of the profitability both of individual novels and of his fiction as a whole, and it was not only in a creative sense that the poetry could be called "the harvest of the novels".[49]

"*Melius fuerat non scribere*. But there it stands." So Hardy commented in his 1912 Preface to *Tess* (xxi) of the sub-title he had added to the first edition. He might have been speaking of his past work in general. He wanted for financial reasons to keep all his books in print; as an artist he was willing and even anxious to subject them to repeated minor revision; but once they had been published in volume form he was not prepared to rewrite or recast them in any fundamental way. An observation on this point survives among other notes which Hardy wrote for possible incorporation in the "Life":

> At one time he thought of re-writing some of his early hurried & immature novels, nobody knowing their faults better than he did. But being convinced that no really live & creative minds ever condescended to such tinkering, it being the mark rather of uninventive & plodding temperaments, he left the faulty novels alone, taking the track of showing his enlarged perceptions by creating entirely new works.[50]

That Hardy may have had Henry James especially in mind is

[353]

suggested by some remarks reported by a visitor to Max Gate in 1920:

> With reference to revision of literary work after it has been published, Hardy held decided views against a man of letters tampering too much with his creations. He was of the opinion that they lost their freshness and spontaneity in the process. He instanced the fastidious retouching in which Meredith and Henry James habitually indulged. He became particularly entertaining when speaking of James's fondness for emendation. Hardy had asked him if he ever saw his work finished, completed. No, James had replied, it was never finished because he was never satisfied with it, and he believed in constant revision. Hardy looked upon that as a sort of 'eternal proof reading.' When it had been necessary for the Wessex novelist to go over his work for new editions, he had only corrected obvious errors, and had retouched very little indeed.[51]

Although Hardy seems to have somewhat underplayed the extent of his own revisions, it is fascinating not only that he should have been aware of this difference between James's practice and his own but that he should have raised the matter in conversation with James himself.

James was of course working on the New York edition of his novels (published in England by Macmillan) at much the same period as Hardy was preparing the Wessex edition. The coincidence is only one of many curious juxtapositions which occur throughout their careers. James's notorious review of *Far from the Madding Crowd* in the New York *Nation*, with its call for novelists to observe the three unities, may conceivably have prompted Hardy's concern for the unities in *The Return of the Native*. On the other hand, it has recently been suggested that *The Portrait of a Lady* may have been influenced by James's reading of *Far from the Madding Crowd*.[52] A. C. Benson records in his diary for April 29, 1904, that he had been talking with Henry James in the smoking-room of the Athenaeum when Hardy came and sat on the other side of him:

I make it a rule *never* to introduce myself to the notice of distinguished men, unless they recognise me; Hardy had looked at
me, then looked away, suffused by a misty smile, and I presently
gathered that this was a recognition—he seemed hurt by my not
speaking to him. . . . Then we had an odd triangular talk. Hardy
could not hear what H. J. said, nor H. J. what Hardy said; and
I had to try and keep the ball going. I felt like Alice between the
two Queens. Hardy talked rather interestingly of Newman . . .
He said very firmly that N. was no logician; that the *Apologia*
was simply a poet's work, with a kind of lattice-work of logic in
places to screen the poetry. We talked of Maxime du Camp
and Flaubert, and H. J. delivered himself very oracularly on the
latter. Then Hardy went away wearily and kindly.[53]

The moment, with its comedy of mutual inaudibility, seems
eloquent of the whole relationship between Hardy and James, as
men and as artists. They first met at least as early as 1880[56] and
often encountered each other in subsequent years. A surviving
letter from James to Hardy suggests that in 1889 there may have
been an attempt to build a closer friendship,[56] and towards the
end of his life James—acknowledging Hardy's contribution to
Edith Wharton's compilation, *The Book of the Homeless*—could
sign himself "your very faithful and thankful old friend".[58] A
previous letter, however, in which James is still begging Hardy to
send Mrs Wharton a poem, betrays in its superbly managed
arabesques of courtesy a degree of uncertainty as to how Hardy
could best be approached and persuaded:

My dear Hardy,
    Your note gives me, for all its noble detachment, courage to
assault you again in sufficient measure just to say that if you *can*
manage between now and the 10th. to distil the liquor of your
poetic genius, in no matter how mild a form, into three or four
blest versicles, on Mrs. Wharton's behalf, by August 10th. (at
which date she tells me she should receive them) you would
enable me to think of you with a still more confirmed and en-
riched admiration, fidelity and gratitude. It is just the stray

sincerities and casual felicities of your muse that that intelligent lady *is* all ready to cherish—so just gently and helpfully over-flow, no matter into how tiny a cup, and believe me yours very constantly

Henry James

P.S. Let me say, to hearten you comparatively, that disgrace-fully void as I am of the rhyming impulse, I shall be reduced to respond to her with ponderous prose—of a sort only appreciable in the clumsy big chunk. I must hew out my block—so see how brevity breathes balmily on *you*![57]

There seems, in fact, to have been no real intimacy between the two men, and their private comments about each other were not entirely devoid of malice. *Later Years* (7–8) quotes the notorious exchange of letters between James and Stevenson about the "vile-ness" of *Tess;* omitted from the published text but still surviving in the typescript is the following comment: "When Hardy read this after James's death he said, 'How indecent of those two virtu-ous females to expose their mental nakedness in such a manner.'"[58] *Early Life* (179) quotes, clearly with arch intent, Hardy's query about James's relationship with Mrs Proctor;[59] again omitted from the published text, however, was the latter part of a note about a Rabelais Club dinner in 1886 at which Hardy "renewed acquaintance" with Henry James, "who has a ponderously warm manner of saying nothing in infinite sentences, and who left suddenly in the midst of the meal because he was placed low down the table, as I was. Rather comical in Henry."[60]

The Book of the Homeless was only the last of several occasions when Hardy and James found themselves publishing in the same places.[61] In 1890 they had both replied to questions asked by George Bainton in compiling his volume, *The Art of Authorship.* "Any studied rules I could not possibly give," Hardy declared, "for I know of none that are of practical utility. A writer's style is according to his temperament, and my impression is that if he has anything to say which is of value, and words to say it with, the style will come of itself."[62] Hardy's response—apparently derived from an idea Horace Moule had first formulated for him more than a quarter of a century earlier[63]—is brief and even meagre, suggesting, like his retreat from James's disquisition on Flaubert, an impatience with all abstract discussions of style and technique. "There isn't any technique about prose, is there?" Hamlin Garland quotes Hardy as saying many years later.[64] James's contribution, not surprisingly, was of a somewhat different kind:

> The question of literary form interests me indeed, but I am afraid I can give no more coherent or logical account of any little success I may have achieved in the cultivation of it than simply in saying that I have always been *fond* of it. If I manage to write with any clearness or concision or grace, it is simply that I have always tried. It isn't easy, and one must always try; for the traps that newspaper scribbling, and every other vulgarity, set for us to-day are innumerable. It is an advantage when the sense of certain differences awakes early. I had that good fortune, which, however, made me compose with mortal slowness at first. But it gave birth to the idea and the ideal of form, and that is a godsend even if one slowly arrives at it. A simple style is really a complicated thing, and in the way of an effort an evolution. I am afraid mine, if I have one, is simply taste and patience.[65]

Though James agrees essentially with Hardy that "the art of authorship" cannot be taught, he nonetheless feels that it can be learned. He is certainly interested enough in the question to worry it a little, sufficiently stimulated by it to write with engaging frankness of his own experience.

Hardy's later description of James as the "Polonius" of novelists[66] sufficiently suggests how he would have responded to James's acknowledgment of a "fondness" for form, and he no doubt felt that his own early experience as a working novelist, compelled by necessity to become "a good hand at a serial", had allowed him little opportunity for a slow, deliberate, disciplined development such as James describes. "Reading H. James's *Reverberator*," notes *Early Life* (227) under a date in the summer of 1888: "After this kind of work one feels inclined to be purposely careless in detail. The great novels of the future will certainly not concern themselves with the minutiae of manners. . . . [sic] James's subjects are those one could be interested in at moments when there is nothing larger to think of." Yet it is of some significance that Hardy, who rarely permitted himself a comment on a contemporary author, should have been reading James at all. Surviving notebooks show that he also read other books of James's, including *Roderick Hudson* and the study of Hawthorne, and he was recorded as saying in 1919 that although he could only read "a page or two" of Meredith, "Henry James he could always read to the end. He had thought of many of the subjects James had chosen independently, *e.g. On the wings of a dove* [sic], a man marrying a woman and knowing that she was going to die."[67] When, in 1903, Hardy first read *The Wings of the Dove*, he told Mrs Henniker that he and Emma had entirely failed to agree on what had actually happened in the novel; James, he added, was nonetheless "a real man of letters" and almost the only one of his contemporaries he could read.[68]

Hardy's respect for James as an artist sprang from a profound artistic engagement of his own. Raymond Williams has demonstrated the inadequacy of identifying Hardy with a "peasant" viewpoint,[69] and it is equally misleading to think of him as a kind of natural rustic genius, untutored, unreflective, divinely spontaneous. Although he seems essentially to have felt, as he told Galsworthy in 1909, that "an ounce of experience is worth a ton of theory",[70] surviving notebooks and published essays testify alike to his interest in contemporary debates about realism and naturalism and, as Morton Dauwen Zabel pointed out, to his need and capacity to evolve some kind of personal aesthetic.[71] Hardy is best seen as striving—consciously enough, but without great clarity of conceptualisation—towards perceived goals quite different in kind from those of James and Meredith. His techniques are lacking both in refinement and in consistency. Eclectically and even opportunistically adopted, they are as likely to be drawn from poetry and the drama as from the novel as traditionally understood—though some of them can perhaps be traced to Hawthorne and other romance-writers. His violent and melodramatic plots, as Virginia Woolf observed in the eloquent essay she wrote on the occasion of Hardy's death, "are part of that wild spirit of poetry which saw with intense irony and grimness that no reading of life can possibly outdo the strangeness of life itself, no symbol of caprice and unreason be too extreme to represent the astonishing circumstances of our existence".[72] Hardy, like his hero Shelley, is very much the romantic artist, bold in scope and expression, working through broad effects for intensification of emotional immediacy. His best novels do not accommodate themselves to a design, whether aesthetic or moral, but strike outwards from a core of experience, reverberate from a single cry of pain.

Meeting Hardy in his old age, Virginia Woolf was impressed by "his freedom, ease and vitality. He seemed very 'Great Victorian' doing the whole thing with a sweep of his hand (they are ordinary smallish, curled up hands) and setting no great stock by literature; but immensely interested in facts; incidents; and somehow, one could imagine, naturally swept off into imagining and creating without a thought of its being difficult or remarkable; becoming obsessed; and living in imagination."[73] As a novelist Hardy had been perpetually alert to "facts" and "incidents", not as concrete expressions of contemporary thought or manners, but as potential precipitants of his Wessex material, narrative cores around which it might be coherently and sequentially organised. In his best work the data and stimuli of the external world are wholly absorbed, transmuted (to adopt Virginia Woolf's phrases) into the stuff of that obsessive imaginative world in which alone he truly lived as an artist.

When Edith Wharton met Hardy at Lady Jeune's in the early 1900s she found him resistant to conversation on other than relatively trivial topics: "He seemed to take little interest in the literary movements of the day, or in fact in any critical discussion of his craft, and I felt that he was completely enclosed in his own creative dream, through which I imagine few voices or influences ever reached him."[74] What Edith Wharton mistook for wilful deafness was perhaps no more—from her post-Jamesian standpoint, no less—than Hardy's sense that theoretical literary dis-

cussion for its own sake was as irrelevant to his own creative purposes as the world of London manners. That in writing his finest
novels he withdrew into "his own creative dream", as into an
impregnable citadel of idiosyncratic artistic integrity, there seems
no doubt. Hardy's "very faults", Vernon Lee suggested at the
conclusion of her ruthless critique of his style, "are probably an
expression of his solitary and matchless grandeur of attitude".[75]
It would perhaps be more appropriate to think of them, not as
"faults", but simply as the means available to Hardy, in his time
and situation, for the realisation of his radically new and individual
vision. As Vernon Lee herself exclaimed, "Stevenson, Meredith,
or Henry James would scarcely be what is wanted for such subject-
matter."[76]

NOTES

ABBREVIATIONS USED IN NOTES

Adams: personal collection of Mr Frederick B. Adams, Jr.

DCM: Dorset County Museum, Dorchester, Dorset.

Personal Writings: Harold Orel, ed., *Thomas Hardy's Personal Writings* (Lawrence, Kansas, 1966)

Purdy: Richard Little Purdy, *Thomas Hardy: A Bibliographical Study* (London, 1954, 1968)

Purdy coll.:   personal collection of Professor Richard L. Purdy.

PRELUDE

The Poor Man and the Lady
1. Quotations in this paragraph from *Early Life*, p. 41.
2. *Chambers's Journal*, March 18, 1865, [161]; repr. *Personal Writings*, p. 159.
3. *Early Life*, p. 75.
4. Simon Nowell-Smith, ed., *Letters to Macmillan* (London, 1967), pp. [129]–130.
5. W. R. Rutland, *Thomas Hardy: A Study of His Writings and Their Background* (Oxford, 1938; reissued, New York, 1962), pp. 114–133.
6. Charles Morgan, *The House of Macmillan (1843–1943)* (London, 1943), pp. 87–88.
7. Purdy, p. 276.
8. Quoted Purdy, p. 275.
9. The case is, however, grossly overstated by Carl J. Weber in the introduction to his edition of *Indiscretion* (Baltimore, 1935; reissued, New York, 1965), pp. 1–20: cf. S. Niemeier, '*Indiscretion and The Poor Man*' (unpublished M.A. thesis, Univ. of Toronto, [1944]).
10. Morgan, *The House of Macmillan*, pp. 88, 88–89.
11. Morgan, pp. 88, 89.
12. Morgan, p. 90.

13. *Tinsleys' Magazine*, 11 (December 1872), 496–497. Since the relevant portion of the manuscript of *A Pair of Blue Eyes* (Berg Collection, New York Public Library) is unfortunately missing, it is impossible to look for physical evidence of the incorporation of material from an earlier manuscript. But there are similarities between this scene and the opening of the second chapter of Part Two of 'An Indiscretion in the Life of an Heiress', the London address of the Swancourts, Chevron Square, reappears as the address of the Allancourts' town house in 'An Indiscretion', while a vestige of that 'outsider's' view mentioned by Macmillan perhaps survives in the first person convention, so unusual in Hardy, with which the scene in *A Pair of Blue Eyes* is introduced: 'We gaze upon the spectacle at six o'clock on this midsummer afternoon . . . ' (152).

14. The deletions from chap. 14 seem not to have been made until the Osgood, McIlvaine edition of 1895, but those from chap. 35 were made as early as the Henry S. King one-volume edition of 1877—perhaps because the chapter had been much criticised in reviews.

15. Morgan, p. 89.

16. Hardy to Clodd, December 5, 1910 (British Museum).

17. Morgan, p. 92.

18. *Early Life*, p. 82.

APPRENTICESHIP

1. Desperate Remedies

1. For details in the first three paragraphs of this chapter see *Early Life*, pp. 76–86, 99–100, 109–110, and Purdy, pp. 4–5, 275–276.

2. Morgan, *The House of Macmillan*, pp. 93–94.

3. On Hardy and Collins see Rutland, *Thomas Hardy : A Study of His Writings and Their Background*, pp. 141–146, and Lawrence O. Jones, '*Desperate Remedies* and the Victorian Sensation Novel', *Nineteenth Century Fiction*, 20 (1965), 35–50.

4. Frederick Dolman, 'An Evening with Thomas Hardy', *Young Man*, 8 (1894), 77. The cutting of the interview in Hardy's 'Personal' scrapbook is annotated '(largely faked)'.

5. 'She, to Him. II' (*Wessex Poems*, p. 17); Purdy, p. 98, associates the same poem with pp. 95–96 of *Desperate Remedies*.

2. *'Ce Saxon autodidacte'*

1. Quoted in Laurence Lerner and John Holmstrom, eds., *Thomas Hardy and His Readers: A Selection of Contemporary Reviews* (London, 1968), pp. [12]–13.

2. *Spectator*, April 22, 1871, 482.

3. 'Mr. Hardy's Novels', *British Quarterly Review*, 73 (1881), 346. For Paul's authorship of this article, see p. 118.

4. Hardy to Paul, April 18, 1881, quoted in C. J. P. Beatty, 'The Part Played by Architecture in the Life and Work of Thomas Hardy (with Particular Reference to the Novels)' (unpub. Ph.D. thesis, University of London, 1963, subsequently referred to as 'Architecture in Hardy') pp. 154–155. It is perhaps worth noting that in revising *A Pair of Blue Eyes* for the 1912 Wessex edn. Hardy changed the status of Stephen Smith's father from the 'journeyman mason' of earlier texts to 'working master-mason' (78).

5. 'The Dorsetshire Labourer', *Longman's Magazine*, 2 (July 1883), 252–269 (*Personal Writings*, pp. 168–189): see pp. 206–214. See also Hardy's letter to the English Folk Dance Society, quoted pp. 55–56.

6. Edwin A. Last, *Thomas Hardy's Neighbours* (Guernsey, C.I., 1969), pp. 185, 186 (paginated as part of series). Cf. *Early Life*, p. 26 ('Thomas Hardy the Second had not the tradesman's soul') and the following passage from a carbon typescript of 'Notes' for the 'Life', now in DCM: 'The building business carried on by T. H. Senior was occasionally extentive [sic], more frequently small, and he did not possess the art of enriching himself [sic] thereby.'

7. *Early Life*, pp. 66. Cf. Samuel C. Chew, *Thomas Hardy: Poet and Novelist*, revised edn. (New York, 1928), p. 8: 'There was no insuperable difficulty in the way of his going to one of the universities. The question was discussed in the family and particulars obtained from one of the Cambridge colleges. But in the end it was thought unnecessary for an architect. It is, therefore, incorrect to read any autobiographical hints into that yearning for academic distinction which is part of the tragedy of Jude Fawley.' This passage, first introduced into the revised edition of Chew's book, is taken almost verbatim from 'Notes on Professor Chew's book' (carbon typescript, DCM). Although these notes, despatched to Chew in September 1922, are ascribed to Florence Hardy, they are based on annotations made by Hardy himself in Chew's original volume of 1921 (DCM).

8. *The Popular Educator*, vol. 2 (London: Cassell, 1853) (DCM), pp. 137–138 and 213–216; on p. iv, below the list of contents, Hardy wrote: 'University of London—137. 213.'

9. F. A. Hedgcock, *Thomas Hardy, penseur et artiste* (Paris, 1911), p. 458, n. 1; Hardy's copy in DCM.

10. See p. 211.

11. Two of these volumes—John M. Moffatt, *The Boys' Book of Science*, 3rd ed., (London, 1843), ins. 'Thomas Hardy/Dec 24th 1849', and Jabez Hogg, ed., *Elements of Experimental and Natural Philosophy* (London, 1853), ins. 'T. Hardy/from his friend Horace./ 1857'—are in DCM. The Timbs volume (London, 1856) was listed (no. 440) in the 1938 William P. Wreden catalogue, 'Books from the Library of Thomas Hardy, O.M.' Hardy's copy of [William Clark,] *The Boys' Own Book* (London, n.d.; see pp. 203, 258–259, for bullfinch and swimming references) was described in Carroll A. Wilson, comp., *A Descriptive Catalogue of the Grolier Club Centenary Exhibition 1940 of the Works of Thomas Hardy, O.M. 1840–1928* (Waterville, Maine, 1940), p. [1], and is now in the Adams collection; cf. *Early Life*, p. 30.

12. Notebook of 1865 in the Purdy collection, others in DCM. The one dated 1867 carries the numeral 'IV' on its front cover.

13. These short titles, to be used as a matter of convenience henceforward, are all derived from headings (not necessarily Hardy's) in the volumes themselves. The 'Trumpet-Major Notebook' is described in Emma Clifford, 'The "Trumpet-Major Notebook" and *The Dynasts*', *Review of English Studies*, n.s.8 (1957), 149–161; Hardy's full heading for the 'Facts' notebook was 'Facts from Newspapers, Histories, Biographies, & other chronicles—(mainly Local)'. This notebook is numbered 'III' on its front cover; 'Literary Notes I', covering the period 1875–1888 (with some earlier material tipped in), and 'Literary Notes II', beginning November 1888, are similarly numbered 'I' and 'II' on their front covers. Evelyn Hardy's edition of *Thomas Hardy's Notebooks* (London, 1955)—properly criticised by George S. Fayen in Lionel Stevenson, ed., *Victorian Fiction: A Guide to Research* (Cambridge, Mass., 1964), p. 352—is based on two other notebooks, 'Memoranda I' and 'Memoranda II', of which the first appears to be a compilation of material selected from earlier notebooks (which were then, presumably, destroyed) while the second covers the period from 1921 onwards. All these notebooks are in DCM, as are Hardy's

'Personal' scrapbook and other scrapbooks of lesser importance. In 1967 Miss Irene Cooper Willis kindly showed me two further items which were then in her custody: a volume, chiefly of newspaper and magazine cuttings, described inside the front cover as 'Literary Notes. III', and a late scrapbook of 'Press Cuttings'.

14. *Early Life*, p. 32.

15. Williams, 'Thomas Hardy', *Critical Quarterly*, 6 (1964), 341.

16. Much (though not all) of Hardy's unpublished correspondence with Noel is at the University of Texas; see especially Hardy's letter of April 3, 1892. For the other correspondents see pp. 177–178 and notes; also Newbolt, *My World As In My Time* (London, 1932), pp. 282–286.

17. Marsh, 'A Number of People: Part I', *Harper's New Monthly Magazine*, 178 (1939), 574: 'I wish I had anything to tell of Thomas Hardy, but he was content to bask in Gosse's beams, and I never heard him say anything that couldn't have been said by the most self-effacing parasite.'

18. Rutland, *Thomas Hardy* (London, 1938), p. 112. The observation is quoted, and much developed, in Allen Tate, 'Hardy's Philosophic Metaphors', *Reason in Madness: Critical Essays* (New York, 1941), 121–124.

3. Under the Greenwood Tree

1. *Spectator*, April 22, 1871, 482.

2. Morgan, *The House of Macmillan*, pp. 94–95.

3. *Saturday Review*, September 30, 1871, 442; partly quoted *Thomas Hardy and His Readers*, pp. 19–21 (here, as on other occasions in the volume, elisions are not always indicated). Purdy, p. 5, describes the review as 'almost certainly' by Moule. The first page of the MS (DCM) is reproduced in *Early Life*, opp. p. 116.

4. Morgan, p. 99.

5. Purdy, pp. 11–12; for remainder of paragraph see Purdy, pp. 331, 7–8, 332.

6. Morgan, pp. 87–88.

7. MS, ff. 42v and 70v.

8. Danby, '*Under the Greenwood Tree*', *Critical Quarterly*, 1 (1959), 6.

9. Charles E. Pascoe, *The Dramatic List* (London, 1880), p. 299. See Purdy, p. 143, and *London Review*, April 13, 1867, 422–423: 'Mrs. Scott-Siddons has a figure admirably suited to the part. . . . [H]er movements are full of elegance and expression . . .'

10. 'In Time of "The Breaking of Nations",' *Moments of Vision*, p. 391.

11. Hardy to unidentified correspondent, September 1, 1889, in Carl J. Weber, ed., *The Letters of Thomas Hardy* (Waterville, Maine, 1954), p. 30.

12. MS, ff. 149, 153, 157.

13. The specific statement, 'nobody being at home at the Manor' (24), seems not to have been added until the Osgood, McIlvaine edn. of 1896. In the Preface to that edn. Hardy recalls that the actual Stinsford choir was accustomed to receive from the manor-house 'ten shillings and a supper' (vi).

14. Most of the changes in Dick's speech were made in the 1896 Osgood, McIlvaine edn. For example, the readings 'o' father's' (1st ed., 'of my father's'), 'a' extra' ('an extra'), 'kip' ('keep'), and 'prented' ('printed') on p. 187 of the Wessex edn. were all introduced in 1896 (p. 241).

15. MS, f. 31.

16. For some interesting observations on this and other aspects of the novel see Harold E. Toliver, 'The Dance under the Greenwood Tree: Hardy's Bucolics', *Nineteenth Century Fiction*, 17 (1962), 57–68.

4. Bockhampton and St Juliot

1. Morgan, *House of Macmillan*, p. 89.

2. Osgood, McIlvaine edn. (London, 1896), p. v; Wessex edn., p. vii, reads: 'fifty or sixty years ago.'

3. *Journal of the English Folk Dance Society* (1927), pp. 53–54. Hardy's letter is quoted in the course of an article headed 'English Country Dances: A Summary of Views as to their Nature and Origin'.

4. See C. J. P. Beatty, 'The Tranter's Cottage in *Under the Greenwood Tree*', *Notes and Queries*, n.s. 10 (1963), 26.

5. M. R. Skilling, *Hardy's Mellstock on the Map* (Dorchester, 1968).

6. C. J. P. Beatty in his introduction to *The Architectural Notebook of Thomas Hardy* (Dorchester, 1966), p. 23, quotes Hardy's reference, in his unpublished 'Notes on Stinsford Church', to 'the disastrous restoration about 1840'. Tipped in between pp. 115 and 116 of the notebook itself (original in DCM) is Hardy's sketch of 'Stinsford Church before the alteration about the year 1842'.

7. *Under the Greenwood Tree*, MS f. 30.

8. Chief sources of information about members of the choir: Reason, *Early Life*, p. 122, *Later Years*, pp. 242–243, and MS f. 3; Keates,

Early Life, pp. 121–123, and Last, *Thomas Hardy's Neighbours*, p. 186; Dart, *Early Life*, pp. 13, 127.

9. 'Facts' notebook, p. 81. For Hardy's reading of the *Dorset County Chronicle* see pp. 237–244.

10 *Dorset County Chronicle*, January 24, 1828, p. 4. This passage is quoted, in part, in an anonymous article, 'Hardys and Keatses: Two Dorset Families', *Dorset Year-Book* for 1928, pp. 135–137. The same article also mentions, p. 136, but without specifying a date, an earlier incident reported in the *Dorset County Chronicle*: 'a disturbance at the Phoenix Inn, Dorchester. The Bockhampton Band were sitting in the kitchen of the inn, when a challenging voice brought John Hardy, drumstick in hand, to the door, where he was attacked by a Fordington player.'

11. Purdy, pp. 12–13. Most of these changes were incorporated into later printings of the Wessex edn. (including the so-called 'Library Edition'), e.g., 'rector' for 'vicar' (2), 'Rectory' for 'Vicarage' (6), 'St. Andrew's church' for 'the nearest church' (112); there are also some additions to the original Wessex text (e.g., p. 8) and the title of Elfride's book, formerly '*The Court of Kellyon Castle*: a romance of the fifteenth century', becomes '*The Court of King Arthur's Castle*: a Romance of Lyonnesse' (38).

12. Paul, 'Mr. Hardy's Novels', 346.

13. Cf. Lois Deacon and Terry Coleman, *Providence and Mr. Hardy* (London, 1966), p. 116.

14. *Early Life*, pp. 122–123. The favourable review of the novel in the *Saturday Review*, August 2, 1873, 158–159, is almost certainly by Moule (Purdy, p. 12n.; *Providence and Mr. Hardy*, p. 116).

15. 'During Saturday night the deceased was very restless, and spoke to the nurse of being afraid of losing his position, because through these attacks of depression he was unable to get through the work.' (*Cambridge Chronicle*, September 27, 1873, p. 8). Cf. *Providence and Mr. Hardy*, pp. 93–95. The official record of the inquest seems not to have survived.

16. 'William Barnes', in Thomas Humphry Ward, ed., *The English Poets, Vol. 5, Browning to Rupert Brooke* (London, 1918), p. 176. (*Personal Writings*, p. 84).

17. 'Reprints—V', *London Mercury*, 6 (1922), 631. The reference to Douglas Cook, editor of the *Saturday Review*, points to a further, though quite incidental, link between Moule and the world of *A Pair of Blue Eyes*. Emma Hardy, in *Some Recollections* (ed. Evelyn

Hardy and Robert Gittings, London, 1961), p. 41, mentions Cook as a regular visitor to Tintagel in the 1860s, while Hardy's diary note for March 9, 1870 (*Early Life*, p. 99), speaks of Cook's 'coming home' to Tintagel to be buried.

18. Hardy presumably thought 'Ave Caesar' (see previous note) representative of Moule at his best. Another poem has recently been reprinted in Lois Deacon, *The Moules and Thomas Hardy* (Guernsey, C. I., 1968), pp. 137–139 (paginated as part of series), and several early pieces appear in the privately printed *Tempora Mutantur: A Memorial of the Fordington Times Society* (London, 1859). For Moule as a reviewer see the article, 'Dorset', *Quarterly Review*, 111 (April 1862), 281–318. In the *Wellesley Index to Victorian Periodicals*, I, 744 (item 1380), this article is attributed to one of Horace's brothers, Frederick John Moule, but a copy in DCM has been annotated by 'CWM' (i.e. Charles Walker Moule): 'This article (Dorset) was written by my dear brother Horace (HMM).'

19. Hardy to George A. B. Dewar, July 24, 1913 (*Grolier Catalogue*, p. 11).

20. 'When I Set Out for Lyonnesse', *Satires of Circumstance*, p. 18.

21. The 2½ pages noted by Purdy, p. 10, as being in Miss Gifford's hand are made up of several separate fragments, of which the first and longest roughly corresponds to p. 58 of the Wessex edn.: MS (Berg Collection), ff. 81–82.

5. *A Pair of Blue Eyes*

1. Purdy, p. 11.

2. Purdy, pp. 12, 332; *Early Life*, p. 118.

3. See *Grolier Catalogue*, p. 8; Hardy's own copy (DCM) of Walter Arthur Copinger, *The Law of Copyright in Works of Literature and Art* (London, 1870) is inscribed 'Thomas Hardy. 1873'.

4. See *Early Life*, pp. 120–121.

5. Purdy, p. 12.

6. The MS is in the Berg Collection: see n. 21 to preceding section.

7. *Early Life*, p. 120.

8. *Early Life*, pp. 121, 122; Purdy, p. 333.

9. Elfride's song, 'O Love, who bewailest' (18), was substituted in the MS (f. 31) for the four-line stanza, 'For his bride a soldier sought her', which Bathsheba sings in *Far from the Madding Crowd* (179).

10. Howells, *Heroines of Fiction* (New York, 1901), II. 177, 188–189; Albert J. Guerard, *Thomas Hardy* (New York, 1949, 1964), pp.

135–138; H. B. Grimsditch, *Character and Environment in the Novels of Thomas Hardy* (London, 1925), pp. 116–119.

11. *Tinsleys' Magazine*, 11 (September 1872), 122.

12. *Tinsleys' Magazine*, 11 (October 1872), 245.

13. Carpenter, *Thomas Hardy* (New York, 1964), p. 48.

14. 1912 postscript to Preface (vi–vii); *Early Life*, p. 119.

15. For Hutton see p. 124 and note. In his letter to Hardy of June 26, 1873 (DCM), Hutton had regretted the conclusion of *A Pair of Blue Eyes*: 'a novel *should end well*.' His next letter, of July 3, 1873 (DCM), expresses agreement with Hardy 'as to the *truth* of her death: but there are two views of a novel—as a work of art & as what that work of art is produced for—the advantage and recreation of the public'.

16. *Spectator*, June 28, 1873, 831; *Saturday Review*, August 2, 1873, 158 (for Moule's authorship see n. 14 to preceding section); *Pall Mall Gazette*, October 25, 1873, 1439.

17. Hardy to H. Macbeth-Raeburn, December 16, 1894 (Adams).

18. Hardy to Dewar, July 24, 1913 (*Grolier Cat.*, p. 11); *Early Life*, pp. 138, 179.

ACHIEVEMENT

I. Far from the Madding Crowd

1. Frederick William Maitland, *The Life and Letters of Leslie Stephen* (London, 1906), p. 271; for Stephen's letter see Maitland, pp. 270–71 (complete text in Purdy, pp. 336–337).

2. For the pre-publication history of the novel see Purdy, pp. 16–17, Maitland, pp. 271–273, and *Early Life*, pp. 126–128, 132.

3. *Grolier Cat.*, p. 16.

4. Hardy to Harrison, July 29, 1901 (Univ. *of Texas*), quoted in Ann Bowden, 'The Thomas Hardy Collection', *Library Chronicle of the University* of Texas, 7, ii (1962), p. 10.

5. *Early Life*, p. 131.

6. Purdy, p. 16.

7. Purdy, pp. 337–338.

8. The pages of rejected MS are in DCM; the final MS as sent to the *Cornhill* is in the possession of Mr Edwin Thorne: for descriptions, see Purdy, pp. 14–16. Hardy wrote to Smith, Elder immediately

(February 18, 1874; letter in DCM) asking for the return of the portion of MS (ff. 2–1 to 2–73) he had recently submitted. Much of the material in the original ff. 2–18 and 2–19 was incorporated in ff. 2–18 and 2–19 of the revised MS, but the last quarter of the original f. 2–19 and the whole of ff. 2–20 to 2–24 were deleted. Baily Pennyways had seen Fanny Robin in Melchester, 'too well-off to be anything but a ruined woman' (f. 2–20), but had nothing further to contribute.

9. Purdy, p. 337.

10. *Cornhill* MS, ff. 3–9 to 3–12; Purdy, p. 15. The additional 3½ pages of MS originally intervened between the last two paragraphs of the chapter (371). In this version Troy returns to the beach only to find his clothes have disappeared; his rescuers then say that their ship, about to begin a six-month voyage, is short-handed, and after much reflection he decides to sail with them.

11. The malthouse conversation in chap. 8 and, especially, chap. 15 shows particularly heavy (and beneficial) revision.

12. Stephen to Hardy, April 13, 1874 (quoted Purdy, p. 339); *Cornhill* MS, f. 2–232.

13. Purdy, pp. 28–30. The fragment of *The Mistress of the Farm* which Professor Purdy located among the Lord Chamberlain's plays (now in the British Museum) has apparently disappeared.

14. Maitland, p. 271.

15. MS leaves (DCM) annotated by Hardy: '(Details of Sheep-rot— omitted from MS. when revised)'; cf. Purdy, p. 16. Boldwood is mentioned in f. 106i; Oak and Troy fight on f. 106j. Robert C. Schweik has recently argued, on the basis of a close analysis of the *Cornhill* MS, that the development of Boldwood's role and the dramatisation of Fanny Robin's story were probably not part of Hardy's original conception: 'The Early Development of Hardy's *Far from the Madding Crowd*', *Texas Studies in Literature and Language*, 9 (1967), 415–428, especially 425–427.

16. *Grolier Cat*, p. 15, lists a copy of *Infantry Sword Exercises* (published by H.M. Stationery Office, 1873) with Hardy's signature on the title page; Hardy also owned (1938 Wreden catalogue, item 342) *Instructions for the Sword, Carbine, Pistol, and Lance Exercise; together with Field Gun Drill. For the Use of the Cavalry* (London, 1871). Since Troy was a cavalryman, the latter volume (published by the Adjutant General's Office, Horse Guards) seems the more relevant, and the instructions there for the cavalry sword exercise

(pp. 8–22) were probably the immediate source of Hardy's descriptive details. They also clarify Troy's remark, 'This may be called Fort meeting Feeble, hey, Boldwood?' (267): 'The recruit having been perfectly instructed in drawing and returning his sword, will now be made acquainted with the strong and weak parts of it; the "Fort" (strong) being the half of the blade near the hilt, the "Feeble" (weak), the half towards the point. . . . From the hilt upwards, in opposing the blade of an adversary, the strength of the defence decreases in proportion as the cut is received towards the point; and *vice versa*, it increases from the point downwards' (pp. 10–11). Cf. R. L. Purdy, ed., *Far from the Madding Crowd* (Boston, 1957), p. 207, n. 1.

17. See Richard C. Carpenter, 'The Mirror and the Sword: Imagery in *Far from the Madding Crowd*', *Nineteenth Century Fiction*, 18 (1964), 342–345.

18. Albert Mordell, ed., *Literary Reviews and Essays by Henry James* (New York, 1958), p. 294; review also quoted in *Thomas Hardy and His Readers*, pp. 28–33.

19. *Early Life*, p. 131.

20. But see Guerard, *Thomas Hardy*, pp. 43–44, on Hardy's onlookers.

21. Hardy's letter, 'Papers of the Manchester Literary Club', *Spectator*, October 15, 1881, 1308 (*Personal Writings*, p. 92).

22. C. J. P. Beatty, 'Architecture in Hardy', p. 244, notes Hardy's focus on four essential buildings: malthouse, homestead, great barn, and church.

23. May O'Rourke, *Thomas Hardy: His Secretary Remembers* (Beaminster, Dorset, 1965), p. 21. Hardy was responding to Miss O'Rourke's suggestion that Stinsford was 'a Gray's Elegy sort of place'. The *Elegy's* image of village life is, of course, far from idyllic, and Hardy may conceivably have been influenced in his choice of title by a passage in Francis George Heath, *The 'Romance' of Peasant Life in the West of England* (London, 1872), p. 6. Heath is concerned to challenge the assumption of city-dwellers that poverty and distress are peculiarly urban phenomena: 'as we wander by gurgling brooks, and through sylvan glades, and listen to the sweet songs of the birds, and see the glad sights which a wise and benificent Creator has spread over the earth, and which are to be seen nowhere in such perfection as they are to be found

"Far from the madding crowd's ignoble strife,"

we cannot imagine that aught but happiness and contentment are the lot of the rustic swain. But nearly all of our native poets in their descriptions of English pastoral life have deceived us by their rose-coloured pictures of the peasants.' On pp. 7–8 Heath uses phrases from the *Elegy* to stress less happy aspects of the labourer's situation and to introduce a discussion of current conditions in Dorsetshire.

24. *Early Life*, p. 131. For the name 'Weatherbury', see 'Recession', section 5, n. 18. In a letter to Thackeray Turner, February 7, 1910 (quoted Beatty, 'Architecture in Hardy', pp. 227–228), Hardy said specifically that St Mary's, Puddletown, was the church of *Far from the Madding Crowd*.

25. Carpenter, 'The Mirror and the Sword', pp. 340–342, has an interesting discussion of this episode.

26. The name Troy also carried local connotations. On the road between Dorchester and Puddletown, at approximately the spot occupied in the novel by the Buck's Head Inn, stood the hamlet of Troy Town: 'Troy-town is, however, another designation for the *maze* or *labyrinth*, constructed by the old inhabitants of Britain with banks of turf, and of which remains have been found in different parts of the kingdom. They are common in Wales, where they are called *Caertroi*, that is, *turning-towns*.' (*A Handbook for Travellers in Wiltshire, Dorsetshire, and Somersetshire* [London: John Murray, 1856], p. 110). The name survives in Troy Town Farm.

27. R. L. Purdy, ed., *Far from the Madding Crowd*, p. xiv.

28. See, for example, Hermann Lea, *Thomas Hardy's Wessex* (London, 1913), pp. 43–44.

29. MS (DCM), ff. 106b–106c.

30. Roy Morrell, *Thomas Hardy: The Will and the Way* (Kuala Lumpur, 1965), p. 59, quotes the opening of the final paragraph of chapter 56 (456) and comments: 'Ahead of Gabriel and Bathsheba is no romance, but a reality that Hardy represents as more valuable, a reality of hard and good work on the two farms.'

2. *Puddletown into Weatherbury*

1. *Cornhill* MS, f. 3–28: *Cornhill*, 30 (November 1874), 624.

2. *Saturday Review*, September 28, 1872, 417; *Times*, January 25, 1875, p. 4 (cf. *Thomas Hardy and His Readers*, pp. 19, 38).

3. *Revue des deux mondes*, 45e année (December 15, 1875), 843.

4. *London*, September 29, 1877, 211, 212.

5. 'The Wessex Labourer', *Examiner*, July 15, 1876, 793–794. The author was almost certainly Charles Kegan Paul: see Paul's letter

to Hardy, April 13, 1877, quoted p. 118. There are several points of similarity with Paul's *British Quarterly Review* article of 1881.

6. *Spectator*, December 19, 1874, 1597–1599: e.g., 'if any one society of agricultural labourers were at all like that which we find here, that class, as a whole, must be a treasure-house of such eccentric shrewdness and profane-minded familiarity with the Bible, as would cancel at once the reputation rural England has got for a heavy, bovine character, and would justify us in believing it to be a rich mine of quaintnesses and oddities, all dashed with a curious flavour of mystical and Biblical transcendentalism' (p. 1597). John Hutton, writing to Hardy on December 23, 1874 (DCM), thought his brother did not know the agricultural poor well enough 'to estimate their intimacy with & constant use of Biblical language nor their quaint good humoured cynicism'.

7. 'The Wessex Labourer', p. 794.

8. Hardy to William Rothenstein, March 11, 1912 (Harvard). Hardy said that his father's recollections of the period had made it familiar to him since childhood. See p. 267 and n.; also Barbara Kerr, *Bound to the Soil: A Social History of Dorset 1750–1918* (London, 1968), pp. 90–119.

9. Hardy had a childhood memory of a boy who died of starvation: *Later Years*, p. 93; H. Rider Haggard, *Rural England* (London, 1902), I, 282. Barbara Kerr, *Bound to the Soil*, p. 116, mentions the death from starvation of a father and son at Sutton Poyntz (the Overcombe of *The Trumpet-Major*) in January 1847.

10. 'The Dorsetshire Labourer', p. 252. (*Personal Writings*, p. 169). Other sources: Arnold White, ed., *The Letters of S.G.O.: A Series of Letters on Public Affairs Written by the Rev. Lord Sidney Godolphin Osborne and Published in 'The Times' 1844–1888*. 2 vols. (London, n.d.), I, 1–4, 14–20, 27–33, 38–44; *Times*, June 18, 1846, p. 5, June 25, 1846, p. 3, July 2, 1846, p. 6; also 'The Peasantry of Dorsetshire', *Ilustrated London News*, September 5, 1846, 156–158. Particularly interesting, both for its arguments and as a source of further references, is William J. Hyde, 'Hardy's View of Realism: A Key to the Rustic Characters', *Victorian Studies*, 2 (1958), [45]–59.

11. *Parliamentary Papers*, Session 1868–69, XIII, 77–[80], 233–[270].

12. *Times*, December 5, 1872, p. 6; for Herbert, see *Early Life*, pp. 224, 238.

13. 'The Dorsetshire Labourer', pp. 264–266 (*Personal Writings*, p. 183).

[375]

14. *Dorset County Chronicle*, February 20, 1873, p. 3. This was not Arch's only visit to Dorchester; he was certainly there again on February 14, 1877 (*Dorset County Chronicle*, February 15, 1877, p. 12), but Hardy was then living in Sturminster Newton, whence he dated a letter to Blackwood on February 13, 1877 (National Library of Scotland).

15. 'The Arcadians of Dorset', *Daily Telegraph*, April 30, 1872, p. 5; attributed to 'Our Special Correspondent'. The article is quoted in full in Francis George Heath, *The English Peasantry* (London, 1874), pp. 27–40.

16. 'The Arcadians of Dorset', p. 5. For interesting historical notes see O. D. Harvey, *Puddletown* (*Thomas Hardy's 'Weatherbury'*), (Puddletown, 1968), esp. pp. 17–36.

17. Purdy, Introduction to *Far from the Madding Crowd*, p. viin.; Weber, 'Chronology in Hardy's Novels', *PMLA*, 53 (1938), 314, and cf. Weber, ed., *Far from the Madding Crowd* (New York, 1959), p. 386. Cf. O. D. Harvey, *Puddletown*, p. 17.

18. *The Mayor of Casterbridge*, p. 253. For the general problem of dating the action of Hardy's novels see pp. 245–247.

19. *Academy*, January 2, 1875, 9.

3. The Hand of Ethelberta

1. Stephen to Hardy, December 2, 1874 (DCM); cf. Purdy, p. 22.

2. Maitland, *Life and Letters of Leslie Stephen*, p. 276; date from original in DCM.

3. Stephen to Hardy, May 20, 1875 (DCM).

4. Compare 1896 edn., p. 6, with first edn., I, 8, and Smith, Elder and Sampson Low one-volume edns., p. 6. Generally speaking, however, the revisions to the 1896 edn. were not as substantial as Purdy, p. 23, suggests, since the major excisions of material from the original chapters 9 and 12 had been made as early as the Smith, Elder one-volume edn. of 1877: compare first edn. I, 102–106 with 1877 edn. p. 64, and first edn. I, 132–135 with 1877 p. 81.

5. In 1856 Murray's *Handbook for . . . Wiltshire, Dorsetshire, and Somersetshire* noted (p. 94): '[Bournemouth] is principally a creation of the last few years, and consists of an irregular cluster of villas scattered through a valley, the centre of which, a pretty fir wood, is laid out as a pleasure-ground. It has, however, lost much of its original beauty by the increase of buildings, and the very questionable taste shown in remodelling the ground.'

6. *Tess*, p. 480.

7. For an excellent historical study, see H. J. Dyos, 'The Speculative Builders and Developers of Victorian London', *Victorian Studies*, 11 (1968), [641]–690. Swanage, where Hardy wrote much of the novel, was the birthplace of John Mowlem who became an important building contractor in London during the early Victorian period: see [J. E. Panton], *A Guide to Swanage, . . . and all Places of Interest in and around the Isle of Purbeck* (Dorchester, n.d.; copy in DCM), p. 20; also Sir Frederick Treves, *Highways and Byways in Dorset*, second edn. (London, 1935), pp. 190–191, and Charles G. Harper, *The Hardy Country* (London, 1904), p. 91.

8. Guerard, *Thomas Hardy*, p. 109.

9. Carpenter, *Thomas Hardy*, p. 56.

10. Cf. Beatty, 'Architecture in Hardy', pp. 285–309. Hardy's poem 'Architectural Masks', *Poems of the Past and the Present* (233), gives the theme an ironic twist.

11. Paul to Hardy, April 13, 1877 (DCM).

12. If, in the 1870s, Chickerell was already known for its brick works, then Hardy may deliberately have evoked it as a village threatened by alien forces. Cf. Marianne R. Dacombe, ed., *Dorset Up Along and Down Along* ([Dorchester, 1935]), p. 47.

13. *Graphic*, April 29, 1876, 419; *Examiner*, May 13, 1876, 546; *Spectator*, April 22, 1876, 532; *Athenaeum*, April 15, 1876, 523.

14. 'Notebook IV': see 'Apprenticeship', section 2, n. 11. The novel itself contains specific reference to Utilitarianism (318–319), and Ethelberta is described as moving from romanticism to 'distorted Benthamism', in the shape of 'a vow to marry for the good of her family' (321).

4. On Native Grounds

1. 'The Wessex Labourer', pp. 793–794.

2. Paul to Hardy, April 13, 1877 (DCM). Paul could conceivably have been referring to the *Examiner* review of *The Hand of Ethelberta*, May 13, 1876, 544–546 (of which Hardy also had a copy in his scrapbook), but the attribution of 'The Wessex Labourer' is confirmed by similarities of argument and phrasing with Paul's 1881 article, 'Mr. Hardy's Novels', and even with his autobiography, *Memories* (London, 1899). William Minto, editor of the *Examiner* between 1874 and 1878, had reviewed *Far from the Madding Crowd* there (December 5, 1874, 1329–1330), and written

to Hardy on November 2, 1875 (DCM), to inquire about the possibility of his supplying a serial to the magazine; he is mentioned in *Early Life*, p. 159.

3. *D.N.B.*, *Supplement 1901–1911*, III, 80–81; F. A. Mumby *The House of Routledge 1834–1934* (London, 1934), pp. 178, 193; Paul, *Memories*, p. 314.

4. Lionel Johnson to John Lane, January 2, 1892 (Texas); cf. Paul, *Memories*, p. 314, and 'Mr. Hardy's Novels', p. 355, on *The Return of the Native* : 'We remember hearing Mr. Hardy say that, when he was writing it, he thought to himself that only Mr. —— among all his probable readers in London would know accurately the district of his story.'

5. *Moments of Vision*, p. 200; Purdy, p. 194. In the MS of *Moments of Vision* (Magdalene College, Cambridge), f. 4, the first line of the second stanza reads 'We were irked by the scene, by each other; yes,' in place of the published 'We were irked by the scene, by our own selves; yes,' (first edn., 1917, p. 4, and all subsequent editions).

6. For Lady Ritchie, see *Early Life*, pp. 129, 132, 137–138, 275; in a letter to Hardy of November 9, [1916] (DCM) she acknowledges the autograph (to be sold for war relief work) requested in a previous letter, and thanks him for remembering earlier times. For Helen Paterson, see *Early Life*, p. 132, and Purdy, p. 220; biographical notes, and an excellent photograph of her in middle-age, can be found in *Happy England, as Painted by Helen Allingham, R.W.S.*, with memoir and descriptions by Marcus B. Huish (London, 1904). Of the illustrations to *Far from the Madding Crowd*, Huish notes: 'The author was fairly complimentary as to the result, although he said it was difficult for two minds to imagine scenes in the same light' (p. 39). Helen Paterson and Lady Ritchie are both mentioned in a letter from Florence Hardy to Howard Bliss, April 21, 1936 (Adams), about this period of Hardy's life.

7. Miss Willis's notes on this conversation of 1937 are contained in a small pocketbook, now in DCM. For 'The Interloper', see *Moments of Vision*, pp. 299–300, and Purdy, p. 200. For the wedding, see Evelyn Hardy, *Thomas Hardy: A Critical Biography* (London, 1954): on September 18, 1874, Hardy wrote to his brother, 'There were only Emma and I, her uncle who married us, and her brother' (p. 143).

8. *Early Life*, pp. 133, 135–136, 141, 142, 145–147. Emma's diary for this period is in DCM, a black notebook headed 'Emma L. Hardy./

1874./West End Cottage./Swanage.' It records the wedding trip, with some notes of later movements, and (at the back) the 1876 visit to Holland and Germany; for extracts, see Evelyn Hardy, 'Emma Hardy's Diaries: Some Foreshadowings of *The Dynasts*', *English*, 14 (1962), [9]–12.

9. Diary, unnumbered page; quoted in Evelyn Hardy, 'Emma Hardy's Diaries', p. 12.
10. Evelyn Hardy, *Thomas Hardy*, p. 143; cf. *Early Life*, p. 136.
11. The excursion, September 13, 1875, was recorded by Emma in her diary, pp. 89–[92]; cf. Beatty, 'Architecture in Hardy', p. 289n.
12. Cf. Sir Frederick Treves, *Highways and Byways in Dorset*, p. 189, and Hermann Lea, *Thomas Hardy's Wessex*, pp. 244–245.
13. Loosely bound typescript, p. [1] (DCM); see *Some Recollections*, pp. 90–91. Emma's diary, p. [70] (see n. 8 above), contains what appear to be trial names and titles.
14. Francis Hueffer to Hardy, January 14, 1878 (DCM). It is of some interest, in view of the possible association of 'An Indiscretion' with *The Poor Man and the Lady*, that Hueffer gave Hardy only until March 10, at the latest, to send in a story.
15. *New Quarterly Magazine*, n.s.2 (1879), [412]–431; Paul to Hardy, October 19, 1879 (DCM).
16. 'Mr. Hardy's Novels', p. 360.
17. Hardy to Paul, April 18, 1881 (quoted 'Architecture in Hardy', pp. 154–155).
18. Paul, *Memories*, p. 259; cf. Paul's article, 'The Condition of the Agricultural Labourer', *Theological Review*, 5 (1868), 107–127.
19. 'Mr. Hardy's Novels', p. 350.
20. The last item of correspondence I have seen is Hardy to Paul, July 27, 1896 (Fales Collection, New York University): Hardy commiserates with Paul on the seriousness of his accident—from which he never recovered.
21. Paul to Hardy, May 29, 1886, December 25, 1891 and November 12, 1882 (all DCM).
22. Paul to Hardy, February 7, 1881 (DCM); it was in the November 12, 1882, letter that Paul confessed his dislike of *A Laodicean*.
23. 'Architecture in Hardy', pp. 26–27; *Early Life*, pp. 40–41.
24. Paul to Hardy, December 25, 1891 (DCM).
25. *Early Life*, p. 156.
26. Hardy to Blackwood, February 13, 1877, and April 12, 1877 (both in National Library of Scotland). The MS could conceivably have

been an early version of *The Woodlanders* (see *Early Life*, pp. 135, 230), but John Paterson, *The Making of 'The Return of the Native'* (Berkeley, 1960), p. 47, suggests on the basis of MS evidence that *The Return of the Native* may originally have been pastoral in character: see p. 130.

27. Maitland, *Life and Letters of Leslie Stephen*, pp. 276–277. Hardy acknowledged return of the MS in a letter to Blackwood of April 26, 1877 (National Library of Scotland).

28. Hardy to editor of *Temple Bar*, June 16, 1877 (Adams); Purdy, p. 27.

29. See *Early Life*, p. 160. Hardy's original pen and ink sketch is in DCM and is briefly described in Donald Morrison, comp., *Exhibition of Hardy's Drawings & Paintings* (Dorchester, [1968]), p. 4. The map was again used as a frontispiece in the Kegan Paul one-volume edn. of 1880; it has recently been reproduced in James Gindin, ed., *The Return of the Native* (New York, 1969), p. [x]. In a letter to Sir Frederick Macmillan of January 17, 1911 (British Museum) Hardy referred to the map as a forerunner of the Wessex map printed in the volumes of the Osgood, McIlvaine edn.

30. See above, p. 36, 73. Hutton's authorship of the *Desperate Remedies* review is confirmed by his letter to Hardy of April 29, 1873 (DCM), in which he apologises for having caused Hardy any distress.

31. Hutton to Hardy, July 3, 1873 (DCM).

32. Hardy to Perkins (i.e., the Rev. T. Perkins, Rector of Turnworth: see *Later Years*, p. 123), April 20, 1900, in Carroll A. Wilson, *Thirteen Author Collections of the Nineteenth Century and Five Centuries of Familiar Quotations*, ed. J. C. S. Wilson and D. A. Randall. 2 vols. (New York, 1950), I, 51. For further 'identifications' of places in the novel, see Lea, *Thomas Hardy's Wessex*, pp. 71–82.

33. Note by Cockerell in his copy of Wessex edn. of *The Return of the Native* (Adams).

34. Paul to Hardy, April 13, 1877 (DCM).

35. 'The Rev. William Barnes, B.D.', *Athenaeum*, October 16, 1886, 502 (*Personal Writings*, p. 101).

36. Gosse to Hardy, October 17, 1886, in Evan Charteris, *The Life and Letters of Sir Edmund Gosse* (London, 1931), p. 201.

37. *Post Office Directory of Dorchester* (London, 1859), p. 611 (Hardy's copy in DCM); cf. *Early Life*, pp. 36–37.

38. The volume is in DCM; cf. Rutland, *Thomas Hardy*, p. 138.

39. *Spectator*, October 15, 1851, 1308 (*Personal Writings*, pp. 92–93).

40. Barnes, *Poems of Rural Life, in the Dorset Dialect : with a Dissertation and Glossary* (London, 1844), p. 11.

41. 'Dorset', pp. 310–318; see 'Apprenticeship', section 4, n. 14.

42. 'The Language of Wessex', *The Marlburian*, 1 (June 7, 1866), 153–154.

43. See above, n. 40, and *Poems of Rural Life, in the Dorset Dialect*, 'Second Edition, the Dissertation and Glossary Enlarged and Corrected' (1848), pp. 7, 9, 12, 13.

44. 'Dorset', p. 282. For Moule's association with *The Marlburian*, see vol. 4 (March 3, 1869), 6: 'All Marlburians were sorry to hear of the unexpected retirement of H. M. Moule, Esq., from the Common Room. His services to the *Marlburian* have been very valuable.' A letter from Moule to the Bursar written after his departure (May 4, 1869) gives no suggestion of his having left under a cloud (I am indebted for this information to Mr. E. G. H. Kempson).

45. Barnes, *Poems of Rural Life in Common English* (London, 1868), p. [v]. This passage was noted in Wilson, *Thirteen Author Collections*, I, 97, and the whole question has recently been discussed in W. J. Keith, 'Thomas Hardy and the Name "Wessex"', *English Language Notes*, 6 (1968), 42–44.

46. Hynes, 'Hardy and Barnes: Notes on Literary Influence', *South Atlantic Quarterly*, 58 (1959), 48. See also Paul Zietlow, 'Thomas Hardy and William Barnes: Two Dorset Poets', *PMLA*, 84 (1969), 291–303.

47. *New Quarterly Magazine*, n.s. 2 (1879), 469 (*Personal Writings*, p. 94).

48. 'William Barnes', in Ward, ed., *The English Poets*, V, 176 (*Personal Writings*, p. 84).

49. 'The Rev. William Barnes, B.D.', p. 502 (*Personal Writings*, p. 105).

50. 'Peasant Life in Dorset', in *Golden Hours* (1872), 480–486; subsequently collected in Heath's *The English Peasant : Studies Historical, Local and Biographic* (London, 1893), pp. 121–132.

51. See above, n. 39, and *Athenaeum*, November 30, 1878, 688 (*Personal Writings*, p. 91).

5. The Return of the Native

1. Paterson, *The Making of 'The Return of the Native'*, p. 167.

2. Dieter Riesner, 'Über die Genesis von Thomas Hardys *The Return of the Native*', *Archiv für das Studium der Neueren Sprachen und Literaturen*, 200 (1963), [53]–59.

3. *Early Life*, p. 160, *Later Years*, p. 235.

4. Entries in Hardy's 'Literary Notes I' notebook, pp. 25–26 (DCM), show that he was reading *King Lear* in 1876; cf. R. E. C. Houghton, 'Hardy and Shakespeare', *Notes and Queries*, n.s.8 (1961), 98.

5. N. Hawthorne, Preface to *The Marble Faun* (Columbus, Ohio, 1968), p. 3.

6. Hardy specifically drew attention to the opening paragraphs of Book Third (197): Hardy to Woolner, April 21, 1880, quoted in Beatty, 'Architecture in Hardy', p. 326; the letter is in Dr Beatty's own collection. Woolner's reply, April 22, 1880, is in the Berg Collection.

7. Cf. Robert C. Schweik, 'Theme, Character, and Perspective in Hardy's *The Return of the Native*', *Philological Quarterly*, 41 (1962), 759–761.

8. Paterson, 'The Return of the Native as Antichristian Document', *Nineteenth Century Fiction*, 14 (1959), 114 n. 6.

9. Cf. Leonard W. Deen, 'Heroism and Pathos in Hardy's *Return of the Native*', *Nineteenth Century Fiction*, 15 (1960), 211.

10. The pattern is reminiscent of Hawthorne's story, 'The Maypole of Merry Mount'.

11. Louis H. Ruegg, 'Farming of Dorsetshire', *Journal of the Royal Agricultural Society of England*, 15 (1854), 453, records the vain attempts of 'Mr. Damen, of Winfrith,' to break up heathland near Dorchester and make it bear good crops. In view of the reference to 'Wildeve's Patch' in the novel (39–40), it is conceivable that Wildeve's first name, Damon, incorporated a local as well as a classical allusion.

12. Clym apparently begins his preaching on the second anniversary of his mother's death. Mrs Yeobright dies on Thursday, August 31, [1843?] (326); Clym first preaches on the Sunday (483), i.e., August 31, following the wedding of Diggory and Thomasin, which apparently takes place on August 25, [1845?]—the 25th of the month after the date on p. 473, which is itself 'almost two months' (467) after the maypole celebrations (458). For discussions of the chronology of the novel, see 'Renewal', section 4, notes 22, 24.

13. Quoted Purdy, p. 26.

14. John Hagan, 'A Note on the Significance of Diggory Venn', *Nineteenth Century Fiction*, 16 (1961), 147–155; Robert Wooster Stallman, 'Hardy's Hour-Glass Novel', *Sewanee Review*, 55 (1947), 283–296.

15. Lord David Cecil, *Hardy the Novelist: An Essay in Criticism* (London, 1943), p. 117, argues that the present marriage between Diggory and Thomasin meets 'the claims of probability'.
16. Paterson, *The Making of 'The Return of the Native'*, p. 30; see also Dale Kramer, 'Unity of Time in *The Return of the Native*', *Notes and Queries*, n.s. 12 (1965), 304–305. Cf. John Paterson, '*The Mayor of Casterbridge* as Tragedy', *Victorian Studies*, 2 (1959), 152, n.1.
17. See n. 3 above; for Clym and Oedipus, see Louis Crompton, 'The Sunburnt God: Ritual and Tragic Myth in *The Return of the Native*', *Boston University Studies in English*, 4 (1960), 238, and C. J. Greshoff, 'A Note on *The Return of the Native*', *Standpunkte*, 18 (1964), 33–35.
18. See especially David J. DeLaura, " 'The Ache of Modernism" in Hardy's Later Novels', *ELH*, 34 (1967), 380–384. Ian Gregor, 'What Kind of Fiction Did Hardy Write?' *Essays in Criticism*, 16 (1966), 299, refers to Clym as 'a slower moving scholar gipsy'.

RECESSION

I. The Trumpet-Major
1. *Early Life*, p. 157, Purdy, p. 27.
2. Irene Cooper Willis pocketbook (DCM): see 'Achievement', section 4, n. 7.
3. *Early Life*, pp. 167, 178, 171, 175–176.
4. Affixed to the first page of Hardy's 'Personal' scrapbook is a cutting from the *Athenaeum*, December 13, 1879, 764, in which both James and Hardy are listed among the 'original members' of the recently-founded Club. See also Simon Nowell-Smith, comp., *The Legend of the Master* (London, 1947), p. xxxvii.
5. 'Trumpet-Major Notebook' (DCM).
6. Hardy to Bentley, April 27, 1878 (Bentley Papers, Univ. of Illinois; copy in Adams coll.).
7. Stephen to Hardy, February 17, 1879 (DCM), partly quoted in Michael Edwards, 'The Making of Hardy's *The Trumpet-Major*' (unpub. M.A. thesis, Univ. of Birmingham, 1967), p. 27; cf. *Early Life*, p. 167.
8. Hardy to Blackwood, June 9, 1879 (National Library of Scotland); Purdy, p. 34.

9. Macleod to Hardy, June 20, 1879 (DCM), quoted in Edwards, 'The Making of Hardy's *The Trumpet-Major*', p. 28. See Purdy, pp. 32–33, and Edwards, pp. 108–110.

10. Hardy to [Isbister?], August 1, 1879, in Weber, ed., *The Letters of Thomas Hardy*, pp. 22–23. Isbister was the publisher of *Good Words*; there seems no foundation for Weber's suggestion that the letter was addressed to A. P. Watt, the literary agent.

11. Purdy, p. 34, *Early Life*, p. 169.

12. Purdy, pp. 32, 34.

13. For descriptions of the MS (Royal Library, Windsor Castle), see Purdy, pp. 33–34; also Edwards, pp. 64–96. On f. 31, e.g., Mrs Garland was originally described as a 'schoolmaster's widow', while the substitution of 'Miller' for 'Farmer' occurs, e.g., on ff. 18, 31. For what appears to be a curious survival of Loveday's earlier occupation, see p. 13 of the novel: 'He had not come about pigs or fowls this time.'

14. For the substitution of 'ma'am' for 'Martha' see, e.g., f. 15.

15. Edwards, p. 91, comes to a similar conclusion. See, e.g., the late addition to f. 185—'conscious that she naturally belonged to a politer grade than his own' (218)—and ff. 21, 81v, 82, 83, 84, etc. The present opening of chap. 2 appears on an inserted leaf, f. 9a, and the evidence of a deleted chapter title on f. 10 suggests that the chapter originally began with the present third paragraph (11). Cf. W. G. Bebbington, *The Original Manuscript of Thomas Hardy's 'The Trumpet-Major'* (Windsor, n.d.), p. 6.

16. MS, f. 65 (74); cf. Bebbington, p. 11.

17. Hardy to [Mrs Rumbold], March 26, 1879 (copy in Adams coll.); Hardy to Blackwood, June 9, 1879 (Nat. Library of Scotland).

18. Maitland, *Life and Letters of Leslie Stephen*, p. 277; *Pall Mall Gazette*, November 23, 1880, p. 12.

19. Guerard, *Thomas Hardy*, pp. 118, 143. Cf. the review in the *Spectator*, December 18, 1880, 1628: 'She is selfish, as Mr. Hardy's heroines are selfish—not wilfully or intellectually, but by dint of her inborn, involuntary, unconscious emotional organism.' John Hutton, writing to Hardy on January 17, 1881 (DCM), identified the reviewer as Julian Hawthorne.

20. For an interesting discussion of the ambiguity of Hardy's handling of time in the novel, see George M. Thomson, 'The Trumpet-Major Chronicle', *Nineteenth Century Fiction*, 17 (1962), 52–56.

2. *The Uses of a Regional Past*

1. David Garnett, ed., *The Letters of T. E. Lawrence* (London, 1938), p. 429.

2. Hardy to Mrs Henniker, October 11, 1899 (DCM).

3. Gosse to Hamo Thornycroft, July 23, 1883: '[Dorchester] is, moreover, as bright and clean as a pin, and full of life; a cavalry and an infantry regiment are stationed in it, and bugling and marching and the loitering coloured military give it quite a foreign air' (Charteris, *Life and Letters of Sir Edmund Gosse*, p. 157).

4. See above, 'Achievement', section 1, n. 16.

5. *Poems of Rural Life in the Dorset Dialect* (London, 1879), p. 329; and see Bernard Jones, ed., *The Poems of William Barnes* (London, 1962), I, xvi–xvii.

6. Hardy to [Sir Henry Ponsonby], December 3, 1880, December 6, 1880, and December 14, 1881 (all in Royal Library, Windsor Castle); quoted Edwards, 'The Making of Hardy's *The Trumpet-Major*', pp. 34–35.

7. Irving Howe, *Thomas Hardy* (New York, 1967), p. [147], draws a comparison with Faulkner; see Michael Millgate, *The Achievement of William Faulkner* (London, 1966), pp. 1–2, 78. For Scott, see Ian Jack, *English Literature, 1815–1832* (Oxford, 1963), pp. 186–187, and Scott's own footnote to Chapter First of *Redgauntlet*. Hardy's grandfather had been a volunteer at the time of Napoleon's invasion threat (*Early Life*, p. 14), and Hardy himself made several visits to Chelsea Hospital to talk with surviving veterans of Waterloo and other battles of the period (*Early Life*, pp. 103, 139–140, etc.). The naming of his heroine was perhaps influenced by local memories of a Major Garland who had distinguished himself at Waterloo: see p. 238, and Peter D. Smith, 'William Cox and *The Trumpet-Major*', *Notes and Queries*, n.s. 14 (1967), 64–65.

8. *Pall Mall Gazette*, November 23, 1880, p. 12.

9. For some relevant background material, see R. Chevenix-Trench, 'Dorset Under Arms in 1803', *Proceedings of the Dorset Natural History and Archaeological Society*, 90 (1969), 303–312. Revisions within the MS, ff. 31, 96, show that Festus was originally conceived as Captain Delalynde, a regular officer in the same regiment of the dragoons as John Loveday. This change in conception is apparently to be associated with what evidence of repagination (e.g., f. 77 formerly numbered f. 57) suggests was a late development of the farcical material revolving upon Uncle Benjy in chapters 6, 7, and 8.

The legendary 'killing by a certain Thomas de la Lynd of a beautiful white hart that the king had run down and spared' is recalled by Hardy in his *New Quarterly Magazine* review of Barnes, p. 470 (*Personal Writings*, p. 95); the passage recurs in *Tess*, p. 10.

10. Stephen to Hardy, February 17, 1879 (DCM); see previous section, n. 7.

11. Though his description of the notebook itself is unsatisfactory, Edwards's thesis contains (pp. 139–142) an exhaustive account of the contents of the 'Trumpet-Major Notebook' and of the ways in which Hardy used it in writing the novel. See also Purdy, p. 34, Emma L. Clifford, 'The "Trumpet-Major Notebook" and *The Dynasts*', *Review of English Studies*, n.s.8 (1957), 149–161 (largely drawn from her 1955 Bristol University Ph.D. thesis, 'Thomas Hardy's View of History', pp. 75–92), and Walter F. Wright, *The Shaping of 'The Dynasts': A Study in Thomas Hardy* (Lincoln, Nebraska, 1967), pp. 128–136, 139–140, etc. For Hardy's part in supplying details for the illustrations, see Purdy, p. 33.

12. Edwards, pp. 165–168. Cf. *The Trumpet-Major*, pp. 116, 117, 118.

13. 'Trumpet-Major Notebook', first gathering, p. [45] (misnumbered 44 by Hardy himself); cf. Wright, *The Making of 'The Dynasts'*, p. 129.

14. *Good Words*, 21 (1880), 507, 730, 795. The chronology of the novel is discussed in Edwards, pp. 279–283.

15. *Early Life*, p. 167.

16. Edwards, pp. 277–278.

17. Elliott Felkin, 'Days with Thomas Hardy: From a 1918–1919 Diary', *Encounter*, 18, iv (1962), p. 30.

3. *A Laodicean*

1. *Early Life*, pp. 181, 182, 184, 187–188; Purdy, pp. 38–40; Hardy to Helen Allingham (née Paterson), June 4, 1880 (Adams); her reply, June 5, 1880 (DCM).

2. Hardy to Gosse, December 30, 1917 (Brotherton Collection, Leeds University).

3. *Grolier Cat.*, p. 23; volume now in Adams collection.

4. Phelps, *Autobiography with Letters* (New York, 1939), pp. 391, 394.

5. Purdy, p. 40.

6. See Beatty, 'Architecture in Hardy', pp. 405–419, and *Architectural Notebook*, pp. 8–9, 17–21.

7. Guerard, *Thomas Hardy*, p. 53.

8. Purdy, pp. 39–40.

9. See p. 116, and n.

10. Quoted Wright, *The Shaping of 'The Dynasts'*, p. 19; the volume, a gift to Hardy from Horace Moule, is in DCM.

11. Macdonnell, *Thomas Hardy* (London, 1894), p. 51.

12. The subject is well covered by Beatty in *Architectural Notebook*, pp. 21–34; cf. 'Architecture in Hardy', pp. 4–70.

13. J. O. Bailey, 'Hardy's "Mephistophelian Visitants"', *PMLA*, 61 (1946), 1156–1159.

14. See *The Hand of Ethelberta*, p. 357.

15. Haight, *George Eliot : A Biography* (Oxford, 1968), p. 496.

4. Politics and Ideas

1. Arnold, *Lectures and Essays in Criticism*, ed. R. H. Super (Ann Arbor, [1962]), p. 230, partly quoted in 'Literary Notes I', p. [150]; cf. *Early Life*, p. 190.

2. 'Literary Notes I', pp. 140–143, [146]–151.

3. *Lectures and Essays in Criticism*, p. 119.

4. *Lectures and Essays in Criticism*, p. 109.

5. Arnold, *Mixed Essays*, second edn. (London, 1880), p. 95.

6. *Mixed Essays*, pp. 79–80, 82–83.

7. 'Trumpet-Major Notebook', 3rd gathering, pp. 35–[42]. Horace Moule's father, the Rev. Henry Moule, was the author of *Two Conversations Between a Clergyman and One of His Parishioners on the Service for the Public Baptism of Infants* (London, 1843).

8. *Early Life*, p. 281.

9. *Early Life*, pp. 175, 217; cf. DeLaura, '"The Ache of Modernism" in Hardy's Later Novels', p. 384 and n. The essay as a whole, pp. 380–399, incorporates a full discussion of Hardy's attitude to Arnold and to Arnold's ideas.

10. 'Literary Notes I', p. 137; cf. James, 'Honoré de Balzac', as collected in *French Poets and Novelists* (London, 1884), p. 88.

11. Hardy to Galsworthy, April 16, 1916, in H.V. Marrot, ed., *The Life and Letters of John Galsworthy* (London, 1935), p. 753; see also Hardy to Galsworthy, March 31, 1916 (Marrot, p. 751).

12. *Later Years*, p. 217; cf. Noyes, *Two Worlds for Memory* (Philadelphia, 1953), pp. 147–155.

13. G. Lowes Dickinson, *J. McT. E. McTaggart* (Cambridge, 1931), p. 101; cf. Hardy to McTaggart, May 23, 1906 (pp. 101–102).

14. D. F. Barber, ed., *Concerning Thomas Hardy: A Composite Portrait from Memory* (London, 1968), p. 150.
15. See, for example, Gosse's essay, 'The Influence of Democracy on Literature', collected in *Questions at Issue* (London, 1893); cf. Paul F. Mattheisen and Michael Millgate, eds., *Transatlantic Dialogue: Selected American Correspondence of Edmund Gosse* (Austin, 1965), pp. 45–47.
16. Marrot, p. 507.
17. *Shop Assistant*, June 21, 1919, 405 (*Personal Writings*, p. 253).
18. Hardy to Morgan, April 5, 1921 (Berg).
19. Hardy to Pearce-Edgecumbe, April 23, 1891 (Texas); cf. Hardy's previous letter, April 21, 1891 (Texas). Pearce-Edgecumbe was narrowly defeated (*Times*, May 9, 1891, p. 7).
20. Draft, Hardy to Joseph Eldridge, June 8, 1892 (DCM). This letter was originally to have appeared in *Later Years* (after '*Easter Sunday*' entry on p. 8), but was deleted from the typescript, pp. 342–343 (DCM: see Purdy, p. 273 and n.) See also Hardy's letter to Mrs Haddon, October 18, 1896, in Weber, ed., *Letters of Thomas Hardy*, pp. 46–47.
21. Hardy to Percy William Bunting [editor of the *Contemporary Review*], October 12, November 5, November 18, 1883, quoted in Robert Liddell Lowe, 'Three New Hardy Letters', *Modern Language Review*, 54 (1959), 396–397.
22. *World*, February 17, 1886, p. 7.
23. 'Literary Notes I', pp. 221–[222].
24. Beatty, 'Architecture in Hardy', pp. 417–419.
25. Cf. Jerome Hamilton Buckley, *The Triumph of Time: A Study of the Victorian Concepts of Time, History, Progress, and Decadence* (Cambridge, Mass. 1966), pp. 18–19.
26. 'The Profitable Reading of Fiction', *Forum* [New York], 5 (1888), p. 64 (*Personal Writings*, p. 118).

5. Two on a Tower

1. *Early Life*, p. 193, Purdy, pp. 43–44. The final stages of composition of *A Laodicean* were also completed at Wimborne: as late as October 5, 1881 (date from postmark), Hardy was writing to Harper's agent, R. R. Bowker, about copy for the final instalment (Library of Congress); cf. Purdy, p. 39.
2. Purdy, p. 44.

3. For the short stories, 'The Honourable Laura' and 'What the Shepherd Saw', see Purdy, pp. 66 and 156.

4. *Early Life*, p. 195. The reference to Greenwich in the novel (220) was a late addition, f. 248v., to the MS (Houghton Library, Harvard).

5. Purdy, p. 44; Hardy wrote in a copy of the 1895 edn.: 'The backgrounds in this novel, by reason of its character, are drawn with a somewhat freer hand than in many others of the series./T. Hardy./ December: 1904' (Sotheby Sale Catalogue, May 29, 1961, lot 17; the volume is now at the University of Texas).

6. Purdy, p. 44.

7. *Athenaeum*, November 18, 1882, 658.

8. James, 'The Question of the Opportunities', collected in Leon Edel, ed., *The American Essays of Henry James* (New York, 1958), pp. 202–203.

9. Cf. Carl J. Weber, 'Ainsworth and Thomas Hardy', *Review of English Studies*, 17 (1941), 193–200; 'The Science of Fiction', *New Review*, 4 (April 1891), 316 (*Personal Writings*, p. 135).

10. 'Literary Notes I', p. [146], where Hardy refers to the novel by its English title, *Transformation*; his copy (London, 1872) is in DCM.

11. Hawthorne, *The Scarlet Letter* (Columbus, Ohio, 1962), p. 37; 'Literary Notes I', p. [146]. Hardy also quoted from the same paragraph: 'The fault was mine. The page of life that was spread out before me seemed dull and commonplace, only because I had not fathomed its deeper import. A better book than I shall ever write was there . . . '

12. Hardy to Gosse, December 4, 1882, quoted Purdy, p. 44, n.

13. Gosse to Hardy, January 1, 1883 (Adams); *Saturday Review*, November 18, 1882, 675.

14. *The Poetry of Astronomy* (London, 1881). In his Preface, p. [v], Proctor wrote: 'Many think that science cannot truly be called science if clothed in poetic garb, and, on the other hand, others seem to fear that a glory must depart from the face of nature if science scrutinise her mysteries too closely. I believe both these fears to be unfounded—that science need not be less exact though poetry underlie its teachings; while, beautiful and glorious though the ordinary aspect of nature may be, a deeper poetry, a more solemn significance, a greater beauty, and a nobler glory can be recognised in the aspect of nature when science lifts the veil which hides it from the unaided vision.'

[389]

15. Tennyson, *Poems* (London, 1833 [1832]), p. 84.
16. As revised for *Poems* (London, 1842) I, 149, 136–137.
17. Wreden Catalogue (1938), item 400. Notes on astronomy attributed to Proctor in 'Literary Notes I', p. 11, apparently date from late 1875.
18. The Transit of Venus (across the face of the sun) occurred in December 1874 for the first time since 1789 (*Annual Register* for 1874, pp. 381–383); an article on the subject was juxtaposed (pp. 1595–1596) to the *Spectator* review of *Far from the Madding Crowd*, December 19, 1874, 1597–1599. There was a second Transit in December 1882, the year of publication of *Two on a Tower*, which must have given the novel a certain element of topicality. For Charborough Park, see *Thomas Hardy's Notebooks*, pp. 61–62 (misquoted and drastically abbreviated from 'Memoranda I'), and Lea, *Thomas Hardy's Wessex*, pp. 194–197; Hardy also drew, especially for the situation of the tower, upon Weatherbury Castle, near Milborne St Andrew: see Lea, pp. 195–196, and Murray's *Handbook*, p. 110.
19. Cf. Carpenter, *Thomas Hardy*, pp. 66–67.
20. The similarities between Viviette and Eustacia are less obvious in editions subsequent to the Osgood, McIlvaine edn. of 1896, which deleted the following paragraph from its former position at the beginning of chapter 14(102): 'Rural solitude, which provides ample themes for the intellect and sweet occupations innumerable for the minor sentiments, often denies a ready object for those stronger passions that enter no less than the others into the human constitution. The suspended pathos finds its remedy in settling on the first intrusive shape that happens to be reasonably well organized for the purpose, disregarding social and other minor accessories. Where the solitude is shadowed by the secret melancholies of the solitary, this natural law is still surer in operation.' (First edn. I, 227, retained in second issue, and in one-vol. Sampson Low edn. of 1882, p. 111; the first edn. text is considerably revised from MS, f. 113, and *Atlantic*, 50 [July 1882], 12.)
21. Ruth A. Firor, *Folkways in Thomas Hardy* (Philadelphia, 1931; reissued, New York, 1962), p. 101; for the 'Planet-Ruler', see *Thomas Hardy's Notebooks*, p. 40 (inaccurately transcribed from 'Memoranda I'). That Hardy deliberately intended the revelation to Swithin to come from the workfolk is suggested by the deletion from the first edn. (I, 202) of an anticipatory passage (at a point

corresponding to the top of Wessex edn. p. 91) which had appeared in the serial, though already shortened there from the version in the MS: *Atlantic*, 50 (July 1882), 6; MS, f. 102.

22. *St James's Gazette*, January 19, 1883, p. 14; see p. 290, and *Personal Writings*, p. 242; also Hardy to Gosse, December 10, 1882 (quoted Purdy, pp. 44–45), and Hardy to Anne Benson Proctor, January 17, 1883 (Berg).

23. In the Osgood, McIlvaine edn. (1895), the second paragraph of the Preface concludes, p. v: 'I was made to suffer in consequence from several eminent pens, such warm epithets as "hazardous", "repulsive," "little short of revolting," "a studied and gratuitous insult," being flung at the precarious volumes.' The deletion was first made from the 1902 Macmillan issue of this edition.

24. Hardy to Gosse, December 10, 1882, quoted Purdy, p. 45.

25. Quoted Purdy, p. 44.

26. Hardy to Francis Thompson, December 31, 1891, quoted *Grolier Cat.*, pp. 34–35; cf. Wilson, *Thirteen Author Collections*, p. 73.

RENEWAL

1. Max Gate

1. Weber, *Hardy in America : A Study of Thomas Hardy and His American Readers* (Waterville, Maine, 1946; reissued, New York, 1966), passim.

2. William H. Rideing, *Many Celebrities and a Few Others* (London, 1912), p. 286.

3. See Mattheisen and Millgate, eds., *Transatlantic Dialogue*, pp. 7–8, 32.

4. Purdy, p. 39; cf. Weber, *Hardy in America*, pp. 44–45.

5. Purdy, pp. 48–49.

6. *Early Life*, p. 205.

7. *Early Life*, pp. 208–209; *Transatlantic Dialogue*, pp. 115–116.

8. *Transatlantic Dialogue*, pp. 38–39; Gosse to Hardy, December 8, 1882 (Adams).

9. Howells to S. L. Clemens, July 10, 1883, in Henry Nash Smith and William M. Gibson, eds., *Mark Twain—Howells Letters* (Cambridge, Mass., 1960), I, 434.

10. Howells to Gosse, June 26, 1883 (*Transatlantic Dialogue*, p. 115). George Du Maurier had illustrated *The Hand of Ethelberta* and *A Laodicean;* [Sir] Hamo Thornycroft, the sculptor, later executed a bust of Hardy (now in DCM).

11. *Harper's Weekly*, March 9, 1912, p. 33, partly quoted in *Personal Writings*, p. 246.

12. Edith Wharton, *A Backward Glance* (New York, 1934), pp. 215–216.

13. See Weber, *Hardy in America*, pp. 152–153.

14. *Early Life*, p. 229; Hardy to Gosse, September 25, 1890 (Adams).

15. Hardy to Henry Hardy, April 20, 1880 (photocopy, Sanders Collection, DCM); Hardy to the agent of the Earl of Ilchester, March 21, 1882 (*Grolier Cat.*, p. 31).

16. Even to Gosse, in a letter of August 18, 1886 (Adams), Hardy referred to life at Max Gate as 'cottage-like'; cf. Hardy to [Alexander], September 16, 1886 (Princeton), and Hardy to Mrs Moulton, July 23, 1890 (quoted *Hardy in America*, p. 129).

17. Hardy to [Library Committee, City of Winchester], February 24, 1915, printed in *Hampshire Observer*, March 12, 1938, p. 4; cf. William Archer, 'Real Conversations. II.—With Mr. Thomas Hardy', *Pall Mall Magazine*, 22 (1901), 536.

18. *World*, February 17, 1886, pp. 6–7.

19. Frederick Dolman, 'An Evening with Thomas Hardy', p. [75].

20. R. R. Bowker, 'London as a Literary Centre. Second Paper: The Novelists', *Harper's New Monthly Magazine*, 77 (1888), 8.

21. Viola Meynell, ed., *Letters of J. M. Barrie* (London, 1942), p. 152.

22. See p. 299–302 and notes.

23. *Early Life*, p. 131.

24. Hardy's name first appears among the list of members in the Club's *Proceedings* for 1882: vol. 4, viii.

25. *Poems of the Past and the Present*, p. 228; *Moments of Vision*, pp. 216–217. For Hardy and the S.P.A.B., see anon., 'Thomas Hardy and "Anti-Scrape"', *Times Literary Supplement*, February 23, 1928, 129, and Beatty, 'Architecture in Hardy', pp. 26–39, 73–84, etc.

26. See Hardy, 'H.J.M. Some Memories and Letters', in H. J. Moule, *Dorchester Antiquities* (Dorchester, 1906), p. 9 (*Personal Writings*, p. 68). Moule's letter about a Dorset book is dated August 24, 1881 (DCM); that it was Hardy who backed out of the scheme is clear from Moule to Hardy, October 3, 1881 (DCM).

27. *Early Life*, p. 210; Gosse to Thornycroft, July 23, 1883 (Charteris, *Life and Letters of Sir Edmund Gosse*, p. 157).

28. 'Some Romano-British Relics Found at Max Gate, Dorchester', *Proceedings of the Dorset Natural History and Antiquarian Field Club*, 11 (1890), [78]–81; previously published as 'The "Find" in Fordington-field', *Dorset County Chronicle*, May 15, 1884, p. 5 (*Personal Writings*, pp. 191–195).

2. *'The Dorsetshire Labourer'*

1. Hardy never collected the essay, and the page references given within parentheses, in this chapter only, are to the first printing in *Longman's Magazine*, 2 (July 1883), 252–269; cf. *Personal Writings*, pp. 168–189.

2. Longman to Richard Jefferies, quoted in Samuel J. Looker and Crichton Porteus, *Richard Jefferies, Man of the Fields: A Biography and Letters* (London, 1965), pp. 125–126. Longman mentioned to Jefferies that he expected a contribution from Hardy.

3. See p. 181 and n.

4. See p. 97 and n.

5. Jefferies, *Hodge and his Masters* (London, 1880), II, 307–312.

6. *Early Life*, p. 175.

7. Collected in *Toilers of the Field* (London 1892), pp. 211–258.

8. That Hardy's observations on this point had nonetheless a certain validity is suggested by a passage (kindly drawn to my attention by Professor W. J. Keith) in Alfred Williams, *A Wiltshire Village* (London, 1912), p. 162: 'The poverty, or very often apparent poverty, of the countryside cottage stands out in greater relief, and is more readily observed by "charitable" persons and intermeddlers than is that of urban districts.'

9. *Poems of Rural Life in the Dorset Dialect* (London, 1879), pp. 5–7.

10 Jefferies, 'The Wiltshire Labourer', *Longman's Magazine*, 3 (November 1883), 52–65; 'John Smith's Shanty', *Fraser's Magazine* n.s.9 (February 1874), [135]–149, and *Toilers of the Field*, pp. 175–210.

11. Hedgcock, *Thomas Hardy, penseur et artiste*, p. 6 (DCM): see 'Apprenticeship', section 3, n. 8.

12. See E. D. Mackerness, ed., *The Journals of George Sturt, 1890–1927* (Cambridge, 1967), pp. 382–383, for Sturt's suggestion that the novel of the agricultural labourer had remained unwritten because: 'The novelist is forced to introduce the employing class,

without whom the labourer's life seems "unconditioned".' I am grateful to Professor Keith for drawing this passage to my attention.

13. See p. 98. Barnes's submission appears in the Appendix, Part Two, to the Second Report (*Parliamentary Papers*, 1868–69, XIII, [242]–[244]); the quotation, p. [244] continues: 'The smallest of our now great farms is beyond his wildest hope, and so he toils without the hope that has led on the poor lad in commercial work to the honourable estate of the high risen merchant.'

14. Kerr, *Bound to the Soil*, p. 155.

15. *Cassell's Saturday Journal*, June 25, 1892, 944.

16. Hunt & Co.'s *Directory of Dorsetshire, with part of Hants and Wilts* (London, 1851), quoted in J. Stevens Cox, ed., *Dorchester in 1851* (Guernsey, C.I.), p. 143 (paginated as part of series).

17. The first part of W. J. Hyde's article, 'Hardy's View of Realism', pp. [45]–53, establishes and documents this point.

18. *Pall Mall Gazette*, January 2, 1892, p. 1.

19. Williams, 'Thomas Hardy', *Critical Quarterly*, 6 (Winter 1964), 349.

20. Arnold Kettle, introd., *Tess of the d'Urbervilles* (New York, 1966), p. xv. Kettle modifies here, and in *Hardy the Novelist: a Reconsideration* (Swansea, [1966]), the more extreme statements of *An Introduction to the English Novel* (London, 1953), II, 49–62.

21. Douglas Brown, for example, relies heavily upon Trevelyan in his analysis of Hardy's 'agricultural theme': *Thomas Hardy* (London, 1954; revised edn., 1961), pp. viii, 39, 50.

22. Fletcher, 'The Great Depression of English Agriculture, 1873–1896', *Economic History Review*, 2nd ser., 13 (1960–61), 431.

23. Jones, 'The Changing Basis of English Agricultural Prosperity, 1853–73', *Agricultural History Review*, 10 (1962), 119.

24. Quoted Fletcher, p. 419; for these developments in general, see Fletcher's entire article, pp. 417–432.

25. Lord Ernle, *English Farming Past and Present*, introd. G. E. Fussell and O. R. McGregor (London, 1961), p. 394; first published 1912.

26. Caird, *English Agriculture in 1850–51* (London, 1852), p. 1.

27. Joseph Darby, 'The Farming of Dorset', *Journal of the Bath and West of England Society*, 3rd ser., 4 (1872), 29, 35.

28. *Parliamentary Papers*, 1882, XV, [30]–[38]; 1895, XVII, 237–[320]. Cf. Kerr, *Bound to the Soil*, pp. 236–237.

29. Darby, p. 36.

30. *Hodge and his Masters*, II, 77; cf. Kerr, pp. 238–242.

31. See E. L. Jones, 'The Agricultural Labour Market in England, 1793–1872', *Economic History Review*, 17 (1964), [322]–338, esp. 337; also J.P.D. Dunbabin, 'The "Revolt of the Field": The Agricultural Labourers' Movement in the 1870s', *Past and Present*, no. 26 (November 1963), pp. [68]–97.

32. Maxwell, 'The "Sociological" Approach to *The Mayor of Casterbridge*', in Maynard Mack and Ian Gregor, eds., *Imagined Worlds: Essays on Some English Novels and Novelists in Honour of John Butt* (London, 1968), pp. 225–236, esp. pp. 233–235. Brown's most extended treatment of the novel is his *Thomas Hardy: The Mayor of Casterbridge* (London, 1962).

33. *Later Years*, p. 146.

34. *Later Years*, p. 146.

35. *Later Years*, pp. 93–94; there are substantial differences between this text (pp. 93–96) of Hardy's letter and that originally published in H. Rider Haggard, *Rural England* (London, 1902), I, 282–285. Hardy's own draft (DCM) coincides precisely with neither.

36. It is neither in *Rural England* nor in Hardy's draft: see previous note.

37. *Later Years*, p. 146.

3. The Mayor of Casterbridge

1. For a full discussion of the MS, see Dieter Riesner, 'Kunstprosa in der Werkstatt: Hardys *The Mayor of Casterbridge* 1884–1912', in Dieter Riesner and Helmut Gneuss, eds., *Festschrift für Walter Hüber* (Berlin, 1964), pp. 267–326.

2. Purdy, however, notes (p. 53) that the serial text was in type by October 20.

3. Purdy, pp. 54–55; Hardy to Howells, November 9, 1886 (quoted Weber, *Hardy in America*, p. 58).

4. Chase, *Thomas Hardy from Serial to Novel* (Minneapolis, 1927; reissued, New York, 1964), pp. [15]–65.

5. *Graphic*, 33 (January 30, 1886), 134.

6. See, e.g., D. A. Dike, 'A Modern Oedipus: *The Mayor of Casterbridge*', *Essays in Criticism*, 2 (1952), 169–179.

7. See, e.g., Douglas Brown, *Thomas Hardy: The Mayor of Casterbridge*, p. 62.

8. The addition of this brief speech of Farfrae's was the most interesting, though not the most substantial, of the changes which Hardy made in the Sampson Low one-volume edition of 1890 (p. 427).

9. For a comment on the role of 'inquisitiveness' in *The Mayor of Casterbridge*, see Robert Kiely, 'Vision and Viewpoint in *The Mayor of Casterbridge*', *Nineteenth Century Fiction*, 23 (1968), 189–200, esp. p. 197.

10. The title only received its final form in the 1912 Wessex edn. In the MS, f. 1 (DCM), it is simply *The Mayor of Casterbridge*; the first edn. has *The Mayor of Casterbridge : The Life and Death of a Man of Character*; the Osgood, McIlvaine edn. of 1895 follows the Sampson Low edn. of 1887 in reading *The Mayor of Casterbridge : A Story of a Man of Character*. Cf. Purdy, p. 52.

4. The Evolution of Wessex

1. Certainly as early as Bertram C. A. Windle, *The Wessex of Thomas Hardy* (London, 1902), p. 4.

2. Keith, 'Critical Approaches to Hardy's Wessex', *Association of Canadian University Teachers of English : Report, 1963*, pp. 22–23. Professor Keith has generously allowed me to read his unpublished 'The Anatomy of Wessex: A Study of Creative Landscape in the Work of Thomas Hardy', in which he notes, (pp. 174–175) that the changes made in this sentence between the serial and the Wessex edn. all introduced references to novels which post-date *The Mayor of Casterbridge*.

3. Hardy to Marston (of Sampson Low, Marston, Searle & Rivington), [1885?] (Purdy coll.); for the revisions to the Osgood, McIlvaine edn. see Purdy, p. 281, and W. J. Keith, 'Thomas Hardy and the Literary Pilgrims', *Nineteenth Century Fiction*, 24 (1969), 84–88.

4. 'Facts' Notebook, pp. 32, 48.

5. 'Facts', pp. 42, 71, 32, 27, 34–35.

6. *Dorset County Chronicle*, December 4, 1828, p. [4]; cf. 'Facts', p. [94].

7. *Dorset County Chronicle*, April 27, 1826, p. [4]; cf. 'Facts', p. 30.

8. Hardy to Douglas, January 28, 1903, in W.M. Parker, 'Hardy's Letters to Sir George Douglas', *English*, 14 (1963), 222.

9. Cf. 'Facts', p. 52.

10. *Dorset County Chronicle*, July 9, 1829; 'Facts', pp. 111–[112].

11. *Dorset County Chronicle*, August 17, 1826, p. [4]; cf. 'Facts', p. 47, where the entries on either side of the obliterated item are to this same issue of the newspaper.

12. See p. 38 and n.; for 'Selling a Wife', see Timbs, p. 122.

13. 'Facts', p. [74]; see also pp. 32–33, 116. I have not been able to consult a copy of the *Dorset County Chronicle* for December 6, 1827.
14. *Dorset County Chronicle*, July 26, 1849, p. [4].
15. According to the *Yeovil Times*, July 31, 1849, p. 4, the arch at Monckton Gate 'was tastefully decorated with Union Jacks, and had a beautiful and tasty [sic] appearance'.
16. Handley C. G. Moule, *Memories of a Vicarage* (London, 1913), pp. 31–32. The Rev. Henry Moule was one of the local committee responsible for arranging the Dorchester ceremony.
17. *Tess of the d'Urbervilles*, pp. ix–x (*Personal Writings*, p. 46).
18. 'Cruchley's Railway & Telegraphic Map of Dorset', on a scale of three miles to the inch (DCM).
19. Hardy's own drawing for the Wessex edn. map (now in DCM) was reproduced in *The Countryman*, 13 (1936), 489–490; it also appears on the endpapers of D. F. Barber, ed., *Concerning Thomas Hardy*.
20. Hardy's letters to Lea about Lea's guidebooks and the photographs for the Wessex edn. are in DCM (Sanders Collection). Hardy praised the accuracy of Lea's *Thomas Hardy's Wessex* in a letter to Harold Child, May 10, 1915 (Adams).
21. [Herman Lea], *A Handbook to the Wessex Country of Thomas Hardy's Novels and Poems* (London, n.d.), pp. [1]–2; cf. Hardy to Lea, June 1, 1905 (DCM).
22. Cf. Lea, *Thomas Hardy's Wessex*, pp. 98, 36. Numerous specific questions of identification are discussed in Beatty, 'Architecture in Hardy', pp. 253n., 360, 364, 391–400, etc. For an excellent general discussion, see Keith, 'Thomas Hardy and the Literary Pilgrims', pp. 80–92, passim.
23. Weber, 'Chronology in Hardy's Novels', *PMLA*, 53 (1938), 320.
24. Weber, *Hardy of Wessex : His Life and Literary Career*, revised edn. (New York, 1965), p. 224.
25. See, however, Albert A. Murphree and Carl F. Strauch, 'The Chronology of *The Return of the Native*', *Modern Language Notes*, 54 (1939), 491–497. F. B. Pinion, in *A Hardy Companion : A Guide to the Works of Thomas Hardy and Their Background* (London, 1968), also has a few modifications to suggest: e.g., he notes (p. 21) the internal clue to the dating of *Under the Greenwood Tree* (see above, p. 57).
26. Weber, 'Chronology', p. 318, *Hardy of Wessex*, p. 149. This misunderstanding disqualifies much of the discussion in Carl J. Weber and F. B. Pinion, '*The Mayor of Casterbridge* : An Anglo-American

Dialogue', *Library Chronicle of the University of Texas*, 8, iii (1967), pp. 3–12. References in Hardy to Candlemas and Lady-Day are (I think invariably) to Old Style, February 14 and April 6: cf. 'The Dorsetshire Labourer', p. 259 (*Personal Writings*, p. 177). As late as 1902 H. Rider Haggard noted in *Rural England*, I, 280: 'In Dorchester an annual hiring fair is held on February 14, that is, old Candlemas Day.' And see above, p. 99.

27. See p. 187 and n.

28. G. M. Young and W. D. Handcock, eds., *English Historical Documents, Vol. XII (1). 1833–1874* (London, 1956), pp. 530–531.

29. David St John Thomas, *A Regional History of the Railways of Great Britain: Volume I. The West Country*, revised edn. (Newton Abbot, 1966). p. 33.

30. See p. 161 and n.

31. 'Trumpet-Major Notebook', 1st gathering, p. 13.

32. Weber, 'Chronology', p. 320.

33. Keith, 'The Anatomy of Wessex' (see n. 2 above), suggests that the relative remoteness of Hardy's setting and its slowness to change made it possible for him to evoke the past by working 'from the life': 'Hardy was in the unique position of being able to communicate a *living* past by recording landscapes and customs which had survived into his own present, and which he was free to adapt and modify to suit his creative needs' (p. 247).

34. Preface to *Far from the Madding Crowd*, p. ix.

35. See n. 18 above. Hardy signed the map 'Th. H./Inv. et Del.' and wrote: 'It is to be understood that this is an imaginative Wessex only, & that the places described under the names here given are not portraits of any real places, but visionary places which may approximate to the real places more or less' (also quoted *Exhibition of Hardy's Drawings & Paintings*, p. 6).

5. The Woodlanders

1. *World*, April 20, 1887, p. 22.

2. *Academy*, April 9, 1887, 251–252; *Dublin Evening Mail*, March 30, 1887, p. 4. There is certainly a discernible resemblance between the Giles-Grace-Fitzpiers pattern and the Gabriel-Bathsheba-Troy pattern, even to such details as the early economic disasters overtaking Giles and Gabriel and the delayed first appearance of Fitzpiers and Troy.

3. *Wessex Poems*, pp. 81–82.

4. *Morning Post*, April 6, 1887, p. 2.

5. Quoted in Hardy, 'H.J.M. Some Memories and Letters', p. 12 (*Personal Writings*, p. 71).

6. Quoted Purdy, p. 74n.

7. Rutland, *Thomas Hardy: A Study of His Writings and Their Background*, p. 212.

8. 'Literary Notes I', pp. 201, [206], 207, [209]–210, etc.

9. *Early Life*, p. 232.

10. Murray's *Handbook*, p. 101. Similar information given in many other sources, including [William Barnes,] *A Guide to Dorchester* (Dorchester, [1864]), p. 22. Henry James had of course used the same name, spelled 'Winterbourne', in *Daisy Miller*, first published in the *Cornhill* in 1878.

11. This seems, indeed, to have been the title he originally intended: see MS, f. 1 (DCM), and Purdy, pp. 56, 57.

12. Writing on July 19, 1889, about a proposed dramatisation of *The Woodlanders*, Hardy observed that 'the conventions of the libraries, etc.' had prevented him from emphasising the implication at the end of the novel that 'the heroine is doomed to an unhappy life with an inconstant husband' (draft DCM, quoted *Early Life*, p. 289). The dramatisers apparently took the hint, since one of them, C. W. Jarvis (see 'Fulfilment', section 4, n. 9), wrote on September 16, 1889 (DCM), to quote the projected ending: '*Fitzpiers* You will come back to me?/*Grace* What else can I do? My father says so, he tells me, every body tells me—to be unhappy.'

13. *Later Years*, p. 42.

14. *Pall Mall Gazette*, May 19, 1887, p. 5.

FULFILMENT

1. Tess of the d'Urbervilles

1. Hardy to Lane, June 30, 1891 (Purdy coll.).

2. See p. 204 and n.; also H. J. Moule to Hardy, December 22, 1886 (DCM), and Purdy, p. 156n.

3. *Dorset County Chronicle*, June 4, 1885, p. 11; cf. the Club's *Proceedings*, 7 ([1886]), 63.

4. *Dorset County Chronicle*, February 28, 1889, p. 5; cf. *Proceedings*, 10 (1889), 20, 26.

5. Comparison of phrasing suggests that H. J. Moule's source may have been [J. C. Panton,] *A Guide to Swanage* (see above, 'Achievement', section 3, n. 7), p. 46: 'It is said that a spectre-coach and four drive out from Wool-bridge House in the gloom of an evening; but lest any reader may wait until evening in order to fathom this mystery, we may add that none can see this ghostly coach of the Turbervilles who have not Turberville blood in their veins.' This same guide (though under a misleading title) is quoted as the source of the Turberville ghost-story in John Symonds Udal's privately printed *Dorsetshire Folk-Lore* (Hertford, 1922), p. 174. It seems clear from the *Tess* MS (British Museum) that the extended references to d'Urberville/Turberville family history were inserted at a relatively late stage of composition, apparently as a result of a perception that these associations could be used as a kind of leit-motif both of heredity and of doom: see, e.g., ff. 254v., 262v., 267, and cf. John Laird, 'The Manuscript of Hardy's *Tess of the d'Urbervilles* and What It Tells Us', *Journal of the Australasian Universities Language and Literature Association*, no. 26 (May 1966), pp. 77–78.

6. Hardy to MacColl, February 9, 1892, quoted in *The Ashley Library: A Catalogue of Printed Books, Manuscripts and Autograph Letters Collected by Thomas James Wise* (London, 1922), II, 168; the published transcription (as with most of the Hardy items in the *Catalogue*) is highly inaccurate, and I have therefore corrected it from the original (British Museum). Cf. Raymond Blathwayt, 'A Chat with the Author of *Tess*', *Black & White*, August 27, 1892, 239 (also in *Thomas Hardy and His Readers*, p. 93).

7. 'Facts' Notebook, pp. 117, 138, 162; these references are all to 1829 or 1830. For a more recent occurrence, see *Dorset County Chronicle*, October 17, 1872, p. 3: 'ACCIDENT.—A collision between two vehicles occurred on the Weymouth road last Saturday evening. As a mail cart driven by Frederick Davis was rounding the corner near the railway gate it ran into a waggon. . . . The driver of the mail cart and his companion were unseated, and in their fall they sustained slight injuries, while the shafts of the vehicle were broken, the horse bolting through South-street and being captured in Pease-lane.'

8. 'SHOCKING SUICIDE.—Captain de Burgess Hodge, of Mat-ford-lodge, Exeter, and formerly of the 12th Lancers, committed suicide at Dartmoor during Saturday night. He had been lodging

at the Saracen's Head Inn, at Dartmoor, and went to bed as usual on Saturday evening. On Sunday morning another person was at breakfast in the house, and observed blood dripping from the ceiling. On his raising an alarm, the household rushed upstairs, and found Captain Hodge, who was 45 years of age, lying dead on the floor, he having shot himself through the head during the night. . . . The deceased left two letters—one addressed to his wife and another to a married lady with whom he was on friendly terms, and who had been with him every evening at the inn where he committed suicide.' (*Dorset County Chronicle*, August 2, 1888, p. 12); volume in DCM.

9. 'Facts' Notebook, pp. 40–41; *Dorset County Chronicle*, July 20, 1826, p. [4]: in an action for damages following a coach accident, the position of the defence was 'that some cottages which were on the road had been removed, and that the coachman was in the habit of fixing his eye on the gable-end of one of these cottages, the absence of which deceived him on the occasion of the accident'; evidence was given that a wheel of the coach had passed over 'part of the foundation of the cottage which was taken down'.

10. Cf. his note on Howells, *Early Life*, p. 314.

11. In the interview in *Cassell's Saturday Journal*, June 25, 1892, for example, Hardy insisted that 'Tess had a real existence', and declared: 'I always like to have a real place in my mind for every scene in a novel. Before writing about it I generally go and see each place; no, one can't do with a picture of it. Local colour is of such importance' (p. 945). Cf. Blathwayt, 'A Chat with the Author of *Tess*', p. 239 (*Thomas Hardy and His Readers*, pp. 92–94).

12. See Purdy, pp. 66–67.

13. David Lodge, *Language of Fiction: Essays in Criticism and Verbal Analysis of the English Novel* (London, 1966), p. 170.

14. Hardy to T. K. Macquoid, October 29, 1891, quoted *Grolier Cat.*, p. 33.

15. Thornycroft wrote to his wife, May 8, 1894, to report Gosse's account of meeting Hardy at the Royal Academy private view the previous Friday, when Hardy said that he had just been 'cheered up by seeing the most beautiful woman in England or rather her whom *I* think the most beautiful woman in England, her on whom I thought when I wrote Tess of the d'Urbervilles. "And who was that?" said Gosse—"Why it was Mrs Hamo Thornycroft" said Thomas Hardy. Now is not that a nice little story & true?' (letter

in possession of Mrs Elfrida Manning). Cf. *Early Life*, pp. 288–289, 293.

16. *Dorset County Chronicle*, August 14, 1856, p. 25. Lady Hester Pinney, *Thomas Hardy and the Birdsmoorgate Murder 1856* (Beaminster, 1966) quotes, p. 2, Hardy's letter to her of January 20, 1926: 'I remember what a fine figure she showed against the sky as she hung in the misty rain, and how the tight black silk gown set off her shape as she wheeled half-round and back.' Recalling the incident to Elliott Felkin ('Days with Thomas Hardy', p. 29), Hardy said that when it began to rain 'I saw—they had put a cloth over the face—how, as the cloth got wet, *her features came through it.* That was extraordinary.' For the possible relationship to *Tess*, see *The Sketch*, November 2, 1904, p. 94, although in the copy inserted in his 'Personal' scrapbook Hardy has deleted the suggestion that he had known the woman executed.

17. Newman Flower, *Just As It Happened* (London, 1950), p. 92.

18. *Later Years*, p. 106; Hardy goes on in the same letter to make a Swiftian 'modest proposal' about using the 'smaller children, say, of overcrowded families' for sporting purposes.

19. Hardy to Douglas, November 8, 1891 (quoted Parker, 'Hardy's Letters to Sir George Douglas', p. 219).

20. Separate notebook leaf (DCM); quoted in *Exhibition of Hardy's Drawings & Paintings*, p. [2].

21. Cf. John Holloway, 'Hardy's Major Fiction', repr. in Albert J. Guerard, ed., *Hardy: A Collection of Critical Essays* (Englewood Cliffs, N.J., 1963), p. 60, and Philip Mahone Griffith, 'The Image of the Trapped Animal in Hardy's *Tess of the d'Urbervilles*', *Tulane Studies in English*, 13 (1963), 85–94.

22. Felkin, 'Days with Thomas Hardy', p. 33.

23. 'The Bride-Night Fire' (formerly 'The Fire at Tranter Sweatley's'), *Wessex Poems*, pp. 94–98. A deletion in the *Tess* MS, f. 117, shows that Hardy originally intended the milkers' ballad about a murderer (p. 141) to have been about a maid who went to a wood and came back a maid no more. For the importance of ballads and oral tradition in Hardy, see Donald Davidson, 'The Traditional Basis of Thomas Hardy's Fiction', *Southern Review*, 6 (1940), 162–178, repr. in Guerard, ed., *Hardy: A Collection of Critical Essays*, pp. 10–23.

24. *National Observer*, November 14, 1891, [673]–675; see Purdy, pp. 69, 77.

25. Cf. Hardy's poem, 'We Field-Women', *Winter Words*, p. 290.

26. [Charlotte M. Yonge], *History of Christian Names* (London, 1863), I, 272, Hardy's copy of a one-volume edition (1884) of this work is in the Colbeck Collection of the University of British Columbia.

27. Cf. F. Max Müller's article, 'Solar Myths', *Nineteenth Century*, 18 (December 1885), 900–922, which Hardy apparently read at the time of its appearance ('Literary Notes I', pp. [200]–201): '*Helio-latry* . . . as a recognition of the supernatural character of the sun as the source of light, warmth, and life, is the most widely spread form of early faith' (p. 907).

28. Johnson, *The Art of Thomas Hardy*, enlarged edn. (London, 1923), esp. pp. 227–249; Schweik, 'Moral Perspectives in *Tess of the d'Urbervilles*', *College English*, 24 (1962), pp. 16–17. For another comment on the end of chap. 13, see Lodge, *Language of Fiction*, pp. 177–178.

29. Cf. John Holloway, *The Victorian Sage* (London, 1953; reissued, New York, 1965), p. 250.

30. Gregor, 'The Novel as Protest: *Tess of the d'Urbervilles* (1891)', in Ian Gregor and Brian Nicholas, *The Moral and the Story* (London, 1962), p. 137.

31. Howe, *Thomas Hardy*, p. 113.

32. See above, p. 268. The sketch map of 'Tess's Country' which Hardy drew for Margaret Deland, the novelist, and her husband was reproduced in *Harper's Monthly Magazine*, 151 (1925), 239, and on the inside cover of the Harper & Brothers pamphlet, *Thomas Hardy: Notes on his Life and Work* (New York, n.d.); original in the Purdy collection. On the general topic of travel and movement in *Tess*, see Tony Tanner, 'Colour and Movement in Hardy's *Tess of the d'Urbervilles*', *Critical Quarterly*, 10 (1968), 231–232, 235–236.

33. Dorothy Van Ghent, *The English Novel: Form and Function* (New York, 1953), p. 201.

34. Cf. the references to 'the fatality of heredity' and 'the fatality of environment' in the first of several passages which Hardy copied out ('Literary Notes I', pp. [196]–[198]) from Vernon Lee, 'A Dialogue on Novels', *Contemporary Review*, 48 (1885), 378–401.

35. Pinion, *A Hardy Companion*, p. 309, points to the relevance of Hardy's poem, 'The Blinded Bird' (*Moments of Vision*, p. 228).

36. Raymond Blathwayt, 'A Chat with the Author of *Tess*', p. 238 (*Thomas Hardy and His Readers*, p. 92), quotes Hardy as saying: 'Do you not see that under *any* circumstances they were doomed to

unhappiness? A sensitive man like Angel Clare could never have been happy with her. After the first few months he would inevitably have thrown her failings in her face.'

37. Brooks, *William Faulkner: The Yoknapatawpha Country* (New Haven, 1963), pp. 29, 32–34.

38. Frederick L. Gwynn and Joseph L. Blotner, eds., *Faulkner in the University: Class Conferences at the University of Virginia. 1957–1958* (Charlottesville, Va., 1959), p. [1].

2   *Candour in English Fiction*

1. E.g., *Pall Mall Gazette*, July 8, 1891, p. 3, and *Spectator*, August 1, 1891, 163–164.

2. Eliot, *After Strange Gods: A Primer of Modern Heresy* (London, 1934), p. 54: '[Hardy] seems to me to have written as nearly for the sake of "self-expression" as a man well can; and the self which he had to express does not strike me as a particularly wholesome or edifying matter of communication.'

3. MS, f. 109v. (Library of Congress); cf. Purdy, p. 65. For Hardy to Clodd, June 27, 1891, see *Ashley Catalogue*, X, 122.

4. *New Review*, 2 (January 1890), 18–19 (*Personal Writings*, pp. 129–130).

5. See Hardy's note in *Wessex Tales*, pp. 286–[287].

6. Wessex edn., p. [399] (DCM).

7. Purdy, pp. 71–73.

8. Arnold to Hardy, November 15, 1889 (DCM).

9. Purdy, pp. 55–56. The decision to serialise *The Woodlanders* in *Macmillan's* had not, presumably, been taken by Mowbray Morris himself. The first approach to Hardy seems to have been made by John Morley during his brief editorship of the magazine (Morley to Hardy, October 15, 1884, in DCM), and even after Morris had become editor it was Frederick Macmillan who communicated to Hardy (letter of March 29, 1886, in DCM) his and Morris's views as to the title of the novel; see p. 259 and n.

10. Morris to Hardy, November 25, 1889 (DCM), partly quoted in Laird, 'The Manuscript of Hardy's *Tess of the d'Urbervilles*', pp. 69–70.

11. Morris to Hardy, September 19, 1886 (DCM).

12. See 'Renewal', section 5, n. 24, and Purdy, pp. 69, 73. Both Purdy and Chase (*Thomas Hardy from Serial to Novel*, p. 76) give, in their

brief references to 'Saturday Night in Arcady', a slightly exaggerated impression of its closeness to the book version of chapters 10 and 11. In fact, the *National Observer* text (in which Tess is referred to simply as 'Big Beauty') differs considerably from any of the other texts and gives only a very abbreviated version of the 'seduction scene', omitting entirely the material which appears in the Wessex edn. on the lower half of p. 87 and on pp. 88–91. 'The Midnight Baptism: A Study in Christianity', published in the *Fortnightly Review*, 55 (May 1891), [695]–701, departs less radically from the book version of chapter 14.

13. [Morris,] 'Candour in English Fiction', *Macmillan's Magazine*, 61 (February 1890), 314–320; see *Wellesley Index*, I, 634, item 2854.

14. [Morris,] 'Culture and Anarchy', *Quarterly Review*, 174 (April 1892), 324, 325, 326; see *Wellesley Index*, I, 773, item 2494.

15. 'Culture and Anarchy', pp. 321, 322.

16. Typescript, pp. 339–340 (DCM): see Purdy, p. 266, and n.

17. Maitland, *Life and Letters of Leslie Stephen*, pp. 275–276; cf. *Early Life*, pp. 130–131.

18. Nowell-Smith, ed., *Letters to Macmillan*, pp. 130–131.

19. Beach, 'Bowdlerized Versions of Hardy', *PMLA*, 36 (1921), 641.

20. *Pall Mall Gazette*, July 10, 1891, p. 2.

21. Weber, *Hardy of Wessex*, p. 121; Purdy, p. 73n.

22. *St James's Gazette*, January 19, 1883, p. 14.

23. Purdy, pp. 90, 89.

24. Hardy to Clement Shorter, January 29, 1892 (quoted Sotheby Sale Catalogue, May 29, 1961, lot 56); cf. the prospectus sent to Tillotson's quoted Purdy, p. 95.

25. Aldrich to Hardy, December 14, 1885 (DCM).

26. Hardy to Massingham, July 1, 1907 (Purdy coll.); to Mrs Henniker, October 22, 1900 (DCM); to Hermann Lea, April 21, 1904 (DCM).

27. Viola Meynell, ed., *Friends of a Lifetime : Letters to Sydney Carlyle Cockerell* (London, 1940), pp. 275–276.

3. *The Well-Beloved*

1. Purdy, pp. 94–95.

2. Hardy to Douglas, March 25, 1897, quoted in Parker, 'Hardy's Letters to Sir George Douglas', p. 220. Where significant inaccuracies occur, as on this and a number of subsequent (indicated) occasions, I have corrected the text from the original in the National Library of Scotland.

3. Hardy to the editor of the *Academy*, March 29, [1897], published in *Academy*, April 3, 1897, 381.

4. Letter to *Academy* cited in n. 3; Guerard, *Thomas Hardy*, p. 68.

5. *Academy*, March 27, 1897, 345.

6. *Early Life*, p. 215.

7. Lois Deacon and Terry Coleman, *Providence and Mr Hardy*, p. 133.

8. *World*, March 24, 1897, p. 13.

9. Typescript, p. 402 (DCM), corresponding to *Later Years*, p. 59.

10. See previous section, p. 291 and n.

11. *Saturday Review*, March 20, 1897, 296; the reviewer was presumably Edmund Gosse: cf. his letter to Hardy of March 16, 1897 (DCM).

12. *Illustrated London News*, December 17, 1892, 775; the punctuation here apparently requires the final 'Ho-ho-ho!' to be authorial.

13. Dated July 7, 1891, in 'Literary Notes II', pp. 63–[64], are a series of notes based on vol. 1 of *The Golden Bough* : this, of course, was the two-volume first edn., London, 1890.

14. Hardy to Swinburne, April 1, 1897, quoted *Later Years*, pp. 60–61; cf. *Ashley Cat.*, X, 169.

15. See Helmut E. Gerber, 'Hardy's *The Well-Beloved* as a Comment on the Well-Despised', *English Language Notes*, I (1963), 49–50.

16. See p. 342; and cf. Evelyn Hardy, *Thomas Hardy : A Critical Biography*, p. 259.

17. Guerard, *Thomas Hardy*, p. 67.

18. Hardy to Mrs Henniker, June 3, 1897 (DCM); to Gosse, April 1, 1897 (Leeds).

19. See, for example, *Early Life*, p. 288, and *Thomas Hardy's Notebooks*, p. 54 (mistranscribed from 'Memoranda I').

20. *Early Life*, p. 42.

21. Typescript, p. 300 (DCM), corresponding to *Early Life*, p. 288.

22. Purdy, pp. 342–348; *Winter Words*, p. 285.

23. Hardy to Emma Lavinia Hardy, [January 24, 1891 ?], in Carl J. Weber, ed., *'Dearest Emmie' : Thomas Hardy's Letters to His First Wife* (London, 1963), p. 13.

24. *Early Life*, p. 223.

25. *'Dearest Emmie'*, p. 3.

26. *Times*, January 11, 1887, p. 9; cf. *Early Life*, p. 242.

27. Typescript, p. 270 (DCM), corresponding to *Early Life*, p. 262.

28. Cf. *Early Life*, p. 284.

29. Cf. *Later Years*, p. 66.

30. The majority of Mrs Tomson's works are listed in *CBEL* (ed. F. W. Bateson), III, 360. Hardy's copy of *The Bird-Bride: A Volume of Ballads and Sonnets* (London, 1889) was inscribed 'Thomas Hardy, with the sincere admiration of G.R.T. June, 89' (Maggs Bros. catalogue 664, 1938, item 197); his copy of *The Poems of Rosamund Marriott Watson* (London, 1912) is still in DCM. John Paterson, *The Making of 'The Return of the Native'*, p. 8, notes that 'Avice' was apparently Hardy's original name for Eustacia Vye, but I take it to be merely coincidental that it should have been suggested in *Notes and Queries*, 169 (December 31, 1935), 446, that Mrs Tomson might have been the 'model' for Eustacia. Since Mrs Tomson was not born until 1860, the idea seems implausible; it does, however, hint at a possible link with some other novel of Hardy's.

31. ' "Graham R. Tomson" ', *Critic* [New York], n.s. 14 (October 25, 1890), 209–210, attributed to ' "Max Eliot," in the Boston *Herald*'.

32. Hardy to Mrs Henniker, July 16, 1893 (DCM).

33. Typescript, p. 271 (DCM), corresponding to *Early Life*, p. 263.

34. *Academy*, March 27, 1897, 345.

35. See n. 3 above.

36. In the serial, *Illustrated London News*, October 15, 1892, 481, Pearston lives on 'Hintock Road'; note, too, the use of the term *'Bien-aimé'* in *The Woodlanders*, p. 314.

37. See, for example, issue of December 17, 1892, 773; the illustrator was Walter Paget.

38. Issue of October 1, 1892, [424].

39. J. H. Lucking, *Railways of Dorset: An Outline of their Establishment, Development and Progress from 1825* ([Lichfield, Staffs.], 1968), pp. 20, 34–35.

40. See also *Early Life*, p. 287. The poems appear in, respectively, *Human Shows*, p. 117, *Winter Words*, p. 226, and *Late Lyrics and Earlier*, p. 161 (see Purdy, p. 224, for a note on the MS).

41. Barber, ed., *Concerning Thomas Hardy*, p. 31.

42. Cf. Hardy's phrases about 'Louie the Buoyant' and 'Louie's life-lit brow' (*Human Shows*, p. 117), and see May O'Rourke, *Thomas Hardy: His Secretary Remembers*, pp. 16–17, 49–52 (a photograph of Louisa Harding c. 1860 appears as a frontispiece). In conversation, July 13, 1967, Miss O'Rourke spoke even more strongly of Louisa Harding's gaiety.

43. Deacon and Coleman, *Providence and Mr Hardy*, pp. 133–134.

44. *Wessex Poems*, pp. 78–79; cf. Purdy, pp. 101–102.

45. The subject is well discussed by F. B. Pinion, *A Hardy Companion*, pp. 435–440. See also the comments by the Rev. O. D. Harvey in *Puddletown (Thomas Hardy's 'Weatherbury')*, pp. 45–[51].

46. Both quotations, *Illustrated London News*, October 15, 1892, 481.

47. Quoted Wright, *The Shaping of 'The Dynasts'*, p. 22.

48. *Poems of the Past and the Present*, pp. 187–189.

49. *Wessex Poems*, p. 107.

4. *Hardy and the Theatre*

1. *Later Years*, pp. 18–20; Purdy, pp. 343–344.

2. Conversation with Florence Hardy recorded by Irene Cooper Willis (pocketbook, DCM).

3. Purdy, p. 342.

4. Hardy to Mrs Henniker, June 3, 1893 (DCM); *Later Years*, p. 21.

5. *Pall Mall Gazette*, August 31, 1892, p. [1] (*Personal Writings*, p. 139).

6. *Weekly Comedy*, November 30, 1889, p. 7.

7. Orel, ed., *Personal Writings*, p. 242.

8. *Weekly Comedy*, November 30, 1889, p. 7.

9. *Early Life*, p. 289, only mentions Grein, but the request to which Hardy was responding came jointly from Grein and Jarvis (dated July 16, 1889, DCM). In a letter of July 23, 1889, to an unidentified correspondent (quoted Maggs Bros. cat. 664, item 246) Hardy speaks of Jarvis as if he were the leading collaborator. See also 'Renewal', section 5, n. 11.

10. Florence Hardy to St John Ervine, July 17, 1926 (Texas).

11. Irving to Hardy, n.d. (DCM).

12. Quoted in Marguerite Roberts, ed., *'Tess' in the Theatre* (Toronto, 1950), p. xxii.

13. C. Archer, *William Archer: Life, Work and Friendships* (London, 1931), p. 322.

14. Frederick Dolman, 'An Evening with Thomas Hardy', p. 76; see 'Apprenticeship', section 1, n. 4.

15. Hardy to Mrs Henniker, December 1, 1893 (DCM).

16. See Purdy, p. 79.

17. 'A Victorian Rehearsal', *Times Literary Supplement*, June 2, 1966, 504.

18. See Purdy, pp. 28–30; also 'Achievement', section 2, n. 13.

19. Purdy, p79.

20. The Adams collection contains a very substantial body of correspondence (much of it conducted through or by Florence Hardy) relating to this episode.

21. Rutland, *Thomas Hardy : A Study of His Writings and Their Background*, pp. 252–253.

22. Archer, 'A Translator-Traitor: Mr. Edmund Gosse and Henrik Ibsen', *Pall Mall Gazette*, January 23, 1891, pp. [1]-2.

23. Ellis, *The New Spirit* (London, 1890), p. 171; cf. 'Literary Notes II', p. [18].

24. This scheme, dated 1897, is the second of four now at the University of Texas.

25. See above, n. 10.

26. Hardy to Ervine, September 9, 1926 (Texas).

27. Roberts, ed., *'Tess' in the Theatre*, pp. xx-xxi.

28. Fischler, 'Theatrical Techniques in Thomas Hardy's Short Stories', *Studies in Short Fiction*, 3 (1966), 435–445.

29. *Tess of the d'Urbervilles*, pp. viii, xi (*Personal Writings*, pp. 45–48); cf. p. 346.

30. Fairley, 'Notes on the Form of *The Dynasts*', *PMLA*, 34 (1919), 402, 403–404.

31. Fairley, pp. 404–405.

32. *Later Years*, p. 165; cf. Purdy, p. 135.

33. 'Facts' notebook, pp. [2]–[4].

34. Pennie, *Britain's Historical Drama* (London, 1832), p. [v]. William Barnes was interested in Pennie: see his letter to J. G. Nichols, February 16, 1849, in the Bodleian.

35. Pennie, p. [v].

5. *Jude the Obscure*

1. Hardy to Mrs Henniker, October 22, 1893 (DCM); cf. Purdy, p. 345.

2. On 'The Spectre of the Real' see Purdy, pp. 346–348. *Later Years*, p. 26, speaks of Hardy's writing poetry in October and November 1893 and, in December, revising the short story, 'An Imaginative Woman'.

3. Hardy to Mrs Henniker, December 1, 1893, and January 15, 1894 (both DCM); to Harper & Brothers, April 7, 1894 (quoted Purdy, p. 90).

4. Purdy, pp. 88–89, 90–91; the novel was post-dated 1896. Cf. Mary

Ellen Chase, *Thomas Hardy from Serial to Novel*, pp. 115–117, and Robert C. Slack, 'The Text of Hardy's *Jude the Obscure*', *Nineteenth Century Fiction*, 11 (1957) 261–275, drawn from his unpub. Ph.D. dissertation, 'A Variorum Edition of Thomas Hardy's *Jude the Obscure*' (Univ. of Pittsburgh, 1953). The manuscript is discussed in John Paterson, 'The Genesis of *Jude the Obscure*', *Studies in Philology*, 57 (1960), 87–98.

5. Cf. Hardy's poem, 'The Recalcitrants' (*Satires of Circumstance*, p. 140)—a title once suggested by Hardy for *Jude* itself (Purdy, p. 87n.).

6. *Jude* MS, f. 1 (Fitzwilliam Museum, Cambridge); cf. Purdy, pp. 87, 89.

7. DeLaura, '"The Ache of Modernism" in Hardy's Later Novels', p. 392n.

8. Bridehead is, however, a Dorset place-name (for the source of the River Bride, near Little Bredy): cf. Murray's *Handbook*, p. 101. Since Hardy had been reading *The Golden Bough* in 1891 (see section 3 above, n. 13) it is perhaps worth noting that Frazer's discussion of the corn-spirit mentions that in parts of Scotland the last handful of standing corn at harvest-time was called 'the Maidenhead or the Head' (I, 345), and that in Scotland and Germany both the last sheaf and the woman who bound it were sometimes called the Bride (I, 346).

9. *Later Years*, p. 42.

10. 'Mr. Hardy's Novels', p. 352.

11. Heilman, 'Hardy's Sue Bridehead', *Nineteenth Century Fiction*, 20 (1966), 307–323; *Later Years*, p. 42.

12. Hardy to Gosse, November 10, 1895, quoted *Later Years*, p. 40.

13. 'The Profitable Reading of Fiction', p. 67 (*Personal Writings*, p. 121).

14. Hardy to Gosse, November 20, 1895, quoted *Later Years*, p. 42.

15. 'Literary Notes I', p. [172].

16. Lagarde, 'A propos de la construction de *Jude the Obscure*', *Caliban*, no. 3 (January 1966), 195.

17. See previous section, n. 24; the first scheme is dated October 24, 1895.

18. Theodore Alois Buckley, trans., *The Tragedies of Sophocles: in English Prose* (London, 1849), p. 53; Hardy underlined most of this passage in his own copy (Adams).

19. Buckley, p. vii.

20. [Gosse], 'Mr. Hardy's New Novel', *St James's Gazette*, November 8, 1895, p. 4.

21. Gosse, 'Mr. Hardy's New Novel', *Cosmopolis*, I (January 1896), 60–69 (partly quoted *Thomas Hardy and His Readers*, pp. 117–122); the letters are quoted in *Later Years*, pp. 40–43. *Thomas Hardy and His Readers* obscures the sequence by omitting the *St James's Gazette* review and printing two of the letters to Gosse *after* the *Cosmopolis* review.

22. Hardy to Gosse, November 10, 1895, quoted *Later Years*, p. 41.

23. See Slack, 'The Text of Hardy's *Jude the Obscure*', pp. 264–268, especially p. 266.

24. See Slack, p. 270.

25. Hardy to Gosse, November 20, 1895, quoted *Later Years*, p. 42. Hardy again speaks of Fielding's Dorset associations in 'Dorset in London', *Society of Dorset Men in London : Year-book, 1908–1909*, p. 7 (*Personal Writings*, p. 224): 'Though not born in the county, he was closely associated with North-East Dorset, having settled for some time at East Stower. That he knew Dorset like a native is apparent to any Dorset man who makes himself familiar with this keen observer's humorous scenes and dialogues.'

26. C. J. P. Beatty has established (*Architectural Notebook*, pp. 30–34) that Hardy directed the restoration of West Knighton Church (not far from Dorchester) in 1893–94, during the composition of *Jude*.

27. 'Mr. Hardy's New Novel' (see n. 21 above), pp. 62–63.

28. Keith, 'The Anatomy of Wessex' (see 'Renewal', section 4, n. 2), p. 230; cf. Ward Hellstrom, 'Hardy's Use of Setting and *Jude the Obscure*', *Victorian Newsletter*, no. 25 (Spring 1964), pp. 11–13.

29. C. B. Tinker and H. F. Lowry, eds., *The Poetical Works of Matthew Arnold* (London, 1950), pp. 256, 261.

AFTERWORD

The End of Prose

1. Hardy to Mrs Henniker, November 10, 1895 (DCM); to Clodd, November 10, 1895 (Leeds). His letter to W. Hatherell, praising the illustration of 'Jude at the Mile-stone', bears the same date (quoted Purdy, p. 88). For the quoted phrase, see *Later Years*, p. 43.

2. Hardy to Douglas, November 20, 1895 (Parker, pp. 219-220).

3. Hardy to Douglas, see n. 2. The reviews, originally published in the *World* [London], November 13, 1895, p. 15, and *Pall Mall Gazette*, November 12, 1895, p. 4, are reprinted (the latter in abridged form) in *Thomas Hardy and His Readers*, pp. 109–111, 113, where 'Hardy the Degenerate' is incorrectly attributed to Jeanette L. Gilder. As *Later Years*, p. 50, makes clear, she was the author of the (signed) review in the December 8 issue of the New York *World*.

4. Hardy to Douglas, January 5, 1896, quoted Parker, p. 220 (punctuation corrected).

5. Hardy to Mrs Henniker, November 30, 1895 (DCM); to Gosse, July 14, 1909 (British Museum).

6. Typescript, p. 378 (DCM), corresponding to *Later Years*, p. 39. Pages 378–379 of the typescript show that the discussion of hostile attacks on *Jude* was once more than a page longer.

7. Cf. William J. Hyde, 'Hardy's Response to the Critics of *Jude*', *Victorian Newsletter*, no. 19, (Spring 1961), pp. [1]–5.

8. *World*, November 13, 1895, p. 15.

9. Anon., 'Thomas Hardy's Wessex', *Bookman*, 1 (1891), 26.

10. Hardy to Douglas, November 16, 1894, quoted Parker, p. 219 (corrected). For the critical works mentioned, see 'Fulfilment', section 1, n. 28, and 'Recession', section 3, n. 11.

11. Hardy to Mrs Henniker, June 3, 1897 (DCM).

12. Barrie, 'Thomas Hardy: The Historian of Wessex', *Contemporary Review*, 56 (1889), 59. The implied reservation about Jefferies as a novelist seems to have been shared by Hardy himself: see W. M. Parker, 'My Visit to Thomas Hardy', *Cornhill*, 66 (1929), 155.

13. Gissing to Algernon Gissing, September 22, 1895, quoted in Purdy, 'George Gissing at Max Gate, 1895', *Yale University Library Gazette*, 17, iii (1943), p. 52. Cf. Archer, 'Real Conversations. II—With Mr. Thomas Hardy', p. 529: 'The town-bred boy will often appreciate nature more than the country boy, but he does not know it in the same sense. He will rush to pick a flower which the country boy does not seem to notice. But it is part of the country boy's life. It grows in his soul—he does not want it in his buttonhole.'

14. Guerard suggests (*Thomas Hardy*, p. 77) that the observation of nature in Hardy's fiction became 'less and less particular'.

15. *Moments of Vision*, p. 409.

16. Martin, 'Thomas Hardy and the Rural Tradition', *Blackfriars*, 30 (1949), 255. In *The Secret People: English Village Life After 1750* (London, 1954), Martin mentions Hardy among the 'cynical

traditionalists' (p. 35) but seems to accept without serious qualification (pp. 17–19) the social evidence offered by the novels.

17. Lynen, *The Pastoral Art of Robert Frost* (New Haven, 1960), pp. 20–21.

18. Gissing to Algernon Gissing, August 4, 1891, in *Letters of George Gissing to Members of his Family*, collected and arranged by Algernon and Ellen Gissing (London, 1927), p. 339.

19. 'The Science of Fiction', p. 317 (*Personal Writings*, p. 136).

20. Interview with Jean Stein vanden Heuvel, quoted in James B. Meriwether and Michael Millgate, eds., *Lion in the Garden : Interviews with William Faulkner, 1926–1962* (New York, 1968), p. 255.

21. Interview in Japan, *Lion in the Garden*, p. 133.

22. Interview with Jean Stein vanden Heuvel, *Lion in the Garden*, p. 251.

23. General Preface, in *Tess of the d'Urbervilles*, pp. viii–ix (*Personal Writings*, p. 45).

24. Paul, 'The Wessex Labourer', p. 793.

25. Faulkner, *The Hamlet* (New York, 1940), p. 207.

26. See e.g., Hardy to Gosse, February 18, 1918, facsimile in *Ashley Cat.*, X, 130–131.

27. 'The Profitable Reading of Fiction', p. 70 (*Personal Writings*, p. 124).

28. *Cassell's Saturday Journal*, June 25, 1892, 944; cf. Hardy's reference to 'the elementary passions' in the General Preface (*Tess*, p. viii; *Personal Writings*, p. 45).

29. Brooks, *William Faulkner*, p. 174.

30. Brooks, p. 174.

31. Drake, '*The Woodlanders* as Traditional Pastoral', *Modern Fiction Studies*, 6 (1960), 251–257.

32. Lynen, *The Pastoral Art of Robert Frost*, pp. 9–13, 56–61, and passim. The discussion in this paragraph is much indebted to Professor Lynen's fine book.

33. Williams, 'Thomas Hardy', p. 350.

34. Williams, pp. 349, 342.

35. 'The Profitable Reading of Fiction', pp. 57–58 (*Personal Writings*, p. 111).

36. Faulkner, *Essays, Speeches and Public Letters*, ed. James B. Meriwether (New York, 1965), p. 120.

37. *Cassell's Saturday Journal*, June 25, 1892, 944.

38. Hardy to Clodd, April 1, 1894, quoted *Ashley Cat.*, X, 123; text corrected from original in British Museum.

39. Barrie, 'Thomas Hardy: The Historian of Wessex', p. 59.

40. General Preface, *Tess*, p. xi (*Personal Writings*, p. 48); cf. Hardy to Harold Child, May 7, 1915 (Adams), and to J. Stanley Little, May 22, 1915 (Princeton).

41. Hardy to Gosse, February 18, 1918: see n. 26 above.

42. Hardy to Clodd, October 8, 1912 (British Museum); cf. Newman Flower, *Just as it Happened*, p. 99.

43. Cf. Hardy to Mrs Henniker, September 25, 1902 (DCM); to Macmillan, July 9, 1902 (quoted Purdy, p. 282).

44. Purdy, pp. 288, 286.

45. See p. 283 and n.

46. Hardy to Douglas, August 27, 1913, quoted Parker, p. 223; cf. Purdy, pp. 155–156.

47. Hardy to Macmillan, May 19, 1894 (British Museum).

48. See, for example, Charles Morgan, *The House of Macmillan*, pp. 154–161, and Simon Nowell-Smith, ed., *Letters to Macmillan*, pp. [129]–134.

49. Brown, *Thomas Hardy*, p. 145, adapting a phrase of Ezra Pound's.

50. These notes are in DCM.

51. Parker, 'My Visit to Thomas Hardy', p. 154.

52. Oscar Cargill, *The Novels of Henry James* (New York, 1961), p. 85; for James's review, see 'Achievement', section 1, n. 18.

53. *The Diary of Arthur Christopher Benson*, ed. Percy Lubbock (London, n.d.), pp. 81–82. See also, for this and other anecdotes of Hardy and James, Nowell-Smith, comp., *The Legend of the Master*, pp. 80, 83, 140, 170.

54. *Early Life*, p. 175.

55. James to Hardy, July 13, [1889] (DCM).

56. James to Hardy, August 10, 1915 (DCM). Copyright, 1971, Alexander R. James. See Purdy, p. 192.

57. James to Hardy, July 21, 1915 (DCM). Copyright, 1971, Alexander R. James.

58. Typescript, p. 340 (DCM). Cf. Dan H. Laurence, 'Henry James and Stevenson Discuss "Vile" Tess', *Colby Library Quarterly*, ser. 3 (1953), 164–168, and Nowell-Smith, comp., *The Legend of the Master*, p. xxxviii.

59. The point is elucidated in Leon Edel, *Henry James: The Conquest of London, 1870-1883* (London, 1962), p. 355.

60. Typescript, p. 242 (DCM), corresponding to *Early Life*, p. 237. For the Rabelais Club, see 'Recession', section 1, n. 4.

61. In 1884, for example, Hardy's 'Interlopers at the Knap' and James's 'The Author of *Beltraffio*' appeared in successive issues of the *English Illustrated Magazine*, while in 1909 Hardy and James both made characteristic statements (in the form of letters to John Galsworthy) on the question of stage censorship: *Times*, August 13, 1909, p. 4 (cf. Purdy, p. 313).

62. Bainton, ed., *The Art of Authorship* (London, 1890), pp. 320–321.

63. Moule to Hardy, July 2, 1863, quoted Deacon and Coleman, *Providence and Mr Hardy*, p. 89.

64. Garland, *Afternoon Neighbours: Further Excerpts from a Literary Log* (New York, 1934), p. 88.

65. Bainton, ed., *The Art of Authorship*, p. 208.

66. *Later Years*, p. 8.

67. 'Literary Notes I', pp. 145–[146]; Elliott Felkin, 'Days with Thomas Hardy', p. 31. Cf. *Later Years*, pp. 168–169.

68. Hardy to Mrs Henniker, March 17, 1903 (DCM).

69. Williams, 'Thomas Hardy', p. 342.

70. Hardy to Galsworthy, July 26, 1902, quoted *Times*, August 13, 1909, p. 4; cf. n. 61 above.

71. Zabel, 'Hardy in Defense of His Art: The Aesthetic of Incongruity', repr. in Guerard, ed., *Hardy: A Collection of Critical Essays*, pp. 24–45.

72. Virginia Woolf, *Collected Essays*, ed. Leonard Woolf (London, 1966), I, 265.

73. Virginia Woolf, *A Writer's Diary*, ed. Leonard Woolf (London, 1953), pp. 93–94.

74. Edith Wharton, *A Backward Glance*, p. 216.

75. Vernon Lee, *The Handling of Words* (London, 1923), p. 241. For an interesting discussion of her analysis, see David Lodge, *Language of Fiction*, pp. 164–176.

76. Vernon Lee, p. 240.

INDEX

INDEX

ABOUT THE AUTHOR

MICHAEL MILLGATE, born in England in 1929, educated at St. Catharine's College, Cambridge, and at the Universities of Michigan and Leeds, was Lecturer in English Literature at Leeds for six years before going to Canada in 1964 to become Chairman of the English Department at York University, Toronto. He is now Professor of English at University College, University of Toronto. He has previously written *William Faulkner, American Social Fiction: James to Cozzens,* and *The Achievement of William Faulkner;* he has also edited texts of Tennyson and Dreiser and been co-editor of *Transatlantic Dialogue: Selected American Correspondence of Edmund Gosse* and *Lion in the Garden: Interviews with William Faulkner, 1926–1962.*